CW01496680

Steam Trains in Your Garden

*Build your own live steam locomotives
and rolling stock*

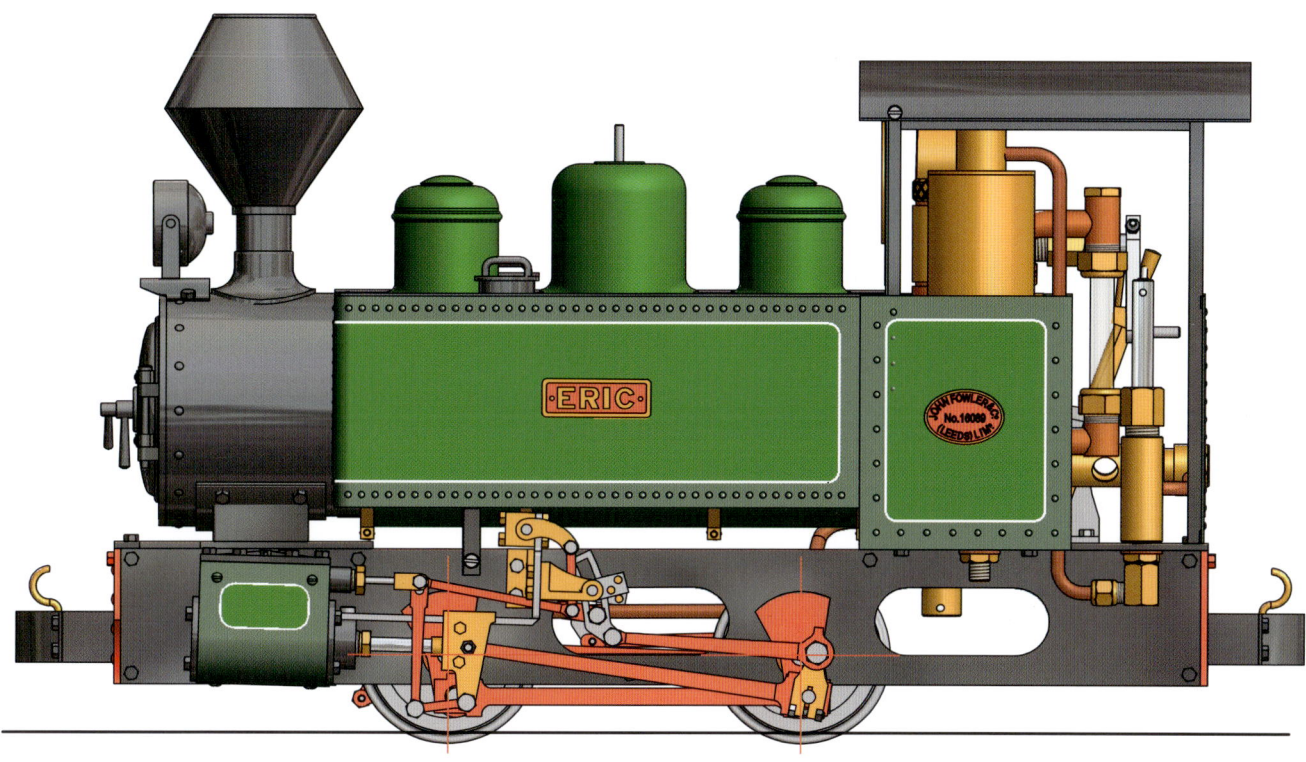

Brian Wilson

British Library Cataloguing-in-Publication-Data: a catalogue record of this work is held by the British Library.

First published 2007
by Australian Model Engineering Magazine Pty Ltd

This printing 2015

ISBN No. 978-1-909358-12-6

CAMDEN MINIATURE STEAM SERVICES
Barrow Farm, Rode, Frome, Somerset BA11 6PS
www.camdenmin.co.uk

Camden stock one of the widest selections of engineering, technical and transportation books to be found; Contact them at the above address for a copy of their latest free Booklist, or see their website.

Layout design & typesetting by David Proctor Publishing Services
Canberra, Australia

Contents

Page

Introduction 7

Gauges and scales: The size of the railway; Background to the locomotive design;
Units; Equipment and materials; Construction sequence.

Part 1 — Building *"Eric"*

Chapter 1 The Chassis 15

Coupling rods; Frame assembly; Tapping small threads; Footplates; Wheels; Axles;
Cranks; Axle bushes; Crank pins; Connecting and coupling rods; Quartering the cranks;
Cylinder assembly; The cylinders; Cylinder covers; Valve chest; Piston and rod; Valve;
Valve rod; Crossheads; Motion bracket and slide bar; Assembling the main motion;
Valve gear; Expansion links; Link brackets; Return crank; Combination lever; Simplified
combination lever; Footplates; Reversing gear; Lifting link; Lifting arms and reverse
lever arm; Weighshaft and bearings; Reversing stand and lever; Finishing the chassis,
Setting the valves and testing on air; Steam inlet fittings; Steam tee; Exhaust tee;
Exhaust pipe; Fitting the pipes and running on air.

Chapter 2 The Smoke Box and Boiler 57

Saddle; Smokebox; Smokebox door assembly; Chimney; Steam and sand domes;
Boiler; Boiler bands; Cladding and insulation.

Chapter 3 The Body 71

Dummy rivets; Soft soldering; Cab sheets; Spectacle plate, Side and back sheets; Cab
frame; Riveting; Side tanks.

Chapter 4 Boiler Fittings, Gas Fittings and Pipework 85

Steam manifold; Manifold centre bolt; Throttle valve body; Making a "D"-bit valve
Spindle; Goodall water filling valve; Pressure gauge; Safety valve; Lubricator steam
piping; Bending pipe; Gas system; Tank; Gas valve; Burner

Chapter 5 Assembling, Painting, and Finishing 101

Assembling and Test Steam; Painting; Single colour paint scheme; Two tone paint
scheme; Lining; Transfers (decals) and finishing; Nameplates

Part 2 — Details and Variations. Other Prototypes

Chapter 6 Slip Eccentric Chassis 111

The rolling chassis; Cylinders and valve chests; Motion bracket and crosshead;
Eccentrics; Eccentric straps; Slip collars; Rocking shaft; Rocking shaft bearings
Setting the valve timing.

Chapter 7 Other Details 117

Crosshead and guide bars; Different wheel arrangements; Saddle tanks; Chimney;
Whistle; Cylinder drain cocks; "Chuff" pipe.

Chapter 8 Other Prototypes 133

The original *"Edwin"*; Manufacturers' works drawings and photographs.

Chapter 9   Laser Cutting and Lost Wax Casting   **139**

Lost wax casting; Laser profiled components.

Chapter 10   Coal Firing   **141**

Coal – fired boiler; Pressure shell; Firebox; Grate and ash pan; Axle pump;
Bypass valve and boiler feed clack; Smokebox fittings.

Chapter 11   Running and Maintenance   **157**

Equipment; Gas firing; Coal firing; After the run; Radio control: Troubleshooting;
Butane burners

Part 3 — Rolling Stock
Simple Wagons and Carriages

Chapter 12   Introduction   **165**

Tools and materials; Design

Chapter 13   Basic 4-Wheel Chassis   **167**

Base; Axle horns; Wheels; Assembling the basic chassis; Casting cosmetic springs;
The pattern; Straight compression spring; Leaf spring; The mould; Pouring the metal

Chapter 14   Wagon and Carriage Body   **173**

An open wagon; Cane wagons; Covered van / Guard's van; Passenger coach;
A tender

Chapter 15   Bogie Wagons   **183**

Casting in whitemetal; Casting in urethane; Chassis; Coach body

Appendix   Alternative Boiler Gauge Glass   **188**

Acknowledgements

A book of this nature is an amalgamation of ideas gathered from many sources over a long period of time. People associated with the live steam hobby are invariably willing to share their knowledge, and thanks are due to all those who have answered my questions and discussed their experiences, in particular the members of the Live Steam Group at AMRA in Brisbane. The garden railway hobby would never have become so popular in Australia without the contribution Gordon Watson of Argyle Locomotives has made over the years, and Paul Trevaskis of Rishon Locomotives has always unselfishly shared his knowledge without hesitation.

Special thanks are due to Don Reinhart who is not a model engineer, but seems to know everything about computers; without his willing and good natured assistance this book could not have been written.

Preface

Narrow gauge railways were used extensively for many different purposes. They were used in sugarcane plantations, logging enterprises, quarries, for Government projects and in all types of factories from breweries to munition works. Many are still operating throughout the world today and they possess a charm and character all of their own. When they are modeled, this charm comes through into the model railway and it is one of the many factors which have sparked the recent increase in their interest.

When my own interest in Garden Railways was awakened, the first step was to purchase a locomotive kit from Gordon Watson of Argyle Locomotives. This kit was a complete set of parts to make *Philladelphia*, a model of a 2 foot gauge Baldwin locomotive which used to run for the Fairymead Sugar Mill in North Queensland, and which is now happily preserved and operational. This excellent kit made an outstanding model, and many of them have been successfully made and are running throughout Australia and overseas.

At the time, this kit seemed to be the only one available. It is distinctly American in appearance, and has inside Stephenson's Valve gear. My preference was more for an English outline locomotive, preferably with Walschaerts Valve gear. After studying which locomotives were used in Australia, it appeared that those from the John Fowler Works of Leeds in England fulfilled these objectives. Many locomotives of varying wheel configurations were supplied by John Fowler and Co. over the years, and when they stopped making steam locomotives around 1935, the Bundaberg Foundry in Queensland acquired the rights to build one of their designs.

Using this design, known as the "Bundaberg Fowler" as a basis, a simple 0-4-0 locomotive called *Edwin* was drawn up in 16mm scale and subsequently serialized as a construction series in *Australian Model Engineering* magazine. This series proved to be far more popular than expected, due no doubt to the surge in interest which was taking place with Garden Railways. Whilst the series was intended for people with some experience with model locomotive building, a large number of beginners started on the project, and many successful locomotives have been completed.

Whilst the original *Edwin* design has proven to make up into a locomotive which runs well and is reasonably straightforward to build, as with all designs, many improvements have subsequently been incorporated. Therefore this book describes how to build an updated version of *Edwin*, the changes being mainly to "beef up" some of the parts to make them less fiddly to construct, and in some cases to improve the wearing qualities. Also improvements have been made to some of the construction methods to make them easier to perform. All of the text and the drawings from the *Edwin* series have been revised or redone.

Our new locomotive is called *Eric*. Once again it is a freelance gas-fired model, this time based on the John Fowler locomotive, Builder's No. 16089, built in 1923 at their factory in Leeds, England. This locomotive was delivered to the State Metal Quarries Railway in New South Wales and is now preserved at the Illawarra Light Railway Museum.

Brian Wilson
Toowoomba Q
May, 2007

Introduction

Model Engineering is one of the world's great pastimes! It is an activity which has been around for decades, caters for all age and skill levels, includes many varied interests and is relatively inexpensive to enjoy.

This book describes an area of model engineering which has enjoyed a huge increase in interest and participation worldwide in recent years. It describes the building of real steam locomotives and rolling stock which can be run in ordinary backyard gardens.

"Ride-on" scale miniature railways have been popular for some time, but lately there has been a growing interest in smaller scale railways. There have always been models built in the smaller sizes, but it was generally a pastime undertaken by a small band of enthusiasts.

The early morning goods moves off on a misty morning on the Brimhillah Railway.

Many people whose interest has been in passenger hauling trains have seen the benefits of modeling in smaller sizes, and also many people have become involved who previously modeled small gauge electric trains.

To cater for the growing interest, some established model railway clubs are building outdoor tracks, and there are many tracks being built in private backyards. Steam-ups take place quite regularly, and they are enjoyable affairs which are free of the problems associated with hauling passengers or handling heavy locomotives.

Locomotives and rolling stock can be purchased ready made, or, as this book describes, built in the home workshop. These days, adequate tools and machinery for the job can be purchased quite cheaply, and the sizes needed are not too large.

Gauges and scales: the size of the railway

If you are making a railway for yourself, then you can make it any size you wish. However, if you want to operate trains with other people, then some standardization is necessary.

The *Gauge* refers to the distance apart of the two tracks, and the *Scale* refers to the relationship of the size of the model to the size of the original railway.

The Garden Railways we are going to describe, have a track gauge of either 32 or 45 millimetres (1¼" or 1¾"). These track gauges have been around for a long time and have been known as Gauge 0 and Gauge 1 respectively. As such, they have generally been used for models of the broad gauge railways which run on mainline tracks, and many different scales have been used. They have always been, and still remain, very popular with enthusiasts.

The author's 7/8ths scale Peckett on the embankment.

Most of the recent increase in interest has been in modeling what are called "narrow gauge" (2' 0" or 2' 6" gauge) prototypes. By applying a scale whereby 16mm on the model represents one foot (305mm) on the prototype (approximately 1:19), we get a track gauge of 32mm. Many tracks are laid to this gauge, but to complicate matters a track gauge of 45mm has become more

A mix of scales in the siding at the AMRA track in Brisbane. A 7/8ths scale Hunslet is ahead of a Queensland PB15 in 1:20.3 scale.

popular, and so the wheel spacing on the models has to be widened accordingly. This can, luckily, be done without upsetting the overall size too much. The well known LGB Railways have a track gauge of 45mm, and therefore are compatible with our trains, even though they are to a slightly different scale.

The railways are often referred to as SM32 and SM45 which simply means: **S**ixteen **M**illimetre scale, **32**mm gauge, or **S**ixteen **M**illimetre scale, **45**mm gauge.

The other scale which fits nicely onto 45mm gauge track is known as "7/8ths Scale". That is, a scale of ⅞ inch to the foot. This is a particularly useful scale when modeling some of the very small prototypes.

The first part of the book describes in detail the building of a 16mm scale locomotive which can be gauged to either 45mm or 32mm. In the second and third part of the book the building of simple rolling stock is also described, based on the series which appeared in *Australian Model Engineering* magazine. These articles have been completely revised along with extra chapters on how to build a coal fired boiler, running and maintenance and various alternative design details for other locomotive prototypes. You should be able to build a working model of almost any narrow gauge locomotive which takes your fancy!

"Edwin" on an early afternoon passenger special.

Units

The introduction of SI units many years ago has not always made it easy for the model engineer. Older machine tools are often graduated in Imperial units. Small taps and dies are still cheaper and more readily available in Imperial sizes than metric, and often material sizes quoted in metric are really only conversions from inches. There is no need for it to be a problem though. Different sizes for materials and threads can be substituted for those given, to suit what stock or tools you have available, so long as the fit of mating parts is allowed for and not adversely affected. For example, the frame spacers which are dimensioned at 5mm could be ³⁄₁₆" or even 6mm or ¼". The threads in the ends could also be different to the stated 6BA, such as 3mm or ⅛" BSW. The main requirement is that the component does its intended job. This principle applies generally throughout the whole design. I therefore make no apology for mixing SI and imperial units throughout the text and drawings!

A conversion chart of equivalents and tapping sizes, etc. is very useful, and should be displayed close by for ready reference. My lathe and most of my drills, taps and dies are Imperial, so Model Engineer and BA threads have largely been used. I believe these threads are still the ones most commonly used in the small sizes. Not too many different ones are needed anyway, and provided you don't break them, once you have them the cost is not too great.

An economical alternative to small BA threads is the use of American threads. In this age of globalization and the internet, these fastenings and their taps and dies are easily obtained direct from the U.S.A. Some equivalents are as follows:

- 6BA : 4-48 UNF
- 8BA : 2-56 UNC
- 10BA : 1-72 UNF

Steve Malone's coal fired John Fowler cane loco "Petrie" tackles the viaduct.

PLEASE NOTE ALL DRAWINGS ARE SHOWN FULL SIZE UNLESS OTHERWISE INDICATED

Paul Blake's Shay waits patiently in the siding on his Pine Creek and Canungra Tramway.

Equipment and materials

All the machining can be done using a drill press and a small lathe, preferably equipped with a vertical slide. A compound vice to bolt onto the drill press table is virtually a necessity and an adequate one can be purchased quite cheaply these days. If you have other equipment, such as a small vertical mill then so much the better. The usual hand tools will be needed and will be referred to in the text. An ideal heating source for boiler work and silver soldering would be a propane gas outfit with a range of tips, say a large, medium and pinpoint.

Many of the turning processes required are

Innisfail No. 8 has a good head of steam meandering through the cane fields.

quite basic, and if you have not had a great deal of experience using tools and machinery in the workshop then start on the more straightforward components of the locomotive and lead on to more complex ones after your experience and confidence grows. If you have never used a lathe before then several books are available to help and many excellent courses are available through technical collegess, TAFE or other providers.

The entire engine can be made without castings, and from materials which may be in the scrap or off cuts bin. Lost wax casting, laser cutting, and etching of plates are processes which are particularly appropriate to working in this scale, and a lot of construction time could be saved by employing some or all of these processes. Some people enjoy the challenge of making almost everything from scratch, whilst others like to speed things up by using as many prepared parts as possible.

To help avoid breaking small taps, and to successfully use a small die, two essential items of equipment are a tailstock tap holder and a die holder, which can also be held in the drill chuck. If you do not already have these, drawings are provided for a pair which will suit 8 and 10BA. Construction of these is quite straightforward and suitable materials should be found in the off cuts bin. If 30mm rod is not available, the diameter of the die holder could be made smaller, although the thread becomes a bit short for the die locking screw. In addition, the shank diameter of taps varies between manufacturers, so you may need to drill other than the ⅛" specified for the tap holder. Make sure that each holder is a free sliding fit in its collar.

One of the great things about model engineering as a hobby is that each person can work to his or her own standard. Whilst normally a person will take as much care as possible to work accurately, we are not making Swiss watches, and steam locomotives are quite forgiving in their need for accuracy. In fact if tolerances are too fine, in some instances things can bind up, and certainly the prototypes were sometimes literally run into the ground with minimal maintenance often resulting in some very loose tolerances. However, when working in small sizes, care has to be taken when

Also on Paul's tramway, his Climax locomotive crosses the timber bridge with a rake of logs.

fitting parts, as an error of say 0.25mm would be 4% of 6mm, but only 1% of 25mm. Therefore in theory, tolerances have to be much less when working in smaller gauges, although in practice average care will produce a free and perfectly satisfactory engine. When our little locomotives are being used, the loads on working parts are less and total running times tend to be less than larger locomotives, thus minimizing wear and reducing the need for absolute precision.

Construction sequence

With a few exceptions where parts have to fit together or be part of an assembly sequence, items can be made in any order at all. If you are a beginner, it is a good idea to make straight-forward pieces first, and then progress to more difficult items as your skills improve.

The descriptions of how to go about making the railway are only suggested methods and there will be many other ways as good or better of making the parts and putting them together. Generally the methods described are for building parts from scratch, although the use of laser cut parts and castings will be discussed in Part 2. There are various general tips on work practices throughout the text which should be found useful.

Part 1

BUILDING *"ERIC"*

Steam Trains in Your Garden

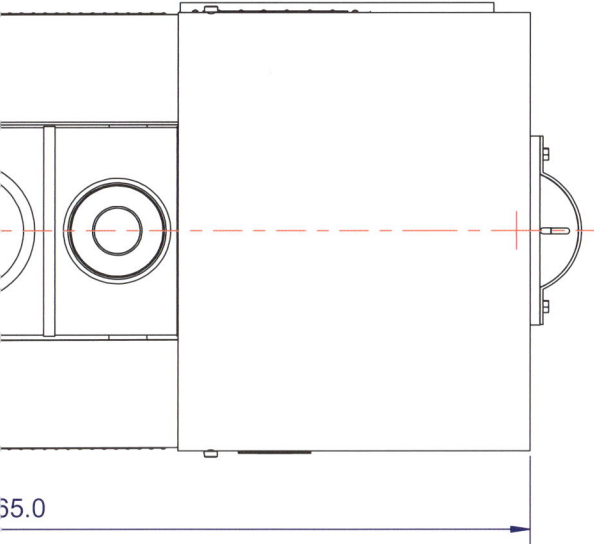

55.0

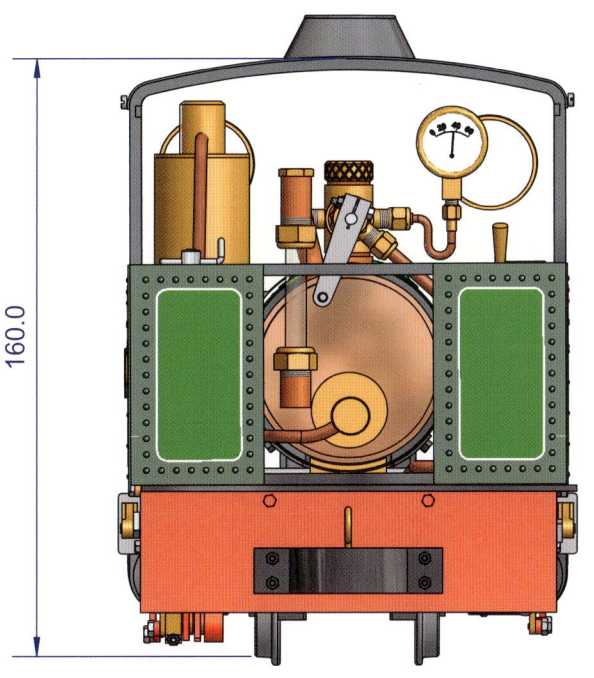

160.0

ERIC

omotive in 16mm scale for 45 and 32mm gauge.
ale: Half Full Size

6089 built 1923 in Leeds. The locomotive was delivered
It is now preserved at the Illawarra Light Railway Museum.

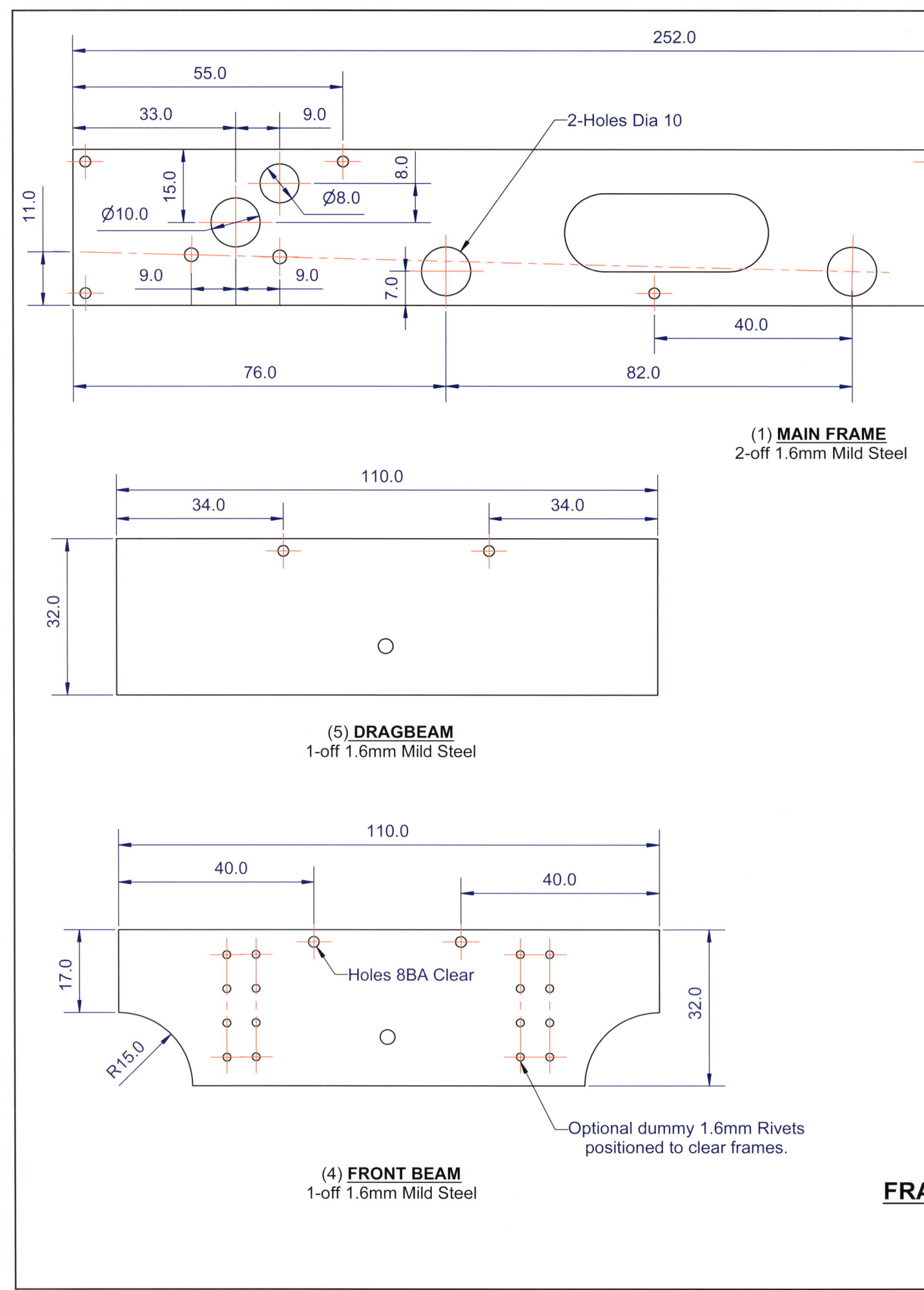

252.0

55.0

33.0 **9.0**

2-Holes Dia 10

11.0

15.0

Ø10.0

Ø8.0

8.0

9.0 **9.0**

7.0

76.0 **82.0**

40.0

(1) MAIN FRAME
2-off 1.6mm Mild Steel

110.0

34.0 **34.0**

32.0

(5) DRAGBEAM
1-off 1.6mm Mild Steel

110.0

40.0 **40.0**

17.0

Holes 8BA Clear

32.0

R15.0

Optional dummy 1.6mm Rivets
positioned to clear frames.

(4) FRONT BEAM
1-off 1.6mm Mild Steel

FRA

75.5

2.5

2.5

32.0

2.5

Ø10.0

Ø12.0

Optional Frame Cutouts

7- Holes 8BA Clear

1.5

Ream 1/4"

4.5

(3) MAIN BUSH
4-off Bronze

60.0

4.0

5.0

8BA

(7) SPACER BAR
7-off Brass

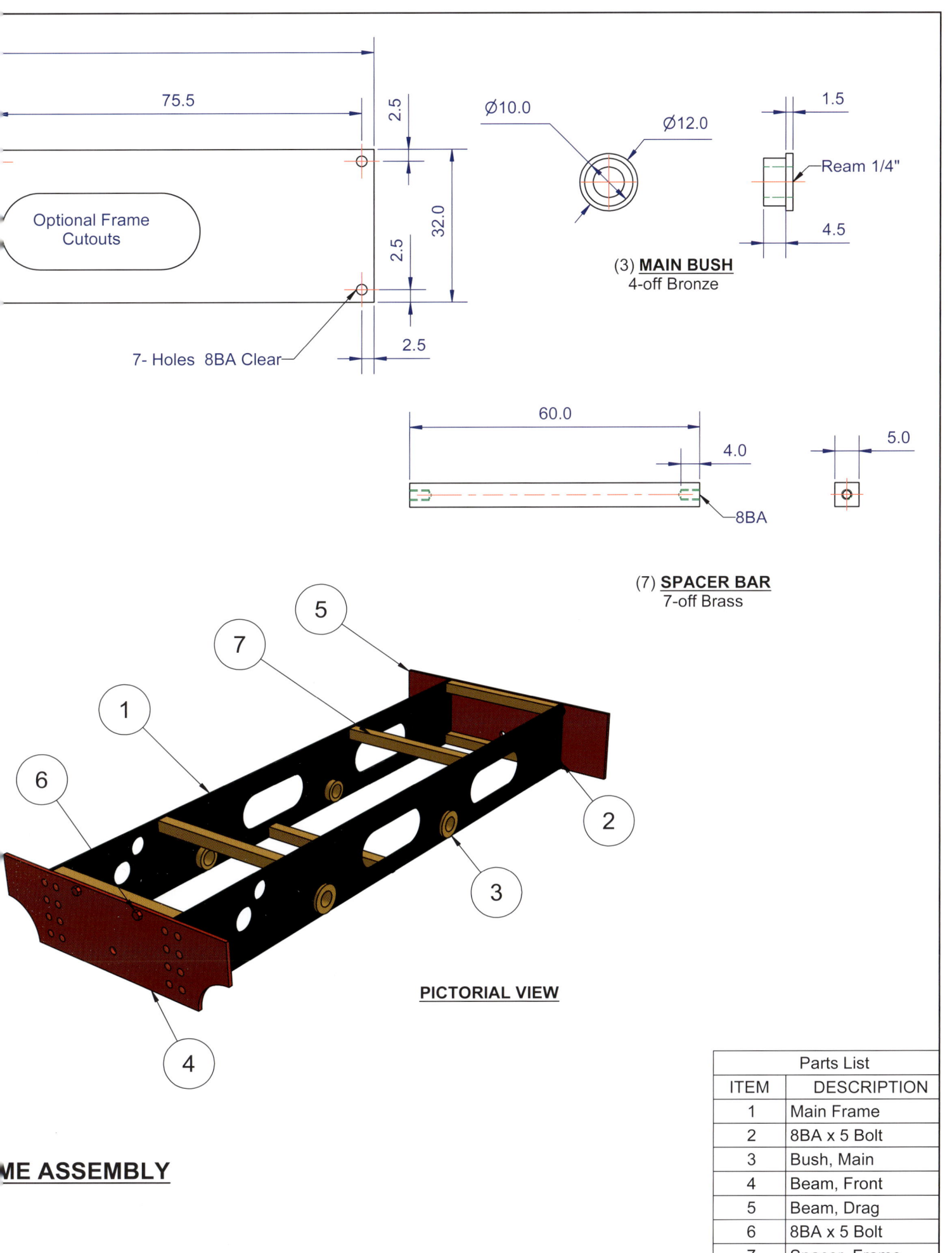

PICTORIAL VIEW

ME ASSEMBLY

Parts List	
ITEM	DESCRIPTION
1	Main Frame
2	8BA x 5 Bolt
3	Bush, Main
4	Beam, Front
5	Beam, Drag
6	8BA x 5 Bolt
7	Spacer, Frame

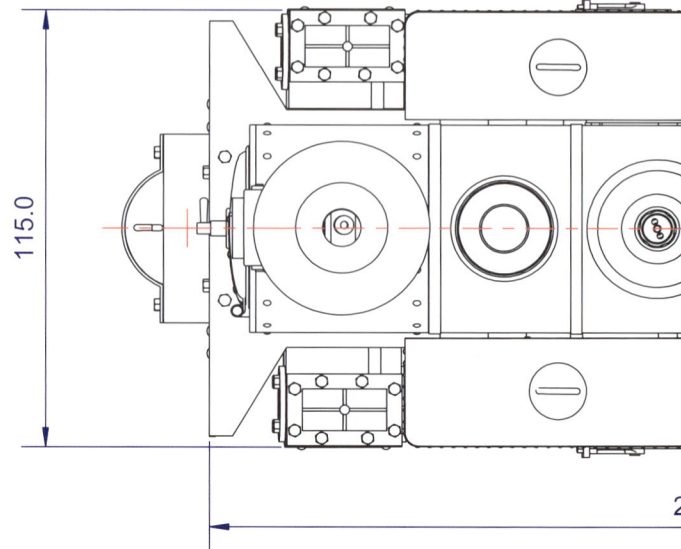

115.0

2

170.0

ERIC

A Freelance John Fowler Style loc
Sc

Based on John Fowler locomotive B/No.
to the State Metal Quaries Railway in N.S.W

CHAPTER 1 – The Chassis

Before making any component, we need to think about accuracy. Which holes, edges or surfaces need to be particularly accurate or true to each other? In this way we can ensure a well made model by making sure that critical fits are accurate. For example, with the frames, the most important holes to position precisely are the ones for the axle bearings. With the other holes, either their position is not so critical, or allowance can be made later to correct any misalignment. The need for accuracy with the bearing holes is so that they will exactly match the position of the holes on the coupling rods. It is not so much that they have to be exactly 82mm apart, but the spacing of the holes must be the same otherwise the rods will bind. Therefore we will start by making the coupling rods, so that they can then be used as a template to accurately drill the holes for the main bearings in the frames.

Coupling rods

Take a piece of 1.6mm mild steel sufficient for the two coupling rods. Make sure the surface is clean and coat with marking blue. (A permanent marker can be used). Make sure one edge is true and mark a centre line 5mm from and parallel to this edge. Mark and centre punch the two bearing holes on one of the rods, but only centre punch one of the holes in the other rod. Draw the outline of the rod with dividers and a scriber and then secure the piece of material in the drill press and drill the three holes dia 5mm. Now cut each rod out, but don't bother cutting to the final profile, just make each a generous rectangle. Put these blanks aside so that we can finish them later and also use them as a template for drilling the bearing holes in the frames.

Frame assembly

You will need a piece of 1.6mm mild steel sheet sufficient for two frame pieces and two buffer beams (about 260 x 100), and about 375mm of 5mm square brass for the spacers. Taking the 1.6mm mild steel, make sure that one long edge is straight then with a try square check an end and if necessary, mark and file it square to the edge. Mark out the two frames and the beams, leaving sufficient clearance for the saw cuts. Saw out the pieces, file to the lines and finally draw file and deburr all edges. The two frame pieces are now fixed together for marking out and drilling.

Coat the outside of the left hand frame with marking blue, then mark out and drill one of the 8BA clearance holes in the corner of each frame and clean out any burrs by using a larger size drill held and turned by hand. (Take care with sharp edges.) On the outside of the hole in the right hand frame, using the drill in the same way, make a small countersink and rivet the two pieces together. If a rivet is not available, an 8BA bolt can be used, cut off and hammered over as a rivet. (Alternatively the pieces can be bolted or super glued together.) Mark out and centre punch the hole in the opposite corner, carefully align the pieces, clamp in the drill press and drill 8BA clear. Place a rivet through this hole in the same way. Finally clean up so that the edges are together and smooth with no burrs. The remaining holes can now be drilled and tapped where necessary. Mark out and drill only the rear set of 10mm bearing holes

We can now drill the forward bearing holes, using the previously made coupling rods as a template. Make a brass plug to be a firm fit into the rear holes on the rod and the frame. Firmly clamp these parts together as shown, place in the drill press, making sure that the rod centres are parallel to the edge of the frame and drill through dia 5mm. Then, making sure that the frames are still clamped down and cannot move, take away the rods and open out the holes in the frames to 10mm.

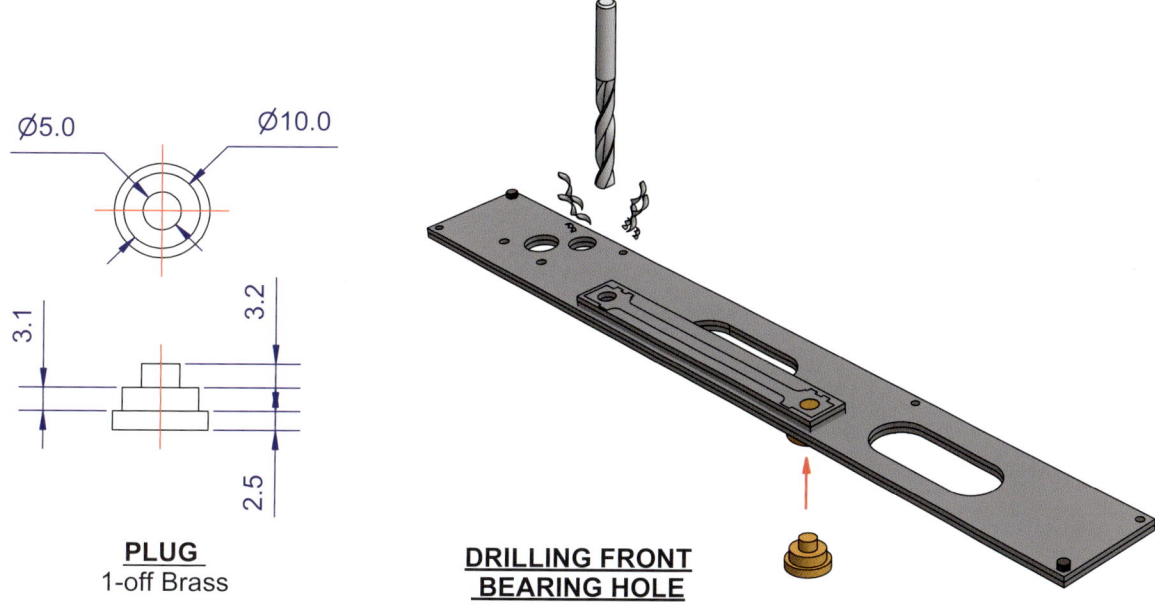

Ø5.0 Ø10.0

3.1 3.2 2.5

PLUG
1-off Brass

DRILLING FRONT BEARING HOLE

Cut out the buffer beams, clean up all edges, mark out and drill the holes then put to one side.

When making the six frame spacers, it is essential that they are all the same length. If you have a graduated hand wheel on your lathe's lead screw, this can be done by using a parting tool. Grip the square brass in the 4-jaw chuck and face off. (It is not necessary to have the material precisely centered for this). Loosen the jaws and move out just enough brass to allow the parting tool to clear the chuck when cutting off 60mm. Wind the parting tool to the end of the work and engage the lead screw. Move the tool by means of the lead screw hand wheel until it just touches the end of the job and note the reading. Measure the width of the parting tool with a micrometer, withdraw the tool and wind it down using the hand wheel a distance of 60mm plus the width of the parting tool and part off. Repeat for each spacer. (You could use your compound slide for this if it has sufficient travel.)

Another way would be to face the first end and then part off each piece slightly longer than required. Measure the length of each accurately with a vernier, noting how much it is oversize then grip in the chuck with the parted off end outermost, bring the parting tool to this end noting the measurement on the compound slide and then move this along the required amount to part off accurately to length.

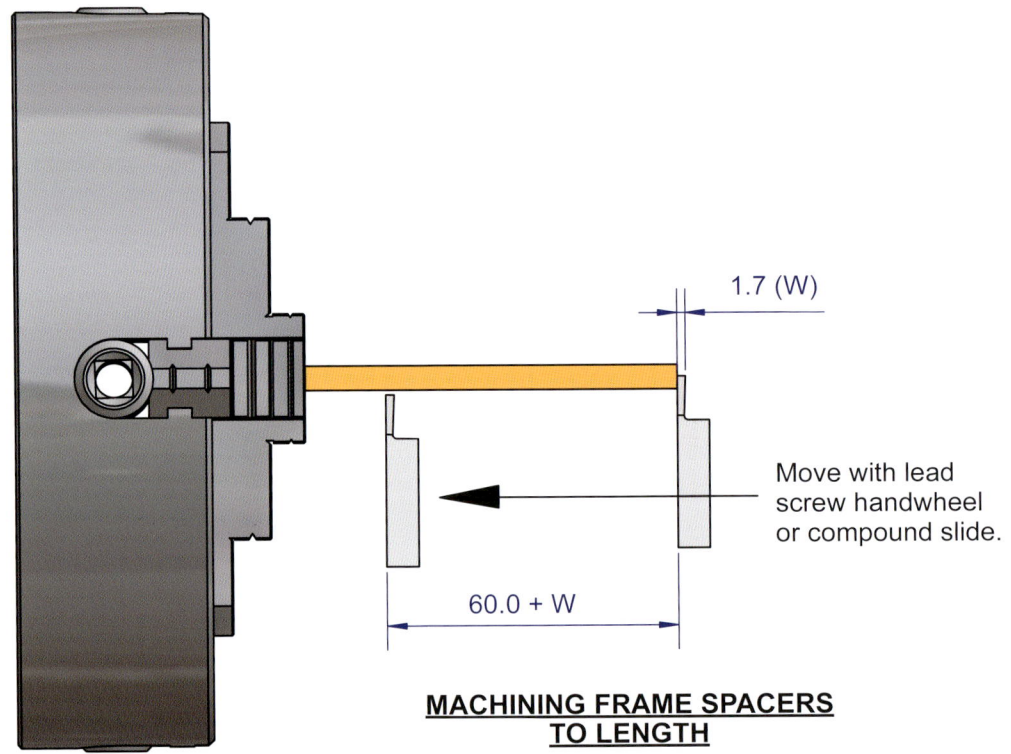

1.7 (W)

Move with lead screw handwheel or compound slide.

60.0 + W

MACHINING FRAME SPACERS TO LENGTH

Tapping small threads

As we need to tap the holes into the ends of the frame spacers, now is a good time to think about tapping small holes without breaking the tap. There are several 8 and 10 BA tapped holes used throughout the model and if we keep breaking taps, then our day will be ruined. To successfully thread a small hole, we need:

(1) A taper and bottoming tap of good quality. (Cheaper ones are usually a poor investment. They often have a poor thread form, are usually made of inferior metal and will almost invariably break).

(2) A drill of the correct tapping size.

(3) Lubricant. (Can be a specialist compound or ordinary oil).

(4) A tap holder which can be mounted in the tailstock or drill press chuck. (**See drawing opposite**).

To cut a thread, firstly make sure the job is firmly clamped or held in a vice, drill the hole, and without moving the job, remove the drill bit from the chuck and grip the tap holder with the taper tap inserted. Apply some lubricant, and gently start the tap using only light finger pressure. As soon as the tap starts to cut, reverse it for half a turn or so and then advance a small amount before reversing again. This process of advancing and reversing must be followed for the entire operation. Do it regularly, as if you go too far, the tap can jam and will break whichever way you turn it. As soon as the taper tap starts to get a bit tight, back it right out and change it for the bottoming tap. Go in with this until it too becomes tight then take out and return to the taper tap again. Throughout all of this you are only using the tips of your fingers. It may seem a little tedious, but I am sure you will agree it is nowhere near as tedious as breaking off a tap! Another consideration is that brass and bronze are much easier to thread than steel (**Photo1.1**).

1.1 — Using the tapping tool to tap a thread into a valve rod

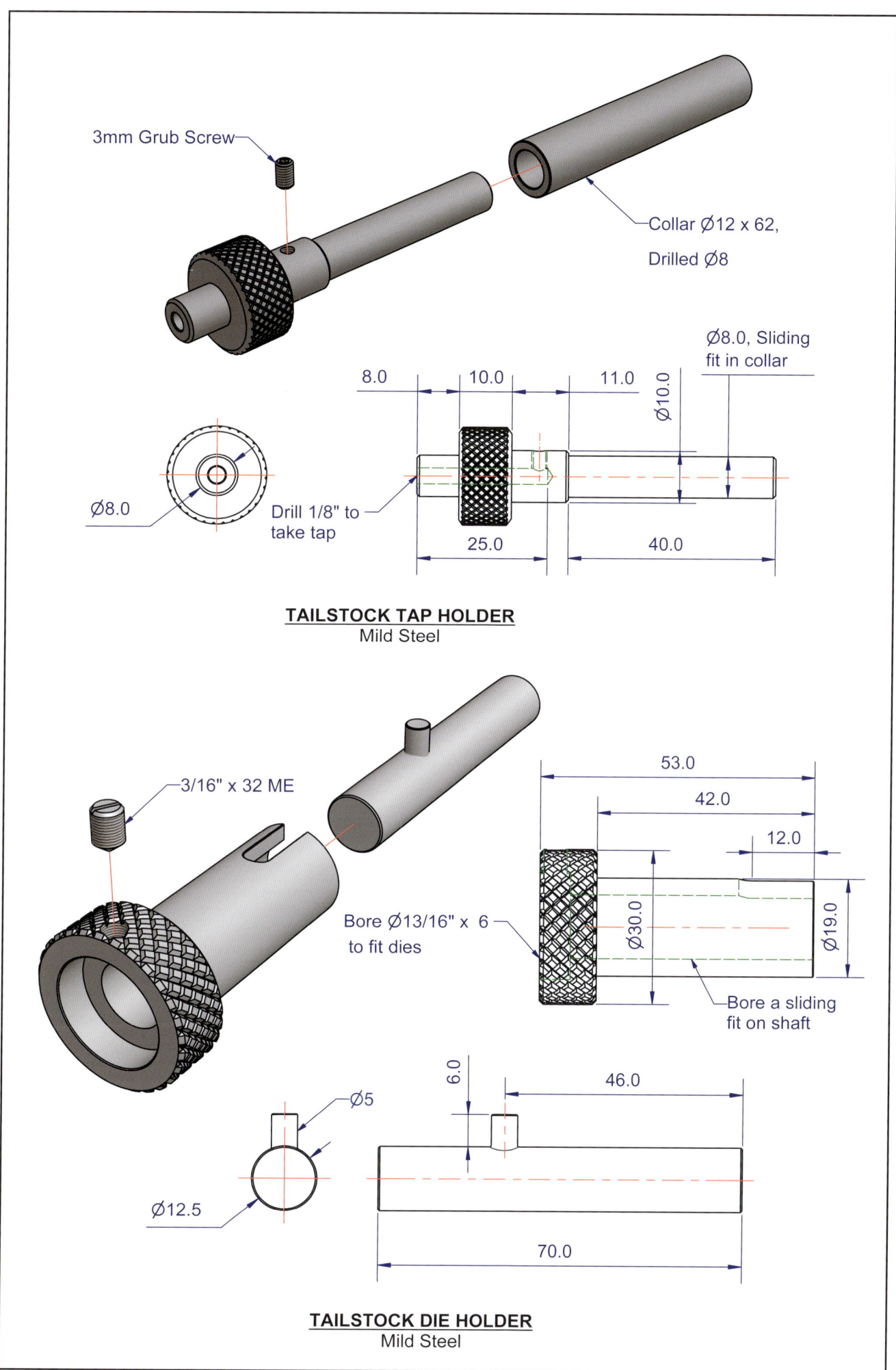

3mm Grub Screw

Collar Ø12 x 62,
Drilled Ø8

Ø8.0, Sliding
fit in collar

8.0   10.0   11.0   Ø10.0

Ø8.0

Drill 1/8" to
take tap

25.0   40.0

TAILSTOCK TAP HOLDER
Mild Steel

3/16" x 32 ME

53.0

42.0

12.0

Bore Ø13/16" x 6
to fit dies

Ø30.0   Ø19.0

Bore a sliding
fit on shaft

Ø5

6.0   46.0

Ø12.5

70.0

TAILSTOCK DIE HOLDER
Mild Steel

To thread the ends of each spacer, it is necessary to have them accurately centered in the 4-jaw. The thread needs to be about 4mm deep. Thread each one as previously described, this time with the tap holder held in the tailstock chuck. It can save time when setting up repetition parts in a 4-jaw chuck to mark two jaws and only undo these each time the job is changed. Whilst the job still needs to be checked for accuracy, it is usually very close to centre using this method.

Bolt the frames together, coat the end spacers with marking blue on the outside faces and place the assembled frames down on a flat surface. (Drill press table, lathe bed or similar). Take the buffer beams and hold them in their position on the ends and using a 1.5mm drill carefully twist it in each hole to mark its location. Take the beam off and centre punch for drilling. As an alternative to rivets, you could drill and tap 4 x 8BA bolt holes in the spacers at the ends of the frames to fix the beams, but rivets have an authentic look and you can't break a tap when using them!

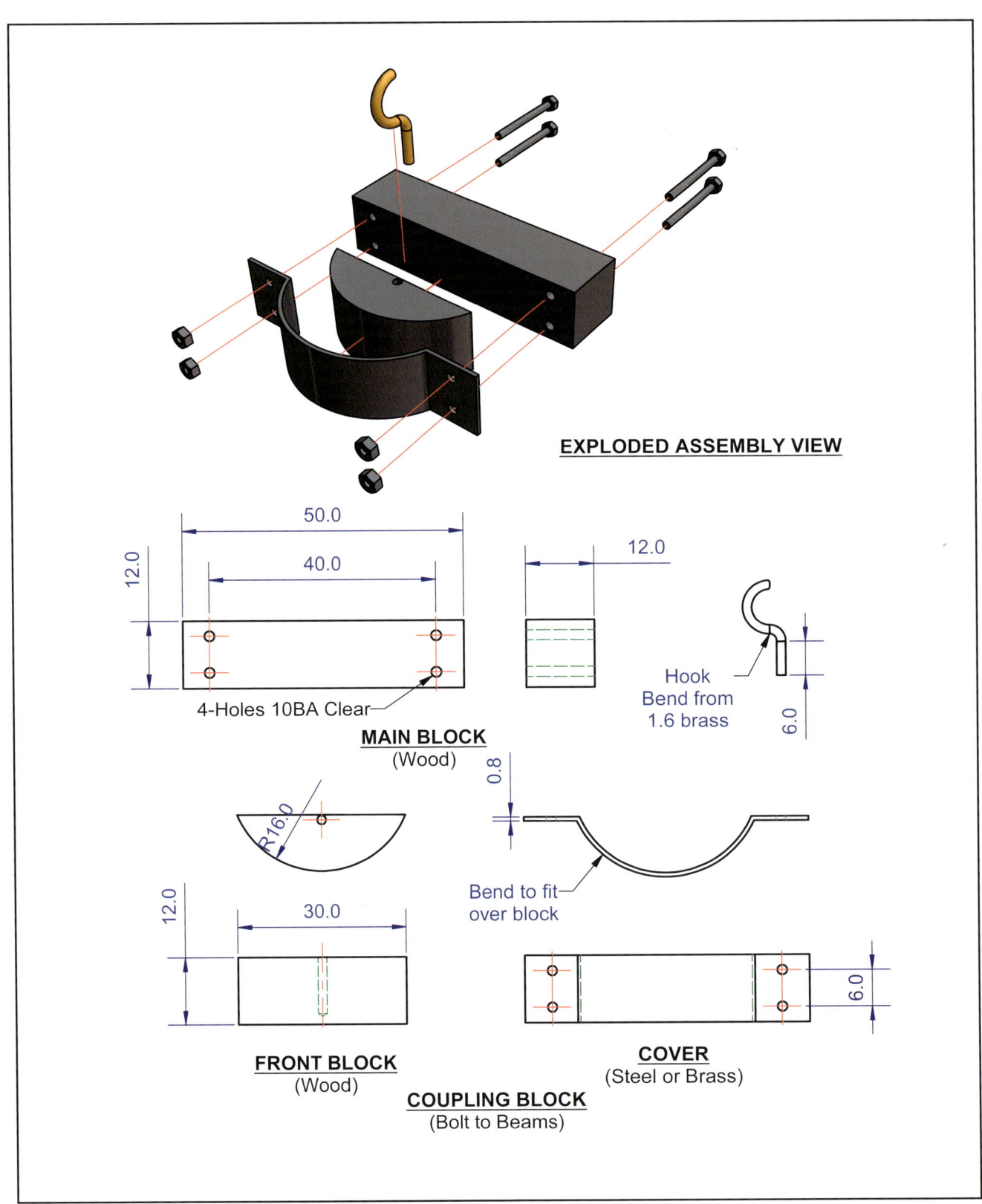

EXPLODED ASSEMBLY VIEW

Hook
Bend from
1.6 brass

4-Holes 10BA Clear

MAIN BLOCK
(Wood)

Bend to fit
over block

FRONT BLOCK
(Wood)

COVER
(Steel or Brass)

COUPLING BLOCK
(Bolt to Beams)

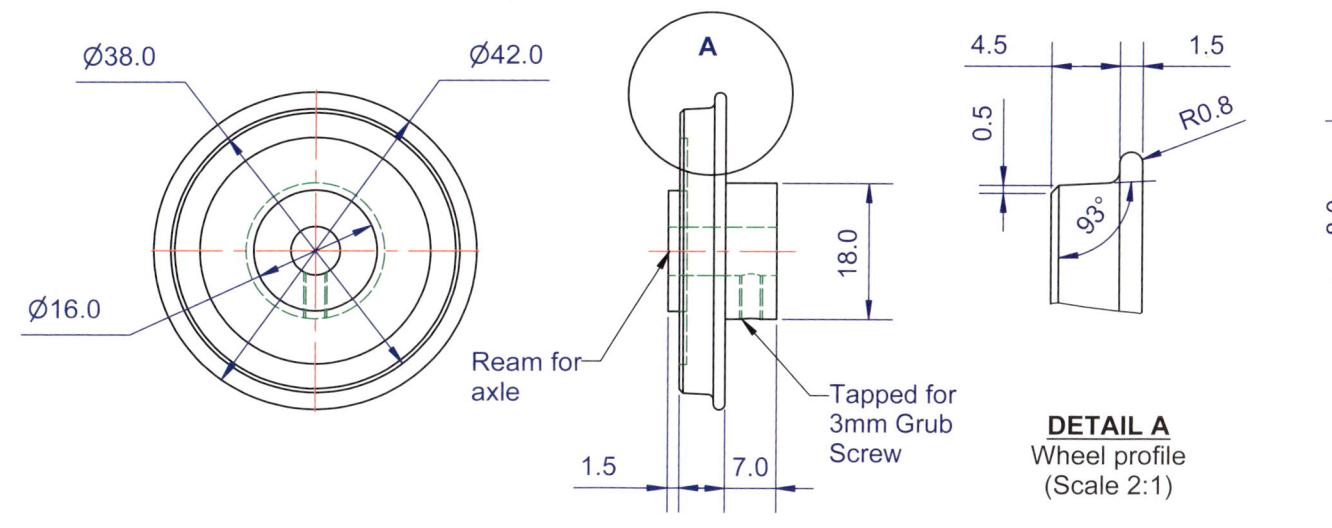

Ø38.0   Ø42.0

Ø16.0

A

4.5   1.5

0.5   R0.8   3.

93°   8.0

18.0

1.5   7.0

Ream for axle

Tapped for 3mm Grub Screw

DETAIL A
Wheel profile
(Scale 2:1)

(8) **WHEEL**
4-off Mild Steel

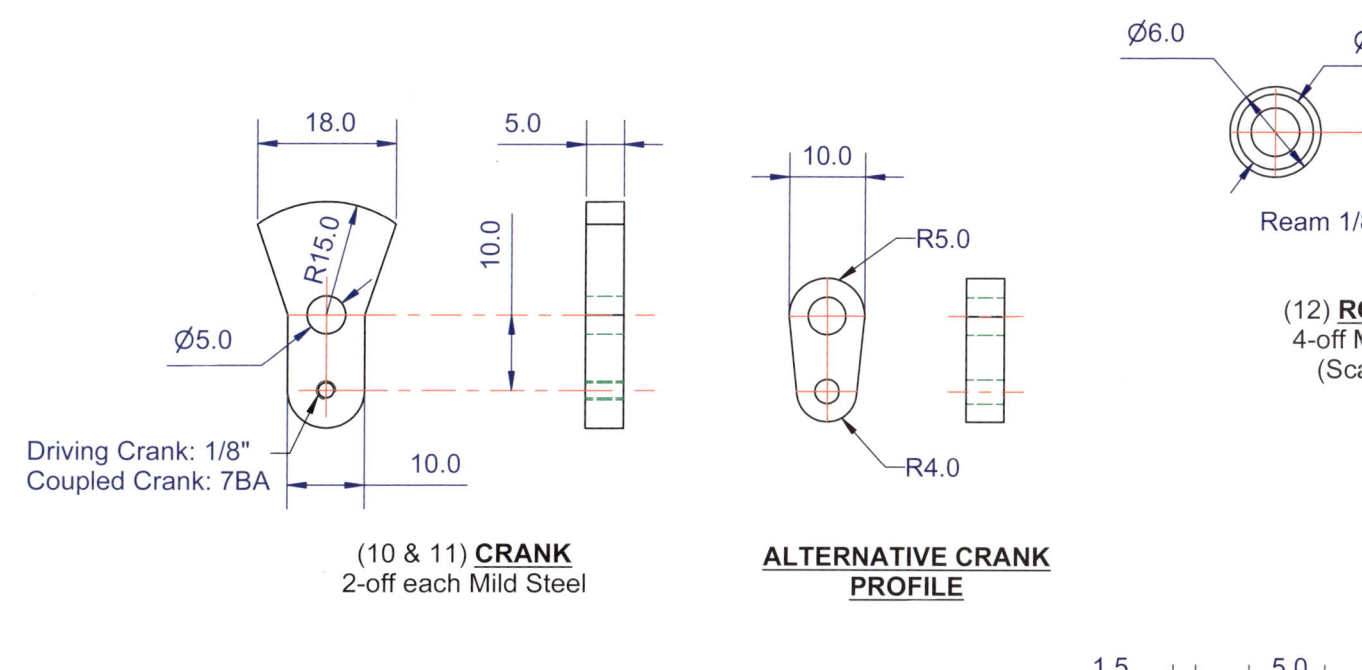

18.0   5.0

R15.0   10.0

Ø5.0

Driving Crank: 1/8"
Coupled Crank: 7BA

10.0

10.0

R5.0

R4.0

Ø6.0   Ø

Ream 1/

(12) **R**
4-off M
(Sca

(10 & 11) **CRANK**
2-off each Mild Steel

**ALTERNATIVE CRANK
PROFILE**

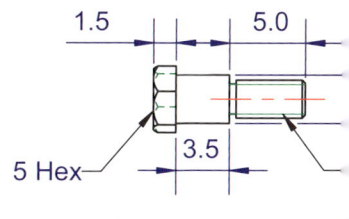

1.5   5.0

3.5

5 Hex

(15) **COUPLED CRAN**
2-off Mild Steel
(Scale 2:1)

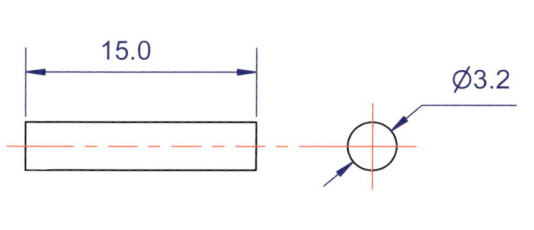

15.0   Ø3.2

(16) **DRIVING CRANK PIN
2-off Mild Steel**
(Scale 2:1)

ROLLING CHASSIS

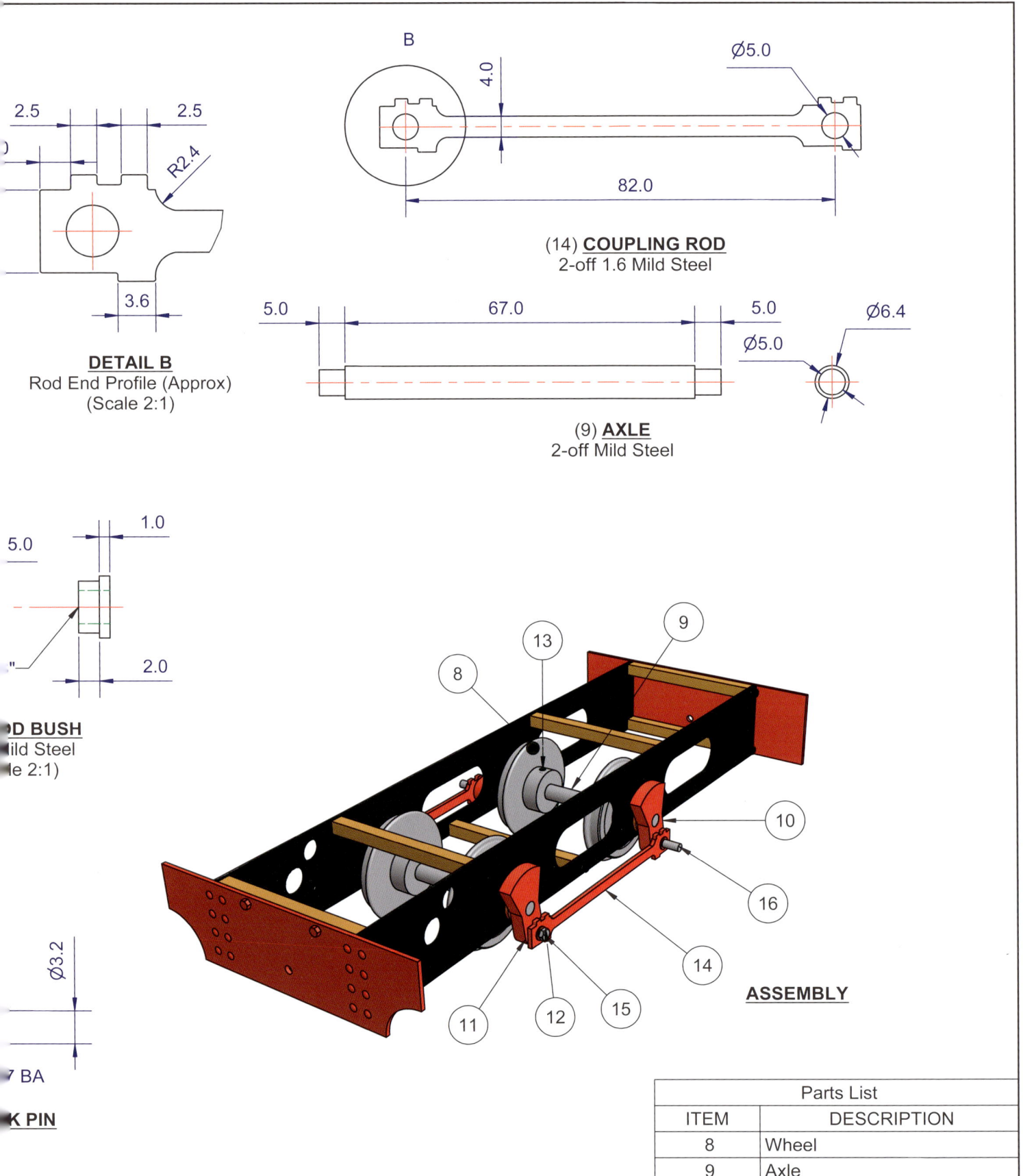

2.5   2.5   R2.4

3.6

DETAIL B
Rod End Profile (Approx)
(Scale 2:1)

B

4.0   Ø5.0

82.0

(14) **COUPLING ROD**
2-off 1.6 Mild Steel

5.0   67.0   5.0   Ø6.4

Ø5.0

(9) **AXLE**
2-off Mild Steel

5.0   1.0

2.0

"

OD BUSH
ild Steel
le (2:1)

Ø3.2

7 BA

K PIN

13   9

8

10

16

14

11   12   15

ASSEMBLY

Parts List	
ITEM	DESCRIPTION
8	Wheel
9	Axle
10	Crank, Driving
11	Crank, Coupled
12	Bush, Rod
13	Grub Screw 3mm x 5
14	Coupling Rod
15	Crank Pin Coupled
16	Crank Pin, Driver

Axle bushes

The axle bushes are made from bronze rod and are a straight-forward turning job. Drill and ream to suit the axles and make them a sliding fit in the frames. They are then inserted into their holes using Loctite®. To make sure they line up, place the axles in position, being careful not to get any adhesive in the wrong place.

Crank pins

The model has several pins in the main running gear and the valve gear. They are shown as being made from mild steel and some of the very small ones are running in mild steel holes, so a word or two about this choice of material might be appropriate before someone starts shaking their head. As far as smooth running and wear resistance in a model of this size goes, the ideal materials to use would probably be either hardened silver steel or stainless steel running in bronze bushes. Where possible, bronze bushes have been used, but it is a bit fiddly in some of the smaller holes, so for the sake of practicability, the bearing is just a hole in the mild steel. The reason mild steel has been specified for the pins, is simply that it is so much easier to machine. Also when you are using your 8 or 10BA die, and you are thinking about how much it has cost you, you will feel a lot better when you know it will last a lot longer if it is not being used to thread hard materials. The other consideration is that the pins are so easy to make in mild steel that they can readily be replaced if they wear. The final decision is of course up to you. If you want to use harder material for the pins then go ahead.

Having said that, the crank pins and eccentric pins can now be made. They are simple turning jobs, so the main thing to consider, particularly for the smaller eccentric pins, and later with the valve gear pins, is to fit them to the holes you are drilling. Whether it is metric or imperial doesn't matter. If you have a reamer, use it, but you probably won't have a reamer smaller than 3mm, so the pins should be made a neat fit in a drilled hole. The threads on the pins are made while the job is held in the lathe, using the tailstock die holder.

Connecting and coupling rods

The coupling rods can now be finished and the connecting rods made. As previously described for the coupling rods, the holes for the connecting rods should be drilled before cutting out the profile. Once the holes for the bearings are drilled, the rods can be cut and filed to shape. This can be done by roughing out with a hacksaw and finishing by filing. If you are going to have a polished finish on the rods, polish them before inserting the bushes, or if they are going to be painted, insert the bushes first and then paint after the Loctite has cured along with the frames as outlined below. The connecting rods need to be offset about 4mm in order to line up with the centreline of the motion. This is readily done by gripping the rod in a vice and carefully bending each end of the rod by hand. If you bend it a little too much, simply "unbend" it. You will find that you don't need to be over particular here.

Because the main bearings are fixed directly into the frames and therefore there are no axle boxes, once the wheel and axle assemblies are in position they can not be easily taken out, so before putting them in it would be a good idea to paint the frames and the wheels while they are still readily accessible. The usual colours for frames are black or red. Red was often used in full size as it is easier to detect cracks in red paint if they occur. The decision is yours, and either way first paint with a good primer. We will say more about painting later, but an etch primer whilst designed for use on non-ferrous metals, does provide a good hard finish which sticks well on steel also. Following the manufacturer's instructions with respect to over coating time lay on the final coat in the colour you have chosen. Be sure to follow all of the paint manufacturer's safety instructions with regard to paints and thinners, as they usually contain some potentially harmful substances.

After the paint has thoroughly dried, we can put together the frame and axle assembly. The tricky bit here is the quartering of the cranks. This simply means that the cranks on each end of the axle have to be fixed at 90 degrees to each other, conventionally with the right hand one leading. Loctite will be used to initially hold the cranks, so care has to taken not to let any adhesive get into the bearings or there is your day ruined again. (If you do have a disaster with Loctite, remember that the bond can be broken down with heating, and then you can have another go).

Quartering the cranks

There are many different ways of quartering the cranks; many articles have been written over time and various jigs have been devised to assist in getting it right. One thing to remember is that the most important thing is not that the cranks are exactly 90 degrees to each other rather than 89 or 91 degrees, but that the angle is the same for both sets of axles. So if you have a favourite way of doing it then by all means go ahead. Every design of model has different requirements, and this one is made a little more awkward by having the axles positioned in the frames, rather than using separate axle boxes. We will describe two methods, the first using a try square and the second using a jig.

Try-square Method: For the driving cranks insert the crank pins into the cranks and secure with Loctite. After the adhesive has cured, the crank pins should also be further secured from moving by drilling through and inserting a 1.6mm dia roll pin. (If roll pins are difficult to obtain, a plain 1.6mm pin can be inserted and lightly riveted or secured with Loctite.) The forward crank pins have a hexagon head which gets in the way for quartering, therefore the best way to get around this is to make a pair of plain temporary crank pins, say ⅛" or even ³⁄₁₆" dia. and around 15mm long. Cut a screwdriver slot in one end and turn and thread the other end 7BA for 5mm. Screw these home firmly for the quartering process.

Next the left hand cranks are secured onto the axles, again using Loctite and then a roll pin. Note that when using the "try square" method of quartering, it is necessary to leave the axles about 1.5mm long on each end for accurate lining up. This extra can then be removed by filing after everything is finished.

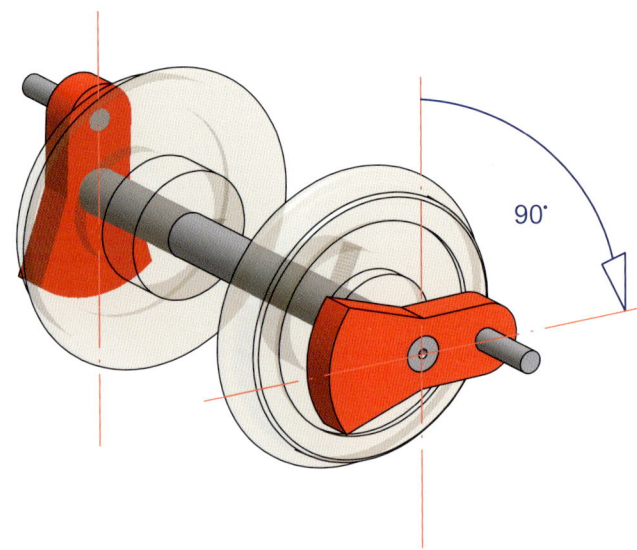

CRANKS QUARTERED

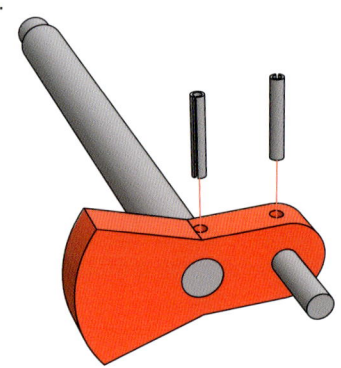

SECURING CRANK AND CRANK PIN WITH ROLL PINS

Slide the axles into their respective bearings making sure not to forget the wheels! To help keep Loctite away from the bearings on the right hand side, very carefully apply a slight smear of thin grease onto the outside of the bush, but do not let it get onto that part of the axle where the crank is to go. On a flat surface, such as the drill press table, place two pieces of packing on either side of the chassis as shown. (These need to be high enough to allow the wheels to turn.) Then pack up the whole frame assembly and lightly clamp it down to prevent it from moving. The datum we are using to set the cranks is a tangent line running from the crank pin to the axle as shown in the diagram. This is lined up on the edge of the packing on the right side and a try square on the left side. Care needs to be taken and you will need your best pair of magnifying glasses. Once you are satisfied everything is right for one axle, remove the crank and carefully apply Loctite to the axle boss and set it up again in position. Let the first axle set before repeating for the other one. If you can lightly clamp things as you go, it will help to avoid bumping something accidentally just when you don't need it.

After the adhesive has cured, you can test whether the quartering has been successful. Place the left hand rod onto the cranks and turn the wheels. Unless you have a major error, the assembly should turn freely. Now place the right hand rod onto the cranks and rotate the motion. Again, it should move freely without any binding or tight spots, but the chances are that there will be tight spots, particularly when the crank pins are right forward or right back. If this is the case, determine whether the distance between the holes in the rod is too short or too long and slightly relieve the front or the back of the forward coupled bearing with a round needle file until the wheels turn freely. After you are satisfied that all is well, drill and pin the cranks and driving pins.

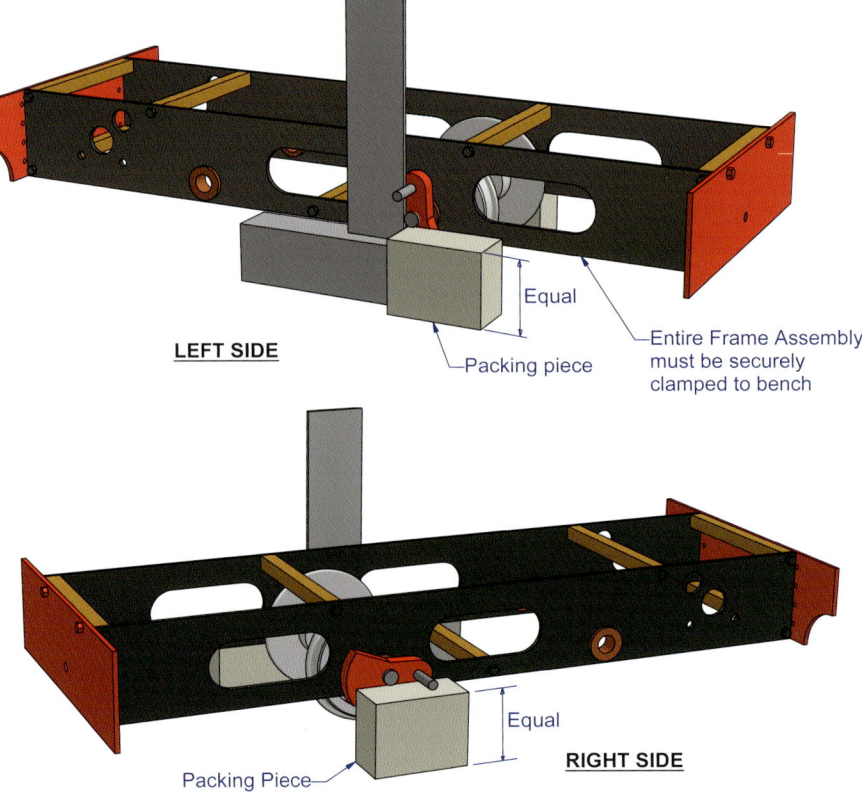

QUARTERING CRANKS
(TRY SQUARE METHOD)

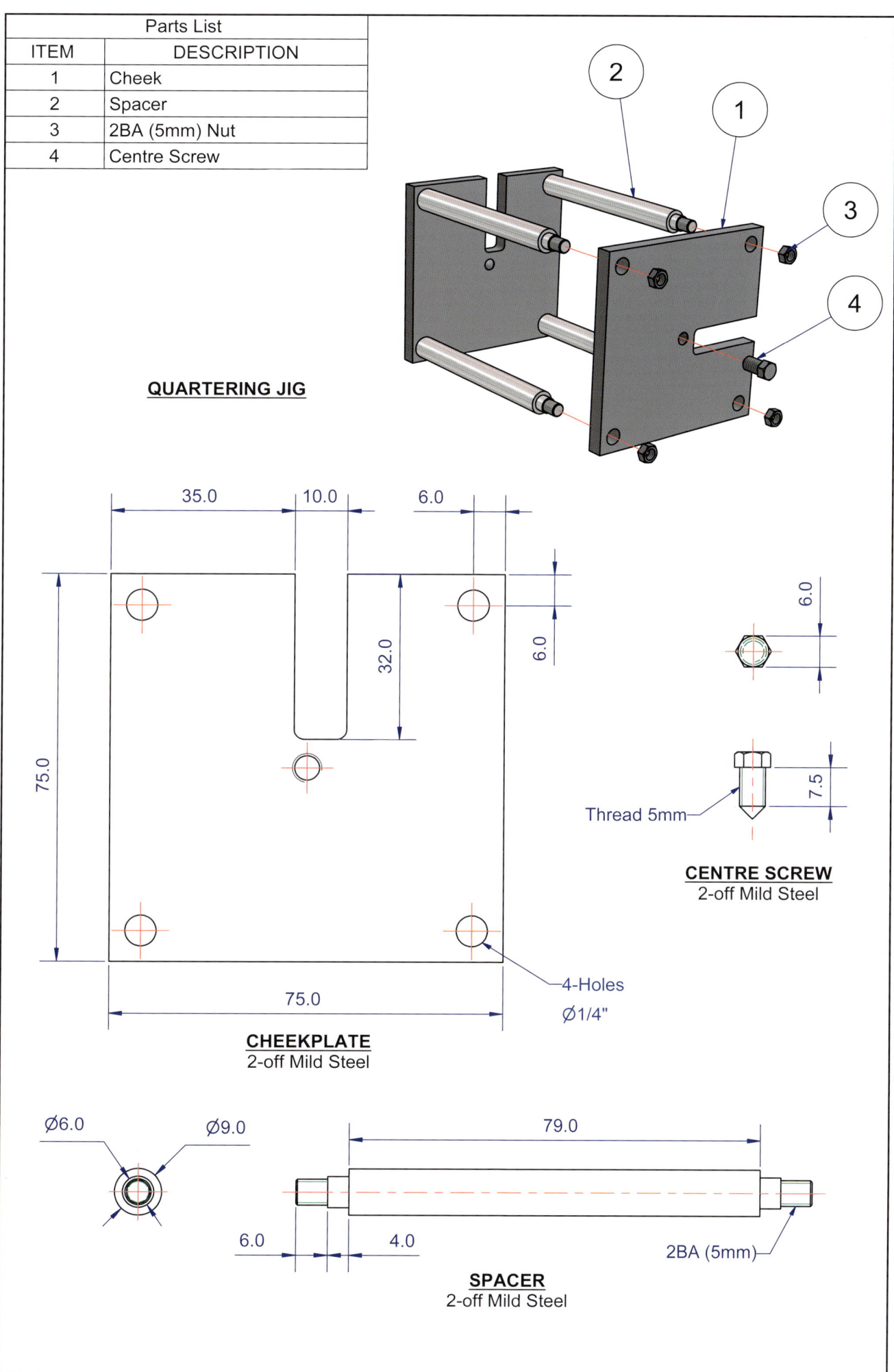

Parts List	
ITEM	DESCRIPTION
1	Cheek
2	Spacer
3	2BA (5mm) Nut
4	Centre Screw

QUARTERING JIG

CHEEKPLATE
2-off Mild Steel

4-Holes
Ø1/4"

CENTRE SCREW
2-off Mild Steel

Thread 5mm

SPACER
2-off Mild Steel

2BA (5mm)

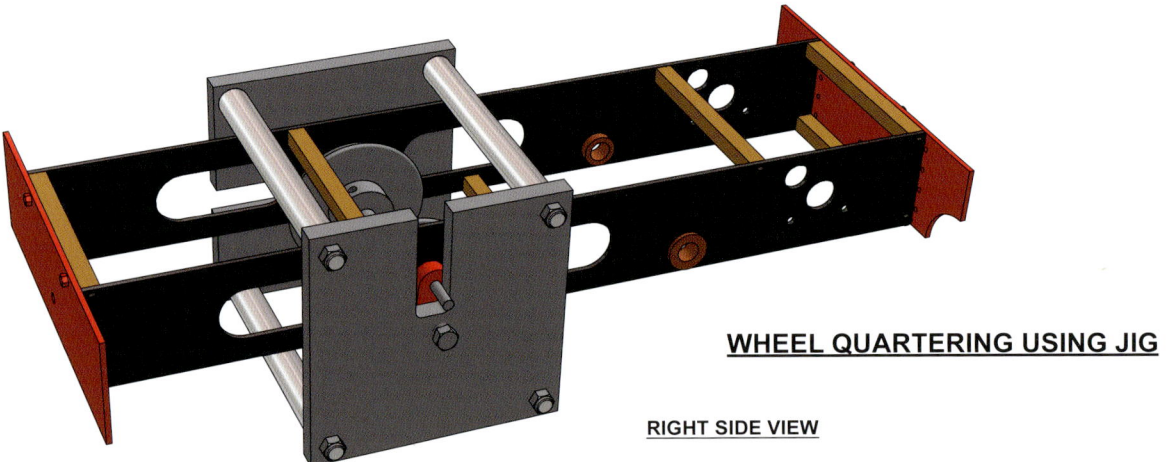

WHEEL QUARTERING USING JIG

RIGHT SIDE VIEW

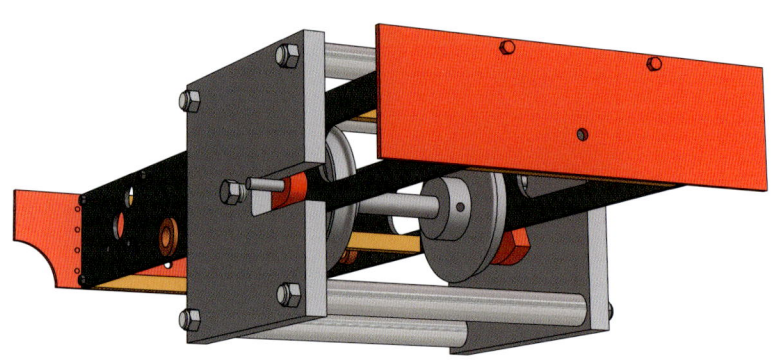

Jig Method: Make the jig shown in the drawing (page 24). The components shown are fairly robust, so you could use smaller sizes for the cheeks and the spacers. The important thing is to have both cheeks identical, and this can be done by preparing the two blanks perfectly square and identical in size and then drilling the centre holes and machining the slot with the two pieces clamped together. The position of the four clamping holes has to be precise, because in use, one cheek is rotated 90 deg. to the other. To use the jig, it will be necessary to drill a small cenre hole in the end of each axle.

LEFT SIDE VIEW

Prepare the axles, cranks, crank pins and wheels as before and do a dry run using the quartering jig to familiarise yourself with how it goes together. It is a bit fiddly and an extra pair of hands might help. Have a couple of open ended spanners or shifters ready to turn the cranks while lining up. Once you are happy that everything is in order, smear a film of grease or oil as before onto the outside face of the main bearing on the side the crank is to be fastened. Coat the axle and the hole in the crank with a minimum of Loctite and reassemble with the jig. The aim is to have each crank pin (or temporary crank pin) touching the forward face of its slot in the quartering jig. (Alternatively, they can touch the back face of the slot, so long as they are both in the same relative position). After the Loctite has hardened, repeat for the other axle. The rods can be assembled onto the crank pins as described previously. (**Photo 1.7**)

1.7 — Using the quartering jig

Cylinder assembly

There are quite a lot of steps in making the cylinders, so they will probably take longer to make than any other part, but that doesn't mean they are any more difficult. They can be made from a suitably sized square or rectangular block of bronze or brass, or cut from a length of 38mm diameter material if using round. The description for each cylinder is the same, the only difference being that they are handed. When finally assembling all the covers and various parts of the cylinders, it is necessary to use gaskets between the faces to ensure a steam tight joint. You can either cut out thin card for gaskets (manila folders are ideal), or use silicone gasket material. If using card, smear some oil on the metal surface and press onto the card to give an imprint. The small holes for 10BA bolts can be cut using a sharp leather punch or similar and the outline cut with sharp scissors. The glands for the piston and valve rods can be sealed by inserting a few twists of PTFE thread tape and screwing the gland nut up firmly but do not overtighten.

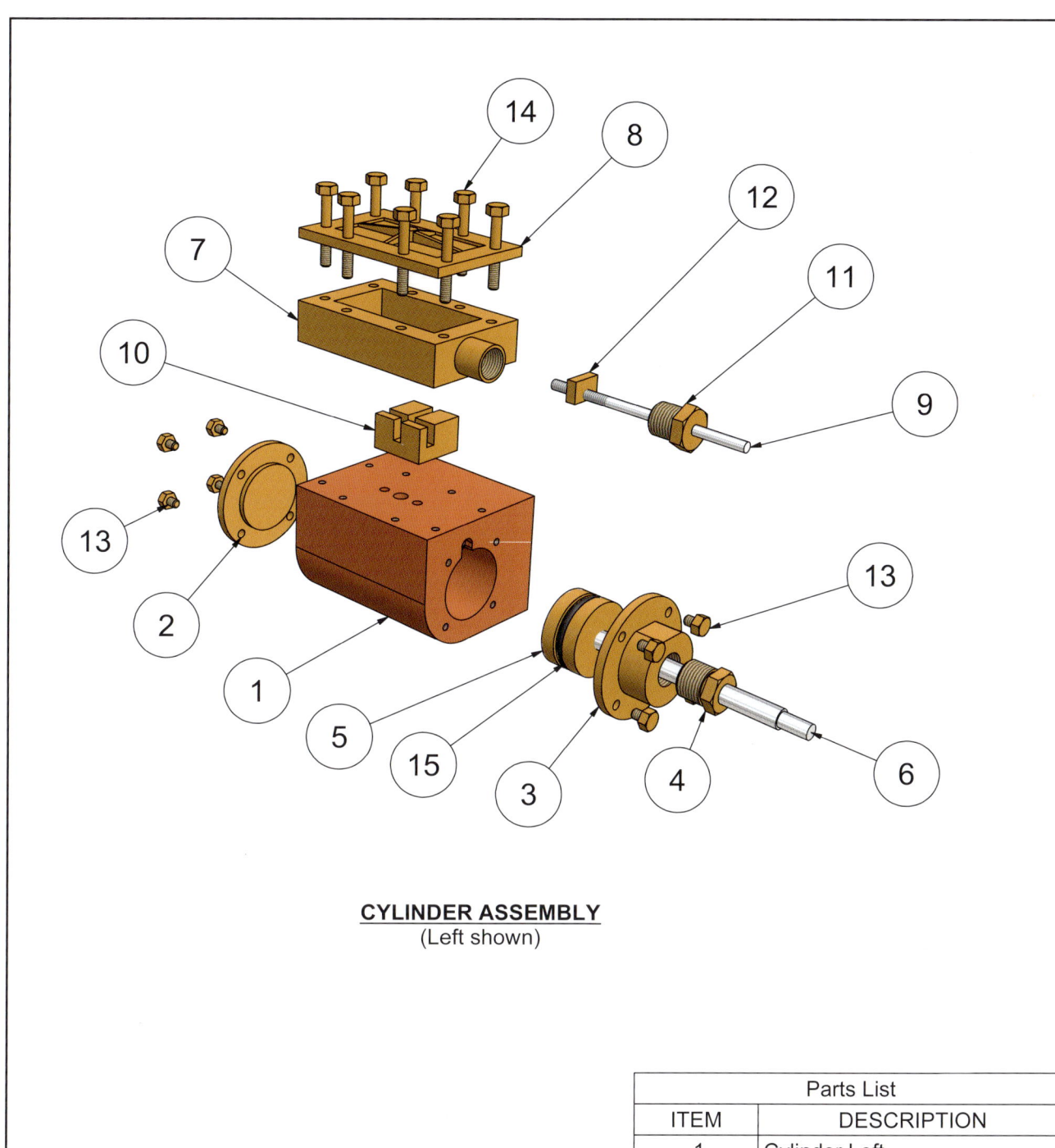

CYLINDER ASSEMBLY
(Left shown)

Parts List	
ITEM	DESCRIPTION
1	Cylinder Left
2	Cylinder Cover Front
3	Cylinder Cover Rear
4	Cylinder Gland Nut
5	Piston
6	Piston Rod
7	Valve Chest
8	Valve Chest Cover
9	Valve Rod
10	Valve
11	Valve Chest Gland
12	Valve nut
13	10BA x 5 Bolt
14	10BA x 12 Bolt
15	O-Ring

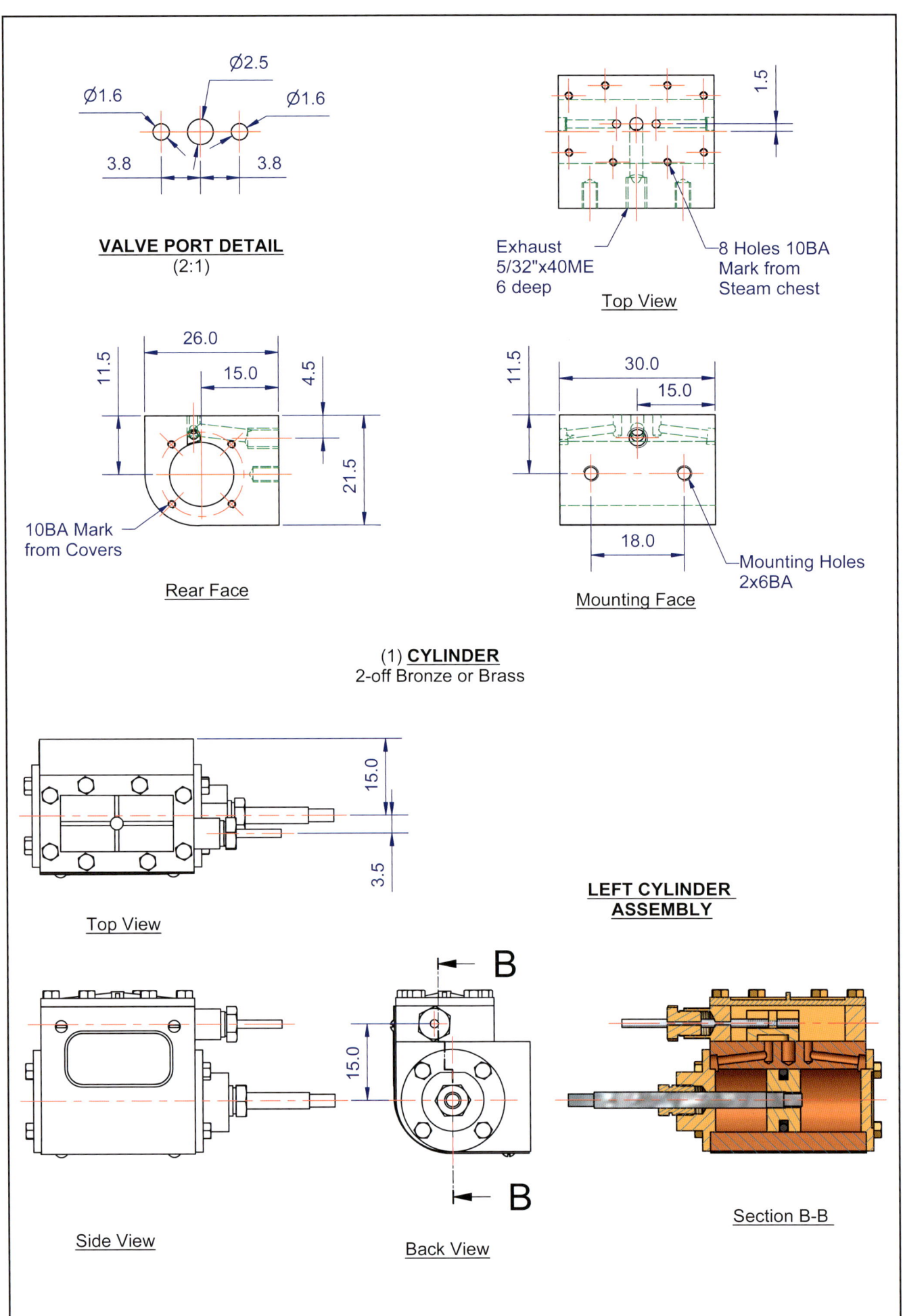

VALVE PORT DETAIL
(2:1)

Ø2.5
Ø1.6   Ø1.6
3.8   3.8

Exhaust
5/32"x40ME
6 deep

8 Holes 10BA
Mark from
Steam chest

Top View

1.5

26.0
15.0
11.5
4.5
21.5

10BA Mark
from Covers

Rear Face

30.0
15.0
11.5
18.0

Mounting Holes
2x6BA

Mounting Face

(1) CYLINDER
2-off Bronze or Brass

15.0
3.5

Top View

**LEFT CYLINDER
ASSEMBLY**

Side View

B
B

15.0

Back View

Section B-B

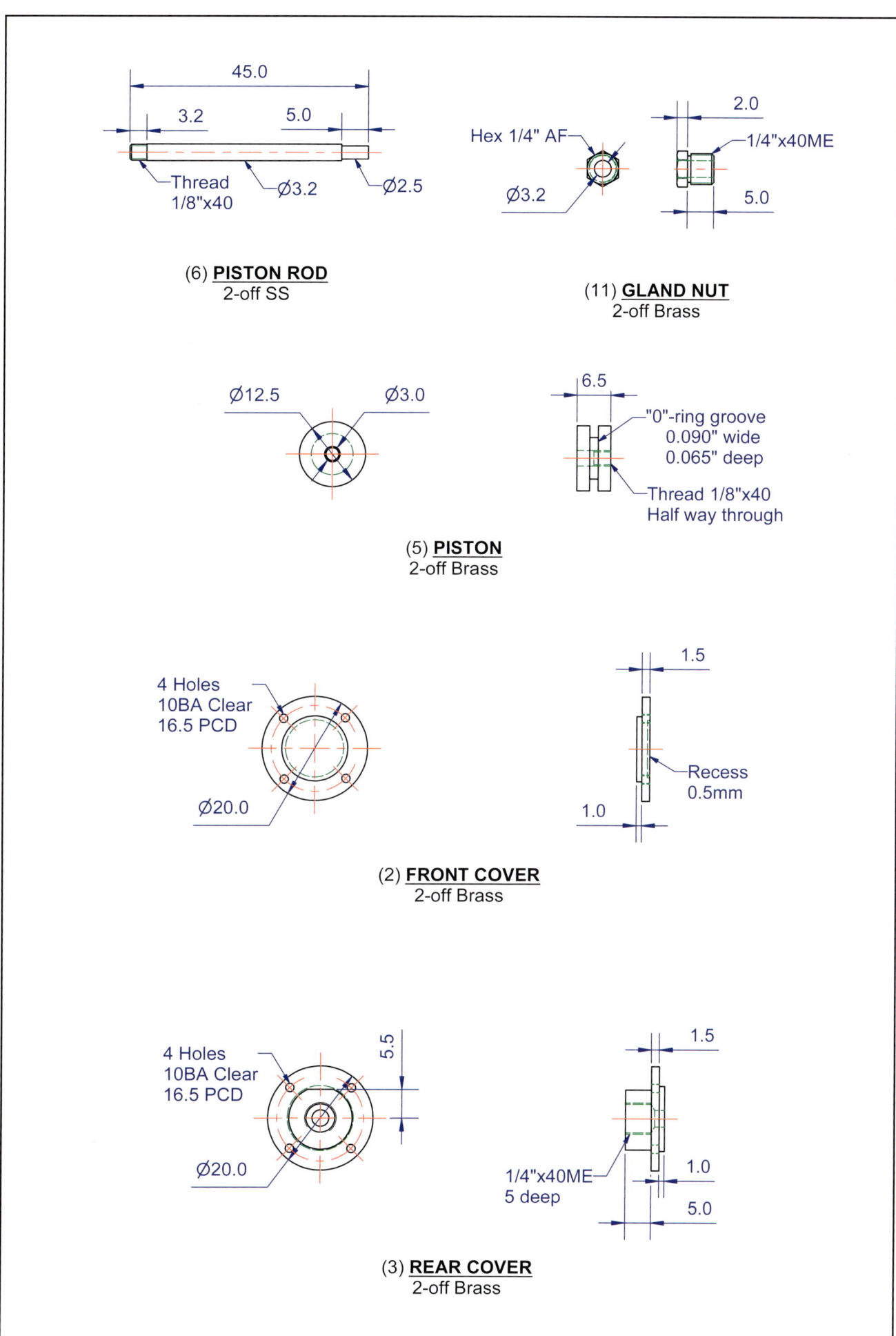

(6) PISTON ROD
2-off SS

Thread 1/8"x40
Ø3.2
Ø2.5
45.0
3.2
5.0

(11) GLAND NUT
2-off Brass

Hex 1/4" AF
Ø3.2
2.0
1/4"x40ME
5.0

(5) PISTON
2-off Brass

Ø12.5
Ø3.0
6.5
"0"-ring groove
0.090" wide
0.065" deep
Thread 1/8"x40
Half way through

(2) FRONT COVER
2-off Brass

4 Holes
10BA Clear
16.5 PCD
Ø20.0
1.5
Recess
0.5mm
1.0

(3) REAR COVER
2-off Brass

4 Holes
10BA Clear
16.5 PCD
5.5
Ø20.0
1.5
1/4"x40ME
5 deep
1.0
5.0

The cylinders

For the cylinders, machine the bronze or brass into two rectangular blocks 30mm x 26mm x 21.5mm. (**Photos 1.8(a) and 8(b)**) To make the block easier to grip, don't shape the curve on the outside of the cylinders until all holes are drilled and ports formed. Make sure that all faces are truly square to each other. Select the best surface for the valve face and coat the surface which will become the back end with marking blue. Mark out and lightly centre pop the centre of the bore. Mount the block in the 4-jaw chuck, placing a thin piece of brass or copper under the jaw which falls on the valve face to prevent marking its surface, and adjust so that the centre pop mark is running exactly at centre. Providing the jaws are in close contact with the work, the valve face and the bolting face should automatically be parallel to the lathe axis. Start the bore with a centre

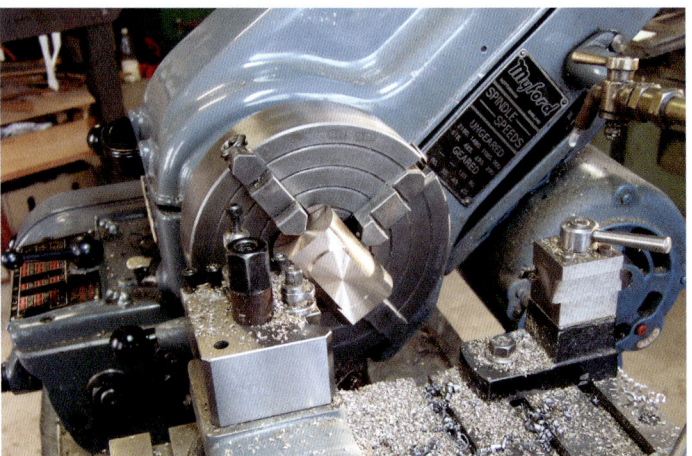

1.8(a) and 1.8(b) — Machining the block for the cylinderd from round rod

drill and drill right through with progressively larger drills, finally reaming out to ½". Take a light cut across the rear face, bringing the block to its finished length of 30mm. This will ensure that the rear face and the bore are true to each other. On the face you have chosen to be the valve face mark out the steam and exhaust ports. Drill these ⅟₁₆" (1.6mm) and ³⁄₃₂" (2.5mm) respectively to a depth of 3mm. Take the block and mark on the outside face a line which shows the position of each angled steam passage running from the end of the cylinder to the bottom of its port hole. (A permanent, fine tipped marker pen is ideal for this.) Using this line as a reference, set the block in the milling machine vice to this angle and drill the steam passages, firstly milling a recess in the end of the cylinder to create a passage for the steam and to form a flat to start the drill. (**Photos 1.9 & 1.10.**) (Make sure this recess is big enough to allow a free flow of steam into, and condensate out of the ends of the cylinder after the end cover is fitted.)

1.9 — Milling recess in end of cylinder   *1.10 — Drilling steam passages*   *1.11 — Drilling exhaust passage*

To drill the exhaust passage, firstly set up the block with the mounting face uppermost and drill and tap ⁵⁄₃₂" x 40 ME thread for a depth of 6mm. Then, mark the exhaust passage with a marker as you did for the steam passages, this time on the end of the block. Mount the block in the vice at an angle to match this line and drill 2mm diameter into the exhaust cavity. Take extra care with this operation and make sure you are doing it on a good day. It would be a shame to drill into the bore! (**Photo 1.11.**) The cylinders can now be put to one side until the valve chest and covers are made.

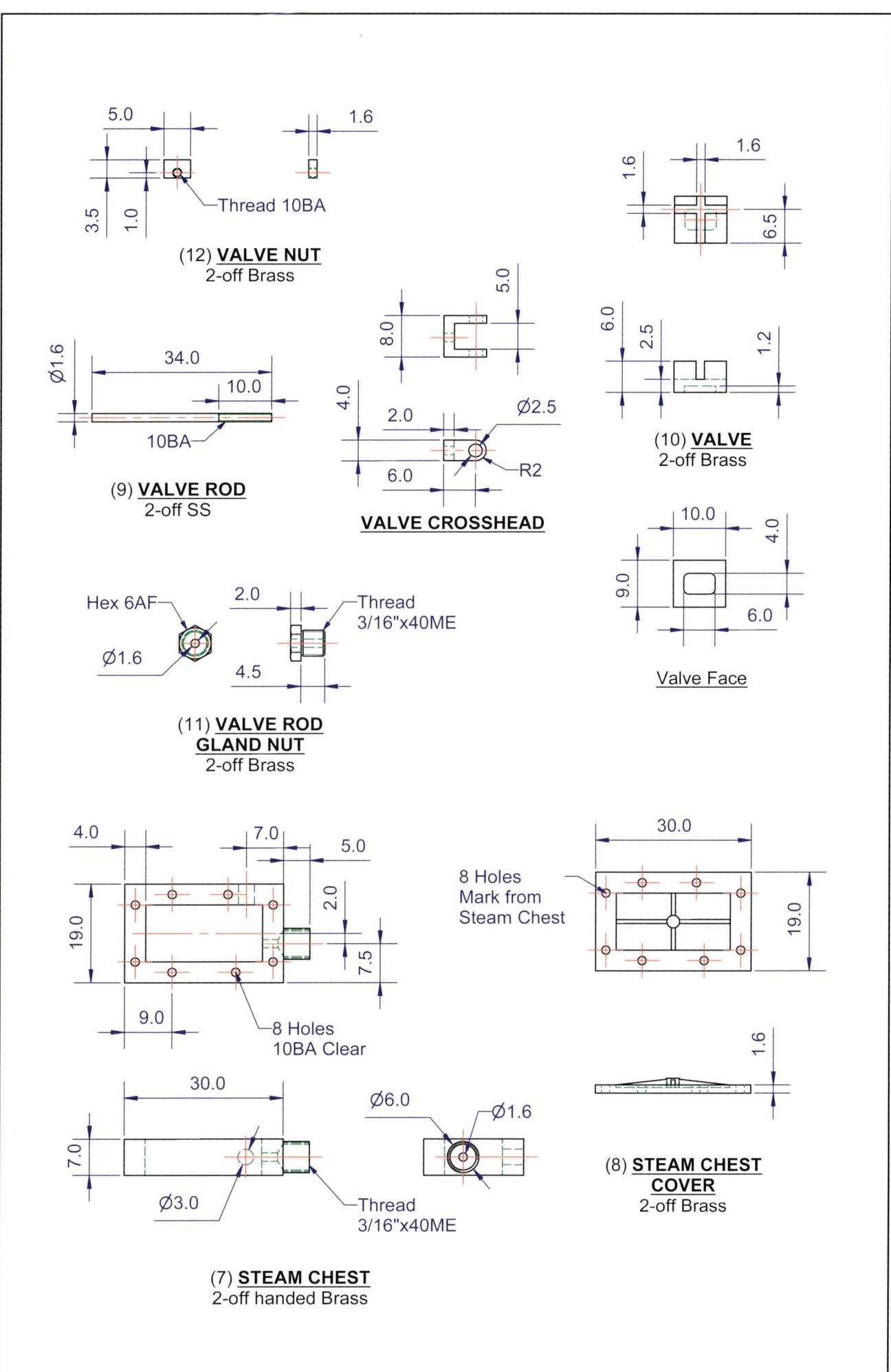

5.0

1.6

Thread 10BA

1.0

3.5

(12) **VALVE NUT**
2-off Brass

1.6

1.6

6.5

Ø1.6

34.0

10.0

10BA

(9) **VALVE ROD**
2-off SS

5.0

8.0

4.0

2.0

6.0

Ø2.5

R2

VALVE CROSSHEAD

6.0

2.5

1.2

(10) **VALVE**
2-off Brass

Hex 6AF

Ø1.6

2.0

4.5

Thread
3/16"x40ME

(11) **VALVE ROD
GLAND NUT**
2-off Brass

10.0

9.0

4.0

6.0

Valve Face

4.0

7.0

5.0

2.0

19.0

7.5

9.0

8 Holes
10BA Clear

30.0

8 Holes
Mark from
Steam Chest

19.0

1.6

(8) **STEAM CHEST
COVER**
2-off Brass

30.0

7.0

Ø3.0

Ø6.0

Ø1.6

Thread
3/16"x40ME

(7) **STEAM CHEST**
2-off handed Brass

Cylinder covers

The front covers are a simple turning and drilling job. For appearance, a small relief can be turned into the forward face.

When making the rear cover it is essential for the bore to be concentric with the mounting spigot which fits into the cylinder, and the small flat on which the guide bar rests much be the correct distance from the centre line (5.5mm). Grip a piece of suitably sized brass in the 3-jaw chuck and turn the rear gland shoulder to 12mm. (Note the exact measurement for this, as we will be using it later). Drill and ream ⅛" to a sufficient depth, say about 12mm, and drill and tap ¼" x 40 for the gland nut. Part off and repeat for the other cover. Make a mandrel by gripping a piece of 10mm brass in the chuck and threading it ¼" x 40 with a ⅛" spigot on the end to match the bore and thread in the end cover. (It is assumed that for the piston rod and valve rod material, the stainless steel will be Imperial sizes, i.e. ⅛" and ¹⁄₁₆" respectively). Screw the end cover tightly onto the mandrel and turn the face, making the 1mm thick shoulder a good fit into the cylinder. To machine the small flat onto which the guide bars rest, grip the cover in the milling machine vice so that the face is held onto the jaw of the vice. Bring an end mill up to the job and from the position where it just touches, take off 0.5mm (check), using hand wheel graduations. This should give a distance to centre of 5.5mm, which can be checked with a vernier. (See drawing).

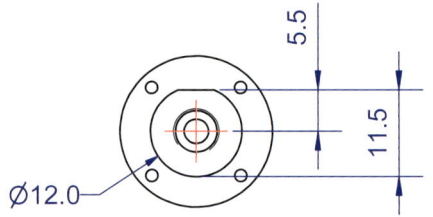

1. Measure original diameter (12.0mm)
2. Measure diameter minus flat (11.5)
3. Centre to flat is therefore: 11.5-6.0 = 5.5mm

MEASURING FLAT FOR GUIDE BAR

Drill the four 10BA clear mounting holes in the covers and finally, with a small end mill remove a small portion of the mounting shoulder from each cover where it lines up with the steam passages. Together with the recesses previously milled in the cylinders, these will ensure a clear passage for the steam and condensate.

Drill and tap the front 6BA mounting hole in the cylinders. (The back one will be spotted through the frames after lining up the cylinders)

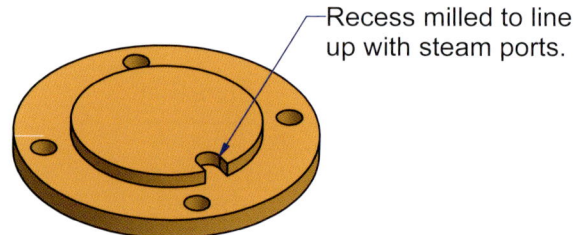

Recess milled to line up with steam ports.

RECESS FOR STEAM PASSAGES

Valve chest

The valve chests are made from brass bar 19mm x 10mm. The guide for the gland can either be made from a separate piece of ¼" round and silver soldered in, or turned from the solid piece. Either way, the bore and gland for the valve rod must be parallel to the faces of the valve chest. Using the method of turning from the solid, cut off a piece of brass about 38mm long and turn down one of the large faces to give a finished thickness of 7mm. Mark out the position for the valve rod hole on the rear face and set up in the 4-jaw chuck with this mark on centre. Drill ¹⁄₁₆" to a sufficient depth (about 12mm) and then drill and tap ³⁄₁₆" x 40 to a depth of 6mm for the gland nut. (**Photo 1.12**.) Turn down to 6mm to form the outside diameter of the guide. (If you use a separate piece, still set up the same way, but drill a 4mm hole to take the turned piece). Remove from the chuck and mark out for the rectangular centre cavity. This can be removed by chain drilling and filing and/or

1.12 — Tapping for the valve chest gland

milling. Mark out and drill the 10BA clearance holes for fixing to the cylinder and the 1/8" diameter hole in the side which will be for the steam pipe. The steam inlet pipe is silver soldered into the valve chest, so the best time to do this would be after all the holes are drilled and before finally assembling it onto the cylinder.

The cover for the valve chest is made from 1.6mm thick brass, making sure that it is nice and flat. Apply marking blue where necessary on the cylinders and the valve chest covers and spot through all of the mounting holes. The valve chest covers and the cylinders are spotted through from the valve chest and the cylinder ends from the front and back covers. Be sure that the flat for the guide bar on the rear cylinder cover is on top and perfectly square. Drill and tap all the mounting holes 10BA into the cylinders. Watch carefully the depth of some of these to avoid breaking through into the bore. (**Photo 1.13**.)

The curved corner of the cylinder can be shaped at this stage. As this is only a cosmetic shape, great accuracy is not needed, so the quickest way to shape it would be to remove the bulk of the material with a cou-

1.13 — Cylinder assemblies nearing completion

ple of hacksaw cuts lengthwise and then file to shape. There are various ways of machining this off, but often with jobs like this you can have it done by hand in the time it takes to work out how to set everything up for machining.

Piston and rod

To ensure that the piston is true to the rod, we rough turn it first and then finish to size after it is finally screwed on to the rod.

Take a piece of 16mm diameter brass rod for the piston and rough turn it to just over ½" (12.5mm) diameter. Drill through with a tapping size drill for ⅛" x 40 and then open 3mm of the hole up to ⅛". Thread the remaining 3.5mm, using the tap holder held in the tailstock and part off, leaving slightly oversize.

As mentioned previously, it is probably more precise for the following operations to set the work up in the 4-jaw chuck unless your 3-jaw is particularly accurate. For the piston rod take a piece of ⅛" diameter stainless steel rod and turn one end to a diameter of 2.5mm for 5mm. Cut the piece to length, turn around and set up to run exactly true and thread ⅛" x 40 for a length of 3.5mm. Now screw on the piston blank as tightly as possible, using some high temperature Loctite to help prevent any future movement. Finish turn the piston to be a sliding fit in the cylinder bore and turn the groove for an 012 "O" ring. Data sheets suggest this should be .090" wide x .065" deep. (2.30mm x 1.65mm). This can be done with a small square tool such as a parting tool. Measure the width of the tool with a micrometer, then carefully run it into the work to the depth of .065", noting the reading on the compound slide. Withdraw the tool and using the graduations on the compound slide, advance the tool a distance of .090" minus the width of the tool bit. Again run the tool into a depth of .065" and then complete the groove according to the width of your tool bit.

Valve

The valve can either be milled from the solid, or it can be made in two pieces silver soldered together which makes cutting the exhaust port easier.

To make it in two parts, take a piece of 1.6mm thick brass and cut out a piece for the valve face. This will be a rectangle 10mm x 9mm. Silver solder this onto a brass block 10mm x 9mm x 4.5mm thick. Clean up the edges, taking care not to touch the sharp edges of the valve face, and cut the two 1.5mm slots to take the valve rod and nut. If you have a slitting saw this can be done in a milling operation, otherwise the slots can be sawn and filed. (Two hacksaw blades held together in a hacksaw frame can make a wide slot about the right size.) It is important to make the nut a good sliding fit and for it to be perpendicular to the valve rod. In operation, the valve has to be allowed to float up and down on the nut so that steam pressure holds the valve onto the valve face.

To make the valve from one piece, make a block 10mm x 9mm x 6mm and mill the exhaust cavity with a small end mill. (The corners of the cavity can be left rounded.)

The slots are then cut in the same way as previously described.

Valve rod

Grip some ¹⁄₁₆" stainless rod in the chuck and thread 10BA for 10mm. Take this slowly, using plenty of cutting lubricant and frequently reversing the die to clear the chips. The stainless tears easily and it is savage on your expensive 10BA die.

The crossheads

The crossheads could be made up from pieces and silver soldered together, but it is probably easier to machine them from a solid block. We need two of them and they are handed, so don't happily make two and find out they are both the same!

Make up two blocks of brass, 15 x 24 x 5.5 and mark out for the piston rod spigot. Mount in the 4-jaw chuck, turn the spigot and drill 2.5mm x 6mm deep for the piston rod. Grip the block vertically in the milling machine

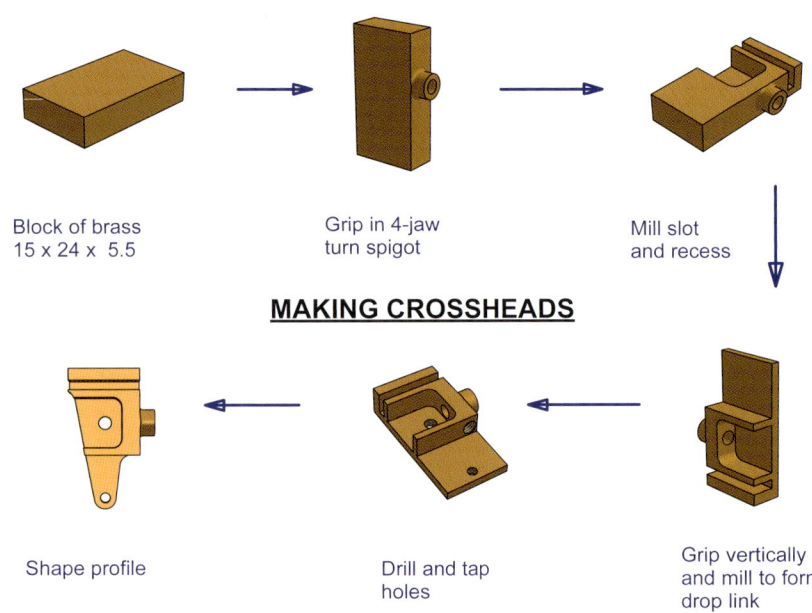

Block of brass
15 x 24 x 5.5

Grip in 4-jaw
turn spigot

Mill slot
and recess

MAKING CROSSHEADS

Shape profile

Drill and tap
holes

Grip vertically
and mill to form
drop link

vice and make the guide bar slot using a slitting saw. Regrip the piece endways and fairly high up in the milling machine vice so as not to squeeze the slot and mill the connecting rod recess using a small end mill. Turn the piece upside down and again gripping vertically mill the cutout which forms the drop link. (You could ease the work on the milling cutter by roughing the bulk of the material out with a hacksaw.) Finally cut away the profile by hand using a hacksaw and files. If you wish, you can soft solder cosmetic bolt heads onto the outside face.

The crosshead pin is turned from 4mm AF hexagon and is screwed into the crosshead from the back with an 8BA nut locking it on the front.

Motion bracket and slide bar

The motion bracket and slide-bar are made in one piece, as it is difficult to find room to fasten a separate slide bar to the bracket with bolts or rivets as might have been done in full size practice. Mark out the bracket onto a piece of mild steel 1.5mm thick. Leave the piece which is shown in the drawing as cross hatched to provide strength while the bar is being bent. It can then be cut away to provide clearance for the valve gear. It is important that the guide bar bends at just the right spot to give the correct distance from the centre of the piston rod to the valve gear, so it would be a good idea to have a few practice attempts on an off cut before tackling the real thing.

Make a saw cut with a fine blade just at or slightly above the point at which you want it to fold, as in the diagram. Obviously the saw cut reduces the strength of the piece, but provided the cut is not too deep, it will still be amply strong enough. A 15mm length of ¼" x ¹⁄₁₆" (6.4mm x 1.6mm) brass angle is riveted to the motion bracket to mount it onto the frames.

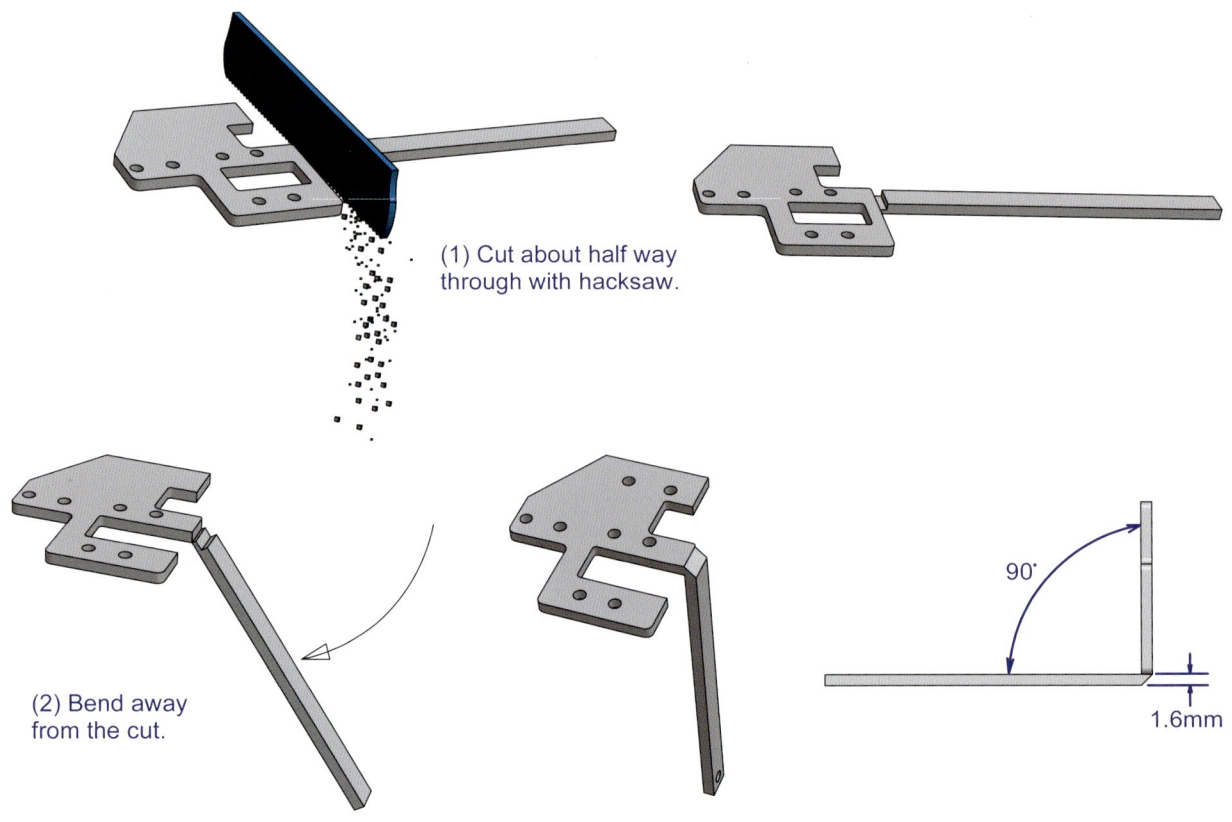

(1) Cut about half way through with hacksaw.

(2) Bend away from the cut.

90°

1.6mm

**BENDING MOTION BRACKET
GUIDE BAR**

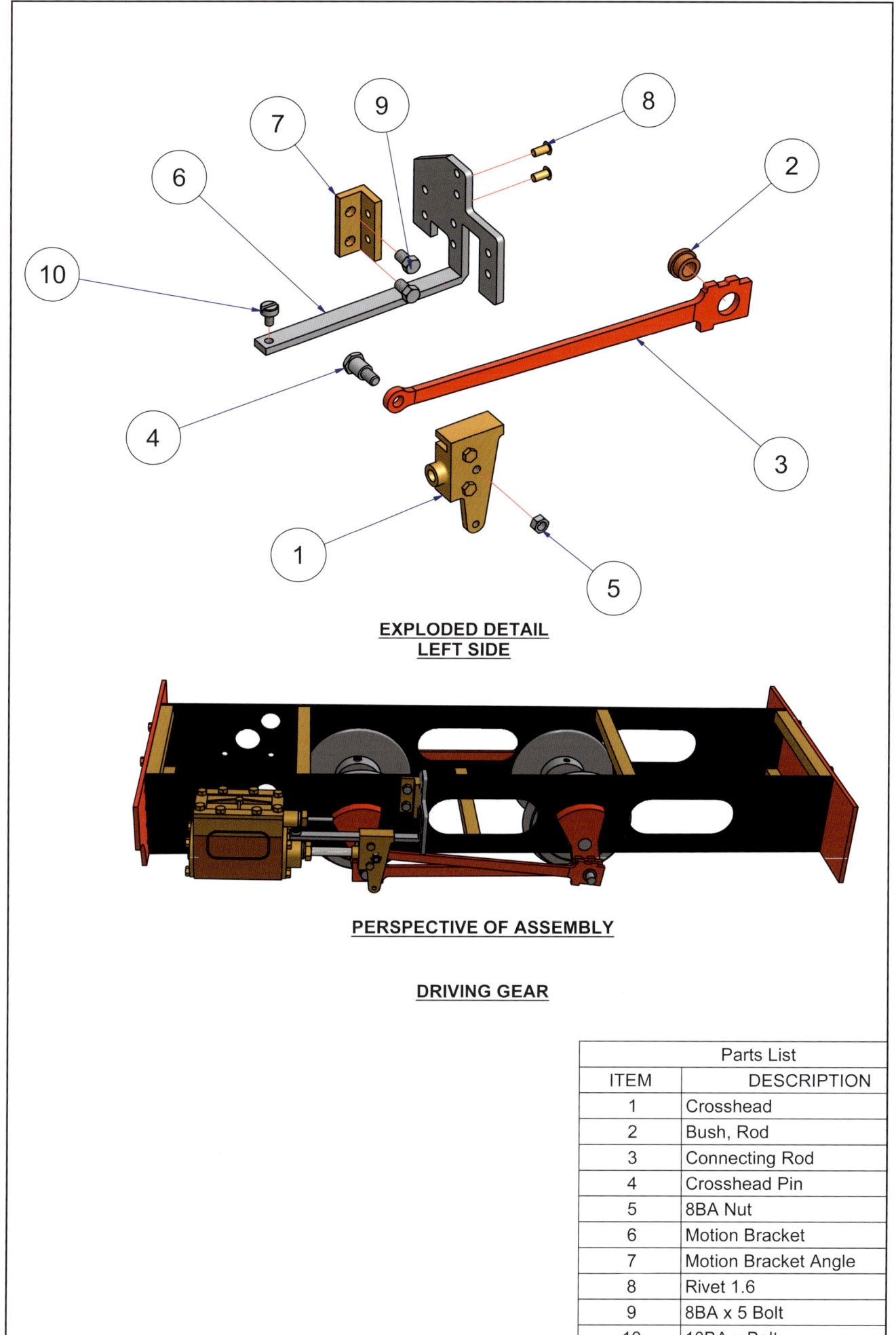

**EXPLODED DETAIL
LEFT SIDE**

PERSPECTIVE OF ASSEMBLY

DRIVING GEAR

Parts List	
ITEM	DESCRIPTION
1	Crosshead
2	Bush, Rod
3	Connecting Rod
4	Crosshead Pin
5	8BA Nut
6	Motion Bracket
7	Motion Bracket Angle
8	Rivet 1.6
9	8BA x 5 Bolt
10	10BA x Bolt

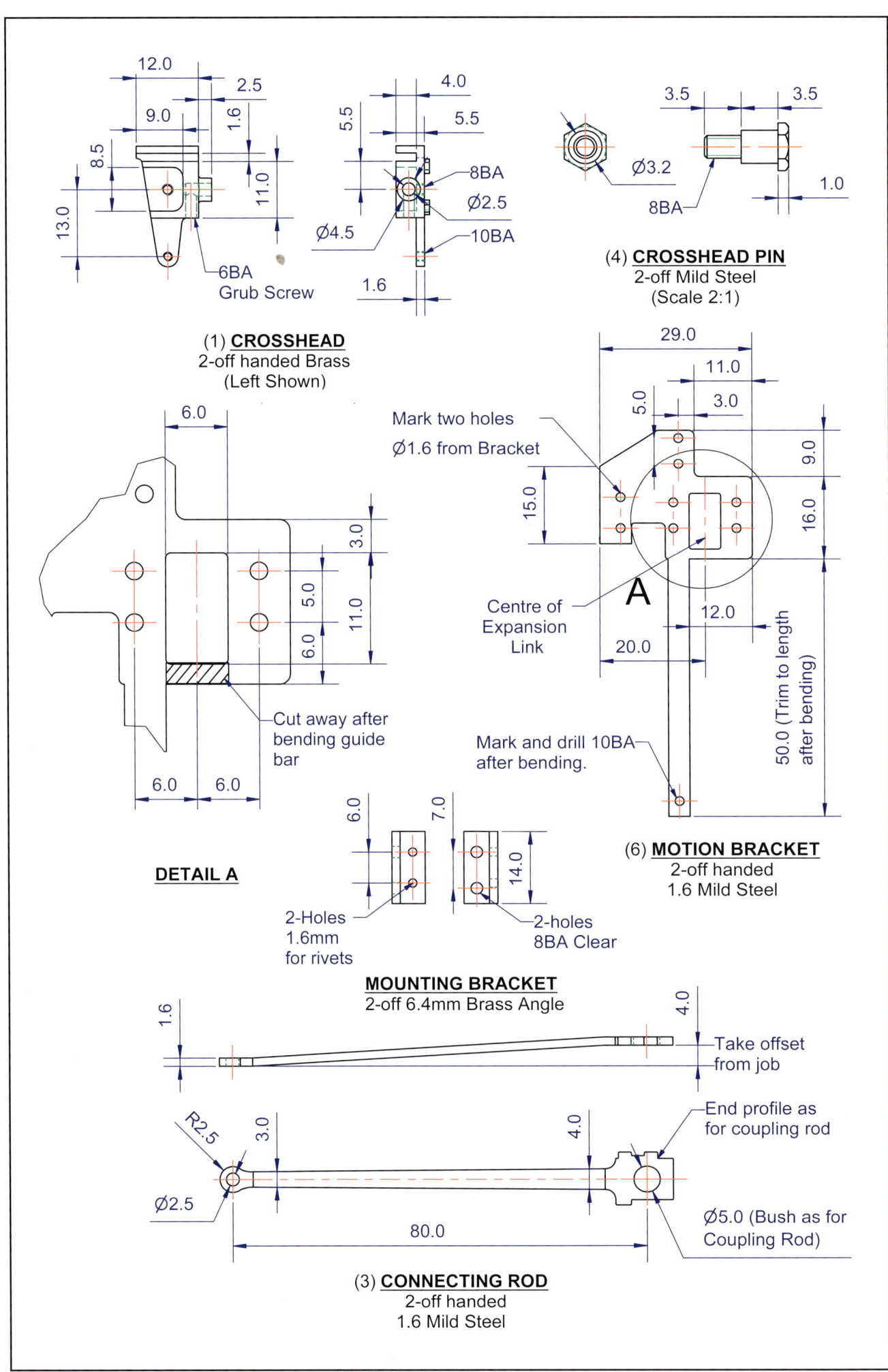

(1) CROSSHEAD
2-off handed Brass
(Left Shown)

6BA
Grub Screw

8BA
Ø2.5
10BA
Ø4.5

(4) CROSSHEAD PIN
2-off Mild Steel
(Scale 2:1)

Ø3.2
8BA

Mark two holes
Ø1.6 from Bracket

Centre of
Expansion
Link

A

Mark and drill 10BA
after bending.

50.0 (Trim to length
after bending)

(6) MOTION BRACKET
2-off handed
1.6 Mild Steel

Cut away after
bending guide
bar

DETAIL A

2-Holes
1.6mm
for rivets

2-holes
8BA Clear

MOUNTING BRACKET
2-off 6.4mm Brass Angle

Take offset
from job

End profile as
for coupling rod

R2.5
Ø2.5

Ø5.0 (Bush as for
Coupling Rod)

(3) CONNECTING ROD
2-off handed
1.6 Mild Steel

Assembling the main motion

We can now assemble the main motion. So far you will have the frames assembled and the wheel and axle assemblies in place with the cranks quartered. At this stage, leave off the footplates as they will only get in the way.

Bolt the rear cover onto the cylinder and insert the piston, rod and O-ring assembly, giving everything a good coating of oil. The piston should move freely back and forth in the cylinder. Make up a pointer from a piece of say, 5mm diameter rod. Drill it to fit firmly over the piston rod at one end and turn a point at the other end, making it just long enough to reach the centre of the rear axle when the piston is about half way or more towards the front of the cylinder. Bolt the cylinder into position with the front mounting bolt and line the pointer up with the centre of the rear axle. Spot through the mounting hole drilled in the frame onto the cylinder for the rear mounting hole. Remove, centre punch, drill and tap 6BA. The cylinder can now be bolted securely in position.

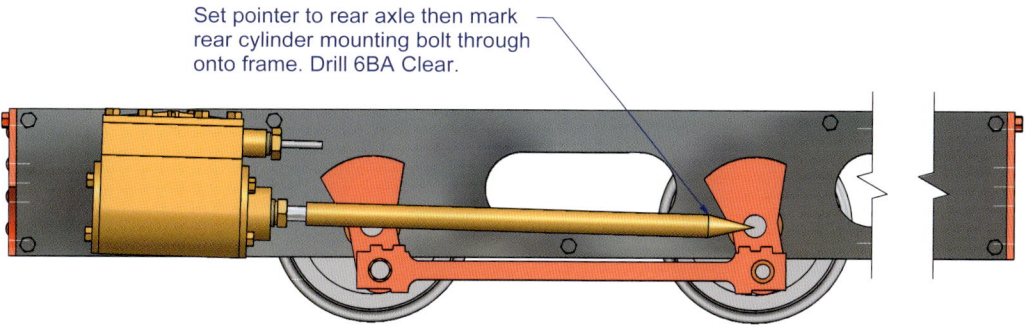

Set pointer to rear axle then mark rear cylinder mounting bolt through onto frame. Drill 6BA Clear.

SETTING UP CYLINDER BLOCKS

Next, to mount the motion bracket, secure the crosshead onto the piston rod, cut the slide bar to length and drill a 10BA clear hole 2.5mm from the front end. Lightly clamp the motion bracket in position on the frame and spot through this hole onto the rear cylinder cover. Drill and tap 10BA, but be very careful as this hole can not be drilled very deeply and it can be easily stripped. Re-position the motion bracket and check that the crosshead moves freely on the guide bar. When you are satisfied that everything lines up, spot the mounting holes through the motion bracket onto the frames for 8BA threads.

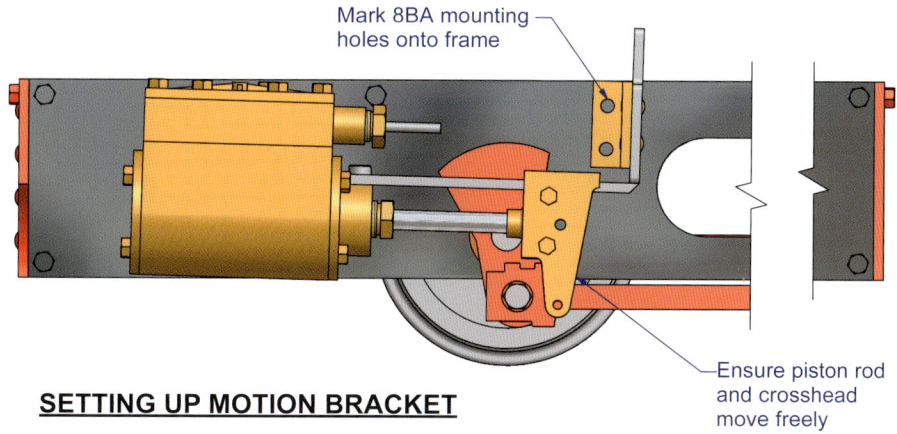

Mark 8BA mounting holes onto frame

Ensure piston rod and crosshead move freely

SETTING UP MOTION BRACKET

The connecting rods can be placed on the cranks and the crosshead pins inserted after which the motion can be tested. Make sure that there is no binding and that the pistons move freely for their full travel.

The Valve Gear

Expansion links

The expansion links which form the central part of Walschaerts valve gear are made up from several pieces of 1.6mm mild steel riveted together. Rather than fasten each one together separately it is a little easier to make them as a pair.

Mark out all the pieces and cut out and drill as shown. When cutting out the central link pieces, it might be easier to leave the part shown with dashed lines until they are finally assembled after which it can be cut away.

Bolt the pieces together with 3mm bolts and nuts and mark out for drilling $\frac{3}{64}$" (1.2mm) for rivets. (**Photo 1.14**) Drill these holes and using a larger drill, countersink the ends of the holes just sufficiently for the rivets by

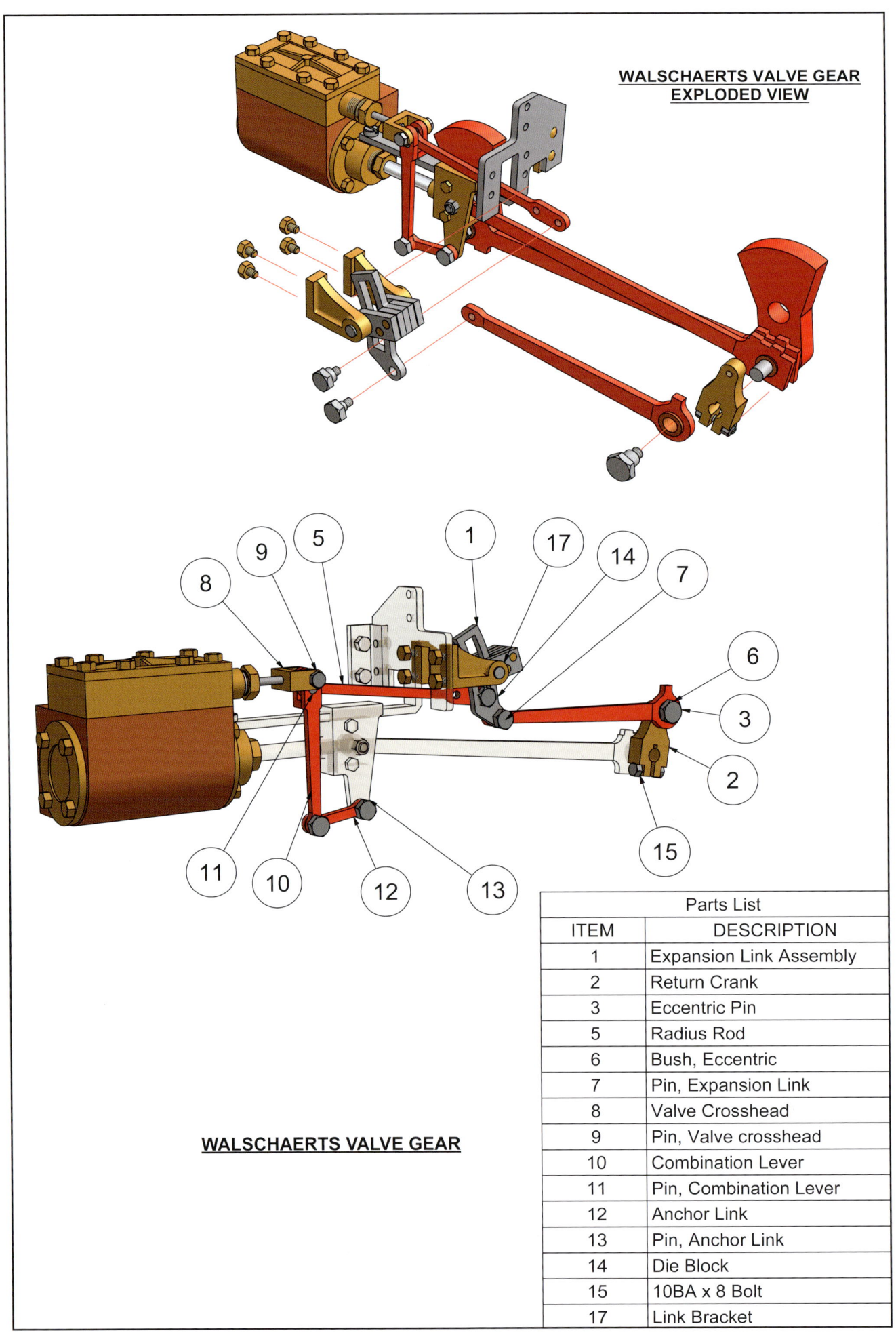

**WALSCHAERTS VALVE GEAR
EXPLODED VIEW**

WALSCHAERTS VALVE GEAR

Parts List	
ITEM	DESCRIPTION
1	Expansion Link Assembly
2	Return Crank
3	Eccentric Pin
5	Radius Rod
6	Bush, Eccentric
7	Pin, Expansion Link
8	Valve Crosshead
9	Pin, Valve crosshead
10	Combination Lever
11	Pin, Combination Lever
12	Anchor Link
13	Pin, Anchor Link
14	Die Block
15	10BA x 8 Bolt
17	Link Bracket

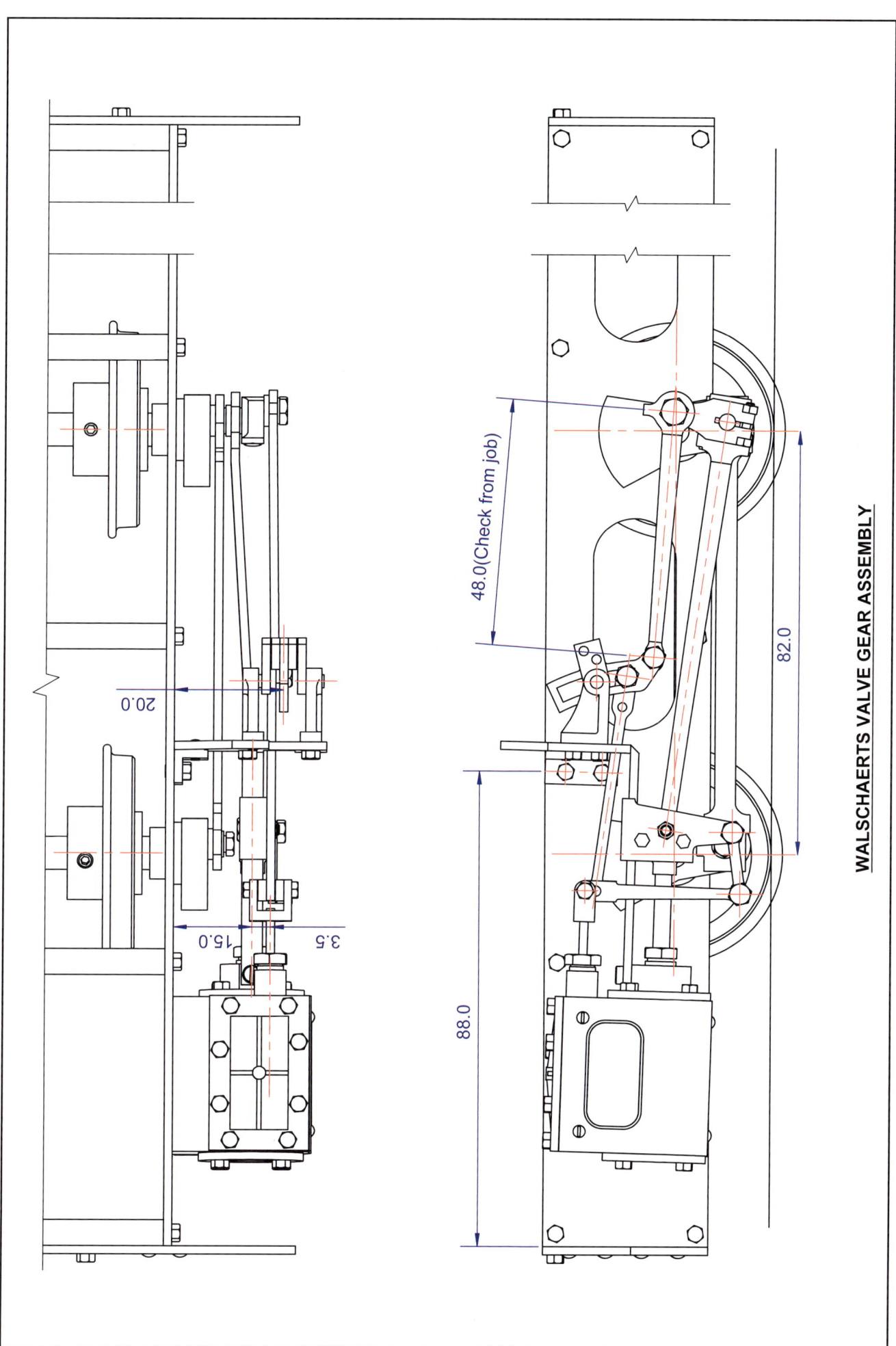

WALSCHAERTS VALVE GEAR ASSEMBLY

20.0

15.0

3.5

88.0

48.0(Check from job)

82.0

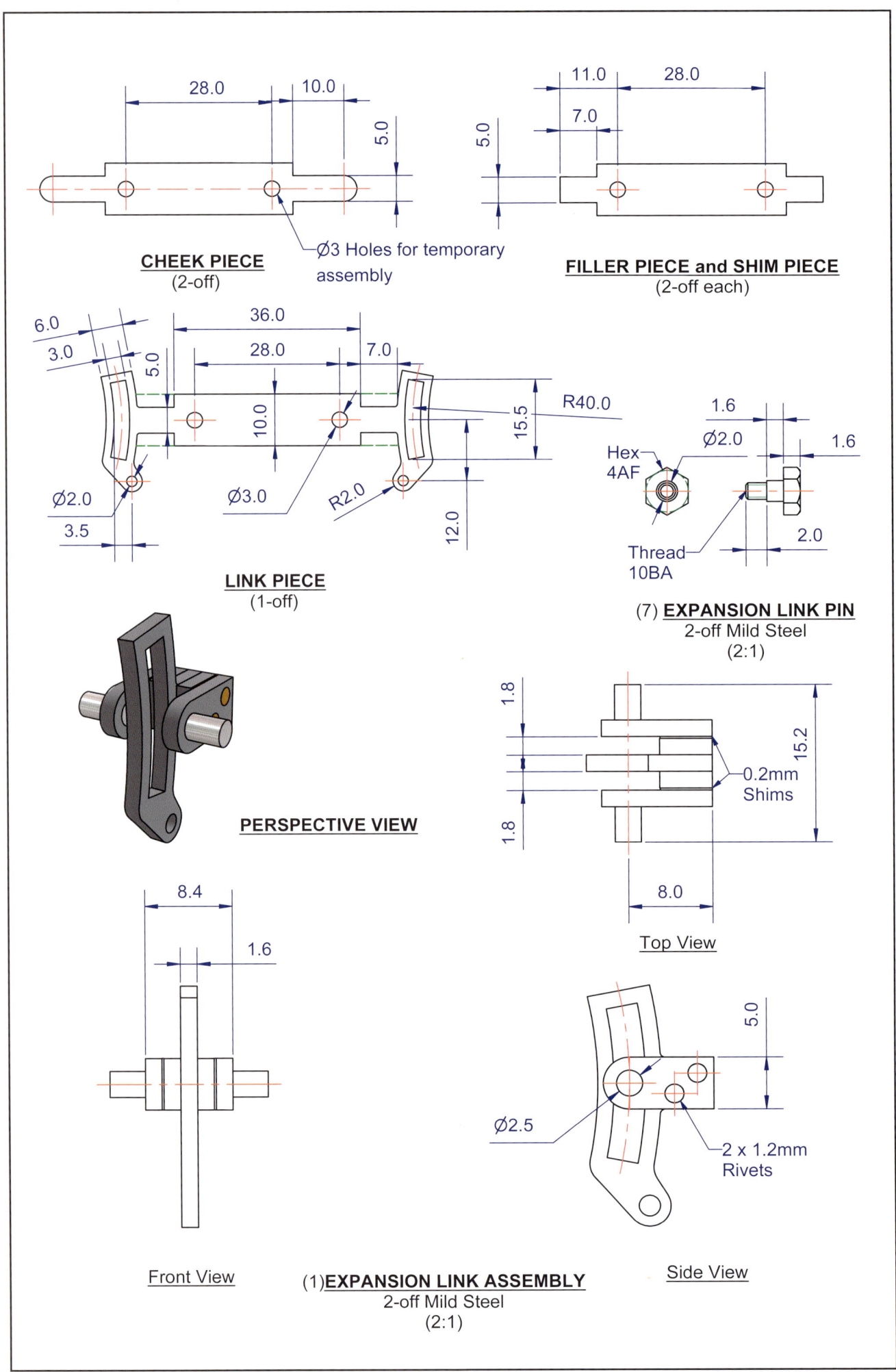

CHEEK PIECE
(2-off)

Ø3 Holes for temporary assembly

FILLER PIECE and SHIM PIECE
(2-off each)

LINK PIECE
(1-off)

Hex 4AF
Ø2.0
Thread 10BA

(7) **EXPANSION LINK PIN**
2-off Mild Steel
(2:1)

R40.0

R2.0

Ø2.0

Ø3.0

PERSPECTIVE VIEW

0.2mm Shims

Top View

Ø2.5

2 x 1.2mm Rivets

Side View

Front View

(1)**EXPANSION LINK ASSEMBLY**
2-off Mild Steel
(2:1)

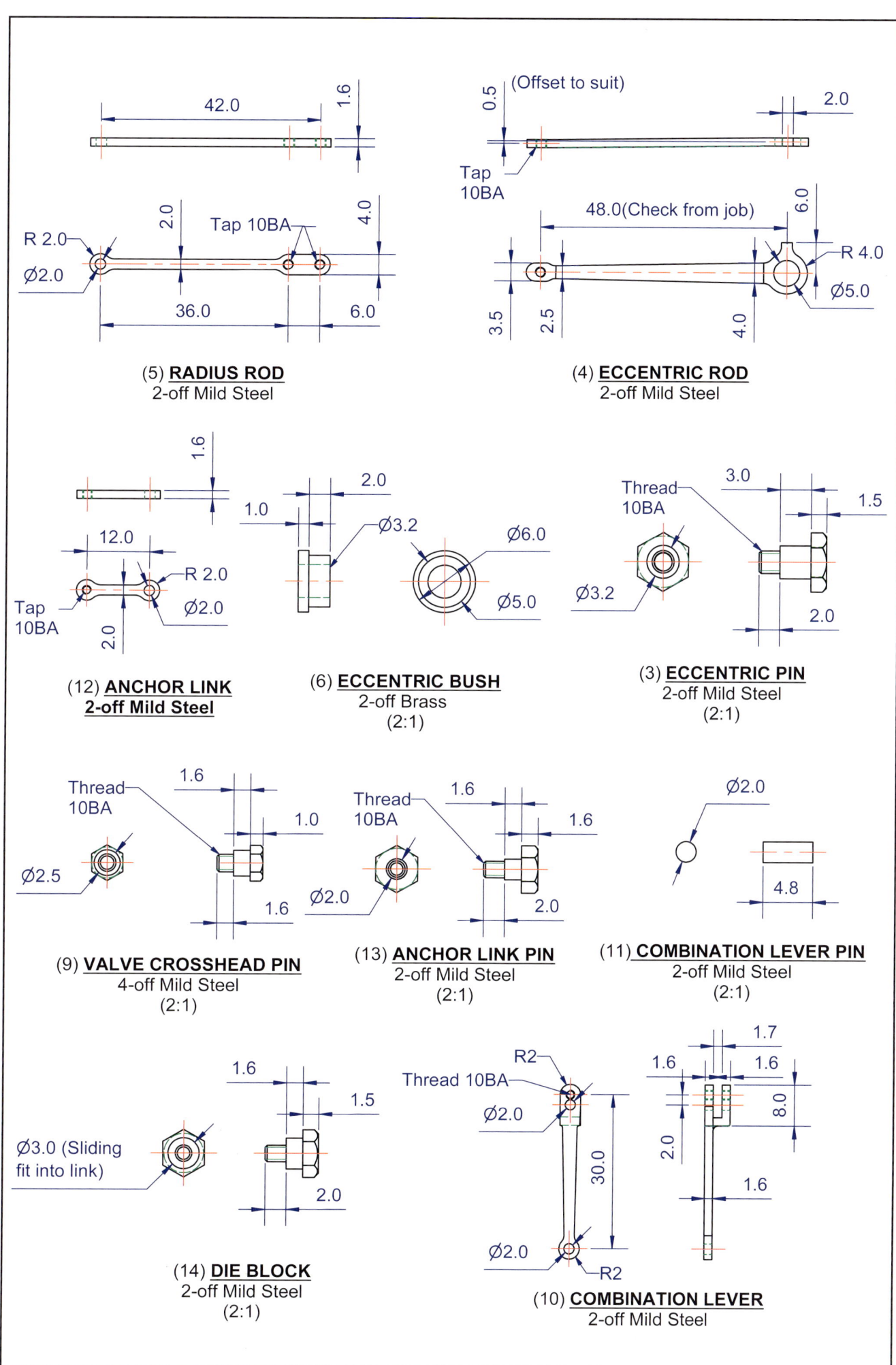

(5) RADIUS ROD
2-off Mild Steel

(4) ECCENTRIC ROD
2-off Mild Steel

(12) ANCHOR LINK
2-off Mild Steel

(6) ECCENTRIC BUSH
2-off Brass
(2:1)

(3) ECCENTRIC PIN
2-off Mild Steel
(2:1)

(9) VALVE CROSSHEAD PIN
4-off Mild Steel
(2:1)

(13) ANCHOR LINK PIN
2-off Mild Steel
(2:1)

(11) COMBINATION LEVER PIN
2-off Mild Steel
(2:1)

(14) DIE BLOCK
2-off Mild Steel
(2:1)

(10) COMBINATION LEVER
2-off Mild Steel

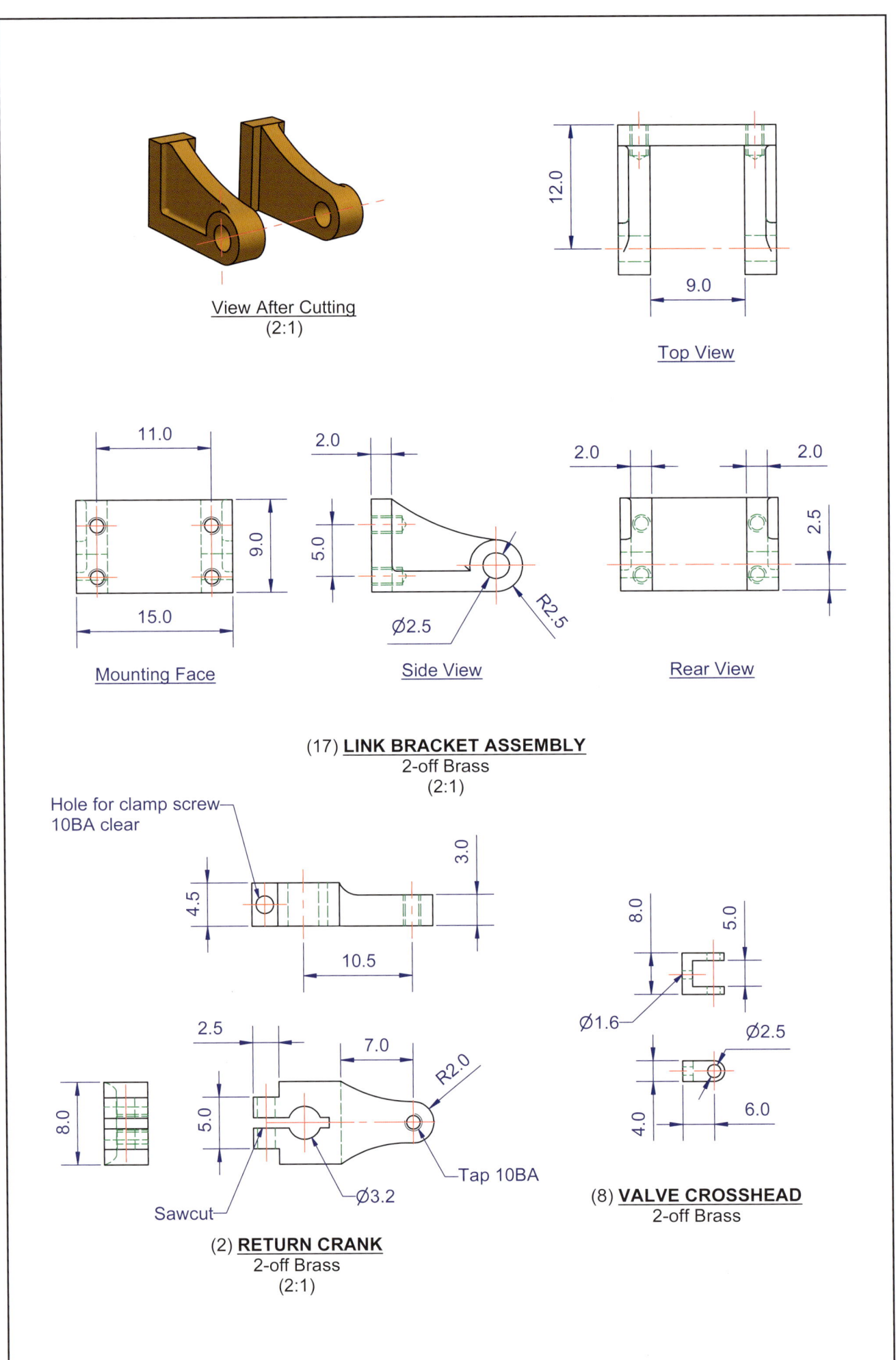

View After Cutting
(2:1)

12.0

9.0

Top View

11.0

9.0

15.0

Mounting Face

2.0

5.0

Ø2.5

R2.5

Side View

2.0

2.0

2.5

Rear View

(17) **LINK BRACKET ASSEMBLY**
2-off Brass
(2:1)

Hole for clamp screw
10BA clear

4.5

3.0

10.5

8.0

Ø1.6

5.0

8.0

2.5

7.0

R2.0

5.0

Sawcut

Ø3.2

Tap 10BA

(2) **RETURN CRANK**
2-off Brass
(2:1)

Ø2.5

4.0

6.0

(8) **VALVE CROSSHEAD**
2-off Brass

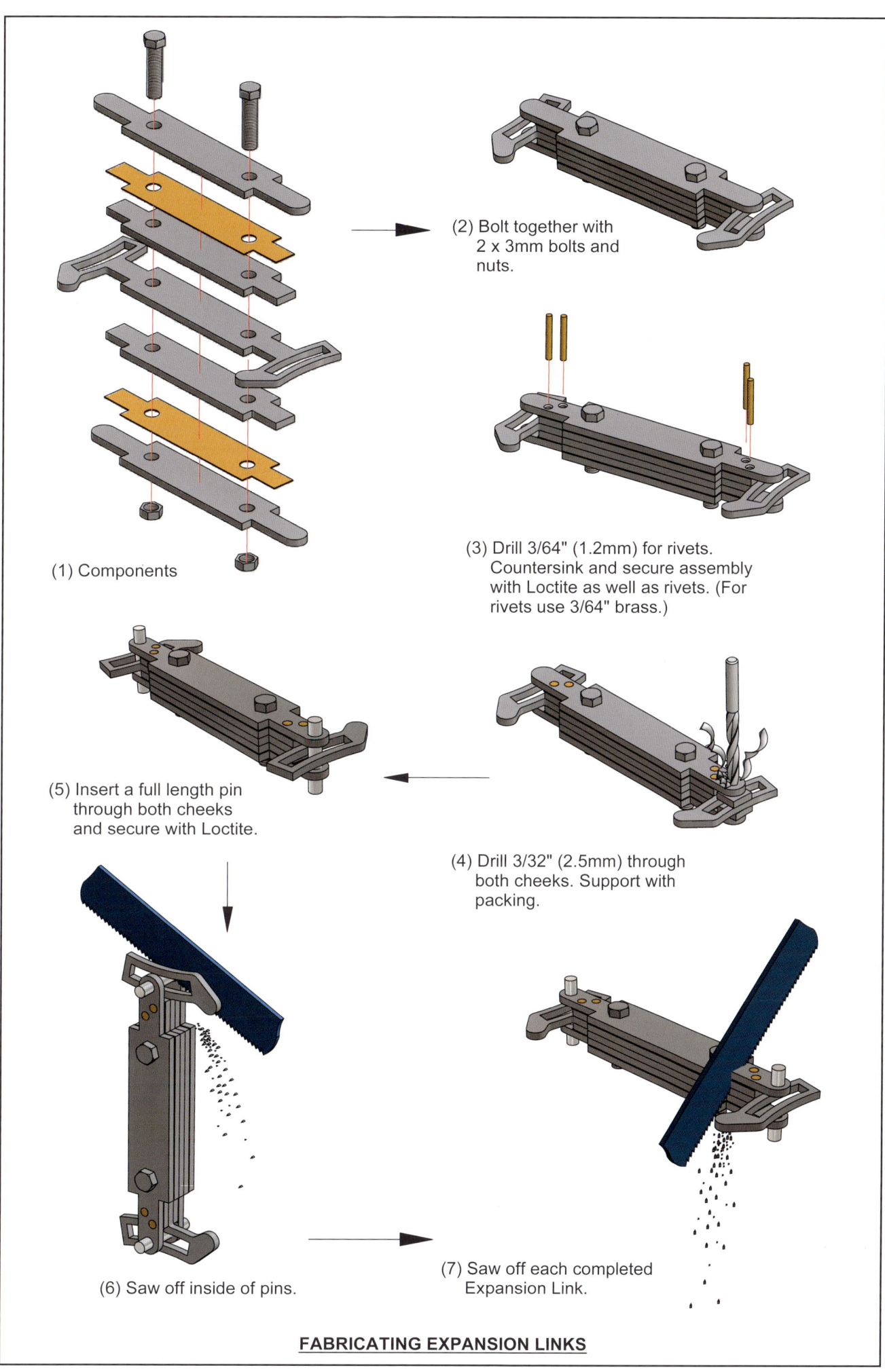

(1) Components

(2) Bolt together with 2 x 3mm bolts and nuts.

(3) Drill 3/64" (1.2mm) for rivets. Countersink and secure assembly with Loctite as well as rivets. (For rivets use 3/64" brass.)

(4) Drill 3/32" (2.5mm) through both cheeks. Support with packing.

(5) Insert a full length pin through both cheeks and secure with Loctite.

(6) Saw off inside of pins.

(7) Saw off each completed Expansion Link.

FABRICATING EXPANSION LINKS

lightly turning the drill by hand. Undo the pieces and clean them thoroughly, making sure there is no swarf between the pieces. Bolt the pieces back together making sure they are in the same order as before, applying some Loctite to help hold everything together. Insert the rivets and peine them over.

Carefully mark out for the pivot pins in the cheeks and placing pieces of packing tightly between the cheeks and the link, drill through ³⁄₃₂" (2.5mm). Check that the cheeks haven't squeezed together, and if they have simply prise them open. Insert full length (15.2mm) pieces for the pins centrally into these holes with Loctite and allow to cure. After curing, saw off the insides of the pins flush with the cheeks and smooth with a file.

Finally saw off each finished expansion link and clean up with a file. Check again that the cheeks haven't squeezed together in the process, the gap between the link and the cheeks needs to be about 1.8mm at least to allow free movement of the radius rods.

1.14 — Drilling expansion links for rivets

Link brackets

Fabricate the Link Brackets from two blocks of brass 15 x 15 x 9mm. Each bracket consists of two pieces, so drilling and tapping the mounting holes when it is still a single piece will ensure that the mounting holes line up after it is cut into two. (**Photo 1.15.**)

Take the block of brass and drill the 2.5mm hole making sure that the hole is perfectly square. Clamp the block onto the motion bracket and mark through for the 10BA mounting holes. The motion bracket will be mounted to the frames when this is done, so the link bracket block can be squared to the frames with a try square. Drill and tap the mounting holes and then the central part can be cut away either with a milling cutter or with hacksaw and file. Mark out and shape the outside profile and then cut the block into its two parts. Bolt the inside half of the bracket onto the motion bracket, the expansion link can be inserted and then the other half can be bolted on. Check that the expansion link is free to move and that everything is lined up correctly.

1.15 — Link brackets fitted to motion brackets before cutting

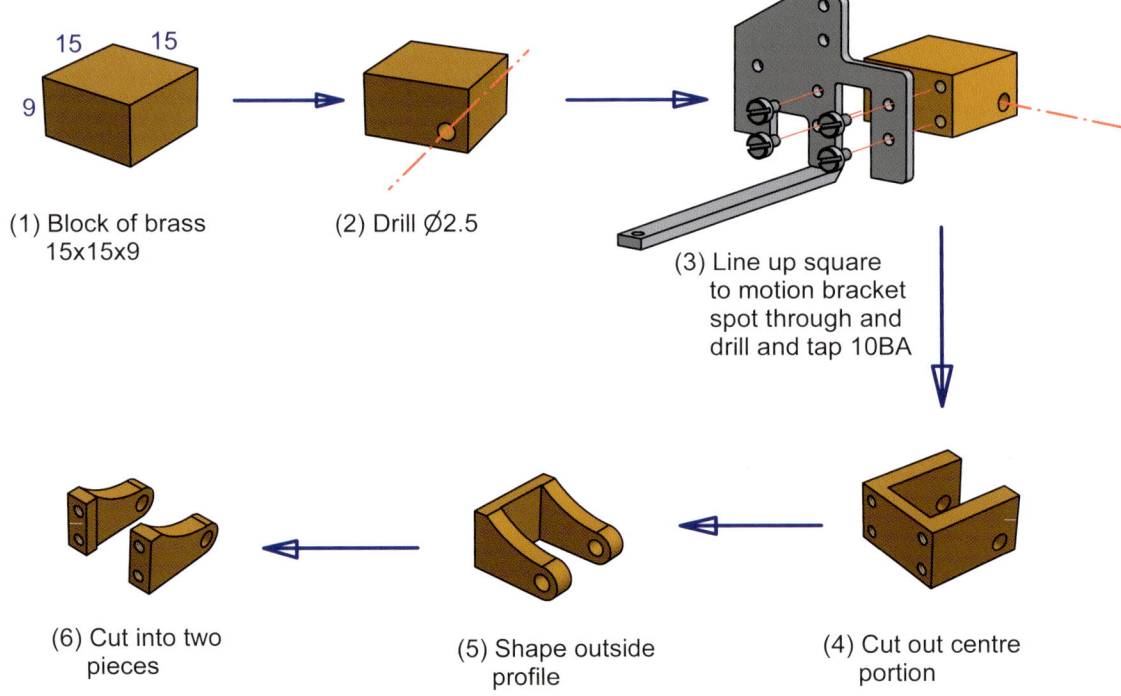

(1) Block of brass 15x15x9

(2) Drill Ø2.5

(3) Line up square to motion bracket spot through and drill and tap 10BA

(4) Cut out centre portion

(5) Shape outside profile

(6) Cut into two pieces

FABRICATING LINK BRACKETS

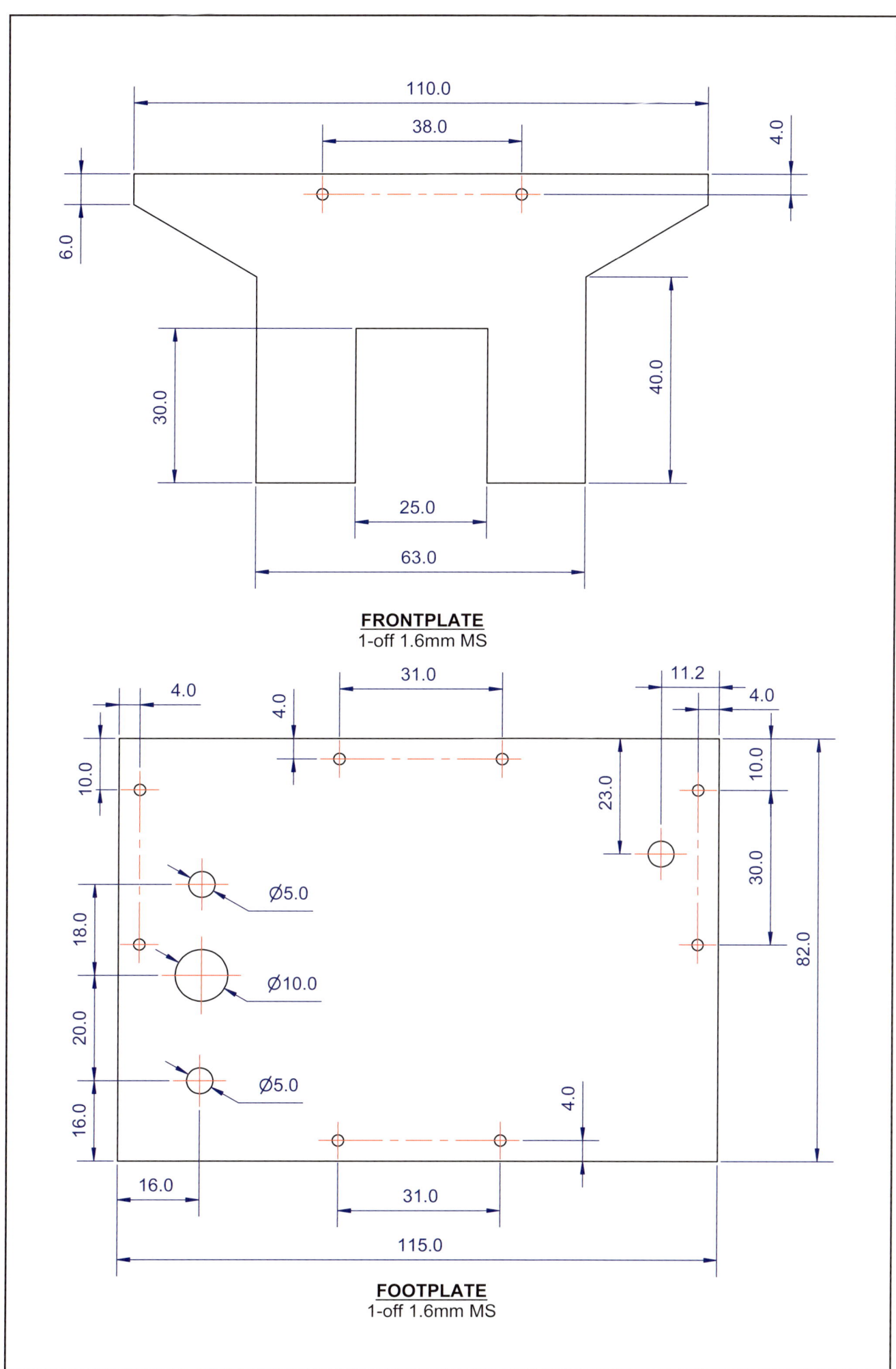

FRONTPLATE
1-off 1.6mm MS

FOOTPLATE
1-off 1.6mm MS

Return crank

The return cranks are made from brass. Drill the hole for the crank and the eccentric pin before shaping the outside, and in the one setting to make sure that they are parallel. Drill the 10BA clear clamping hole and make the cut outs for the clamping bolt and nut. Take the saw cut through to the opposite side of the crank hole as shown to assist with the clamping action. After the valve gear is set the return crank will be pinned onto the crank pin to prevent any chance of it moving and upsetting the valve timing.

Combination lever

Take two pieces of mild steel, 35 x 4 x 1.6mm and 8 x 4 x 3.5mm and silver solder them together, making sure there is a good fillet of solder at the join. Drill and tap the holes and then mill the slot in the top using a slitting saw. Shape the outside profile.

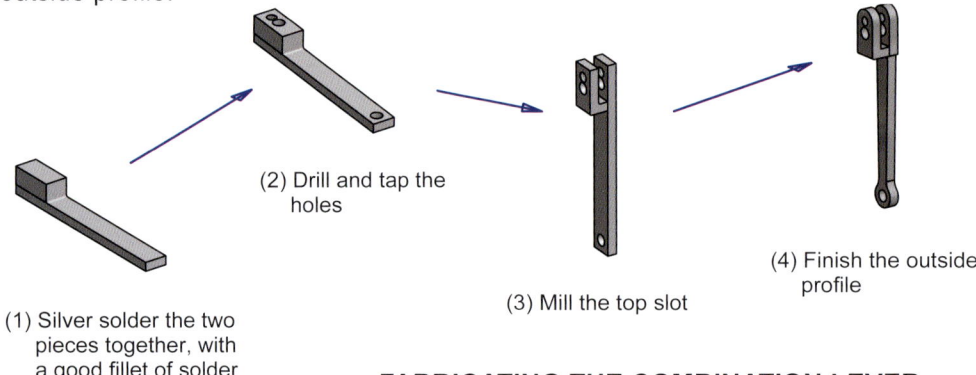

(2) Drill and tap the holes

(4) Finish the outside profile

(3) Mill the top slot

(1) Silver solder the two pieces together, with a good fillet of solder (or cut from solid)

FABRICATING THE COMBINATION LEVER

Simplified combination lever

A simplified arrangement for the combination lever is given which avoids the soldering and milling work. These parts are made in the same way as other rods and offset by bending as shown. The valve crosshead is silver soldered onto the side of the valve rod.

All of the remaining pieces of valve gear, that is the rods and pins, are straight forward exercises and the technique applied to the main motion rods of drilling the holes before shaping the outside profile should be applied. When making the die block, make the 3mm diameter section which slides in the expansion link slightly longer than 1.6mm so that when it is tightened into the radius rod it will slide up and down freely. In this area clearances are very tight, so some careful filing and fitting will be necessary to give the right clearances. Do not drill the front hole in the eccentric rod where it goes onto the pin at the bottom of the expansion link, instead leave an elongated section at the front and this hole will be drilled later when setting the valve gear. The elongated section provides allowance for some variation in where this hole will be drilled.

Footplates

The front and rear plates are cut from 1.6mm mild steel plate, making sure everything is square. Holes for mounting the lubricator and gas system can be drilled where shown on the drawing and the reversing lever can be positioned and the 8BA mounting holes drilled and tapped. The cutout for the steam pipes on the front plate can be done by chain drilling and filing. Bolt on the cab footplate but leave the front plate off for now until after the chassis has been tested by running on air.

Reversing gear

In full size, the purpose of the reversing gear is to raise and lower the die block in the expansion link which in turn puts the valve gear in forward or reverse. In addition to this, the gear can be "linked up" which means that the die block is moved in from the extreme position towards the centre of the link which restricts the valve movement and gives more efficient use of the steam.

In our model we are only interested in moving the valve gear into forward or reverse, so the reverse lever is provided with only three positions: forward, reverse and mid-gear.

Lifting link

The lifting links are made from 1.6mm mild steel and as with the other rods, mark out the holes and drill and tap them before shaping the outside profile. Turn and thread the pins and turn the small spacer. Remember clearances in this area are very tight

Lifting arms and reverse lever arm

Again, the lifting arms are a handed pair, so don't make two the same! Fabricate them by silver soldering the 5mm diameter boss onto a piece of 1.6mm brass. Grip the boss in the 3-jaw chuck and locate the centre,

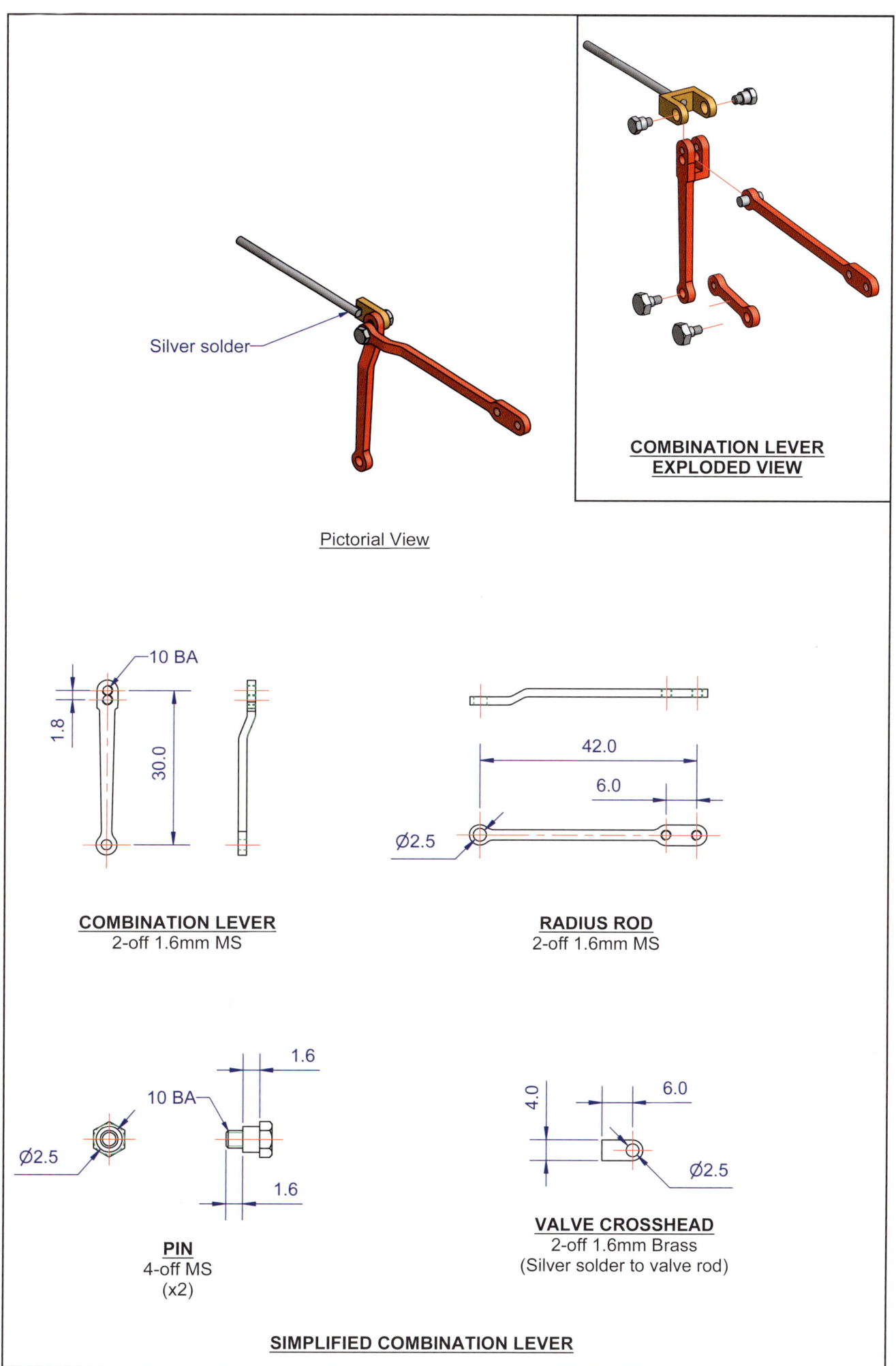

Silver solder

**COMBINATION LEVER
EXPLODED VIEW**

Pictorial View

10 BA

1.8

30.0

COMBINATION LEVER
2-off 1.6mm MS

42.0

6.0

Ø2.5

RADIUS ROD
2-off 1.6mm MS

10 BA

1.6

1.6

Ø2.5

PIN
4-off MS
(x2)

4.0

6.0

Ø2.5

VALVE CROSSHEAD
2-off 1.6mm Brass
(Silver solder to valve rod)

SIMPLIFIED COMBINATION LEVER

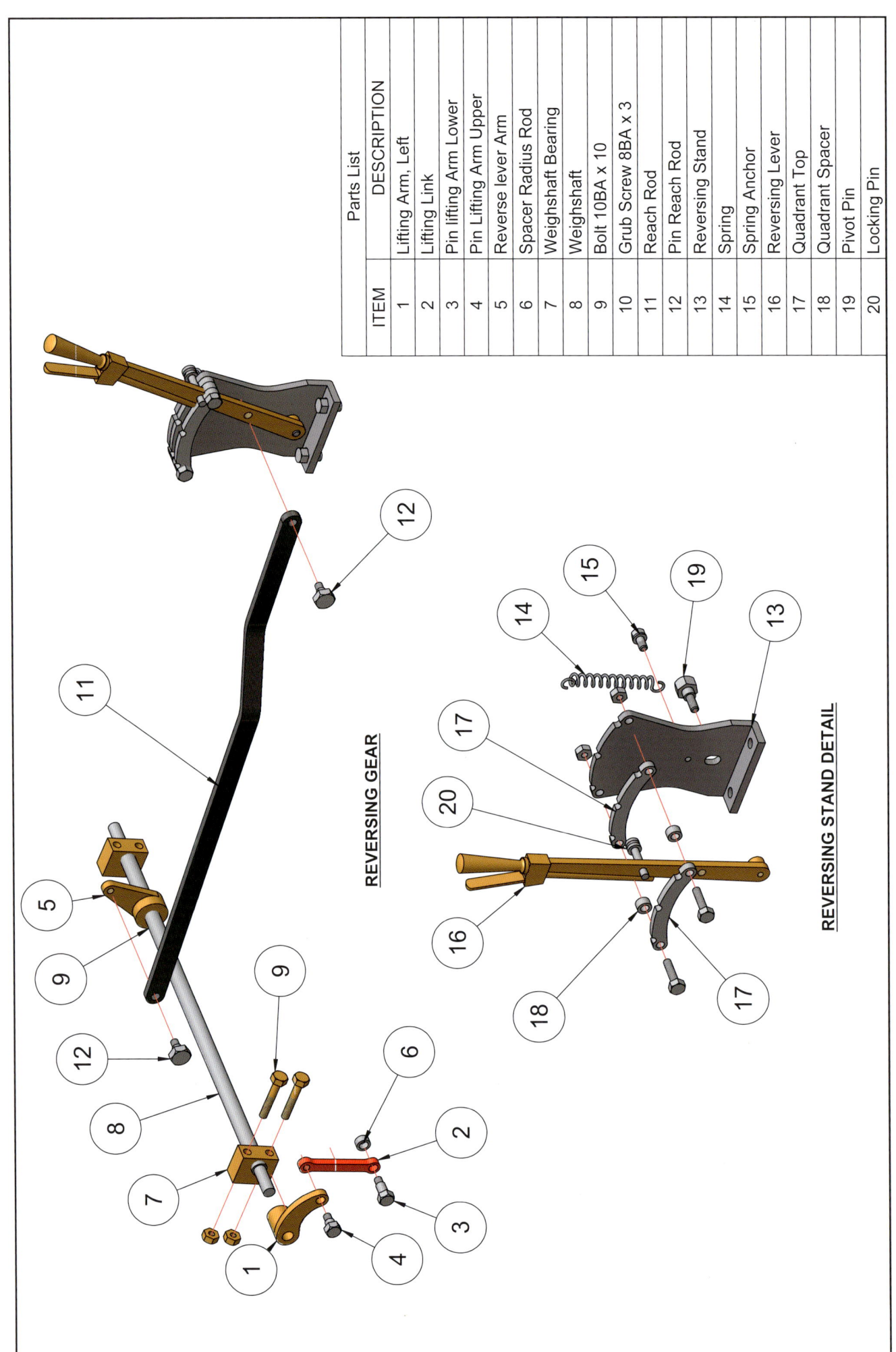

Parts List	
ITEM	DESCRIPTION
1	Lifting Arm, Left
2	Lifting Link
3	Pin lifting Arm Lower
4	Pin Lifting Arm Upper
5	Reverse lever Arm
6	Spacer Radius Rod
7	Weighshaft Bearing
8	Weighshaft
9	Bolt 10BA x 10
10	Grub Screw 8BA x 3
11	Reach Rod
12	Pin Reach Rod
13	Reversing Stand
14	Spring
15	Spring Anchor
16	Reversing Lever
17	Quadrant Top
18	Quadrant Spacer
19	Pivot Pin
20	Locking Pin

REVERSING GEAR

REVERSING STAND DETAIL

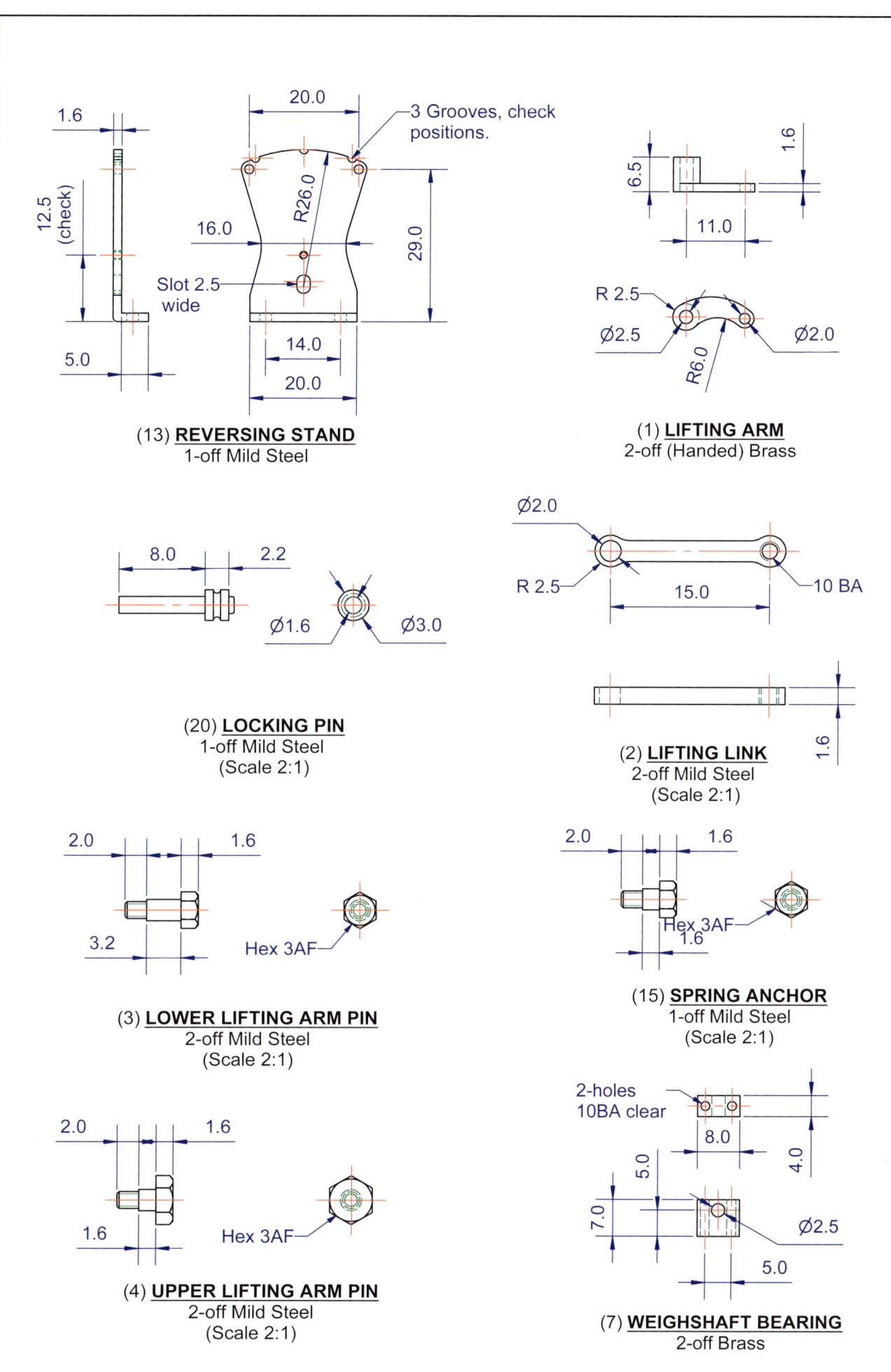

(13) **REVERSING STAND**
1-off Mild Steel

(1) **LIFTING ARM**
2-off (Handed) Brass

(20) **LOCKING PIN**
1-off Mild Steel
(Scale 2:1)

(2) **LIFTING LINK**
2-off Mild Steel
(Scale 2:1)

(3) **LOWER LIFTING ARM PIN**
2-off Mild Steel
(Scale 2:1)

(15) **SPRING ANCHOR**
1-off Mild Steel
(Scale 2:1)

(4) **UPPER LIFTING ARM PIN**
2-off Mild Steel
(Scale 2:1)

(7) **WEIGHSHAFT BEARING**
2-off Brass

from which the 11mm hole distance can be marked. Drill the boss 2.5mm, remove from the chuck, drill the 2mm hole for the lifting links and then shape the outside. The reverse lever arm can be fabricated in the same way

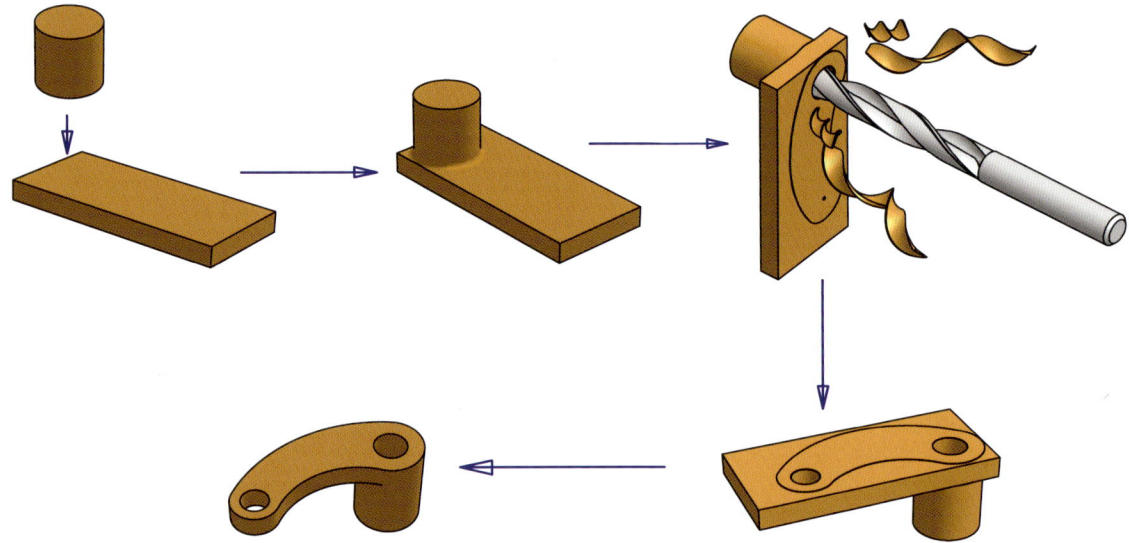

FABRICATING THE COMBINATION LEVER

Weighshaft and bearings

Make the two rectangular brass blocks for the weighshaft bearings and drill the holes for the weighshaft and the mounting bolts. The holes for the mounting bolts should be spotted through from the motion brackets. Make sure all of these holes are square to each other. Mount the bearings temporarily and check the dimensions for the weighshaft, making any adjustments necessary and turn the shoulders on the ends of the weighshaft.

The lifting arms need to be pinned onto the weighshaft to prevent any chance of movement after the valves are set. Do this by drilling through the boss and shaft and inserting a 1.6mm roll pin or a 1.6mm plain pin held in with Loctite. Do one end now and the other end after setting up all the reversing gear.

Reversing stand and lever

The reversing stand and quadrants are made from 1.6mm mild steel. Make a hacksaw cut part way through the stand so that when the base is bent over it will form a good sharp bend. The reverse lever itself can be fabricated from brass or mild steel or a combination of both. The position of the holes is important, but the handle is cosmetic and can be any shape you like. Fit the parts of the stand together making sure that the lever moves freely backwards and forwards, and that it is free to move up and down in the slot at the bottom. Make sure the spring pulls the lever firmly down to the bottom of the slot. Don't file the locating slots on the quadrant yet, that is done shortly. The reach rod is made from 1.6mm mild steel about 4mm wide. Obtain the final length and the bend positions from the job.

Assemble all the parts of the reversing gear, the expansion links and associated parts of the valve gear. We can now pin the other lifting arm. By moving the reversing lever, the die block under the lifting arm which has been pinned should move up and down freely in its link and evenly either side of centre. Move it to the top of its travel and going to the lifting arm which has not been pinned, move it also to the top of its travel. Mark on the weighshaft where the arm is located, remove from the chassis and making sure the bearings and reverse lever arm are in position, drill and pin the lifting arm. Refit and check that everything runs smoothly and evenly.

The positions for the locating pin on the reversing lever can now be established and the slots filed using a small round needle file. Try to position these slots so that the die block is not hard against the end of the expansion link, as in operation there needs to be some free movement.

Finishing the chassis, setting the valves and testing on air

Now comes the exciting part where we can watch all our hard work come together to produce a working chassis!

Because of the small scale of things and the large number of component parts which make up the whole valve movement, it is difficult to have the valve gear working precisely as it should and some compromises may have to be made. Let us remind ourselves, however, that the objective is to produce a fun locomotive which is run for enjoyment and not to haul huge loads for profit or passengers to a tight schedule. Having said that, if you have taken reasonable care there should be no major problems and the locomotive should run well and give many hours of trouble-free service. Remember we are making a steam engine, not a Swiss watch!

Set the return crank as closely as possible in its position on the crank pin and lightly tighten the clamp

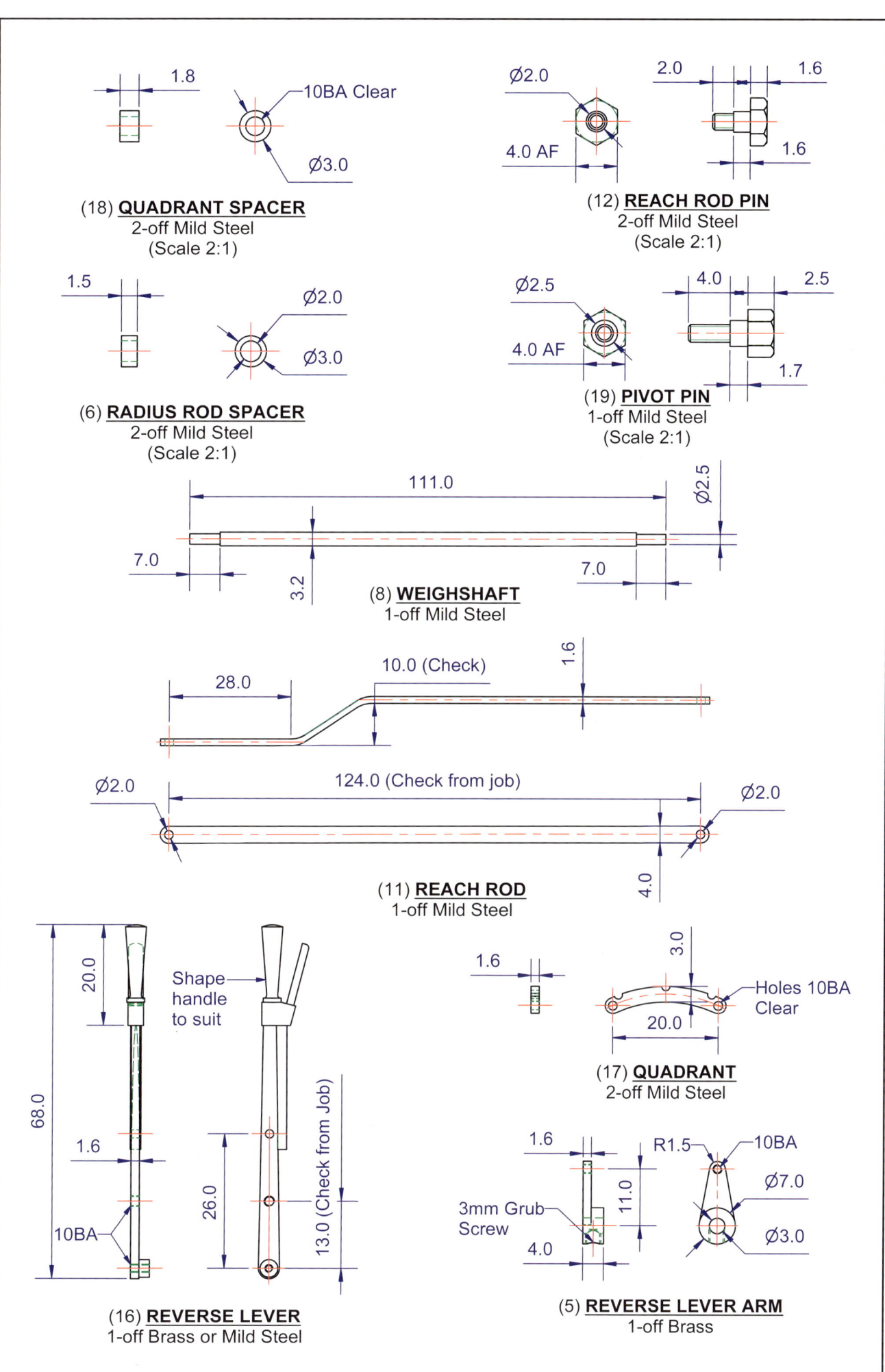

1.8

10BA Clear

Ø3.0

(18) QUADRANT SPACER
2-off Mild Steel
(Scale 2:1)

Ø2.0

2.0 **1.6**

4.0 AF

1.6

(12) REACH ROD PIN
2-off Mild Steel
(Scale 2:1)

1.5

Ø2.0

Ø3.0

(6) RADIUS ROD SPACER
2-off Mild Steel
(Scale 2:1)

Ø2.5

4.0 **2.5**

4.0 AF

1.7

(19) PIVOT PIN
1-off Mild Steel
(Scale 2:1)

111.0

Ø2.5

7.0

3.2

7.0

(8) WEIGHSHAFT
1-off Mild Steel

28.0

10.0 (Check)

1.6

Ø2.0

124.0 (Check from job)

Ø2.0

4.0

(11) REACH ROD
1-off Mild Steel

20.0

Shape
handle
to suit

68.0

1.6

26.0

13.0 (Check from Job)

10BA

(16) REVERSE LEVER
1-off Brass or Mild Steel

1.6

3.0

Holes 10BA
Clear

20.0

(17) QUADRANT
2-off Mild Steel

1.6

R1.5 **10BA**

11.0

Ø7.0

3mm Grub
Screw

4.0

Ø3.0

(5) REVERSE LEVER ARM
1-off Brass

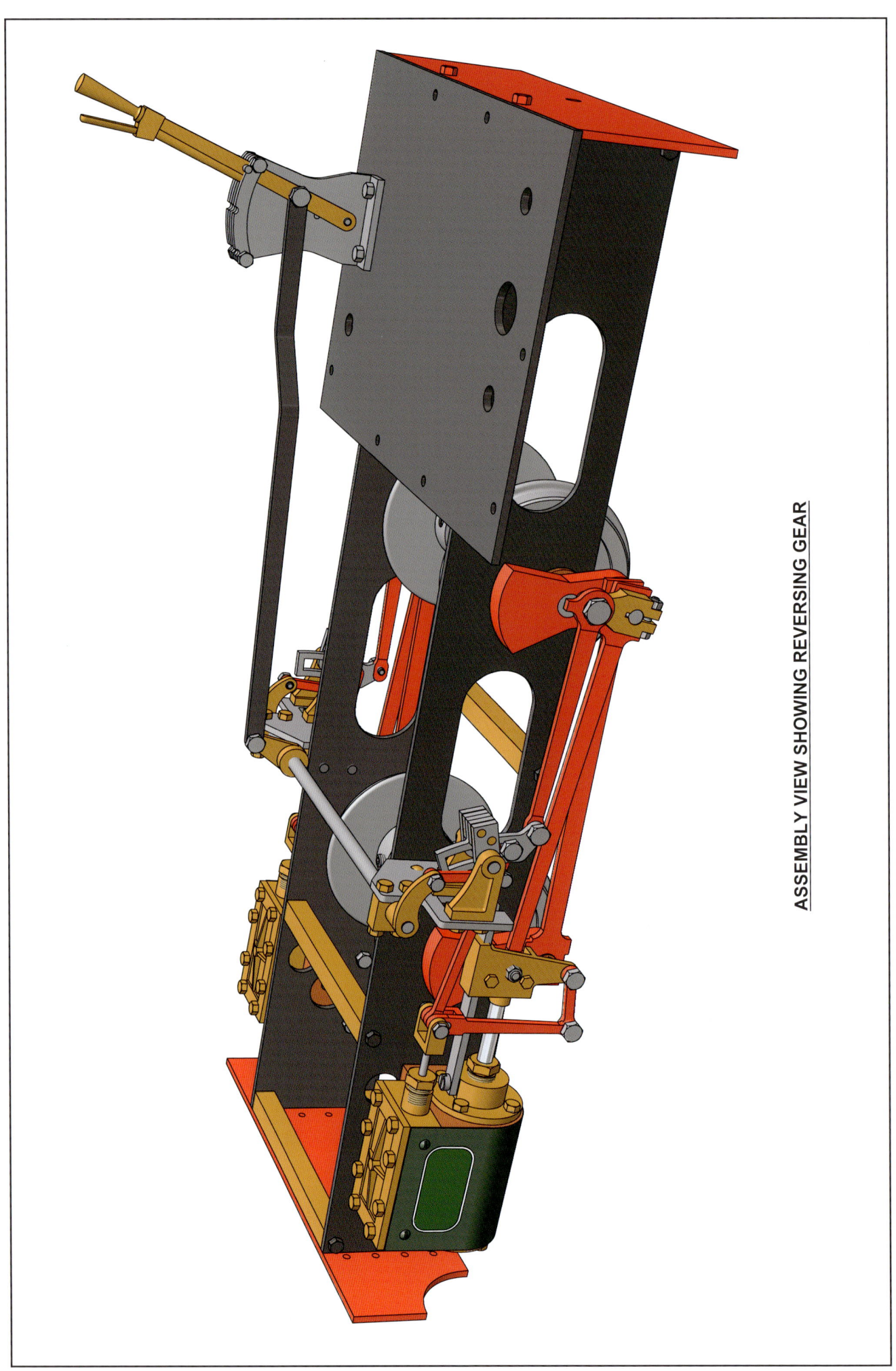

ASSEMBLY VIEW SHOWING REVERSING GEAR

screw. The eccentric pin should lead the crank pin by 90 degrees, and be running on a pitch circle of about 7.5mm. (Make a dummy pointer as shown in the drawing to screw into the 10BA thread in place of the eccentric pin.) Place the main crank on back dead centre and the expansion link in mid position. That is, when the radius rod is moved up and down, there is no movement of the valve. Now, take the distance between the centre of the offset hole at the bottom of the expansion link and the centre of the hole in the return crank pin. (Dividers or vernier callipers can be used for this). Repeat this with the main crank at forward dead centre. Both measurements should be exactly the same. If they are not, then adjust the setting of the return crank until they are. When these measurements are the same, this also is the length of the eccentric rod, i.e. the distance apart of the holes. The eccentric rod can now be made and fitted. Repeat for the other side. (Don't be alarmed if the eccentric rods are slightly different in length.)

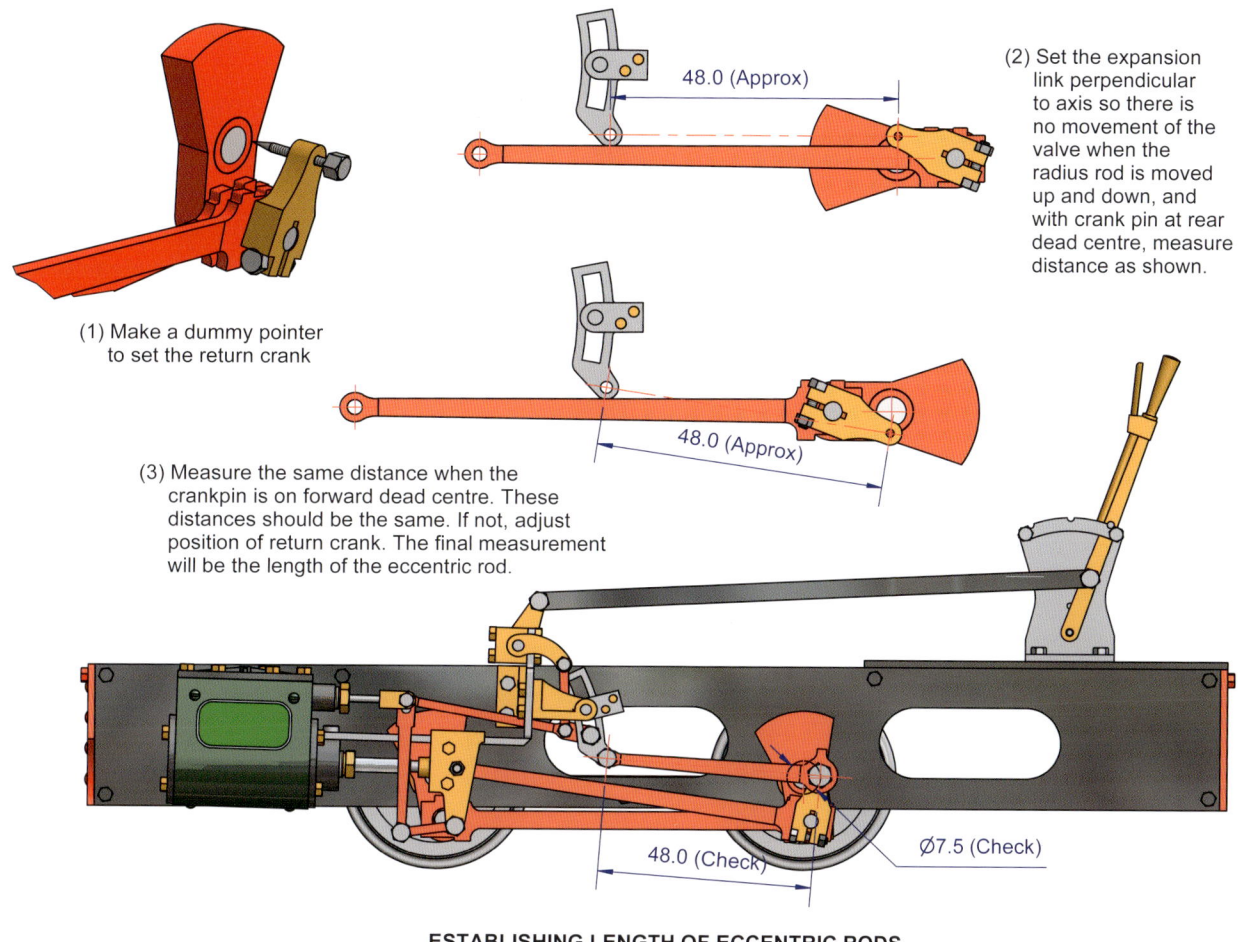

(1) Make a dummy pointer to set the return crank

48.0 (Approx)

(2) Set the expansion link perpendicular to axis so there is no movement of the valve when the radius rod is moved up and down, and with crank pin at rear dead centre, measure distance as shown.

48.0 (Approx)

(3) Measure the same distance when the crankpin is on forward dead centre. These distances should be the same. If not, adjust position of return crank. The final measurement will be the length of the eccentric rod.

48.0 (Check)

Ø7.5 (Check)

ESTABLISHING LENGTH OF ECCENTRIC RODS
(Not to Scale)

Finally, the valves themselves can be set on their spindles. What we are after here is for the valve to admit steam to each end of the cylinder in turn. Steam admission should start at the beginning of the piston stroke and shut off sometime before full stroke.

Leave the covers off the valve chests, and bolt the chests on with a couple of bolts with packing under the heads. Put the reverse lever into forward gear position (the lever will be back) and taking each side in turn, watch the action of the valve as the motion is rotated. As the crank moves to forward dead centre, (that is the piston is right forward) you should see the valve moving back and just cracking open the front steam port. As you continue turning, the valve continues to move back and uncover the port until it is fully, or nearly fully uncovered. The valve then changes direction and starts to move forward until the port is fully covered, at roughly three quarters of the full piston stroke. After this the crank will come to back dead centre and the valve should perform the same action over the rear steam port.

Adjust the valve to achieve this by disconnecting the valve crosshead and screwing the nut until the valve movement is equal over both the ports. The total valve movement should be about 3.5 to 4mm. Check both forward and reverse, and even out any discrepancies which may have been caused by slight inaccuracies along the way. If you have difficulty getting forward and reverse the same, then set the valve to favour the forward direction. If there are major problems getting it right, then double check the length and setting of the eccentrics. When you are satisfied, place a few drops of oil into the valve chests and bolt the covers on.

The final job before testing on air is to make the steam and exhaust lines into the cylinders.

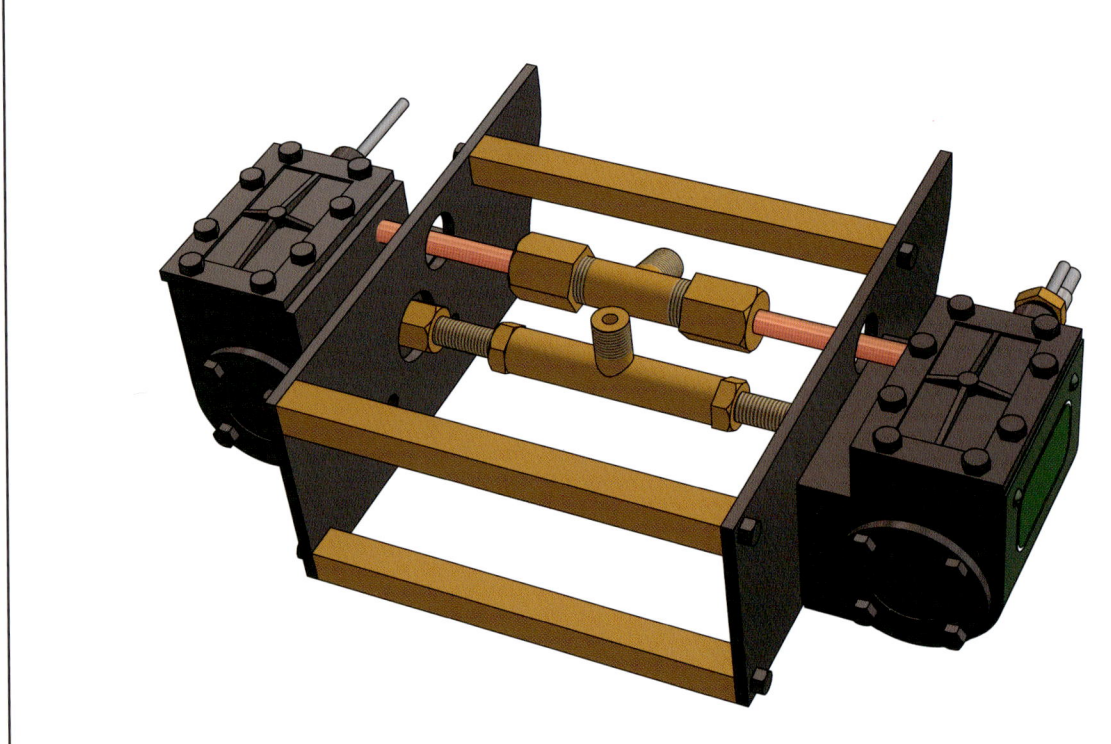

**PERSPECTIVE VIEW
OF ASSEMBLY**

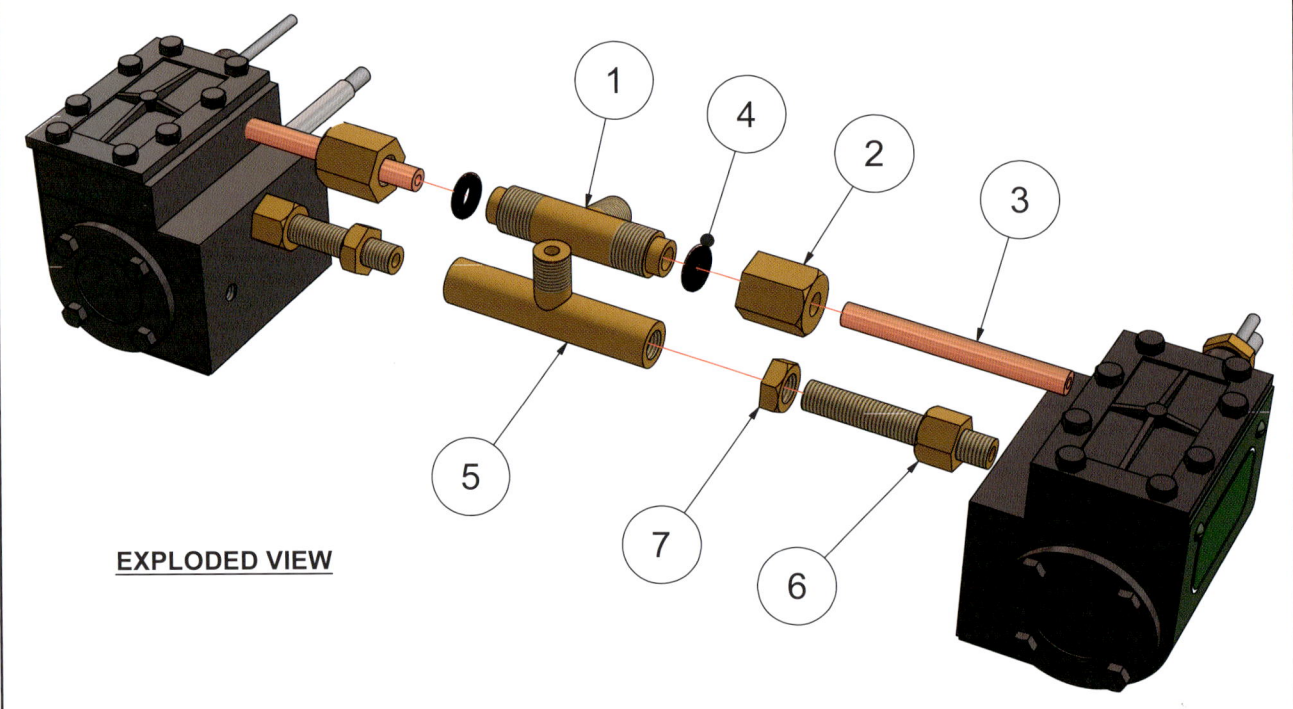

EXPLODED VIEW

Parts List	
ITEM	DESCRIPTION
1	Steam Tee
2	Nut, Steam
3	Steam Pipe
4	O-Ring 1/8" ID
5	Exhaust Tee
6	Exhaust Pipe
7	Nut, Exhaust

**STEAM AND EXHAUST CONNECTIONS
TO CYLINDERS**

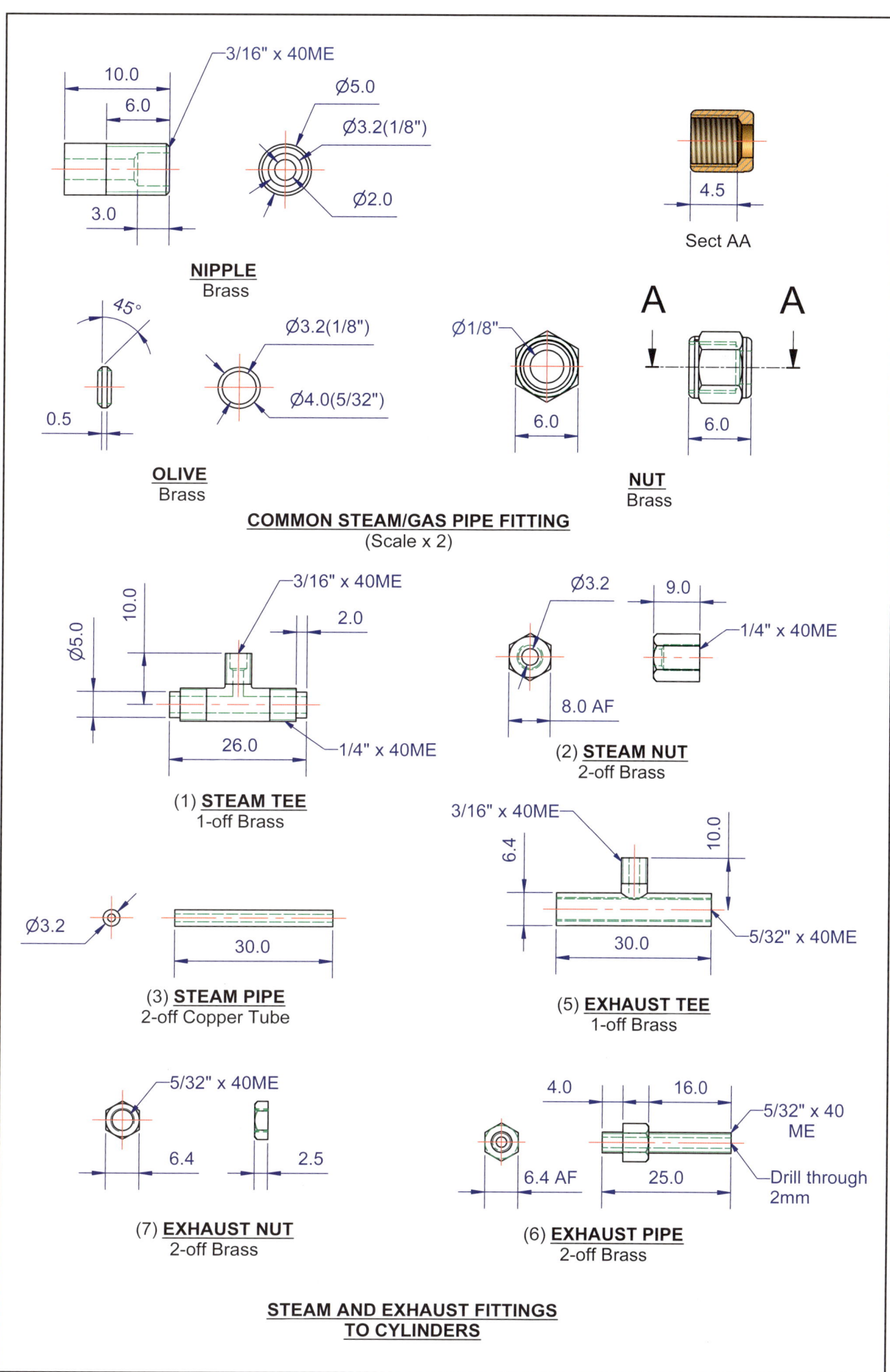

3/16" x 40ME

10.0

6.0

Ø5.0

Ø3.2(1/8")

Ø2.0

3.0

4.5

Sect AA

NIPPLE
Brass

45°

Ø3.2(1/8")

Ø4.0(5/32")

0.5

Ø1/8"

6.0

A   A

6.0

OLIVE
Brass

NUT
Brass

COMMON STEAM/GAS PIPE FITTING
(Scale x 2)

3/16" x 40ME

10.0

2.0

Ø5.0

26.0

1/4" x 40ME

(1) STEAM TEE
1-off Brass

Ø3.2

9.0

1/4" x 40ME

8.0 AF

(2) STEAM NUT
2-off Brass

Ø3.2

30.0

(3) STEAM PIPE
2-off Copper Tube

3/16" x 40ME

6.4

10.0

30.0

5/32" x 40ME

(5) EXHAUST TEE
1-off Brass

5/32" x 40ME

6.4

2.5

(7) EXHAUST NUT
2-off Brass

4.0

16.0

5/32" x 40 ME

6.4 AF

25.0

Drill through 2mm

(6) EXHAUST PIPE
2-off Brass

STEAM AND EXHAUST FITTINGS
TO CYLINDERS

Steam inlet fittings

For all of the steam and gas fittings on the locomotive where ⅛' copper pipe is used a common style of compression fitting will be used. The inlet to the steam tee is the first of these to make, so when doing this it would be a good idea to make as many as are needed in total and a few spares as well. (About 10 should do.) Also the nuts and olives should be made, in that way you can set up a small production line to speed things up.

Nipple

Grip some ³⁄₁₆" (5mm) round brass in the 3-jaw chuck and thread ³⁄₁₆ x 40ME for 6mm. Drill ⅛" for a depth of 3mm and then drill 2mm for about 12mm. Part off at 10mm.

Nut

Grip some ¼" hexagon in the 3-jaw chuck and drill ³⁄₁₆" x 40ME tapping size for 4.5mm. Drill ⅛" for about 7mm. Chamfer the corners of the hexagon or turn a cosmetic shape as shown in the drawing. Part off at 6mm, reverse in the chuck and shape the corners in the same way.

Olive

For these you will need some ⁵⁄₃₂" diameter brass which is obtainable from hobby shops. (They stock a variety of small size sections of brass in the "K&S" range.) Grip the brass in the 3-jaw chuck with about 12mm protruding and drill ⅛" for around 10mm. (Make sure you start the hole running true with a centre drill and use a good ⅛" drill to avoid wandering off centre as you drill.) Place a short length of ⅛" brass or steel in the tailstock chuck and place it into the hole you have just drilled to support the small pieces as we cut them off. Part the olives off with a tool sharpened to a point of about 45 degrees as shown.

To use these unions, slide the nut onto the length of copper pipe, then the olive onto the end, place the pipe in the ⅛" hole in the nipple and tighten up. These fittings can be done up and undone many times.

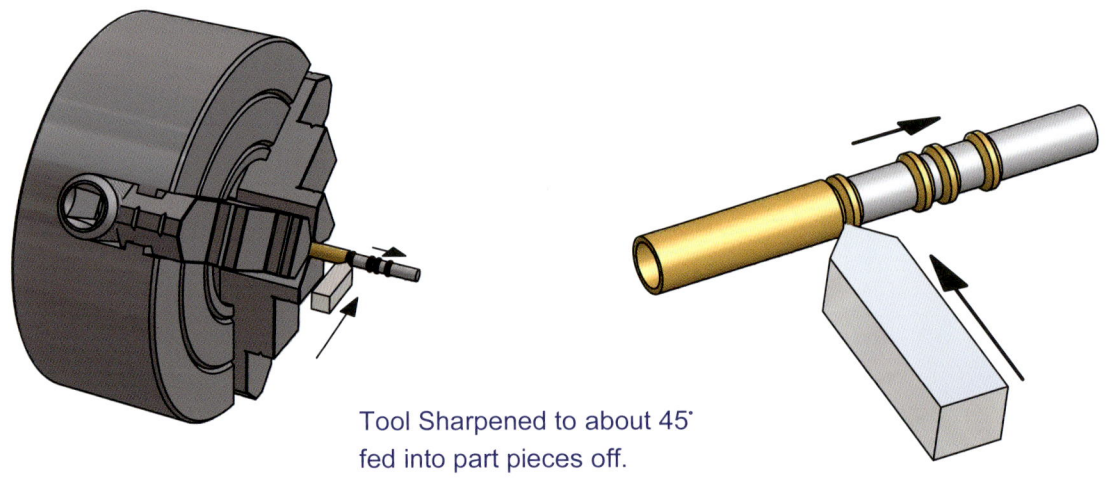

Tool Sharpened to about 45˚
fed into part pieces off.

PARTING OFF OLIVES FOR STEAM/GAS PIPES

Steam tee

The Steam Tee is fabricated from brass. For the main cross piece place some ¼" (6.4mm) diameter brass in the 3-jaw chuck and drill ⅛" to a depth of about 30mm. Thread ¼" x 40ME for 7mm then turn off the first 2mm of the thread forming a clean shoulder to take the O-ring. Part off to 26mm, reverse in the chuck and turn and thread this end in the same manner. Centre punch for a hole in the centre and grip in the drill press vice. Drill a ³⁄₁₆" hole to take the nipple. It is a good idea to start this hole with a centre drill and then drill in just deep enough for the nipple to enter fully, don't go right through to the bore of the cross piece. During this process the drill may wobble around a little, but as we will be silver soldering, it doesn't matter if the fit is a bit loose.

Position the nipple in the hole and silver solder. Again grip in the vice and clean the bore through the nipple with a 2mm drill, then grip the fitting in the lathe by the cross piece and clean the bore right through with a ⅛" drill.

Exhaust tee

Because the wall of the exhaust tee is so thin it would be difficult to join the two pieces in the same way we did for the steam tee. In this case, firstly drill the ³⁄₁₆" hole into the centre of the blank cross piece and silver solder the nipple in place. (This nipple is slightly different as there is no 1/8" hole drilled in the end.) After this, mount in the 3-jaw chuck and drill right through the cross piece, drilling firstly half way through and then

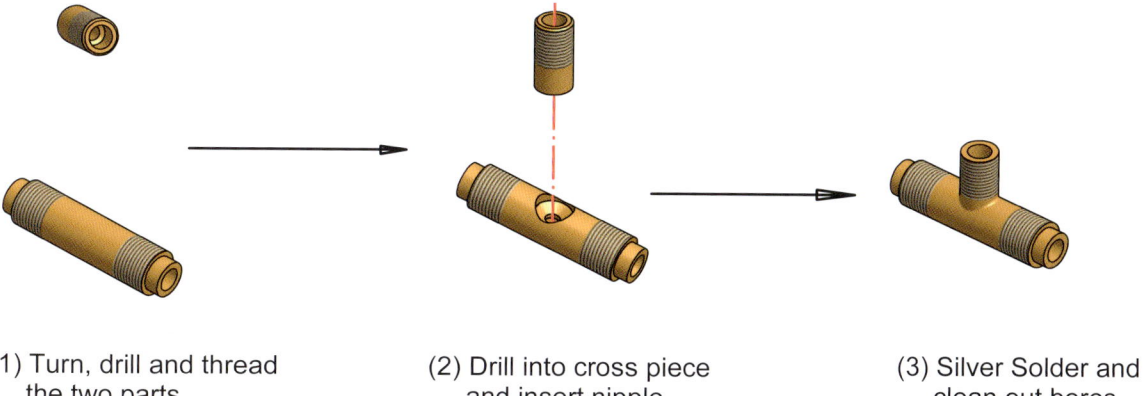

(1) Turn, drill and thread
the two parts

(2) Drill into cross piece
and insert nipple.

(3) Silver Solder and
clean out bores.

FABRICATING STEAM TEE

(Exhaust Tee Similar)

reversing to drill all the way just in case there are voids from the silver soldering which might throw the drill off course. Thread the hole ⁵⁄₃₂" x 40ME.

Exhaust pipe

The exhaust pipe that screws into the cylinders is made by taking a piece of ¼" brass hexagon and threading both ends to the lengths shown. Drill right through with a 2mm drill.

Fitting the pipes and running on air

Space is a bit tight for fitting the steam and exhaust pipes, so you will need to do some juggling around. Do the exhaust pipes first. Screw the lock nuts onto the long end of each exhaust pipe then screw one exhaust pipe into its cylinder using some thread tape or sealant to ensure it is steam tight. Take the exhaust tee and screw it fully onto this exhaust pipe which should leave sufficient room to get the other exhaust pipe screwed into the opposite cylinder. After this is done, screw back the tee onto the second exhaust pipe until it is midway between the frames. Nip up the locknuts.

To fit the steam tee you will need to bend one of the ⅛" copper steam pipes slightly to one side. Place the nuts and O-rings onto the pipes and slide the tee onto the pipe. Straighten the pipe up and slide the tee so that it is also centered between the frames. Nip up the nuts just sufficiently to squeeze the O-rings and make a seal.

When assembling the steam pipe from the boiler, the nipple on the steam tee will be pointing backwards and down, but to test on air we can leave it pointing up.

Finally make up a temporary fitting to join your air line to the steam tee and we are ready to have a run.

Mount the chassis onto a couple of wooden blocks under the ends to raise the wheels off the bench and clamp down with a G-clamp or similar. (**Photo 1.16**) Oil the wheels, rods and all parts of the motion.

1.16 — Running the chassis on air. Let's hope the bolt isn't from somewhere important!

Run up the compressor and set the pressure to about 100 kPa (20 psi). With the valve gear set in forward, gradually open the air valve. If everything is set up correctly (of course it will be!) your chassis should spring into life. At this stage everything will be a bit tight, so you may need a bit more pressure and you may need to turn it over by hand to get it started. Also, air doesn't expand while it is working in the same way as steam so the motion won't run as smoothly. Try the gear in both forward and reverse. After making any necessary adjustments to get it turning nicely, run slowly for about half an hour or so, oiling frequently. By now it should be starting to run a little more smoothly as the parts are wearing in. An hour or two should be enough and then you have to stop playing and get on with the rest of the locomotive.

Parts List	
ITEM	DESCRIPTION
1	Smokebox
2	Saddle
3	Chimney Base
4	Chimney
5	Spark Arrestor
6	Rivets, Dummy
7	8BA x 5 Bolt
8	Smokebox Door
9	Smokebox Door Hinges
10	Smokebox Door back
11	Hinge Blocks
12	Hinge Pin
13	Door Insert Ring
14	Dart 1
15	Dart 2
16	Headlight Bracket
17	Headlight
18	Reflector
19	Globe
20	10BA x 5 Bolt

SMOKEBOX ASSEMBLY EXPLODED

Steam Trains in Your Garden

CHAPTER 2 – The Smoke Box and Boiler

Saddle

The saddle is fabricated from two pieces. The curved part can be rolled from a piece of approximately 1.6mm thick sheet or can be cut from a piece of tube. If the tube isn't quite the correct size, it can be opened up or closed in to suit. An off cut of copper boiler tube would be ideal and this would need to be opened up slightly to match the curve on the outside of the smokebox. Cut and bend to shape the base piece to be a nice fit onto the underneath of the curve and silver solder together. Cut out the opening and drill the holes.

Smokebox

The smokebox can be rolled up from sheet, but it is easier to use a piece of tubing or a threaded black iron socket. (**Photo 2.1**). Turn to size and mark out for the cutout and mounting holes from the saddle. Cut the piece out and drill and tap the four mounting holes 8BA. Bolt the saddle onto the smokebox and drill a 10BA clear hole underneath which is also marked through and drilled into the front plate to secure the smokebox to the chassis. Stand the smokebox on a table and mark out the hole for the chimney, making sure that it is placed exactly above the vertical exhaust pipe. When drilling, make it the correct size to fit the turned down end of the bottom of the chimney pipe (12mm) and also take care as it is a bit thin to drill through. Building up to the final size with smaller drills and making sure the job is very firmly supported can help to minimize the chance of a disaster.

2.1 — Threaded socket before (right) and after (left) turning to size

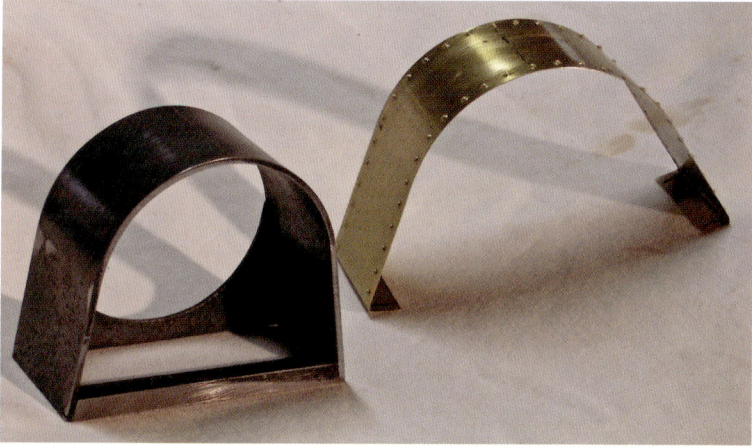
2.2 — Rivets embossed in an overlay for a Hunslet style smoke box

If you want to put a couple of rows of dummy rivets around the smokebox, now is a good time to drill for these. They are purely cosmetic although they do add a nice touch. Once the holes are drilled the rivets can be cut short and inserted with a little epoxy or super glue which is adequate to hold them until they are painted, when the paint will also help to hold them in. Another way to apply dummy rivets is to wrap a sheet of thin shim around the smokebox with the rivet heads embossed in it. (We will talk about embossing rivets later in the body work section). The shim is cut short and held under the edges of the saddle by the four mounting bolts. If this method is used, put epoxy glue under the top part to bind it while drilling for the chimney, otherwise the drill will catch the shim and spoil all your nice rivet work! The glue will burn away after it has done its job. (**Photo 2.2**)

Smoke box door assembly

The smoke box door assembly is an important contributor to the good looks and authenticity of a locomotive. For this locomotive we have an English style of door, the most distinctive parts being the hinges and darts. For our purposes we don't need to make the door open on the hinges, it is easier to just make the whole assembly a push fit into the front of the smoke box.

Start with the backing plate which is a piece of 1.6mm mild steel 55mm diameter. Mark out the 55mm diameter with dividers and drill a hole ¼" in the centre. Roughly cut the outside to size with a hacksaw and then mount the piece in the 3-jaw chuck on a ¼" bolt, tightening up with a washer and nut. Turn the outside to 55mm. Take an off cut of 2" (50.8mm) copper boiler tube about 5mm long, clean up in the lathe and silver solder it centrally onto what will become the back of the door backing plate.

The door itself will need to be turned from a piece of brass or mild steel 2" (50mm) diameter. Grip in the 3-jaw chuck and turn the curved profile of the front and the three diameters for the darts. If your lathe is big

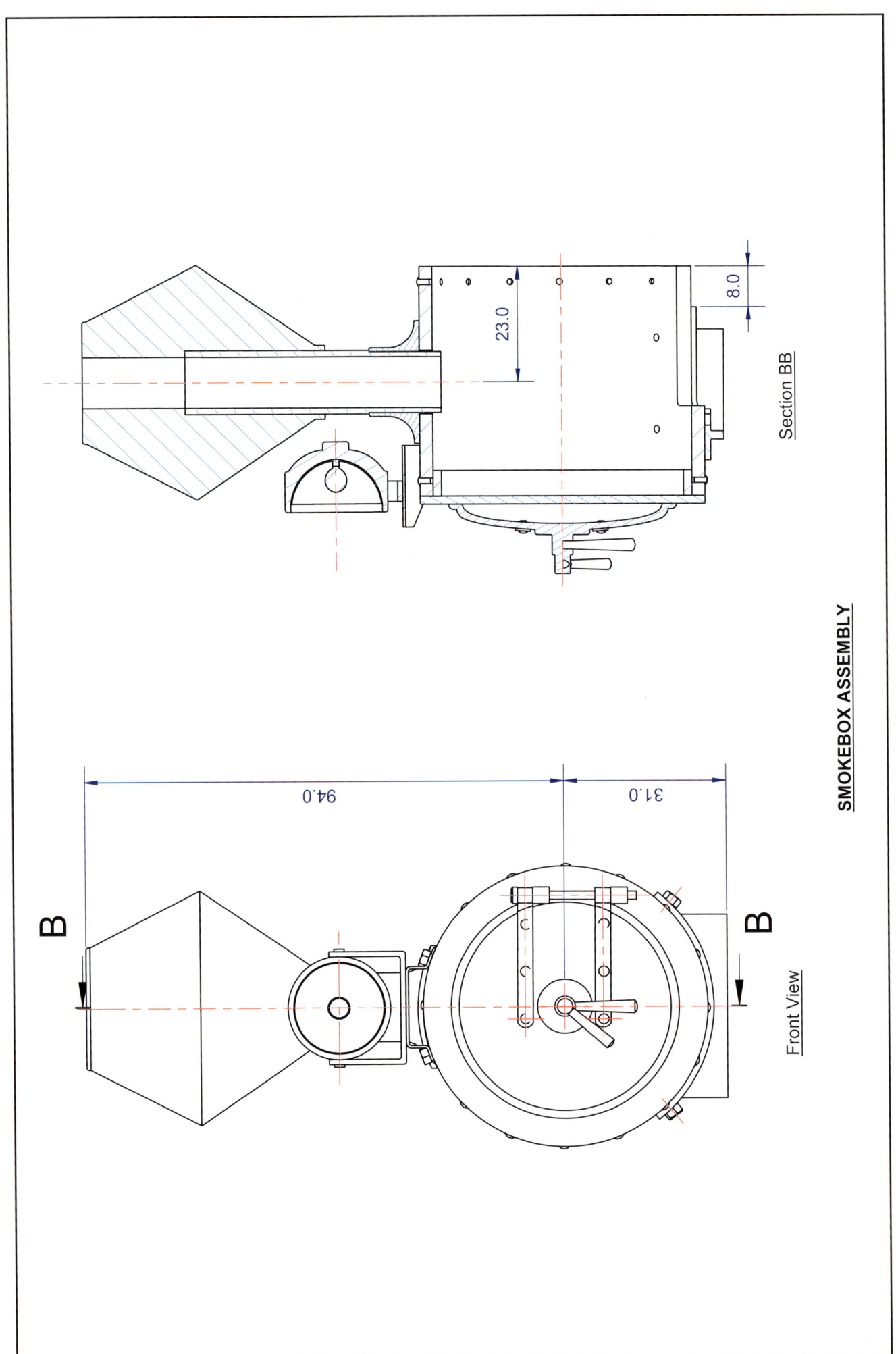

Section BB

8.0

23.0

94.0

31.0

B

B

Front View

SMOKEBOX ASSEMBLY

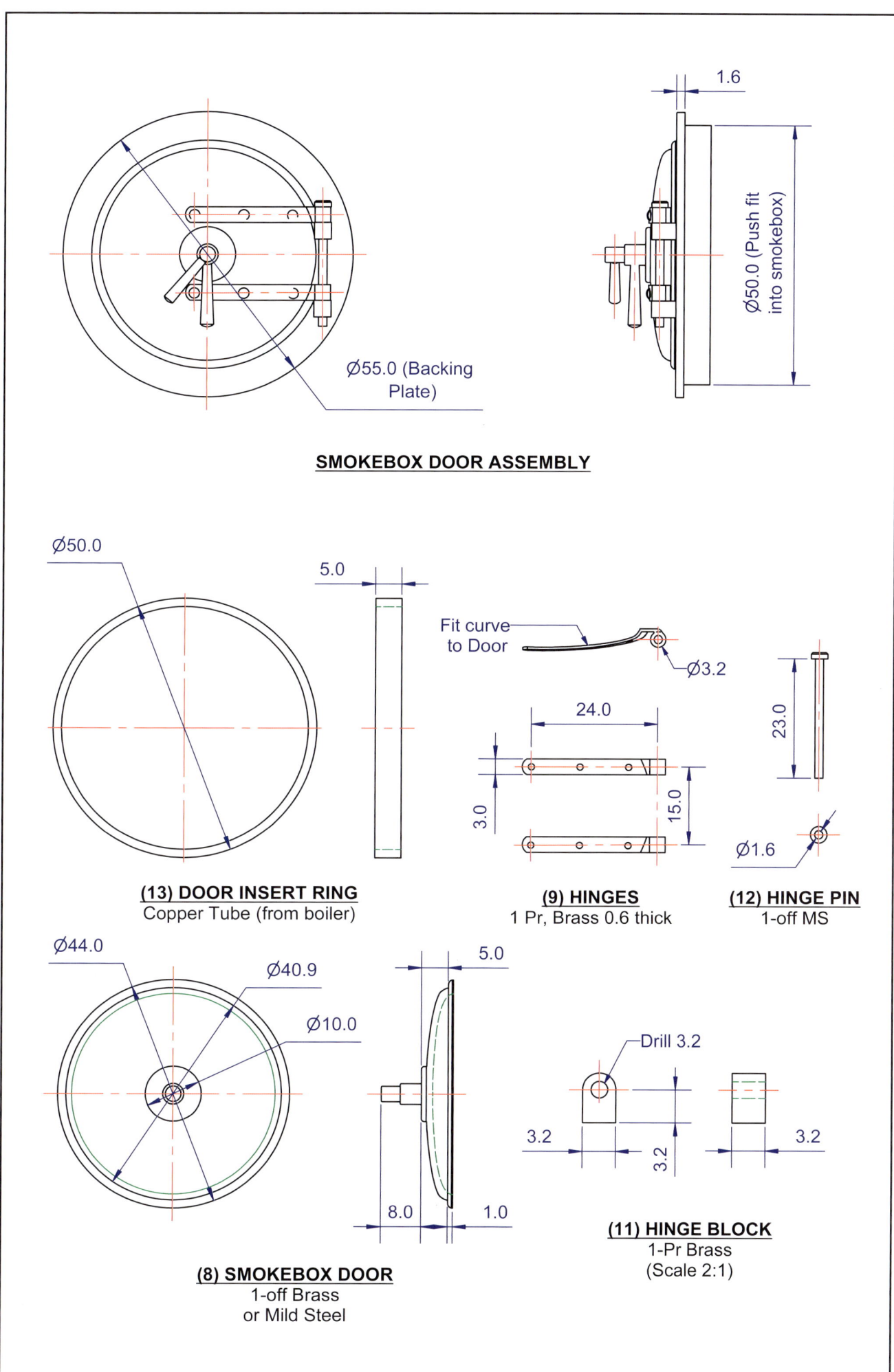

SMOKEBOX DOOR ASSEMBLY

Ø55.0 (Backing Plate)

1.6

Ø50.0 (Push fit into smokebox)

Ø50.0

5.0

(13) DOOR INSERT RING
Copper Tube (from boiler)

Fit curve to Door

Ø3.2

24.0

3.0

15.0

(9) HINGES
1 Pr, Brass 0.6 thick

23.0

Ø1.6

(12) HINGE PIN
1-off MS

Ø44.0

Ø40.9

Ø10.0

5.0

8.0

1.0

(8) SMOKEBOX DOOR
1-off Brass
or Mild Steel

Drill 3.2

3.2

3.2

3.2

(11) HINGE BLOCK
1-Pr Brass
(Scale 2:1)

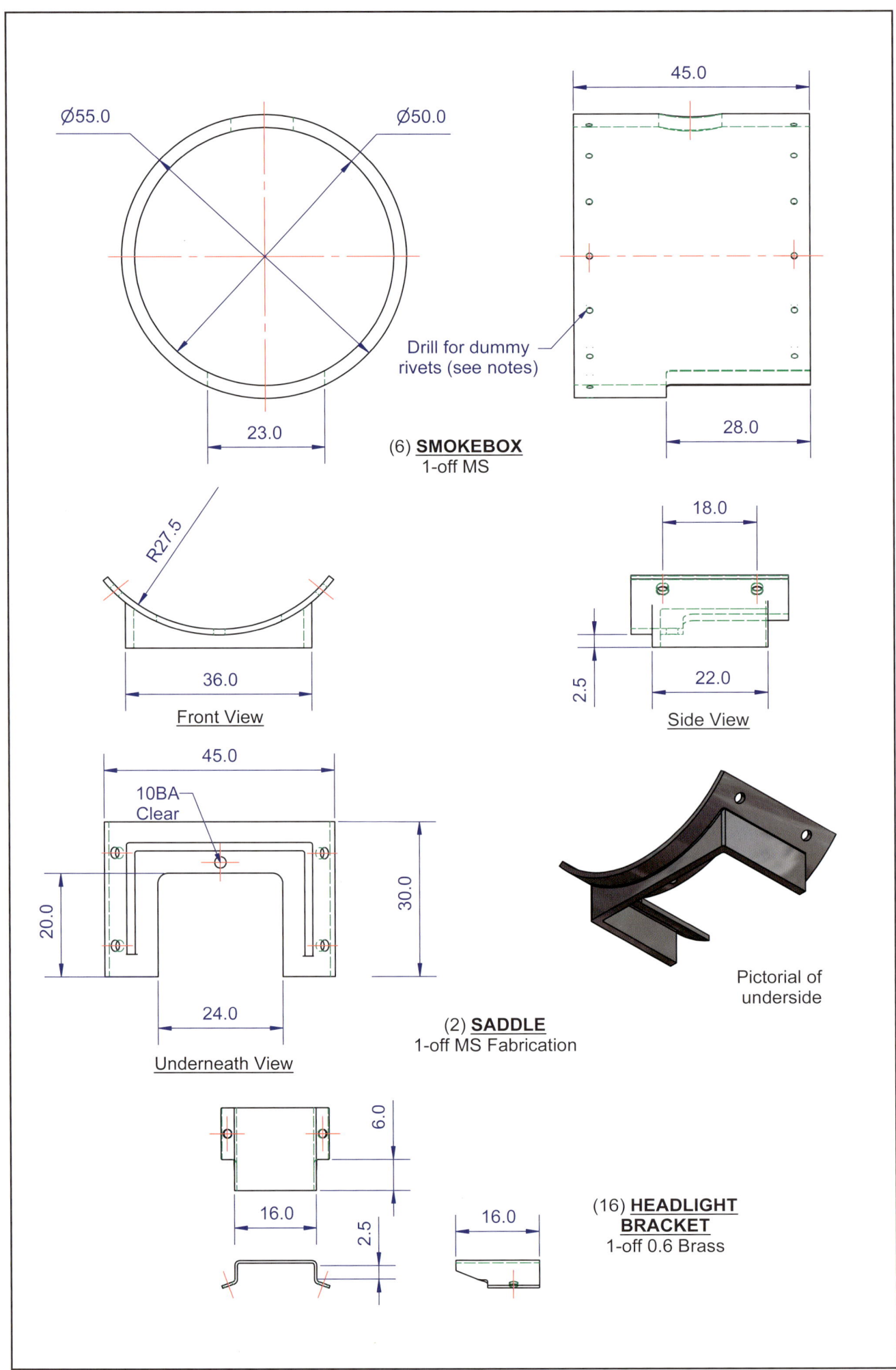

Ø55.0

Ø50.0

Drill for dummy rivets (see notes)

23.0

45.0

28.0

(6) **SMOKEBOX**
1-off MS

R27.5

36.0

Front View

18.0

22.0

2.5

Side View

45.0

10BA Clear

20.0

30.0

24.0

Underneath View

(2) **SADDLE**
1-off MS Fabrication

Pictorial of underside

6.0

16.0

2.5

16.0

(16) **HEADLIGHT BRACKET**
1-off 0.6 Brass

enough, part this piece off, otherwise cut off with a hacksaw and grip carefully in the chuck by the small diameter of the rear dart. Turn the back flat and scallop out the inside a little to make sure the door fits flush onto the backing plate. It will be necessary to do these operations very carefully with light cuts as there is not much for the chuck to grip onto.

The hinges, while they look a bit fiddly, are really quite easy to make. Cut a couple of strips of 0.6mm thick brass 3mm wide and using pliers with a good sharp edge, bend and twist the pieces until they are a close fit onto the door. Mark them out for rivet holes, drill, mark through onto the door and drill again and rivet in place, leaving them long at the hinge end to be trimmed off later.

The little hinge blocks and the hinge bearings can be made and all assembled in their correct order onto the hinge pin. Turn the two dart handles and carefully drill the spigot in the door at the correct position and angles and insert these. Lay the door down and place the hinge assembly into position and silver solder. Use solder sparingly otherwise there will be unsightly blobs, the solder only has to hold things together not do any hard work. This area gets very hot in use, so soft solder would not be up to the task, you must use silver solder.

Chimney

The chimney consists of three pieces, the base, the central tube and the outer dummy spark arrestor.

If you have a piece of brass tubing the correct size, the central tube can be made from this, otherwise drill some ½" brass 10mm and turn one end to 12mm for a length of 14mm.

The dummy spark arrestor can be made from any material of suitable diameter, but as it is a rather large lump of metal, aluminium would be ideal. If you have a length longer than required, it can be drilled and turned in the one setting by gripping in the 3-jaw chuck, drilling and then setting over the compound slide to turn the two angles (approximately 27 deg and 34 deg), or if you only have a piece which is just long enough, it can be drilled and then gripped with a mandrel to turn the two angles. As these angles are purely cosmetic they do not have to be exact.

The chimney base involves a little more work, but is one of those pieces which, if well made, looks good on the locomotive. Take a piece of 1" (25.4mm) brass rod longer than required, say no less than 50mm, and grip horizontally in the milling machine vice. (Some vices have a groove to facilitate this.) Set up a fly cutter or boring tool in the machine and cut the 27.5mm radius to match the smoke box shell.

Remove the piece, set it up in the 3-jaw chuck in the lathe and turn the 5mm radius and outside diameter of the top part. Drill 12mm for a depth of about 16mm. We now have to finish shaping the 5mm fillet to blend with the smoke box curve. The only way to do this is to file carefully by hand using a combination of round or half round files of suitable size. Part the piece off and then finish by rubbing with a strip of emery cloth and finally buffing.

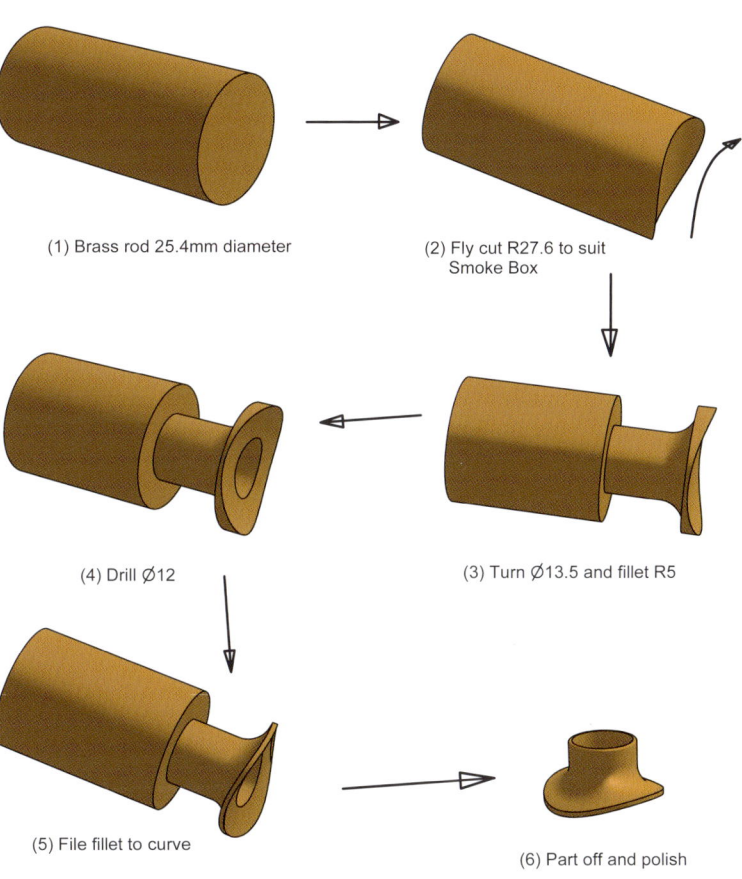

(1) Brass rod 25.4mm diameter

(2) Fly cut R27.6 to suit Smoke Box

(3) Turn Ø13.5 and fillet R5

(4) Drill Ø12

(5) File fillet to curve

(6) Part off and polish

SHAPING CHIMNEY BASE

Steam and sand domes

There are a number of different ways in which the domes can be made, depending on how big your lathe is and what materials you have to hand. Also the curve on the bottom has to be fitted to the outside of the cladding of your finished boiler, so although making these is described here, you may wish to wait until the boiler is finished before going ahead.

They could be turned in a similar way to the chimney base, but in addition they need to be held securely in the chuck while turning the tops.

Using a piece longer than required, grip in the milling machine chuck and cut the bottom curve to fit the boiler with a fly cutter. Turn the outside including the 2 or 3mm fillet. Drill and thread around ½" or 12mm for

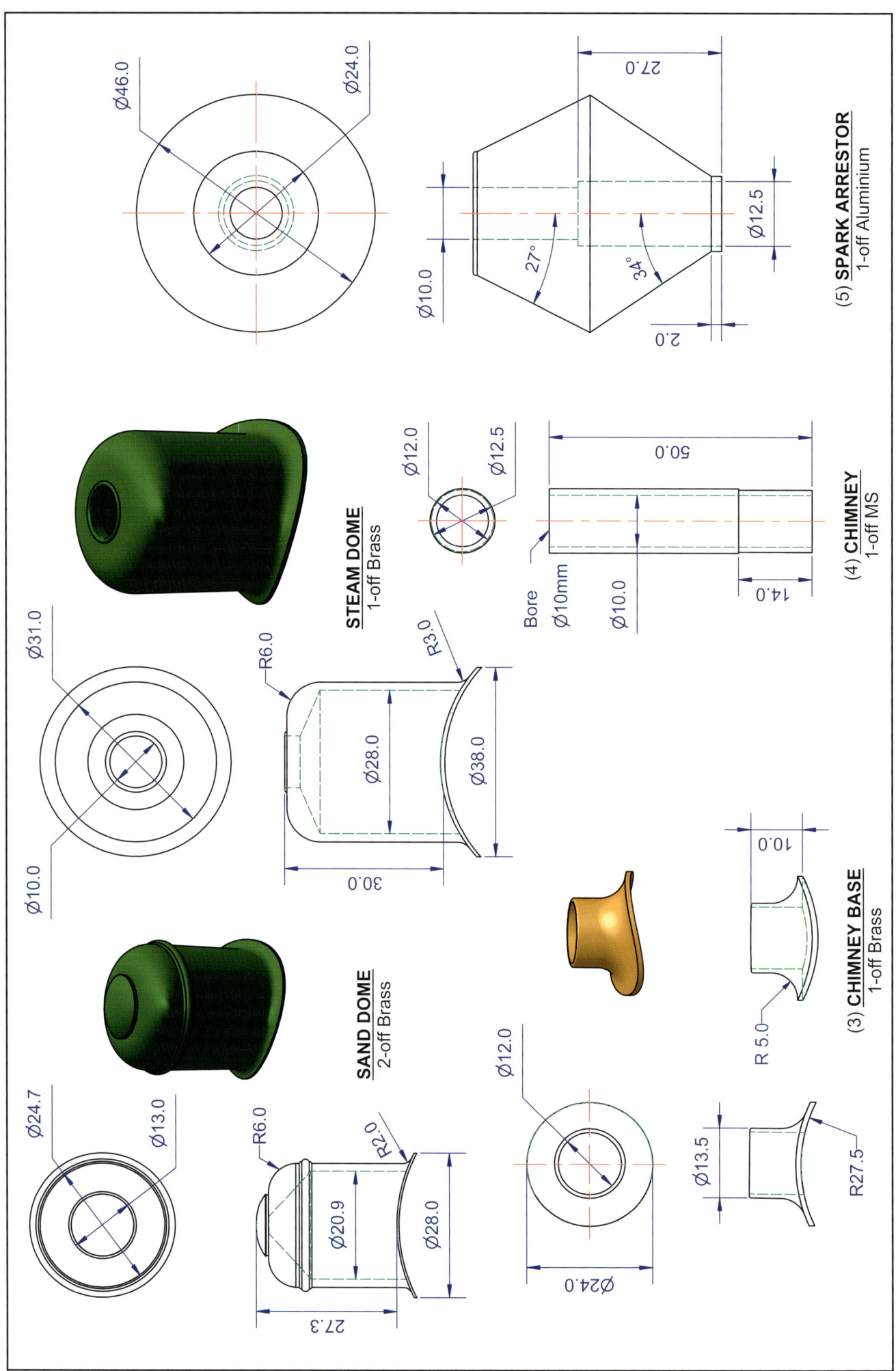

Ø46.0

Ø24.0

(5) SPARK ARRESTOR
1-off Aluminium

27.0

Ø10.0

27°

34°

Ø12.5

2.0

STEAM DOME
1-off Brass

Ø12.0

Ø12.5

R6.0

R3.0

Ø28.0

Ø38.0

30.0

Bore
Ø10mm

Ø10.0

(4) CHIMNEY
1-off MS

50.0

14.0

Ø31.0

Ø10.0

SAND DOME
2-off Brass

(3) CHIMNEY BASE
1-off Brass

10.0

R 5.0

Ø24.7

Ø13.0

R6.0

R2.0

Ø20.9

Ø28.0

27.3

Ø12.0

Ø24.0

Ø13.5

R27.5

screwing onto a mandrel. Turn the mandrel from some mild steel stock about ¾" diameter, making a thread about ½" (12mm) diameter by 10mm long. Screw the work piece onto the mandrel and turn the outside profile. Drill the hole in the end in the case of the steam dome and turn the end profile for the sand domes. Remove from the chuck together with the mandrel, grip in the vice and file the fillet. Finally drill out the thread to be a loose fit over the boiler bush which will be ½" (12mm).

The foregoing describes making the domes from a solid piece, so they would finish up quite heavy. This in itself doesn't matter, but it is very

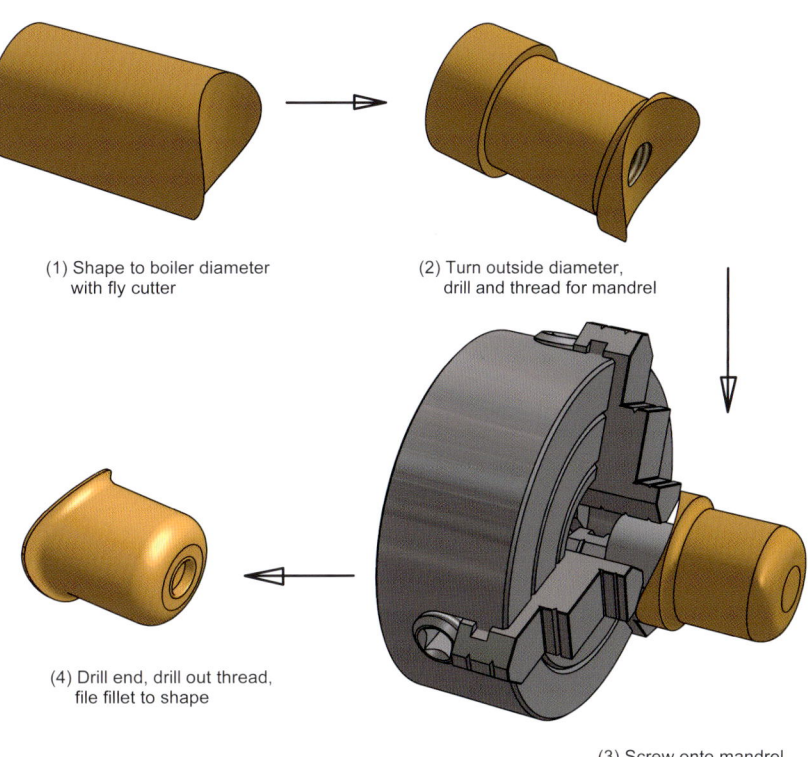

(1) Shape to boiler diameter with fly cutter

(2) Turn outside diameter, drill and thread for mandrel

(4) Drill end, drill out thread, file fillet to shape

(3) Screw onto mandrel and turn outside profile

SHAPING DOME

Tap with Mallet

SHAPING THE FILLET WHEN USING TUBING

wasteful of material, so they could be made in two parts. The bottom part could be made from tubing, leaving the fillet off and then turning a top piece to suit and soldering together. This is much easier, but the domes really look much better if they have a nice fillet where they meet the boiler. It is possible to make the fillet with tubing by shaping the end to fit the curve of the boiler and then annealing and tapping onto a conical shape such as a large lathe centre. This a little difficult to get right and might need some practice on some tubing off cuts first. You will need to do some panel beating and general rocking back and forth to get a nice fillet all the way around.

Boiler

People are sometimes frightened off when it comes to making the boiler. However if a few basic rules and concepts are followed, it can be the easiest part of the whole locomotive!

As far as boilers go, this one is quite basic. It is gas fired, and has one flue tube. The design follows the guidelines of the AMBSC Code Part 3 — Sub-Miniature Boilers. Before making it, you should verify the design with a club boiler inspector or appropriate authority, and make sure that you fully understand all of the requirements for making and using a model boiler. The materials used should be as specified in the Standard and the manufacturer's instructions with regard to the materials and equipment used to make the boiler must be thoroughly understood and followed during construction. Care must be taken and appropriate precautions followed when using acid pickle to clean the copper. The steps of construction outlined here are suggestions only and it is the builder's responsibility to make sure that the steps are thoroughly understood, taken in a safe order and are within his or her ability to carry out.

For boiler making you will need a heating source, the most ideal for a small boiler being an air/propane torch with pinpoint, medium and large tips. Make sure to follow all manufacturers' instructions and wear protective clothing as specified. An acid pickle will be needed and commonly dilute sulphuric acid is used. A cheaper and safer alternative to use is citric acid, which can be obtained from a Home Brew shop. You may need to leave the job in the pickle bath a little longer, but the benefits may be worth this inconvenience. A good hearth area is needed and this can be made up from fire bricks or other heat resistant materials. Its purpose is to reflect heat back into the job as well as protect the surrounding area.

There are two alternative ways to operate the boiler in a locomotive of this size. The first is to use a gas tank which runs out of fuel before the water level becomes too low in the boiler in which case a gauge glass to show the water level is not essential. The second is to use a larger gas tank which gives a longer run, and then top up the water level while firing by using a plastic "squeeze" bottle feeding through a "Goodall" non-return valve.

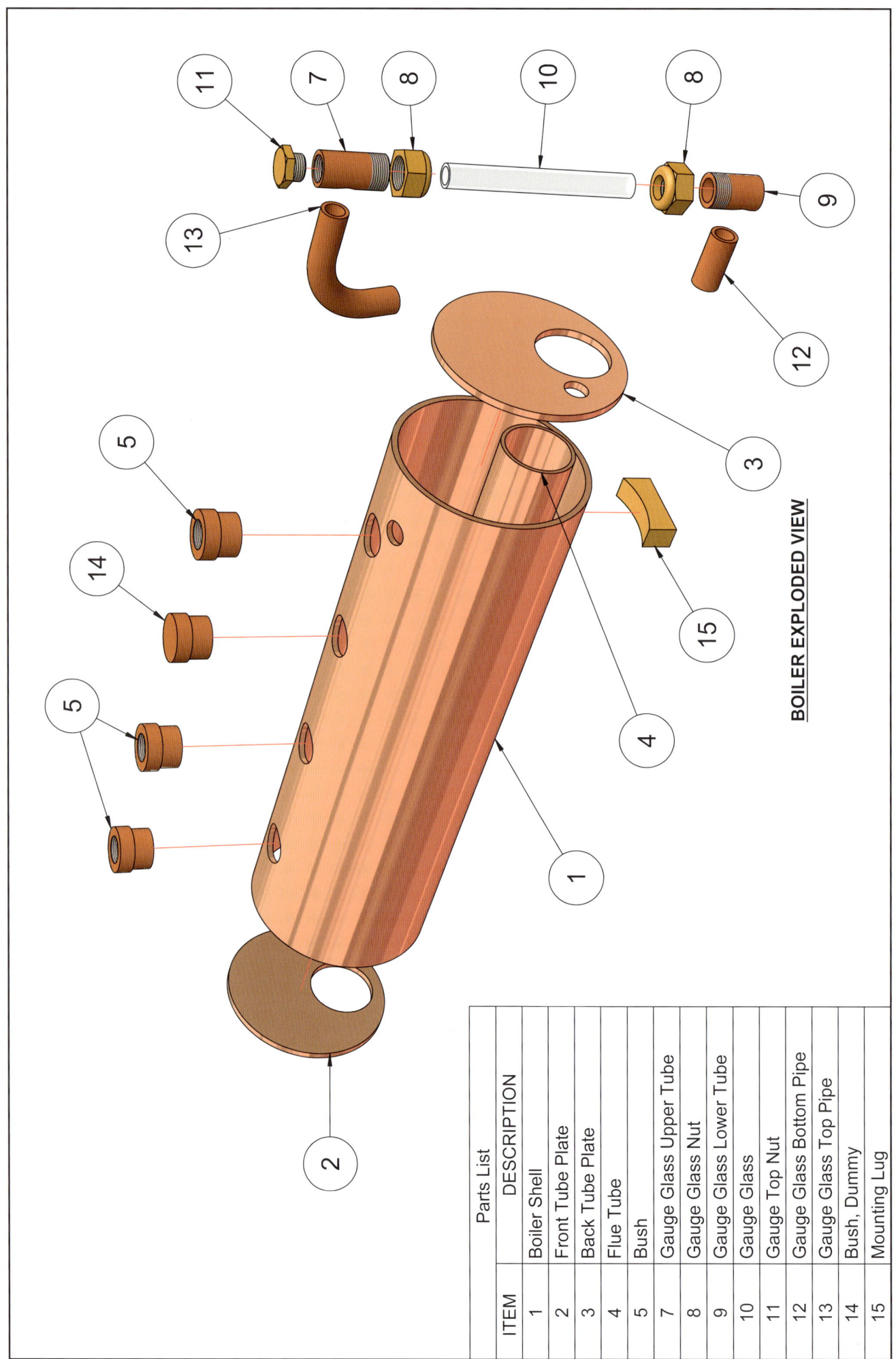

BOILER EXPLODED VIEW

Parts List	
ITEM	DESCRIPTION
1	Boiler Shell
2	Front Tube Plate
3	Back Tube Plate
4	Flue Tube
5	Bush
7	Gauge Glass Upper Tube
8	Gauge Glass Nut
9	Gauge Glass Lower Tube
10	Gauge Glass
11	Gauge Top Nut
12	Gauge Glass Bottom Pipe
13	Gauge Glass Top Pipe
14	Bush, Dummy
15	Mounting Lug

The drawings for the boiler and fittings show one with a gauge glass included where the inlet pipes to the glass are soldered into the boiler shell. it is possible to use a different type of gauge glass mounting where the inlet pipes to the glass are attached to the boiler by means of screwed bushes. Either can be used, but we will describe the soldered type in the notes.

Cut and prepare all the materials and turn the bushes for the safety valve, steam manifold and steam dome from bronze. (**Photo 2.3**) The sizes given here will need to be checked and if necessary, adjustments made to suit your materials. Generally, the copper available is still made in Imperial sizes, so the tube plates will be $\frac{1}{16}$" thick. Two discs around 38mm diameter are required. These should be marked out (a fine tipped permanent marker

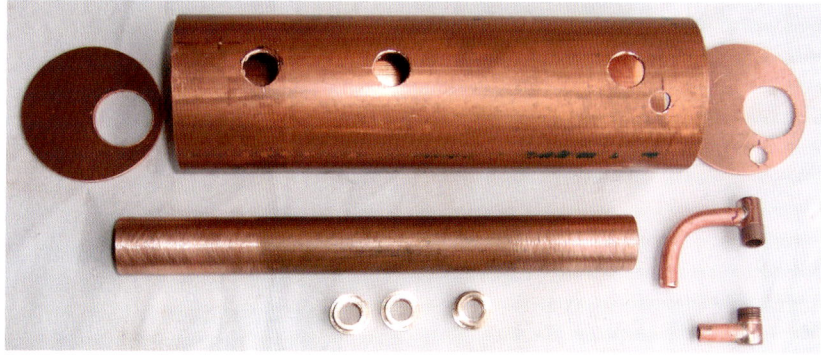

2.3 — Boiler components

is ideal) and the 19mm diameter holes for the flue tube and the ¼" hole in the back plate for the water gauge drilled. The tube plates are then cut out and should be made a neat fit in the barrel. These plates do not have flanges so therefore they must be a firm fit in the end of the barrel so that they remain in place when soldering. It is tempting to turn the plates in the lathe to be a neat fit in the barrel, but if this is done they will either be too loose or too tight. If they are too tight the solder will not flow around the joint properly. The best way to fit the end plates is to file or grind the discs so that the edges are a bit "wavy" and can lock into place with high spots around the circumference. This way there will be ample room for the solder to flow. To drill the holes in the top of the barrel for the bushes, cut and shape a piece of hardwood to support the tube as the drill breaks through. (**Photo 2.4**)

The boiler is now ready for soldering, but first let us mention a few basic principles which will help to produce a good result. Firstly, the joints to be soldered should be a good fit and be adequately supported when heating. There is nothing much worse than being halfway through a soldering job when the heat expands or moves the pieces and everything collapses, or worse, slips and solders itself out of position. Secondly, the joints to be soldered must be clean and well fluxed; and thirdly, adequate heat must be applied to enable the solder to flow freely, but not so much that the joint becomes overheated. When heating at any stage, always apply flux to previously soldered joints, or areas where solder is to be applied in the future.

2.4 — Drilling the boiler barrell

A useful property of a silver soldered joint is that when soldering a piece which is near a previously soldered area, provided that the area is not overheated, the solder will flow into the new joint without melting solder in the previously soldered area.

The suggested sequence of heating and soldering stages is:
(1)   The front tube plate together with the flue tube into the barrel.
(2)   Back tube plate and the flue tube.
(3)   The bushes.
(4)   The gauge glass pipes.

(1)   Apply flux to all parts of the barrel which are to be soldered. Apply flux to both ends of the flue tube and to both sides of the front tube plate where it is to be soldered. Assemble these three pieces in their relative positions (making sure the flue hole is at the bottom) and stand the assembly upright on the back end of the barrel onto a couple of pieces of packing. Cut short lengths of solder rod about 20mm long and place around the joints as well as having a stick of solder ready to feed into the joint as necessary. You must apply sufficient solder to completely fill the joint and form a nice fillet. (Don't even start to think about the price of silver solder as the joint hungrily consumes it!)

   Apply heat using the large burner tip. Keep the flame moving around the whole job at first, gradually concentrating on the end where the solder is to flow. When the correct temperature is reached, the solder will flow freely into the joints and you can top it up with the stick of solder as required. As soon as a good fillet of solder is evident around both joints remove the heat and let the job cool until

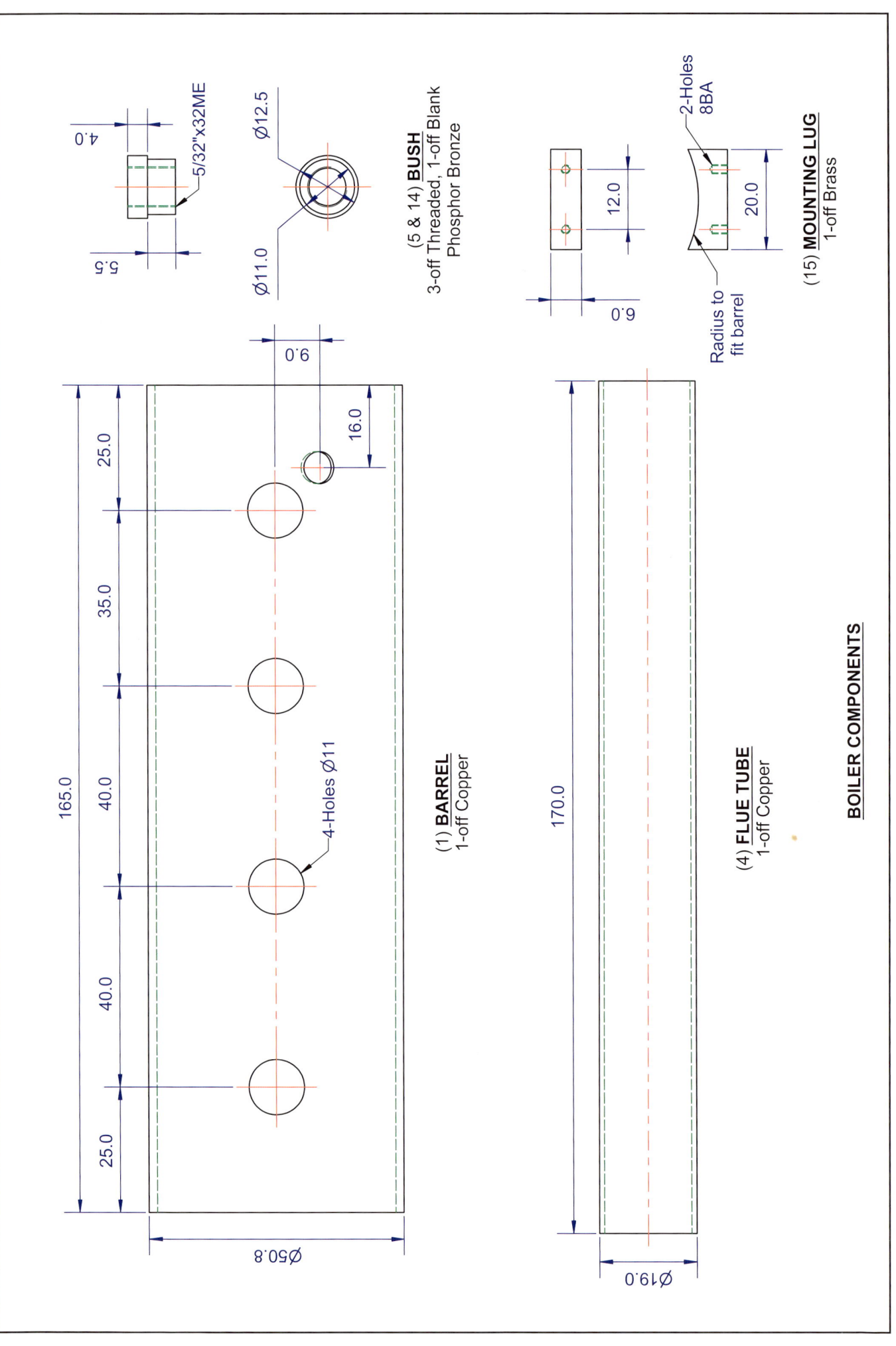

4.0

5.5

5/32"x32ME

Ø12.5

Ø11.0

(5 & 14) **BUSH**
3-off Threaded, 1-off Blank
Phosphor Bronze

9.0

16.0

25.0

35.0

40.0

40.0

25.0

165.0

4-Holes Ø11

Ø50.8

(1) **BARREL**
1-off Copper

12.0

6.0

2-Holes
8BA

20.0

Radius to
fit barrel

(15) **MOUNTING LUG**
1-off Brass

170.0

Ø19.0

(4) **FLUE TUBE**
1-off Copper

BOILER COMPONENTS

it is only warm and then carefully place in the pickle bath. Leave in the pickle until the copper is clean, then take it out and thoroughly rinse in water and examine the joint. If all appears well we can proceed to the next step.

(2) Apply flux to the joints you have just soldered and also to every part where solder is to be applied. Insert the rear tube plate into the barrel making sure the hole is at the bottom and the plate is square to the end. If the flue tube is slightly out of line it can be bent easily into position. Place solder around the joints as before (**Photo 2.5**) and apply heat, again pickling and checking when finished.

(3) Whilst the bushes could have been soldered during the last heating, it is probably safer to do them in a separate step. Apply flux again and insert the bushes. Place the boiler horizontally and solder the bushes in. They should have a neat fillet of solder all the way around. Cool, pickle and clean.

(4) Soldering the gauge glass pipes in position can be a bit tricky and there are different sequences which can be used, but the following should give good results. Firstly solder together the top and bottom tubes and pipes away from the boiler as can be seen in **photo 2.3**. (Note that the top pieces are at an angle when looking from the back.) Insert the two pipes, making sure that they are a tight fit in their respective holes. If loose, they can be flared out a little. So that the glass will line up later, insert a length of

2.5 — The boiler fluxed, solder applied and ready for heating. (The bushes could have been left out until the next step

metal (aluminium would be ideal) into the position where the glass will later fit and apply flux to these joints and to all previously soldered ones as well. Apply heat and solder the two pipes into position in the shell and back tube plate. Heat very carefully and only apply sufficient heat to thoroughly run the solder into the two joints. As long as the area is not overheated, the previously soldered joints will not be disturbed.

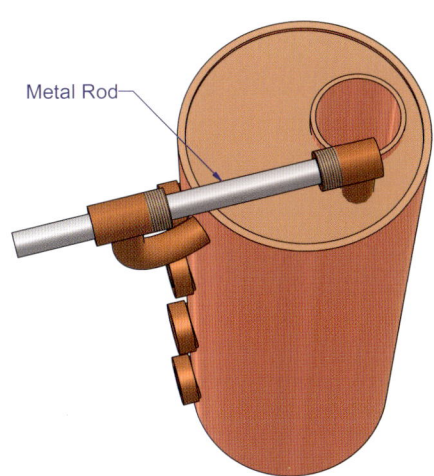

LINING UP GAUGE GLASS TUBES FOR SOLDERING

Clean the boiler up with steel wool or a plastic scouring pad to remove any flux residue and generally spruce things up. The mounting bracket can be fixed on later using high melting point soft solder. (That is, the soft solder which has a small silver content.)

Now would be a good time to cold water test your boiler to twice the working pressure. (35psi or 250kpa). You can do this yourself with a set up similar to that shown, (**Photo 2.6**) but the final test should be done in consultation with a club boiler inspector.

When tested, the boiler must have no leaks whatsoever. If any leaks do show up then apply flux to the whole boiler and reheat the area where the leak is until the solder again flows. You can add a little extra solder, but do not just heat the area up inadequately and blob more solder over the top of the leak. The job must be reheated sufficiently to allow the existing solder to flow.

Well Done! Once the boiler has satisfied its hydrostatic test, and no further silver soldering is necessary, set it up in the smokebox and mark the position for the mounting lug which fastens through the cab floor. The boiler will be fixed by this lug at the rear and will be free to slide in the smoke box as it expands with heating.

Make the mounting lug from some brass about 6mm

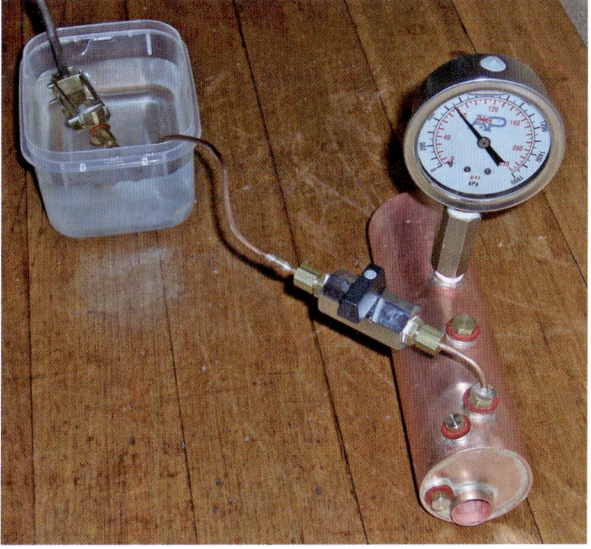

2.6 — Testing the boiler with cold water to 2 x working pressure

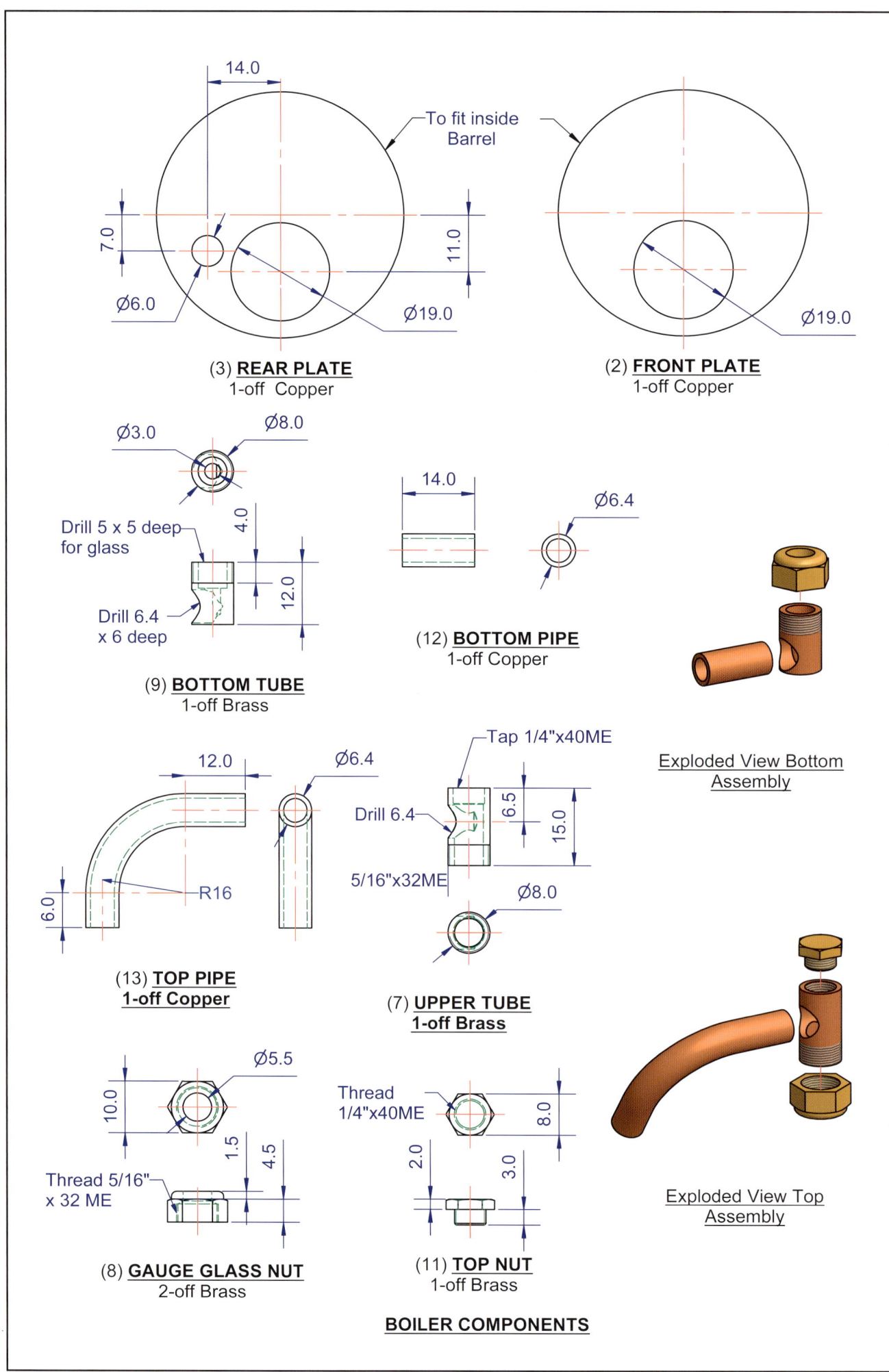

(3) **REAR PLATE**
1-off Copper

14.0

7.0

Ø6.0

Ø19.0

11.0

To fit inside Barrel

(2) **FRONT PLATE**
1-off Copper

Ø19.0

Ø3.0   Ø8.0

Drill 5 x 5 deep
for glass

Drill 6.4
x 6 deep

4.0

12.0

(9) **BOTTOM TUBE**
1-off Brass

14.0   Ø6.4

(12) **BOTTOM PIPE**
1-off Copper

Exploded View Bottom
Assembly

12.0   Ø6.4

R16

6.0

(13) **TOP PIPE**
1-off Copper

Tap 1/4"x40ME

Drill 6.4

5/16"x32ME

6.5

15.0

Ø8.0

(7) **UPPER TUBE**
1-off Brass

Exploded View Top
Assembly

Ø5.5

10.0

Thread 5/16"
x 32 ME

1.5

4.5

(8) **GAUGE GLASS NUT**
2-off Brass

Thread
1/4"x40ME

8.0

2.0   3.0

(11) **TOP NUT**
1-off Brass

BOILER COMPONENTS

thick. Make its height so that the boiler is level when resting in the smoke box and shape its curved top to fit the boiler. Drill two 8BA clear holes in the footplate and tap the mounting lug to suit. Solder the mounting lug into position on the bottom of the boiler using high melting point soft solder.

Boiler bands, cladding and insulation

As in full size practice, we will put some insulation around the boiler and hold it in position using cladding held in place with boiler bands.

For insulation felt sheet can be used as found in craft shops. Simply wrap the felt around the boiler a couple of times, cutting out holes for the bushes and mounting lug. After cutting, it can be held in place temporarily while fitting the cladding with white woodworking glue (PVA).

The cladding is made from 0.2mm thick hard or semi hard shim brass. Measure the circumference of the boiler plus lagging, and the length from just behind the smoke box to the back end of the boiler and cut out a rectangle of shim to these sizes. Draw a centreline lengthwise and mark the positions of the bush holes and the gauge glass hole. Drill these holes using a wood cutting spade bit which has spurs. This ensures a good clean cut to the edges of the holes. Never try to drill sheet metal without thoroughly supporting it. (**Photo 2.7**) Not only does this method give a good edge to a hole, but it prevents the drill grabbing and twisting the sheet around the drill and possibly you, with disastrous results! A good way to drill the cladding is to sandwich it between two pieces of wood where the top piece is cut to the same size as the metal sheet and the holes positions are marked out for drilling on the wood.

2.7 — Drilling sheet metal

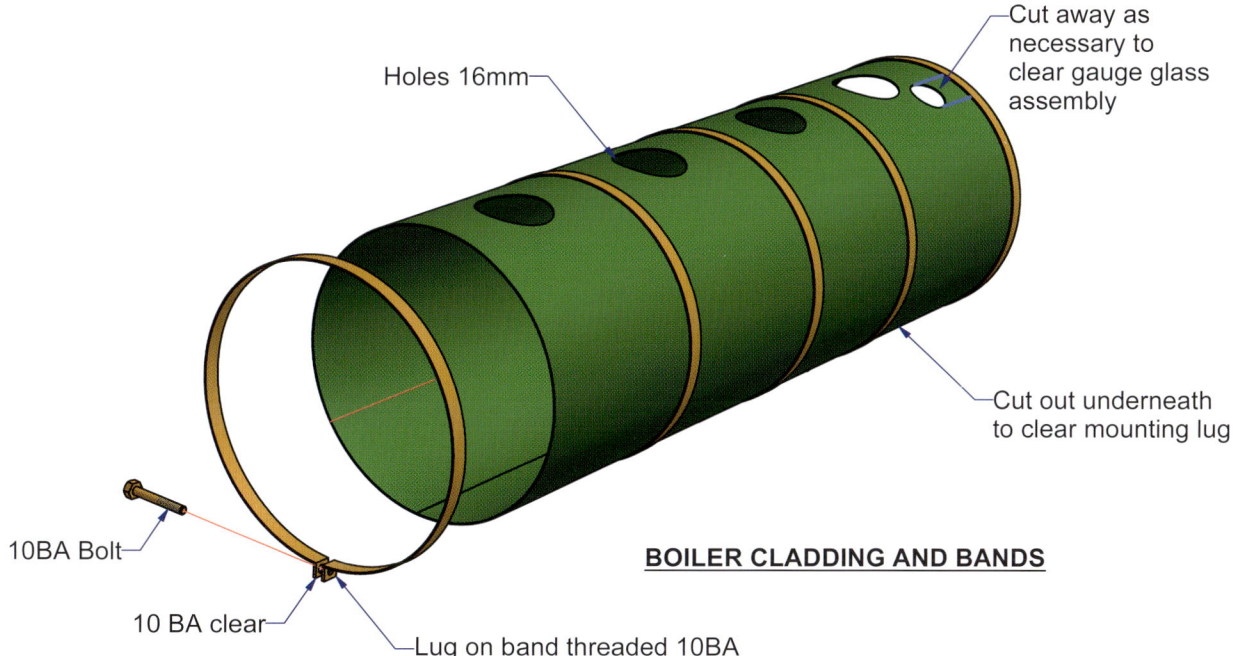

Holes 16mm

Cut away as necessary to clear gauge glass assembly

Cut out underneath to clear mounting lug

10BA Bolt

10 BA clear

Lug on band threaded 10BA

BOILER CLADDING AND BANDS

Drill the holes for the boiler bushes around 16mm which will give plenty of clearance around the bushes, but will still leave the edges of the holes covered by the domes. Cut away the cladding underneath in way of the mounting lug and wrap the cladding around the boiler holding it in place temporarily with strips of masking tape or similar.

The boiler bands are cut from the same 0.2mm brass shim. On a straight edge of the sheet mark out a strip 3mm wide and cut off with sharp tinsnips. Wrap it around the boiler and cladding to determine the length to cut it. Fold each end as shown in the

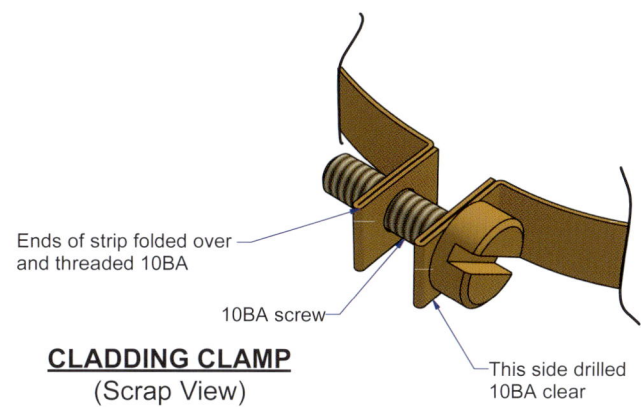

Ends of strip folded over and threaded 10BA

10BA screw

CLADDING CLAMP
(Scrap View)

This side drilled 10BA clear

2.8 — Boiler cladding and bands

diagram making it so that the tightening screw almost, but not completely closes the end of the clamp together.

You may find it easier to make the cladding in two pieces, joining at the spectacle plate. This would make it easier to make the cut outs around the mounting lug and the gauge glass. (**Photo2.8**) shows this. (Note that this boiler is slightly different from the one we are describing in that it has one less bush on top.)

CHAPTER 3 – The Body

The body consists of two main parts: The cab assembly and the side tanks. The completed cab assembly bolts or screws onto the cab footplate and the side tanks are each held by a bracket onto the frame and a bolt or two through the spectacle plate.

The sheeting for the cab and tanks is 0.8mm brass throughout. (You could use another thickness such as 0.6mm as long as the end result is stiff enough.) When cutting this material care has to be taken not to distort it. While tinsnips can cut material of this thickness, they distort it rather badly so it has to be cut either with a guillotine, band saw, hacksaw or a combination of these. Both the band saw blade and the hacksaw blade need to have fine teeth to avoid catching the thin sheet, and for any long cuts a hacksaw blade has to be held in a sheet saw frame, otherwise the back of the hacksaw frame gets in the way. The work must be well supported along the length of the cut and this can be done by clamping a piece of wood along the edge of the bench. (**Photo 3.1**)

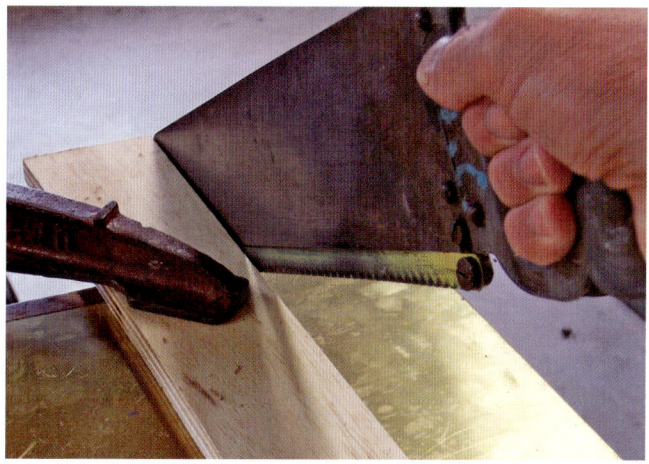

3.1 — Cutting sheet metal with a sheet saw

Dummy rivets

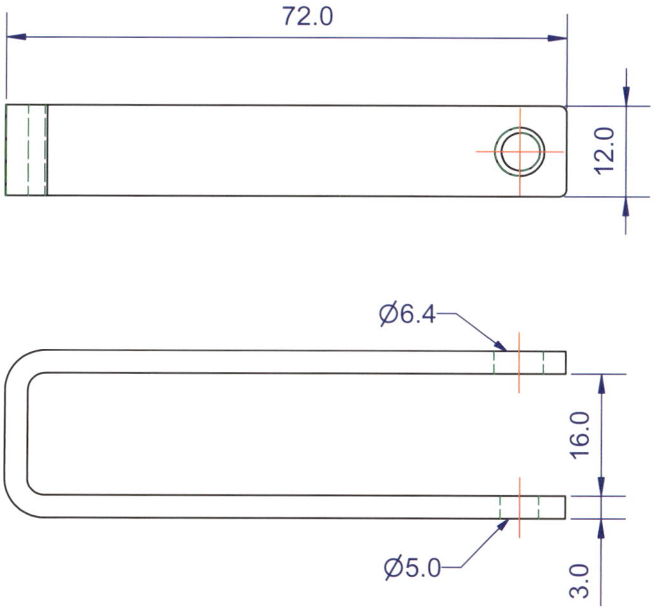

72.0
12.0
Ø6.4
16.0
Ø5.0
3.0

BODY
1-off Mild Steel

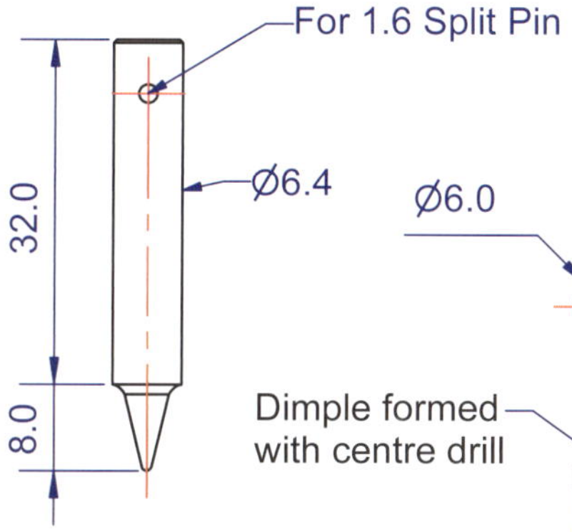

For 1.6 Split Pin
Ø6.4
32.0
8.0

PUNCH
1-off Silver Steel

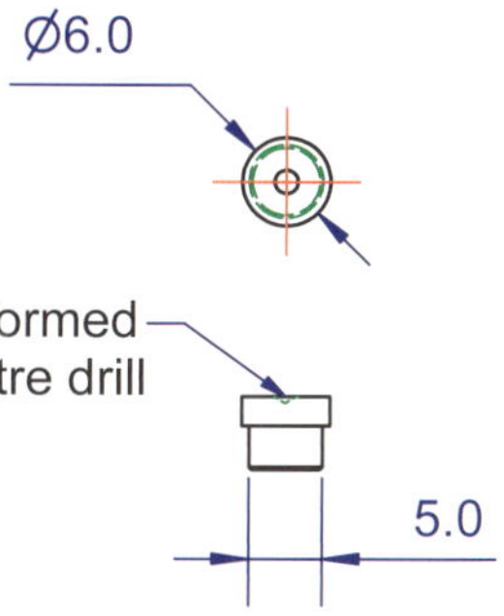

Ø6.0
Dimple formed with centre drill
5.0

ANVIL
1-off Silver Steel

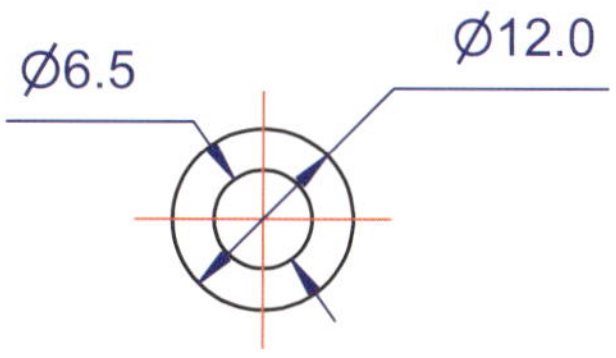

Ø6.5
Ø12.0

WASHER
Brass 2mm thick

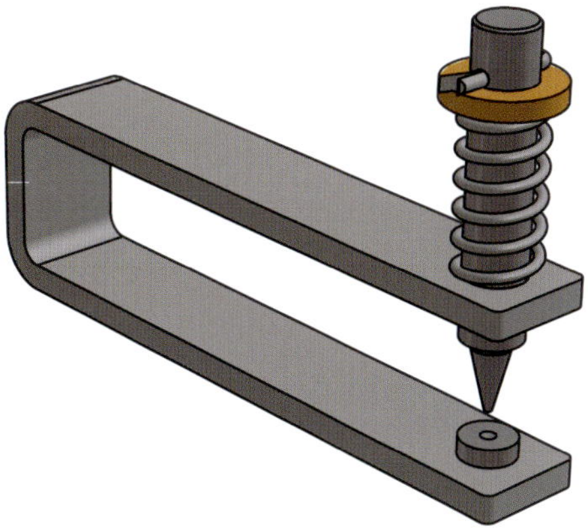

RIVET TOOL

Rear View

Front View

CAB ASSEMBLY
Perspective Views

Steam Trains in Your Garden

When the prototype for this locomotive was built, welding wasn't what it is today and the plate work was largely held together with rows of rivets. Because they gave the locomotives such a distinctive appearance, it is worth trying to achieve this look on our model. Small rivets are available, but it is a very tedious operation to try and use the large numbers required and also to use small enough ones means a very small drill is needed, and that most probably means broken drills! What does work very well is a rivet punch. This is a small home made tool which punches a little dimple from the back of the sheet which from the front looks very much like the head of a rivet. There are different designs around, but the following one will work well on the 0.8mm sheet.

3.2 — Using the dummy rivet punch

The tool can be made closely to the sizes shown, but can be made longer or shorter to suit your purposes. If you wish to rivet along the inside of a large sheet, the body will need to be made longer and if you are only going to use the tool on the edges of a sheet then it could be made shorter. The silver steel punch and anvil will need to be hardened and tempered. (**Photo 3.2**)

The tool is held in the drill press vice supported underneath with a block of metal or wood and with the rivet point sticking out the distance that the rivets will be from the edge of the sheet. The dummy rivet is punched by pressing down on the top of the punch with the drill press. The correct pressure to be applied will soon be determined and the rivet spacing can either be marked off with a marker along a line or the sheet can be progressed along so that the rivet dome just punched rests against the edge of the anvil.

How many rivets you punch is up to you. Generally, there were more rivets placed along seams which had to be watertight such as tanks, than purely structural rivets for cab sheets. The numbers that were used can be determined from photographs. A lot of locomotives had no rivets at all on their tanks as they approached the end of their working life, the tanks having been repaired or replaced so many times that they finished up with fully welded tanks.

Soft soldering

When assembling the body sheets and framing, occasionally pieces can be held together with a few genuine rivets or bolts, but mostly soft solder is used. This is another process which some people have difficulty with, but if a few basic rules are adhered to, it becomes a very simple and quick way of working.

Firstly, the way soft solder works here is that it we use it in much the same way as an adhesive. It doesn't melt into or become part of the parent metal, but rather adheres to it. The pieces need to be thoroughly clean and free of grease and oil and we need a good surface area of contact and a good fit between pieces. The solder flows into the joint by capillary action, not by magic or by hope.

Secondly, in order for the solder to flow it needs to be fluid enough and that means hot enough to melt and be a liquid. Not only must the solder itself be heated sufficiently for this to happen, but the job must also be hot enough. It is no good having liquid solder flowing into a cold joint and immediately solidifying part way into the joint. An all too common sight is to see blobs of solder splattered over a joint where the solder has been heated adequately, but not the job and the molten solder has been dripped onto the joint in the hope that it will all stick together.

Thirdly, the joints we are soldering need to be held together securely while soldering. This can be done in a variety of ways either permanently with rivets or bolts, or temporarily with masking or packaging tape being careful to place the tape so that it doesn't burn too much. (**Photo 3.3**) Some parts

3.3 — Soft soldering a saddle tank using a combination of tape and a clamp to hold the pieces in position

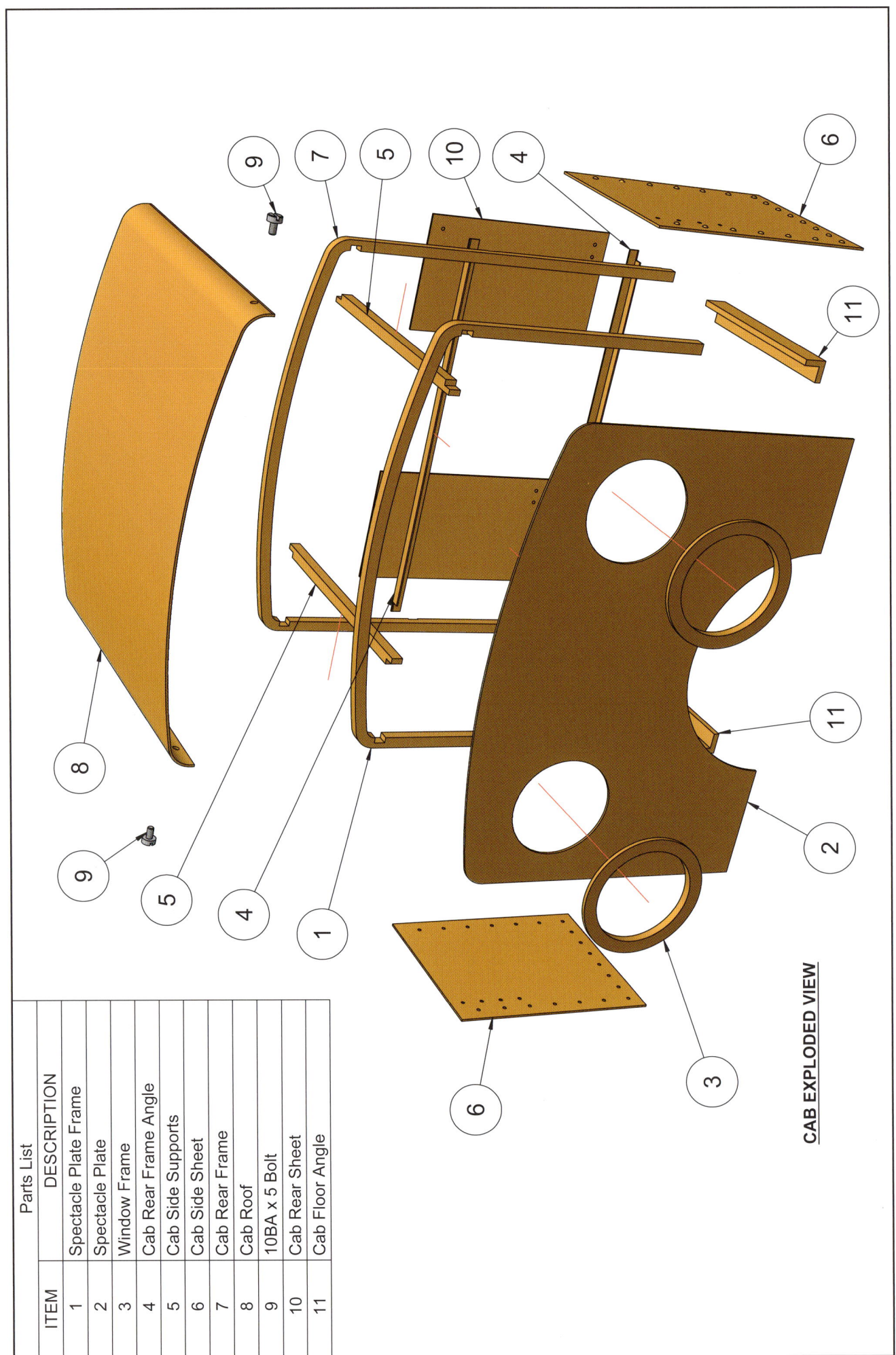

Parts List		
ITEM	DESCRIPTION	
1	Spectacle Plate Frame	
2	Spectacle Plate	
3	Window Frame	
4	Cab Rear Frame Angle	
5	Cab Side Supports	
6	Cab Side Sheet	
7	Cab Rear Frame	
8	Cab Roof	
9	10BA x 5 Bolt	
10	Cab Rear Sheet	
11	Cab Floor Angle	

CAB EXPLODED VIEW

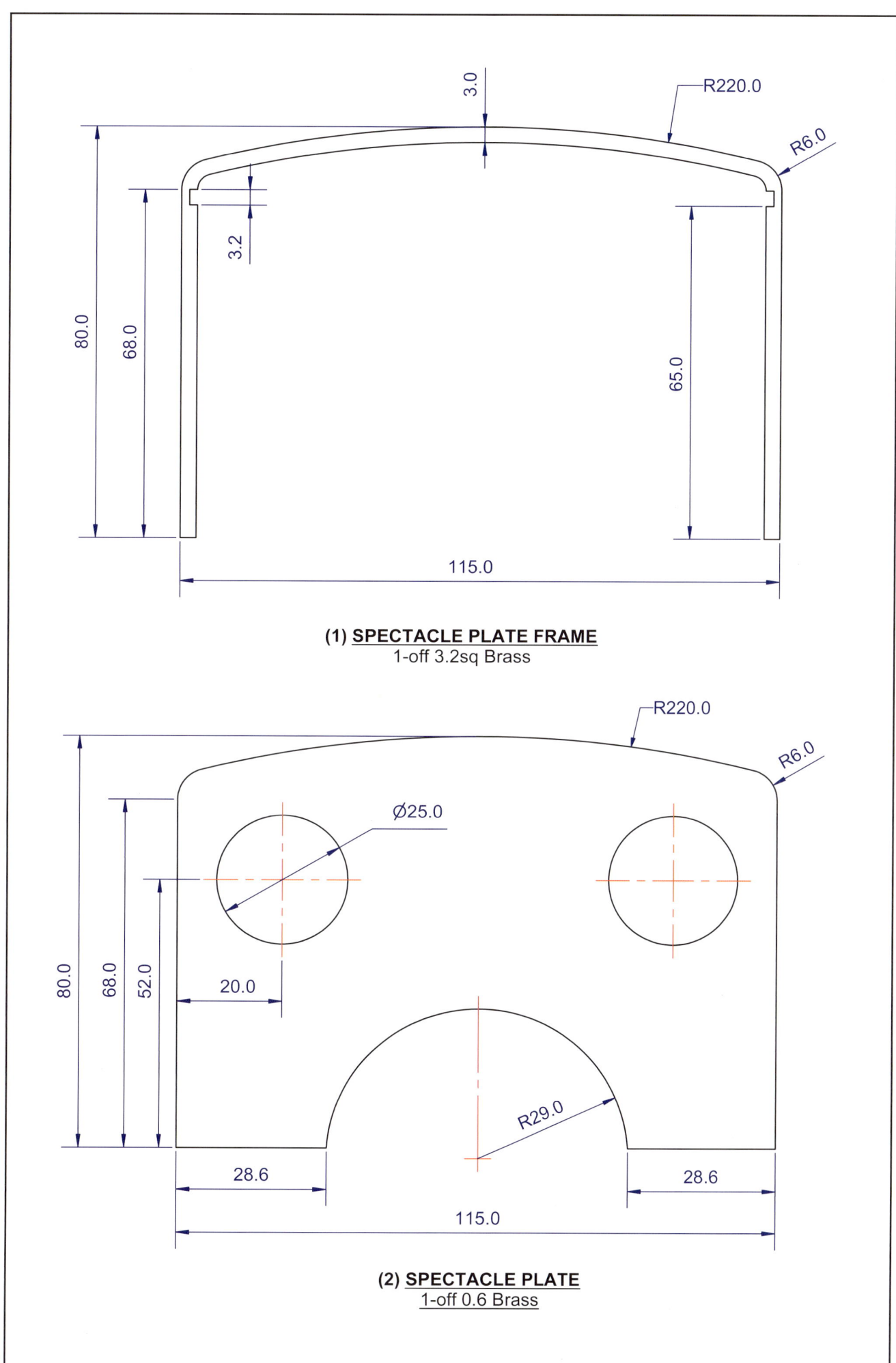

(1) SPECTACLE PLATE FRAME
1-off 3.2sq Brass

(2) SPECTACLE PLATE
1-off 0.6 Brass

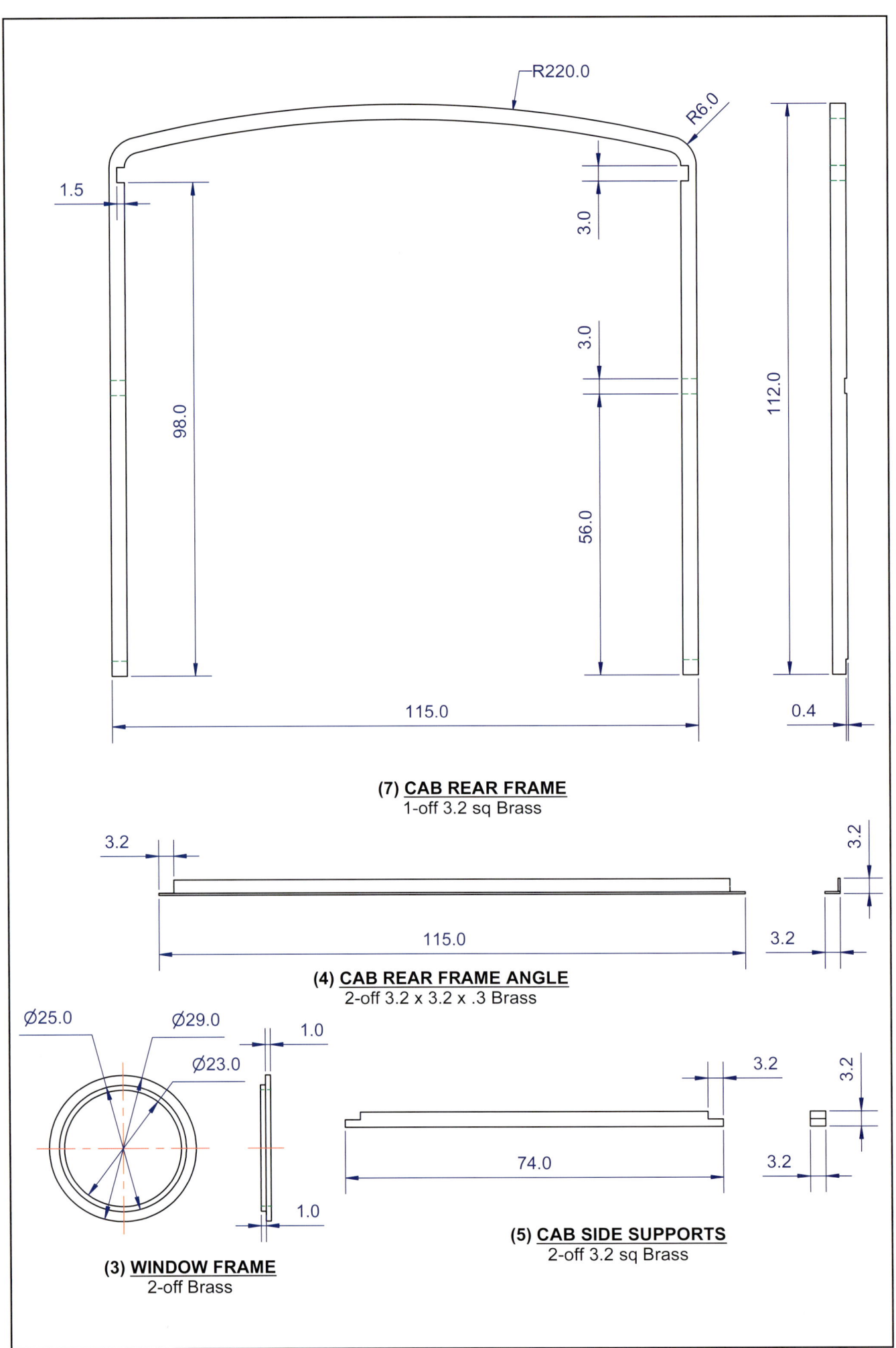

R220.0

R6.0

1.5

3.0

3.0

98.0

56.0

112.0

115.0

0.4

(7) CAB REAR FRAME
1-off 3.2 sq Brass

3.2

3.2

115.0

3.2

(4) CAB REAR FRAME ANGLE
2-off 3.2 x 3.2 x .3 Brass

Ø25.0

Ø29.0

Ø23.0

1.0

1.0

3.2

3.2

74.0

3.2

(5) CAB SIDE SUPPORTS
2-off 3.2 sq Brass

(3) WINDOW FRAME
2-off Brass

can be clamped but a problem with that is that the clamp can act as a heat sink and take the heat away from the joint. A technique which can be used with tape or clamps is to tack solder the joint while it is held with tape and then remove the tape before soldering fully. Even superglue can be used sparingly in some situations.

Heat can be applied by a gas torch or old fashioned solid soldering iron, but in this size the best way is a hefty electric soldering iron. One which draws at least about 80 Watts is ideal. The tip must be tinned which means that it must have a coating of solder. If the bit is not tinned, or it needs a clean up simply clean the tip with a file so that the copper shows brightly, heat the bit, apply flux and then wipe solder over it so that it appears bright and shiny with a coating of solder.

To solder a joint, apply flux liberally then hold the bit against the job so that heat flows into the job. The flux keeps the joint clean and free of oxides as it is heated. Be patient and hold the bit there until the job is hot enough so that when you apply solder it will flow readily into the joint. Slowly slide the bit along the joint feeding in more solder as necessary to fill the joint and form a nice neat fillet.

The Cab Sheets

Spectacle plate, side and back sheets

Cut these four pieces from 0.8mm brass. Making sure they are square, clean up the edges to remove any burrs and punch for the dummy rivets. On the side sheets mark out and drill for the four genuine 1.6mm rivets.

Mark out the spectacle plate and drill the two round window cut outs. Use the same technique as described for the boiler cladding where the metal is sandwiched between two pieces of wood and drilled with a spurred spade bit, or they could be chain drilled and filed with a round or half round file. Cut out the section which fits over the boiler by chain drilling and filing. When filing this thin material, grip it near its edge between two pieces of wood held in the vice. (**Photo 3.4**)

Turn two pieces of brass for the window frames. Make these a firm fit so they can be forced in after painting. If they are a bit loose they can be held in with a little epoxy.

3.4 — Filing thin material

Cab frame

The frame is made up from ⅛" (3.2mm) square brass and ⅛" brass angle. These sizes of brass are readily available in most hobby shops.

Although some sort of a jig could be made up to bend the frames for the curve of the roof, it is hardly worth it, because it is really quite easy to bend up by hand. A suggestion is to initially cut the pieces longer than required and work from the centre, starting with the large radius bend for the roof, bending around a former such as a piece of pipe of approximately the correct radius and truing up by hand using the drawing as a template. Once you are satisfied with this curve, the two sharp bends which bring the sides down vertically can be bent by hand around a piece of 6mm rod. After these bends are done, cut out the sections for the side supports. Don't cut the frames before bending or they will bend at that spot rather than where you want them to bend!

Cut the two side supports to length and cut the ends to fit neatly into the cut outs in the two frames.

The pieces of angle which take the rear sheets across the back of the cab are shown as 3.2 x 0.3mm brass angle. This size is quite satisfactory, but if you wish you can use other sizes of angle with the same result. The two short pieces of angle at the bottom of the two side sheets are 1.6mm thick as these are threaded to take the holding down bolts through from under the footplate.

Riveting

Riveting is a good way of holding pieces together for soldering and also for certain situations the rivets can be used alone without soldering. As discussed previously, we don't need rows and rows of rivets, but just the minimum number to hold things together. We can use two types of rivets and for our purposes 1/16" diameter is ideal. There are ones with a head which are purchased from model engineering suppliers or we can use plain lengths of 1/16" brass rod cut to length. The diagram illustrates using headed rivets. If using plain lengths of rod, countersink both sides of the hole, insert the rivet, rest the bottom end of the rivet on a firm surface and lightly

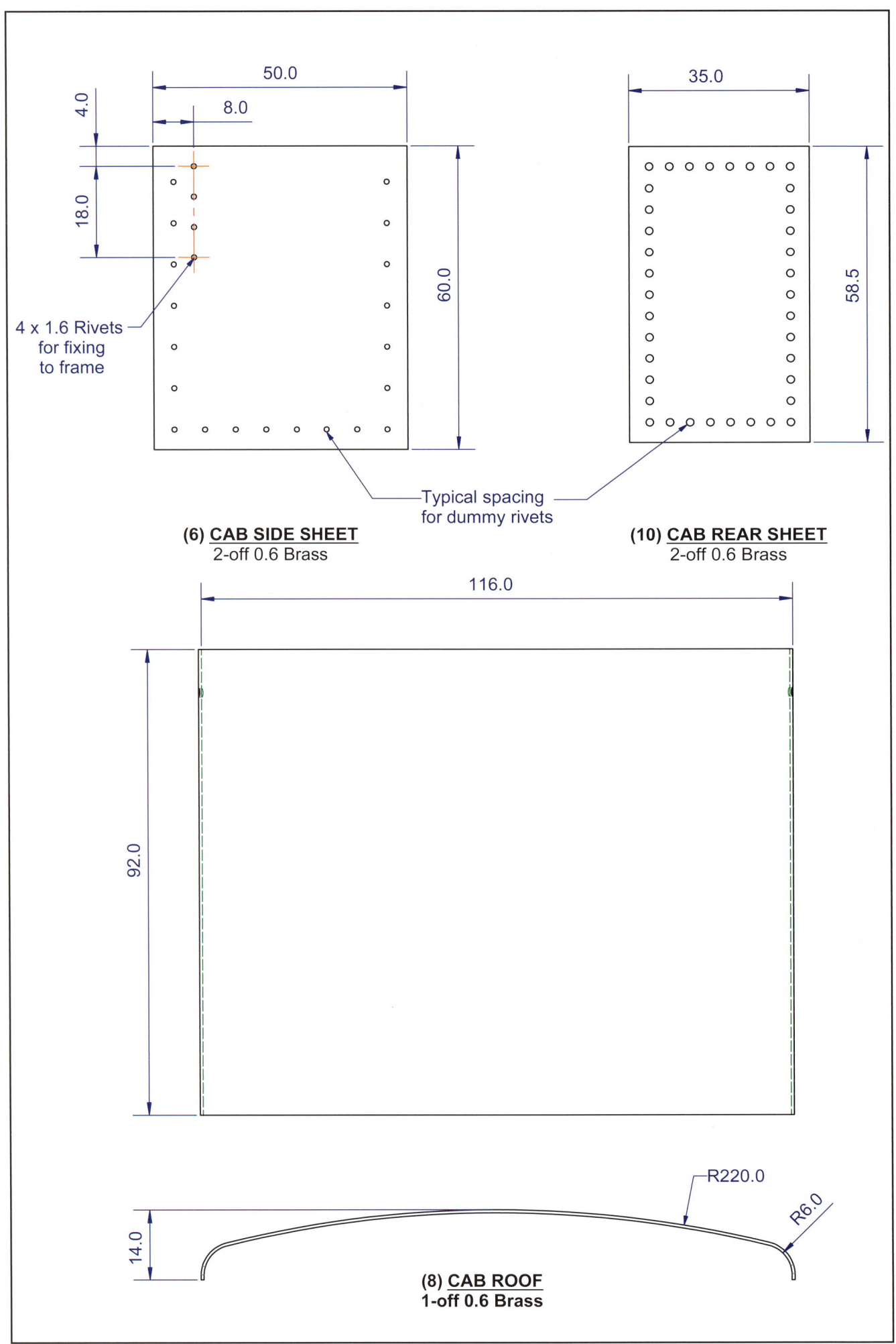

50.0

8.0

4.0

18.0

4 x 1.6 Rivets
for fixing
to frame

60.0

Typical spacing
for dummy rivets

(6) CAB SIDE SHEET
2-off 0.6 Brass

35.0

58.5

(10) CAB REAR SHEET
2-off 0.6 Brass

116.0

92.0

R220.0

R6.0

14.0

(8) CAB ROOF
1-off 0.6 Brass

tap the top over with a hammer, turn the job over and tap the other side and repeat this process until the rivet is firm and fills the countersink on both sides.

Start assembling the cab by riveting the pieces of angle onto the bottom of the side sheets. (Drill out the two corner dummy rivets.) Then rivet the side sheets onto the front frame with four rivets each side. Note that the front frame does not go all the way down to the footplate, so allow for this when positioning the pieces. There is no need to solder the sides onto the frame, but it would be a good idea to solder the angle pieces onto the bottom edge.

Place the spectacle plate into position, hold with some tape and solder onto the frame, then assemble the back frame and sheets and solder these together.

If you have made the side supports a tight fit in the frames, it might be possible to assemble the front and back sections together for soldering without any other clamping, but as is more likely they don't hold together, a headless rivet can be placed in each of the four joints before giving a good fill of solder. When doing this last operation, the cab frame should be stood on a flat surface to make sure it sits squarely.

The final piece for the cab is the roof and unless you have a set of rollers, this can be done satisfactorily by hand. When curving a sheet like this you have to bend smoothly and evenly so it doesn't kink, and often a better result can be obtained by bending it to a tighter radius than required and then easing it back to the desired radius.

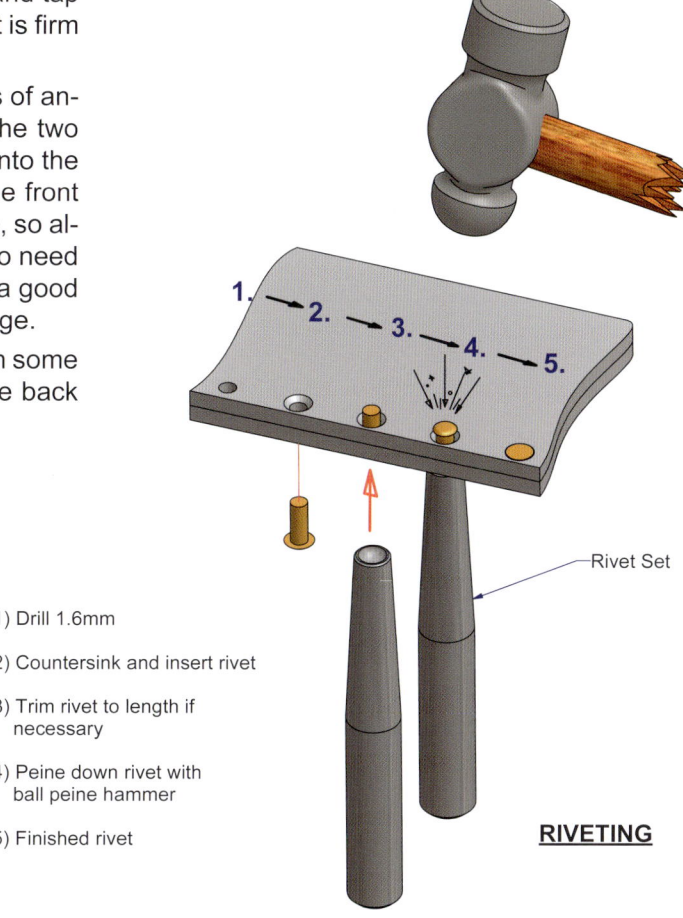

(1) Drill 1.6mm

(2) Countersink and insert rivet

(3) Trim rivet to length if necessary

(4) Peine down rivet with ball peine hammer

(5) Finished rivet

RIVETING

Cut a piece of 0.8mm brass sheet to size and clean up all the edges. You will need a curved former such as a piece of pipe around 150mm diameter. Place the centreline on the former and push down on both sides. You should finish up with a curve which follows the profile in the drawing, but which flattens out a little on each end. It is almost impossible to fold a sheet like this right to the edges, but in this case it doesn't matter as the side edges have a further sharper curve. Bend this tighter curve over a piece of brass or mild steel about 6 to 8mm diameter held in the vice as shown in the diagram.

In order to access the fittings in the cab for filling gas and steam oil it is necessary to remove or lift the roof. This can be done by placing the formed roof into position and marking at the front where the hinge point will be. Drill these two places 10BA clear,

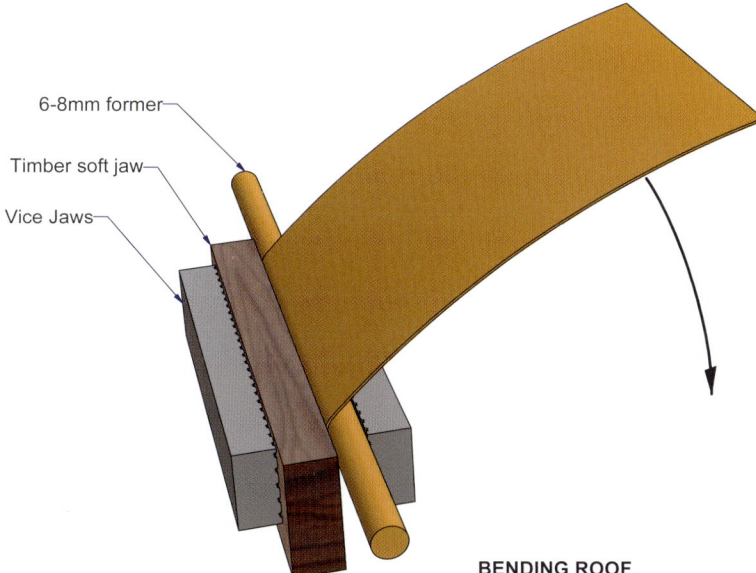

BENDING ROOF

replace the roof and mark through onto the frame for drilling and tapping 10BA. Fit a 10BA bolt and washer to each side forming a hinge to tilt the roof forward.

Another method for making the roof removable is to solder four brass tabs onto the underside which fit snugly down onto the top of the frame. Shape these as shown in the diagram so that they bend outwards forming a slight spring.

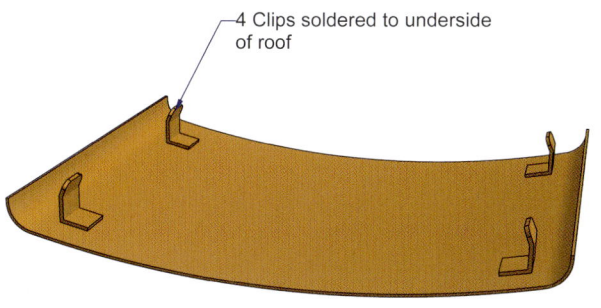

HOLD DOWN CLIPS FOR ROOF

Outer and Top

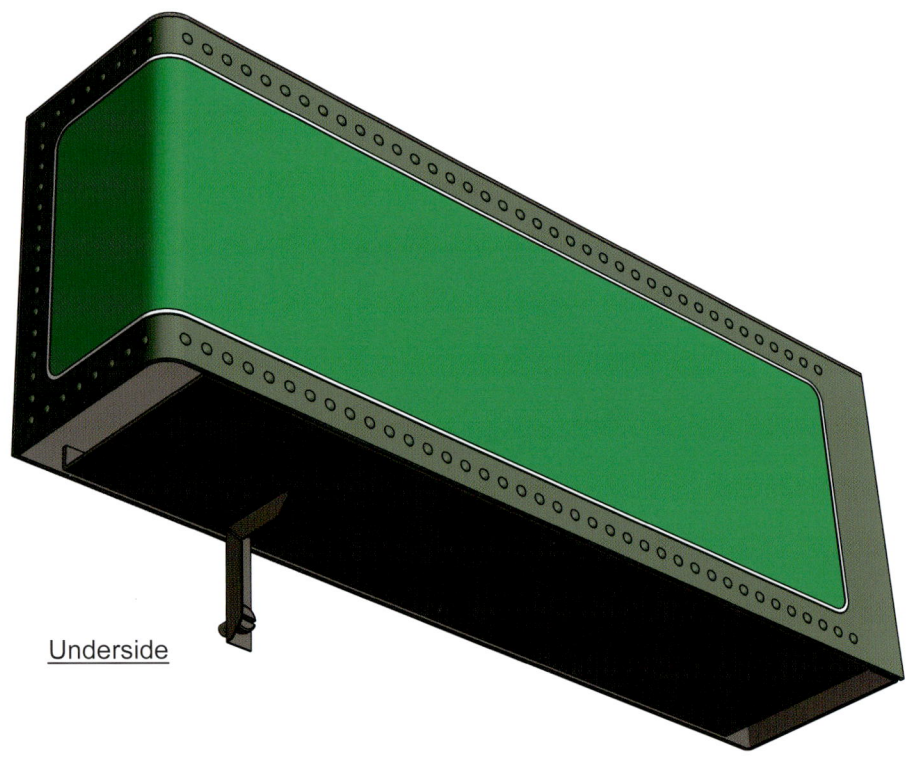

Underside

TANK PERSPECTIVE VIEW
(Left Hand Tank)

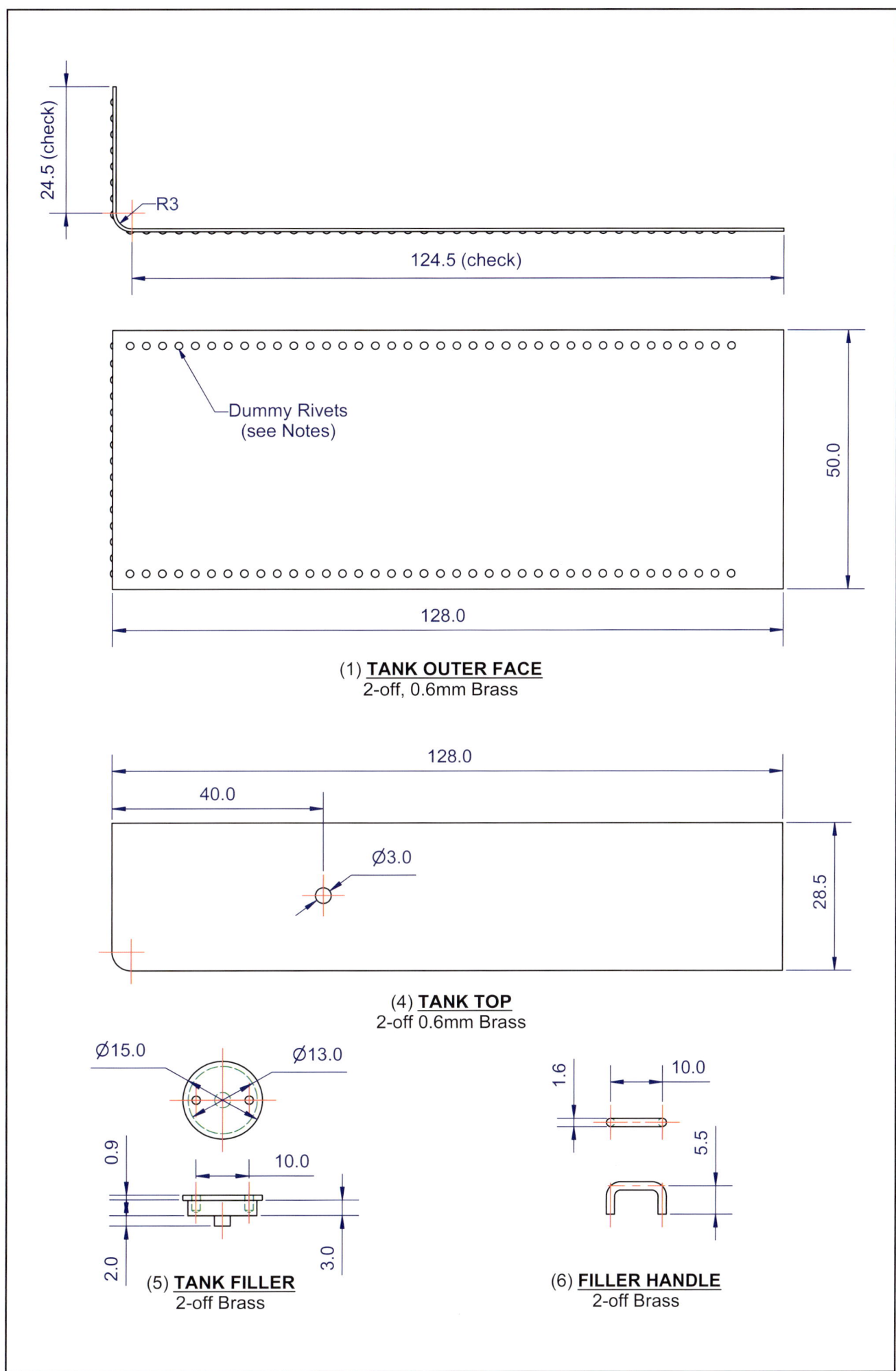

24.5 (check)

R3

124.5 (check)

Dummy Rivets
(see Notes)

50.0

128.0

(1) **TANK OUTER FACE**
2-off, 0.6mm Brass

128.0

40.0

Ø3.0

28.5

(4) **TANK TOP**
2-off 0.6mm Brass

Ø15.0   Ø13.0

0.9

10.0

2.0   3.0

(5) **TANK FILLER**
2-off Brass

1.6   10.0

5.5

(6) **FILLER HANDLE**
2-off Brass

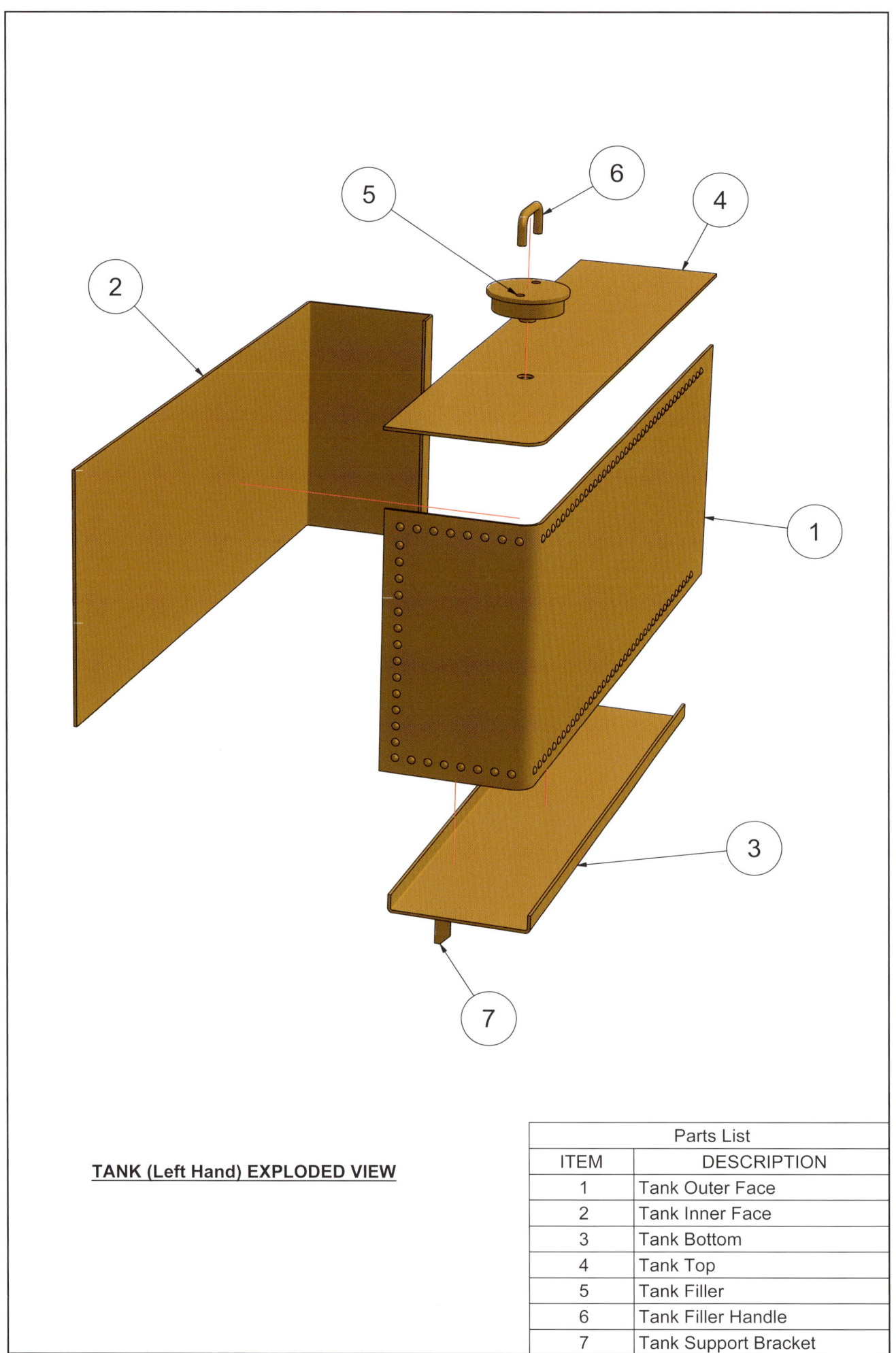

TANK (Left Hand) EXPLODED VIEW

Parts List	
ITEM	DESCRIPTION
1	Tank Outer Face
2	Tank Inner Face
3	Tank Bottom
4	Tank Top
5	Tank Filler
6	Tank Filler Handle
7	Tank Support Bracket

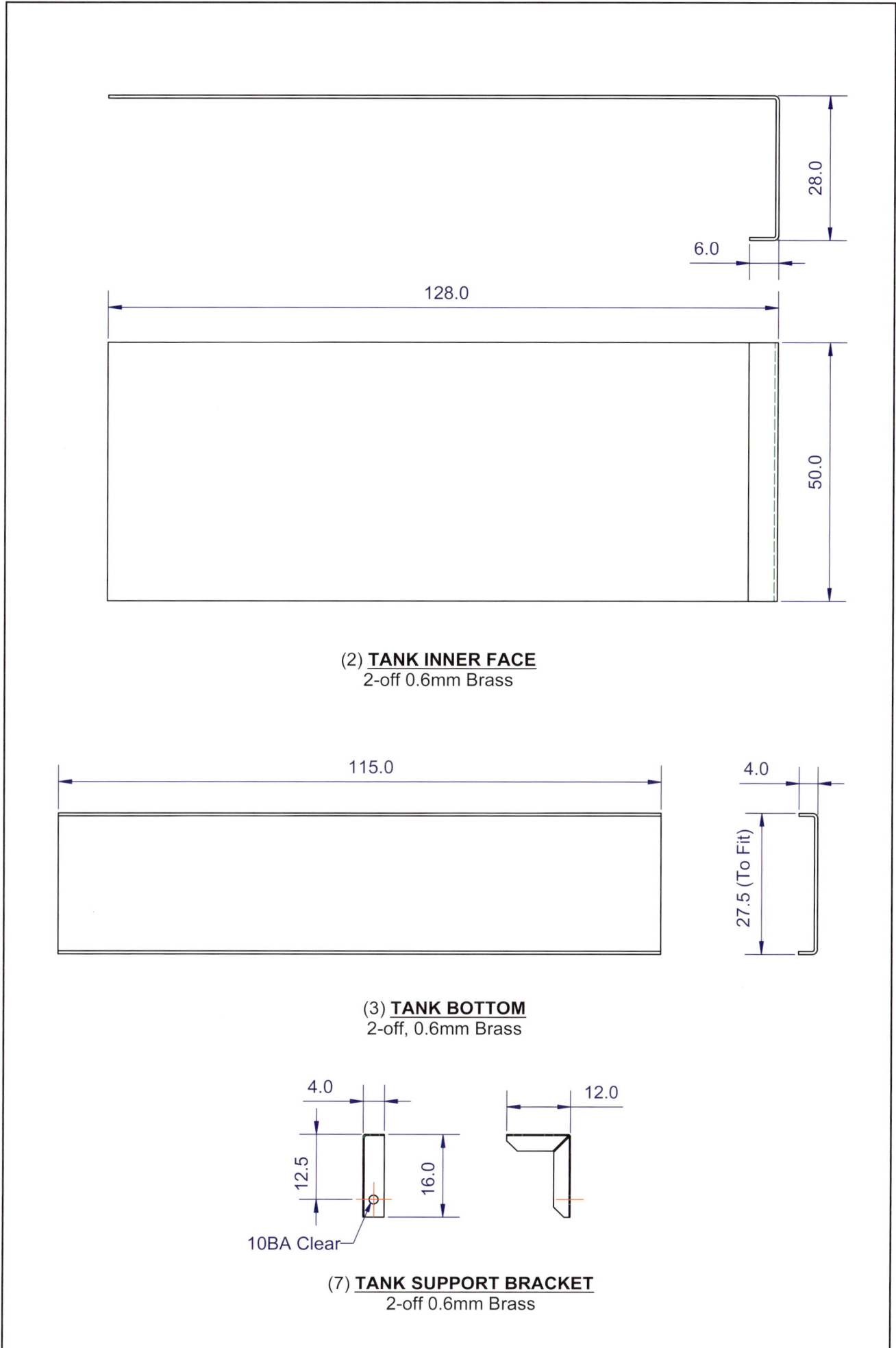

(2) **TANK INNER FACE**
2-off 0.6mm Brass

(3) **TANK BOTTOM**
2-off, 0.6mm Brass

10BA Clear

(7) **TANK SUPPORT BRACKET**
2-off 0.6mm Brass

Side tanks

The side tanks are made up from 0.8mm brass and are both the same except they are handed. (Again, don't make two identical tanks!)

Start with the outer face, making it a millimeter or two longer than required so that after making the curved bend at the front, it can be trimmed off accurately. This curve can be done in a similar way to the edges of the roof by gripping the sheet in the vice and bending over a 6mm diameter rod. Press the dummy rivets before bending.

Next make the inner faces. To make nice sharp bends in the brass sheet, grip it between blocks of wood in the vice and press over by hand. A final tap with another block of wood will ensure a good bend. The inner face could be made with an extra fold at the front to solder to the front of the outer piece, but a butt joint with a good fillet of solder will prove adequate.

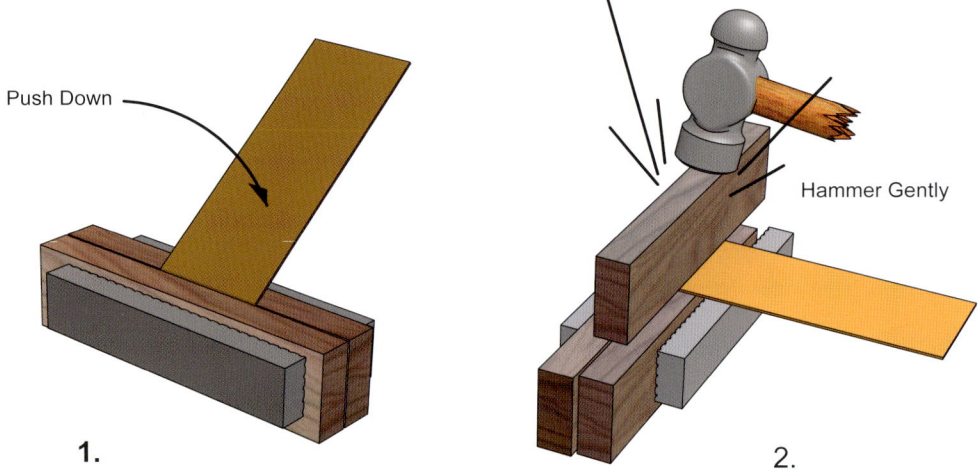

BENDING TANK SHEETS

The rest of the pieces for the tanks are simply made up by cutting to size and bending, noting that the bottom piece is left short on the ends for convenience. Mark out the top last to be a neat fit onto the top of the tank and this can be soldered in position or made removable by soldering on some tabs similar to those described for the roof. If you fit radio gear into the tanks the top will need to be removable. The tank filler is a dummy and is made up and soldered in position.

The tank can be held together with tape for soldering, and as it doesn't have to hold water, you don't have to do continuous runs of solder, it can be simply tacked in several places.

The tank is mounted by placing a 10BA screw from the support bracket through into the frame, either tapped or with a nut, and with two 10BA screws through the spectacle plate. A convenient way to have these would be to drill the rear tank face 10BA clear, insert the screws from inside the tank and solder in position. This way the nuts can be screwed on from inside the cab. Alternatively you could solder a doubling piece onto the inside of the back face of the tank and drill and thread 10BA, screwed in from inside the cab.

CHAPTER 4
Boiler Fittings, Gas System & Pipe Work

There are lots of small parts to be made here, but nothing is too difficult, so it just means patiently working through the various components.

Steam manifold

The Steam Manifold sits on top of the boiler and is the distribution point for steam to the throttle, pressure gauge and whistle.

For the body of the manifold, grip some ½" (12.5mm) diameter brass in the lathe, drill through 8mm diameter and part off to 18mm. For the Valve Socket, use a piece of the same material and turn a 10mm diameter shoulder for 3mm, thread through ⁵⁄₁₆" x 32 ME and part off. Turn the two steam outlet nipples. (You may have made these before).

Drill the body section 10mm and 3mm, making sure it is gripped firmly when drilling the larger hole.

Assemble the pieces, silver solder, and if necessary clean through the holes with a drill.

Manifold centre bolt

Turn down some ½" (12.5mm) brass (hexagon could be used) to ⁵⁄₁₆" for 22mm and thread ⁵⁄₁₆" x 32 ME for around 9mm. Drill 3mm 18 deep and turn the steam groove on the outside. Check the position of this groove, as it needs to line up with the throttle and this could vary from that shown on the drawing, depending on the thickness of the washers that you use. Knurl, part off and drill through 3mm at the position of the steam groove.

Throttle valve body

The only tricky thing with the throttle is making sure that the length of the valve spindle matches the throttle body exactly so that the valve seats properly. Check the measurements given to ensure they are correct for your job. Also we have to make the valve seat by inserting a "D"-bit to square up the bottom of the hole.

Making a "D"-bit

The "D"-Bit is made from silver steel which is a carbon steel that can be hardened. The diameter for this piece should be about 4mm so that it fits into the tapping size hole for ³⁄₁₆" x 40 ME. Make it around 75mm long, face the end and reduce the diameter down exactly halfway for a length of about 15mm either by milling or filing. Relieve the end with clearances as shown in the drawing to provide a cutting edge and then harden and temper the cutting end. The "D"-Bit is fed into the end of a previously drilled hole to give it a square bottom and provide a seat for a valve spindle.

Grip some 9mm (³⁄₈") brass hexagon in the chuck, turn the outside and thread ⁵⁄₁₆" x 32 ME for 7.5mm. Drill the tapping size for ³⁄₁₆" x 40 ME (4.0mm) to a

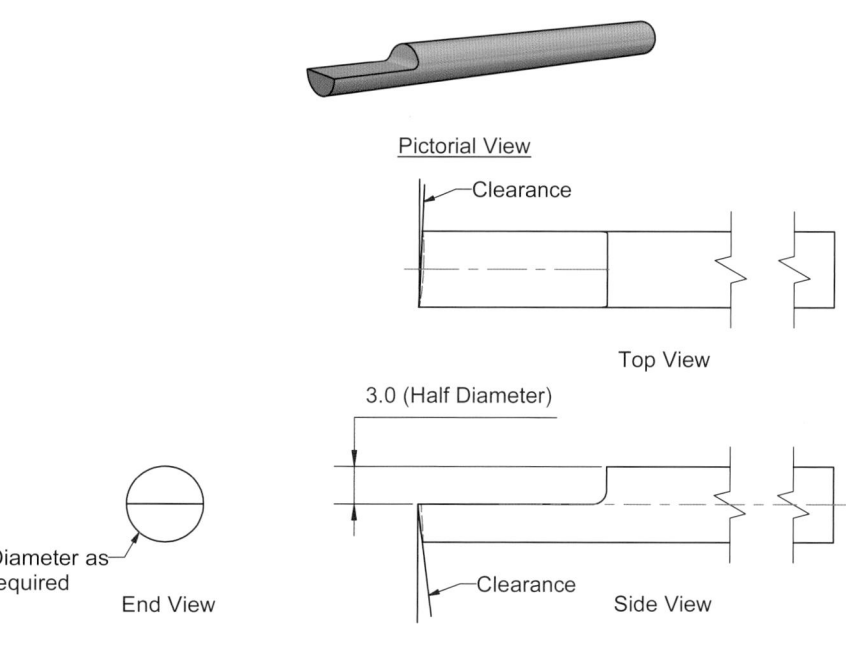

Pictorial View

Top View

"D"- BIT
Silver Steel, Hardened and Tempered

depth of about 20mm and then drill 2.5mm for a further 8mm. Make the valve seat by inserting the "D"-Bit into the last millimeter or two of the 4mm hole to a depth of 22mm. Using a ³⁄₁₆" bit, drill out the start of the thread to a depth of about 2.5mm to ensure that the spindle screws right home.

Part off to 27mm, reverse in the chuck and thread ⁵⁄₁₆" x 32 ME for 14mm and then turn the 5mm shoulder for a length of 3mm.

Remove from the lathe and drill a 3mm hole into one of the flats of the hexagon into which a steam outlet nipple is silver soldered.

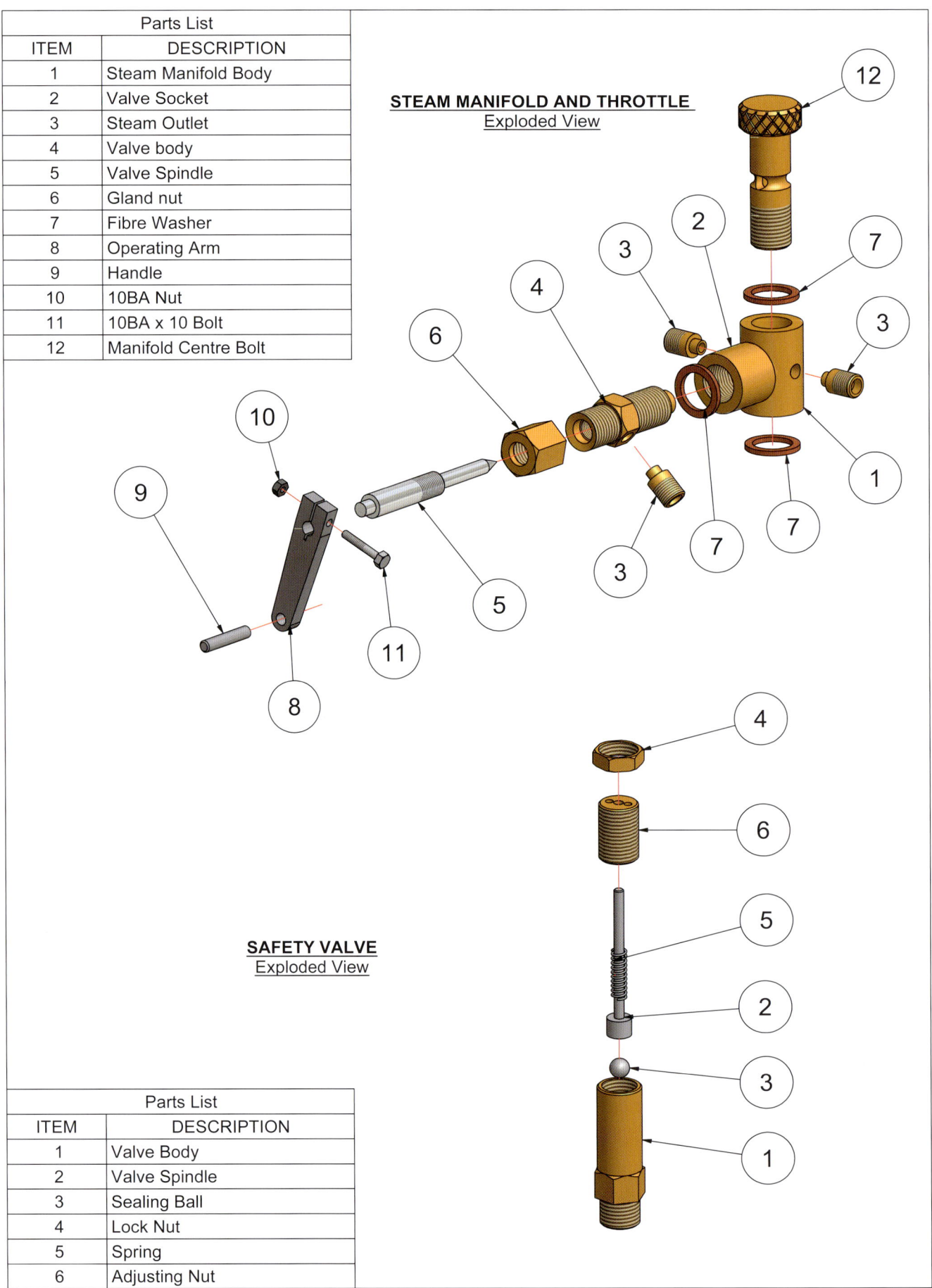

Parts List

ITEM	DESCRIPTION
1	Steam Manifold Body
2	Valve Socket
3	Steam Outlet
4	Valve body
5	Valve Spindle
6	Gland nut
7	Fibre Washer
8	Operating Arm
9	Handle
10	10BA Nut
11	10BA x 10 Bolt
12	Manifold Centre Bolt

STEAM MANIFOLD AND THROTTLE
Exploded View

SAFETY VALVE
Exploded View

Parts List

ITEM	DESCRIPTION
1	Valve Body
2	Valve Spindle
3	Sealing Ball
4	Lock Nut
5	Spring
6	Adjusting Nut

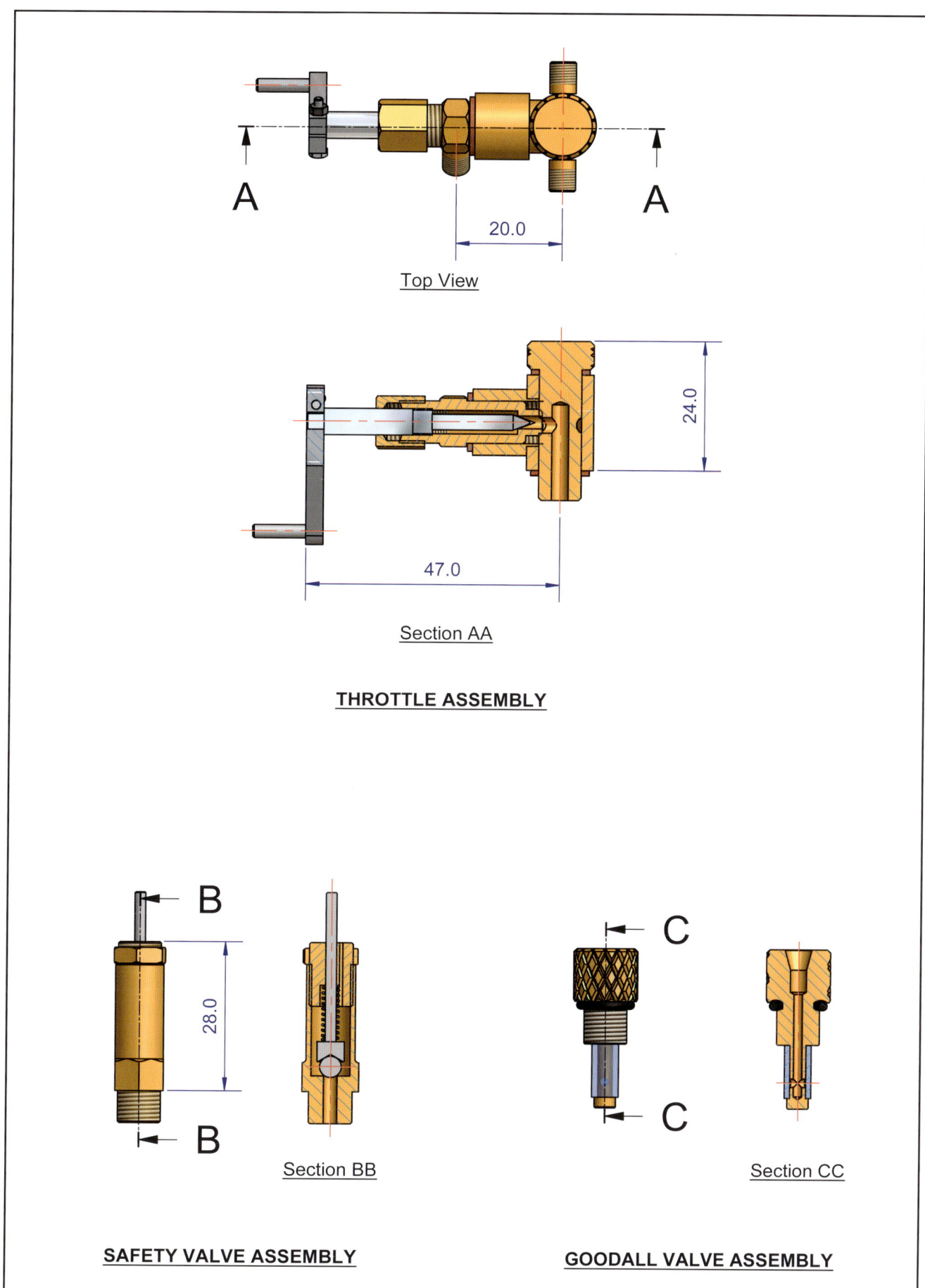

20.0

Top View

24.0

47.0

Section AA

THROTTLE ASSEMBLY

B

28.0

B

Section BB

C

C

Section CC

SAFETY VALVE ASSEMBLY

GOODALL VALVE ASSEMBLY

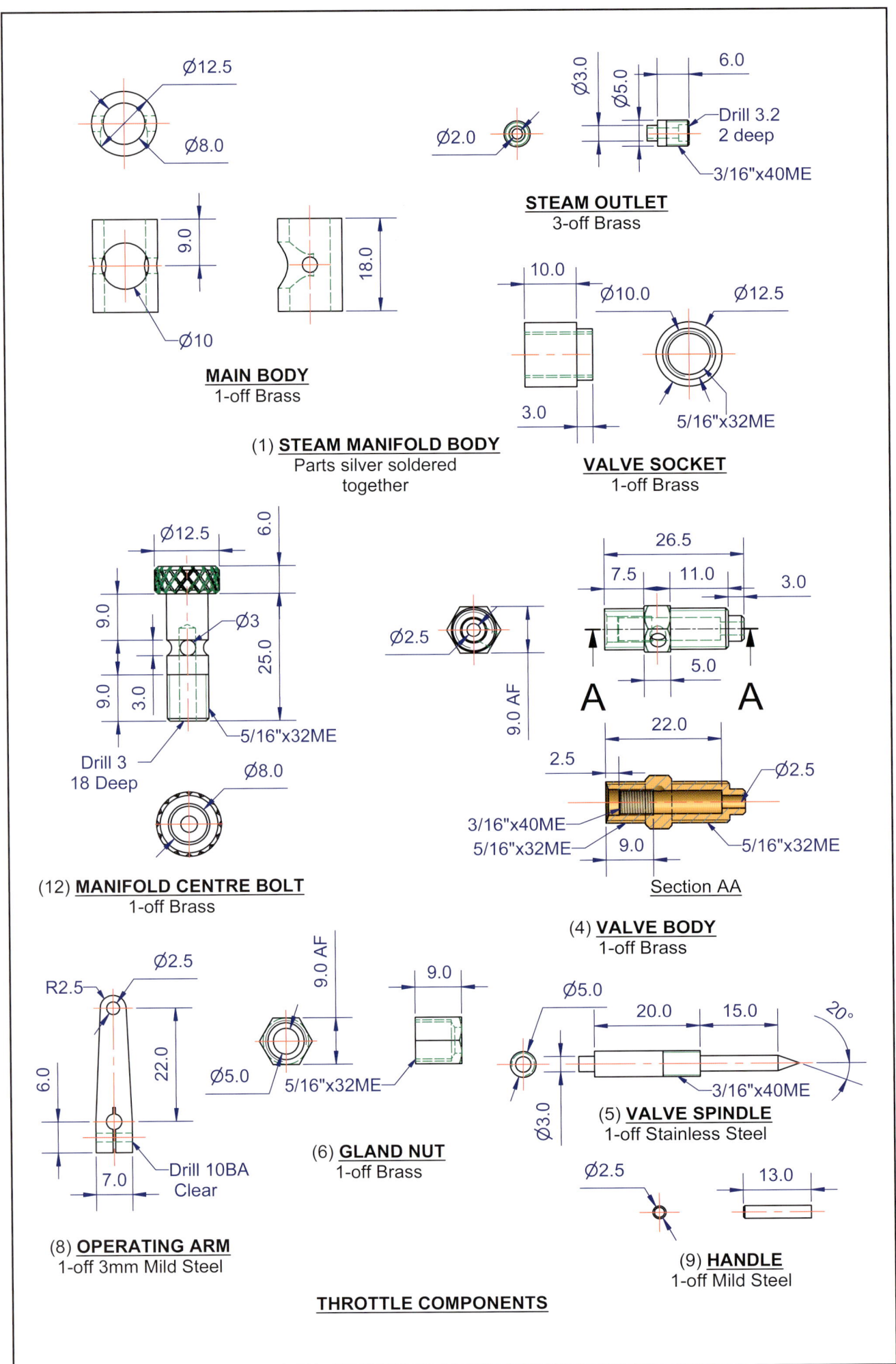

Ø12.5

Ø8.0

Ø2.0

Ø3.0

Ø5.0

6.0

Drill 3.2
2 deep

3/16"x40ME

STEAM OUTLET
3-off Brass

9.0

18.0

Ø10

10.0

Ø10.0

Ø12.5

3.0

5/16"x32ME

MAIN BODY
1-off Brass

(1) **STEAM MANIFOLD BODY**
Parts silver soldered
together

VALVE SOCKET
1-off Brass

Ø12.5

6.0

9.0

Ø3

9.0

3.0

25.0

5/16"x32ME

Drill 3
18 Deep

Ø8.0

26.5

7.5

11.0

3.0

Ø2.5

9.0 AF

5.0

A   A

22.0

2.5

Ø2.5

3/16"x40ME
5/16"x32ME   9.0   5/16"x32ME

Section AA

(12) **MANIFOLD CENTRE BOLT**
1-off Brass

(4) **VALVE BODY**
1-off Brass

R2.5

Ø2.5

9.0 AF

9.0

22.0

6.0

Ø5.0

5/16"x32ME

Drill 10BA
Clear

7.0

(6) **GLAND NUT**
1-off Brass

Ø5.0

20.0   15.0

20°

Ø3.0

3/16"x40ME

(5) **VALVE SPINDLE**
1-off Stainless Steel

Ø2.5

13.0

(8) **OPERATING ARM**
1-off 3mm Mild Steel

(9) **HANDLE**
1-off Mild Steel

THROTTLE COMPONENTS

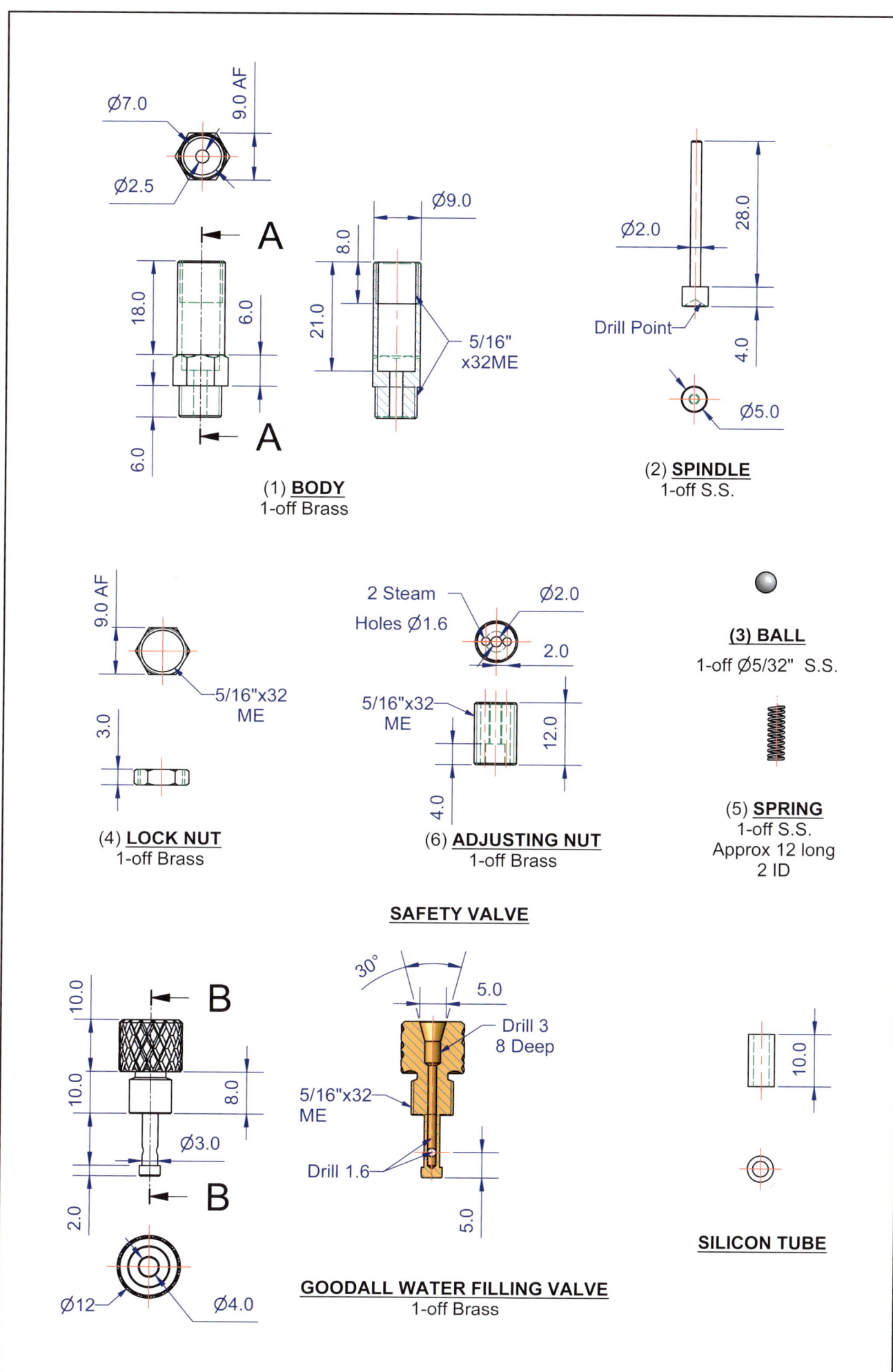

Ø7.0
9.0 AF
Ø2.5

A
A

18.0
6.0
6.0

8.0
21.0
Ø9.0

5/16"
x32ME

(1) BODY
1-off Brass

Ø2.0
28.0
Drill Point
4.0
Ø5.0

(2) SPINDLE
1-off S.S.

9.0 AF
5/16"x32 ME
3.0

(4) LOCK NUT
1-off Brass

2 Steam
Holes Ø1.6
Ø2.0
2.0
5/16"x32 ME
12.0
4.0

(6) ADJUSTING NUT
1-off Brass

(3) BALL
1-off Ø5/32" S.S.

(5) SPRING
1-off S.S.
Approx 12 long
2 ID

SAFETY VALVE

10.0
B
B
10.0
8.0
Ø3.0
2.0
Ø12
Ø4.0

30°
5.0
Drill 3
8 Deep
5/16"x32 ME
Drill 1.6
5.0

GOODALL WATER FILLING VALVE
1-off Brass

10.0

SILICON TUBE

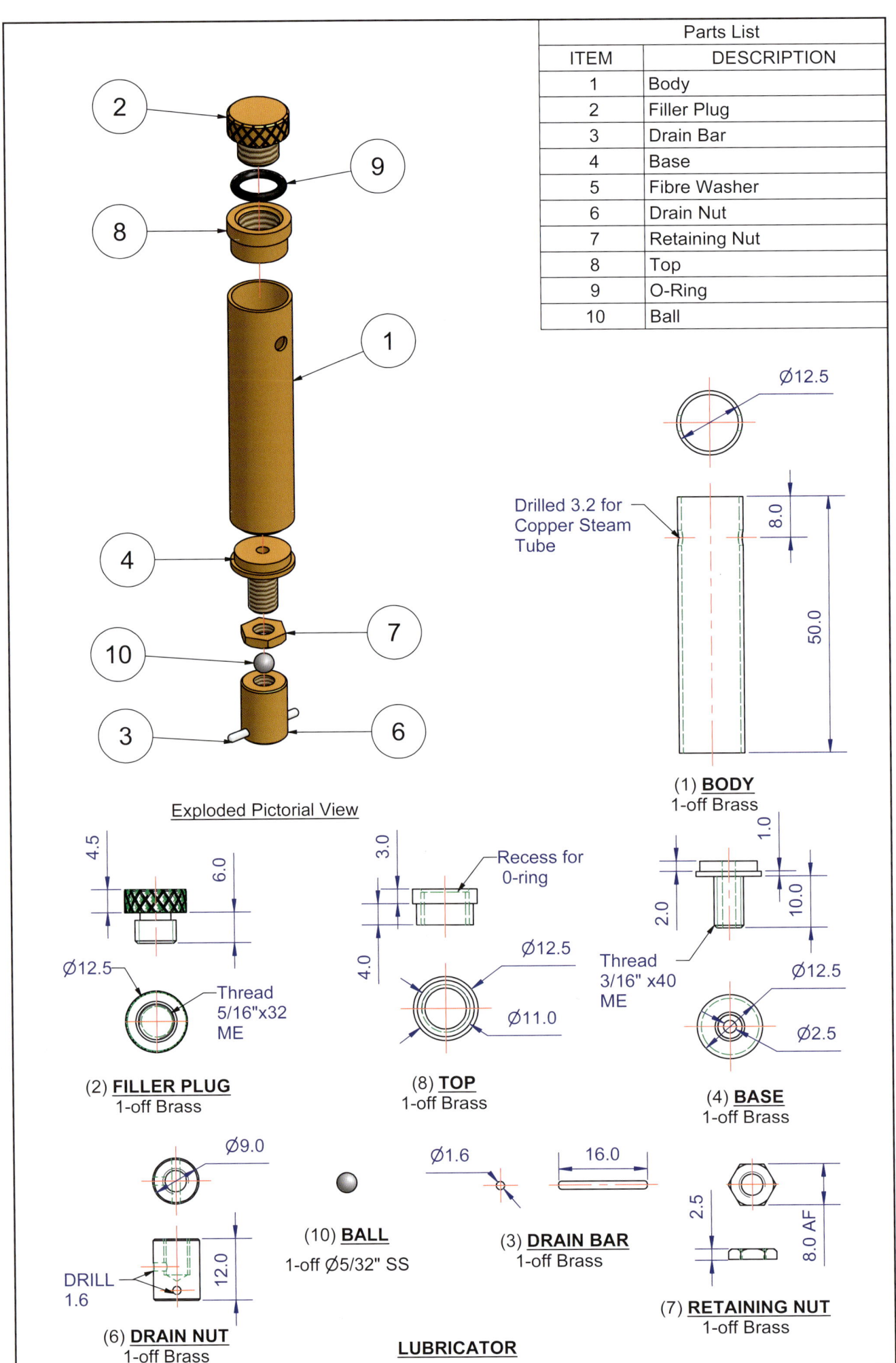

Parts List	
ITEM	DESCRIPTION
1	Body
2	Filler Plug
3	Drain Bar
4	Base
5	Fibre Washer
6	Drain Nut
7	Retaining Nut
8	Top
9	O-Ring
10	Ball

Exploded Pictorial View

Ø12.5

Drilled 3.2 for
Copper Steam
Tube

8.0

50.0

(1) **BODY**
1-off Brass

4.5

6.0

Ø12.5

Thread
5/16"x32
ME

(2) **FILLER PLUG**
1-off Brass

3.0

Recess for
0-ring

4.0

Ø12.5

Ø11.0

(8) **TOP**
1-off Brass

1.0

2.0

10.0

Thread
3/16" x40
ME

Ø12.5

Ø2.5

(4) **BASE**
1-off Brass

Ø9.0

DRILL
1.6

12.0

(6) **DRAIN NUT**
1-off Brass

(10) **BALL**
1-off Ø5/32" SS

Ø1.6

16.0

(3) **DRAIN BAR**
1-off Brass

2.5

8.0 AF

(7) **RETAINING NUT**
1-off Brass

LUBRICATOR

Valve spindle

The valve spindle is ideally made from stainless steel, but could be made from bronze which is a lot easier to turn and a lot kinder to your expensive dies. Either way, insert a length of ³⁄₁₆" (5mm) diameter into the chuck and turn the 15mm stem to 3mm and the 20 degree valve point. Angle the compound slide over to do this. Thread ³⁄₁₆" x 40 ME for 7mm, bearing in mind that the valve will seat part way along this tapered end, again make sure that the measurements are correct for the position of the thread on the spindle to enable the valve to seat fully. Part off, reverse in the chuck and turn the 3mm shoulder for the operating arm.

Turn the gland packing nut from ³⁄₈" (9mm) AF hexagon brass, seal it with a few twists of thread tape and make the operating arm and handle from mild steel.

When the valve body is screwed into the manifold, use one or two fibre washers as required to allow the steam outlet to be angled in the correct direction.

Goodall water filling valve

The Goodall Water Filling Valve is a non return valve which allows the boiler to be topped up with water from a plastic squeeze bottle whilst under steam. It works in a similar way to old style tyre valves.

It is a straightforward turning job from ½" diameter brass. The little shoulder on the end stops the silicone tubing from slipping off. (**Photo 4.1**). You may want to vary the taper at the top to suit the fitting on your squeeze bottle. Alternatively, you can make the fitting on your water bottle to fit the valve.

4.1 — "Goodall" water filling valve

Pressure gauge

The pressure gauge is a commercial item and comes in either ½" or ¾" diameter. The smaller one is closer to scale size, but as our eyes get older and aren't to scale, the larger one is far easier to read. It must be fitted with a siphon loop which in use fills with condensate and keeps hot steam away from the gauge. Make this pipe from ⅛" copper and carefully drill one end to insert the tail fitting on the pressure gauge. Soft solder this in as silver solder would overheat the gauge. (**Photo 4.2**).

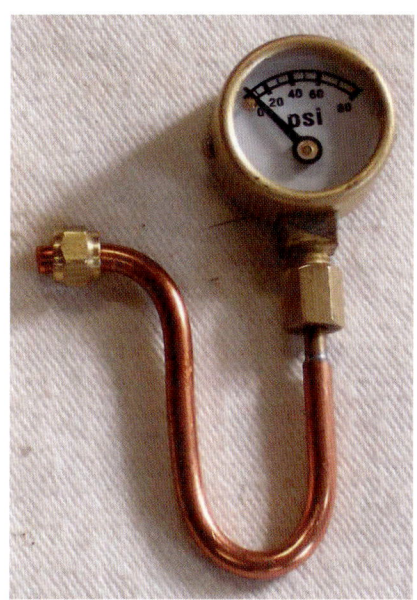

4.2 — Pressure gauge and siphon tube

Safety valve

Grip a length of ³⁄₈" (9mm) AF brass in the chuck and turn the hexagon off the outside for a distance of 18mm. Drill with ⁵⁄₁₆" x 32 ME tapping drill to a depth of 20mm and thread for 8mm. Drill a further 12mm from the bottom of this hole with a 2.5mm drill and then insert a "D"- Bit to form the valve seat at a depth of 21mm and part the piece off to 30mm.

Reverse in the chuck and thread ⁵⁄₁₆" x 32 ME for 6mm. Both the safety valve and the Goodall valve can be screwed in using either a fibre washer or an "O" – ring. If you use an "O" – ring, turn a small retaining groove as shown in the drawing of the Goodall valve, whereas if a fibre washer is used the face should be left flat, although it is a good idea to relieve the last few threads with a parting tool.

The spindle can be made up by silver soldering a length of 2mm stainless rod into the cap. This cap has a hollow made with a drill point to retain the ball. The spring must be stainless and a good source for these is Schrader tyre valves obtainable from your favourite bike shop. There are two types of Schrader valve, one has a long spindle and the other a short one. The long spindled one is the one we need here and they are used in high pressure tyres for cycles

Make the adjusting nut by threading a length of ⁵⁄₁₆" brass for about 14mm then drilling right through 2mm. Drill 4mm by 4mm deep to form a recess for the spring and then part off. Drill two 1.6mm holes down either side of the centre hole for the steam to escape. There is not much room here so accuracy is essential.

The safety valve is completed with a 3mm thick lock nut which locks the adjusting nut at the correct blow off pressure.

Lubricator

The lubricator is of a type known as a displacement lubricator. The steam pipe to the cylinders passes through it and has a tiny hole in the top (1mm or less). It is filled with steam oil and works because as the steam flows through the pipe, a little of it condenses into the lubricator body as water which eventually sinks to the bottom of the lubricator. As it does so, it displaces some oil which passes into the steam line and flows

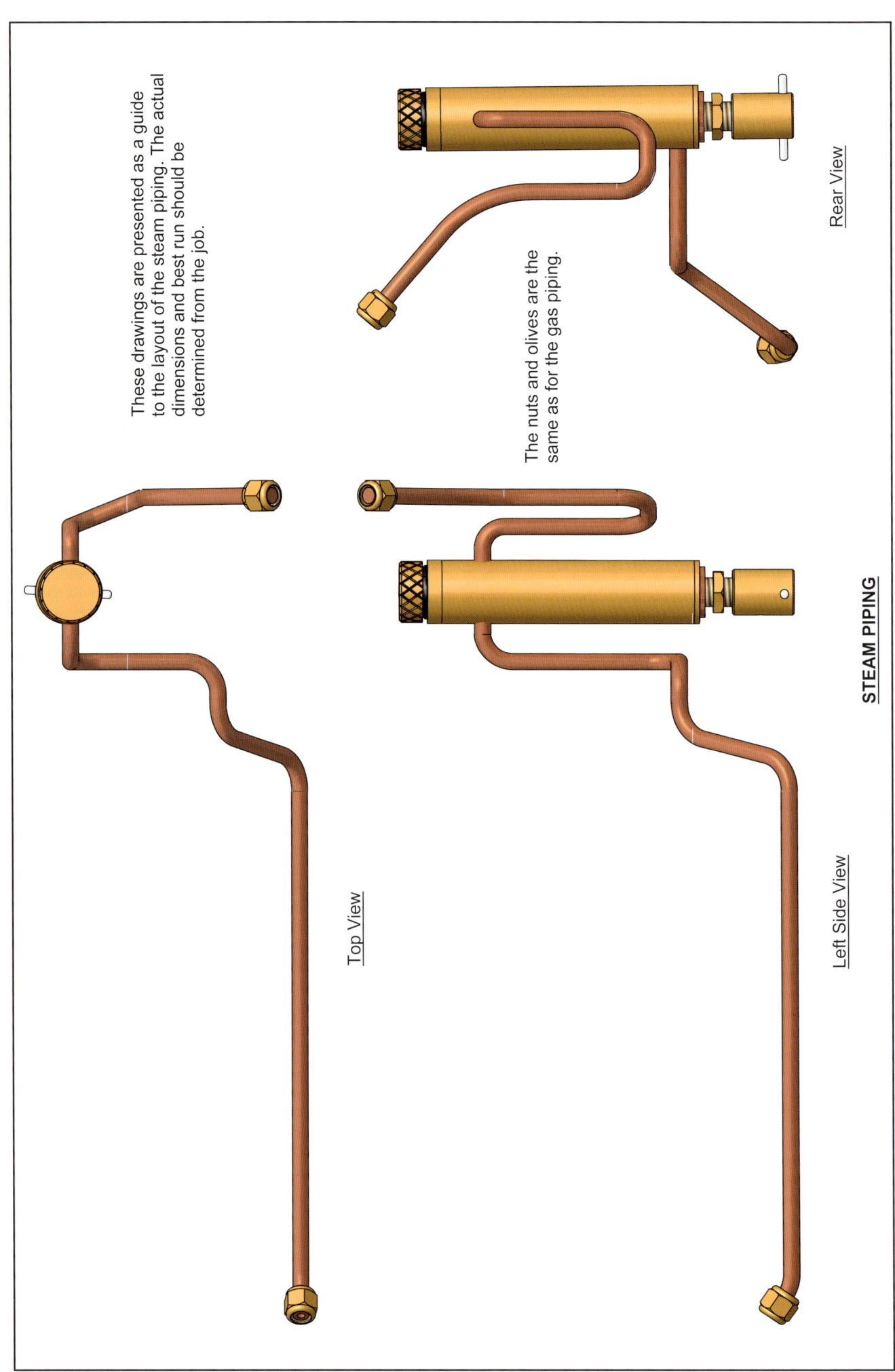

These drawings are presented as a guide to the layout of the steam piping. The actual dimensions and best run should be determined from the job.

The nuts and olives are the same as for the gas piping.

Rear View

Top View

Left Side View

STEAM PIPING

to the cylinders. Its operation can be a bit erratic, but generally they work quite well. After a run, the water is drained out of the bottom and it is topped up with fresh oil. (**Photo 4.3**)

For the body, cut a length of ½" brass tube and face both ends. Drill ⅛" right through for the copper steam pipe. All the other components are straightforward. Everything is silver soldered together although the short length of bar for the drain rod can be secured in place with Loctite. The top can be a simulated brake handle type as in the photo or a simple knurled one.

The threaded portion at the bottom passes through the cab footplate and is held in position with a lock nut and fibre washer.

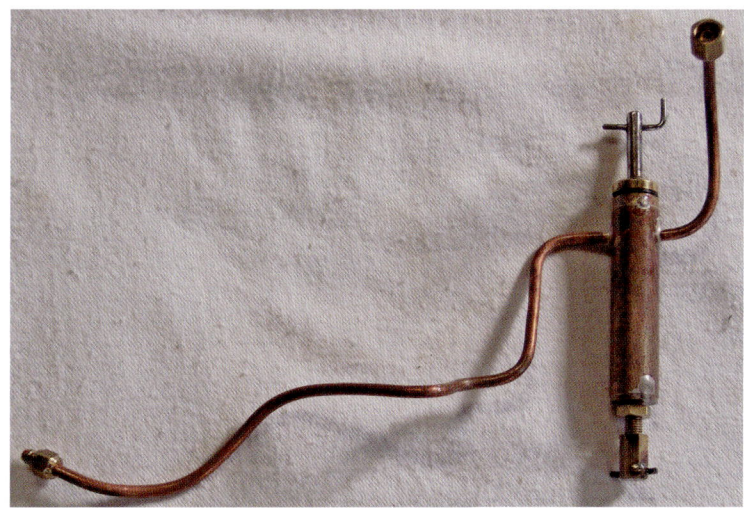
4.3 — Lubricator and piping

The drain nut containing the ball then screws on after this. To drain the water simply unscrew the drain a couple of turns, which lets the ball off its seat and allows the water to escape through the 1.6mm hole.

Steam piping

The steam piping is made up from ⅛" copper pipe. Copper pipe seems to vary quite a lot in size these days and it might be 3mm or ⅛" or something in between. When making your fittings, be aware of this and try to allow for any variation. Also the pipe can be manufactured by drawing through dies and if any grooves form on the outside of the pipe in this process, it will be impossible to get the olives to seal, so again check that there are no grooves on the outside of the pipe.

Making the nuts and olives has been described in the section on the steam inlet for the cylinders so if you haven't already made these, make up as many as you need with a few spares. Setting up the pipe runs is a bit fiddly and you may even wish to break the run and insert a coupling, although by careful juggling you should be able to avoid this and have a single run.

Take a reasonably straight piece of tubing and allowing plenty of length both ends, pass it into the lubricator and silver solder around both entry points. Very carefully drill the oil entry hole into the top of the steam pipe inside the lubricator.

Drawings are given as a guide to the pipe runs. These are approximate only and you will need to do the bends for your particular situation. One way of determining the run is to bend some wire along the path and use this as a template to make the bends in the pipe.

Bending pipe

Before making any bends, make sure the tubing is annealed. It is usually soft when purchased, but as copper is worked it "work hardens" so as you are making bends the material hardens. If you need to bend and unbend a section a few times it will need to be annealed again. To anneal the copper pipe simply heat it to a dull red heat and then quench out in water. This can be repeated as often as required.

Slight bends can be made by using your fingers, but tight bends need to

DRILLING OIL INLET HOLE

be done in a former so that the pipe doesn't kink or close up. A very simple bender can be made from a piece of 16mm diameter mild steel. Turn a groove so that the tubing is a neat fit and deep enough to support the sides of the tube when bending. The bending radius will be close to the inside diameter of the groove.

After making the bends, the tubing can be cut to length and the pipe unions temporarily fitted.

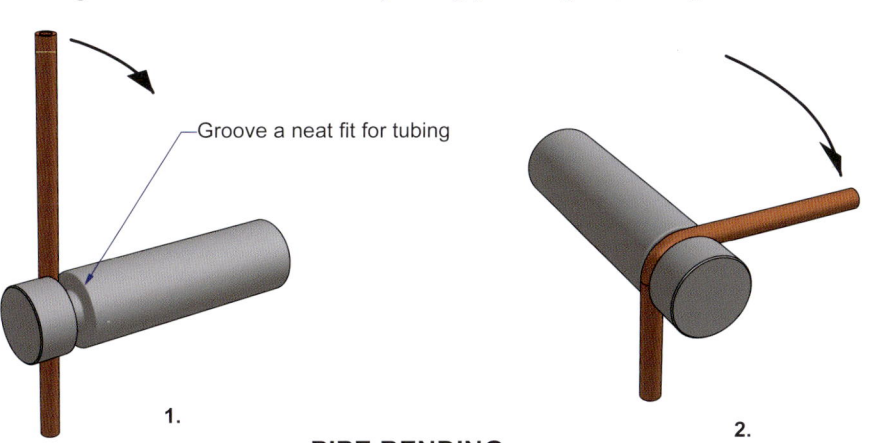

Groove a neat fit for tubing

1.

2.

PIPE BENDING

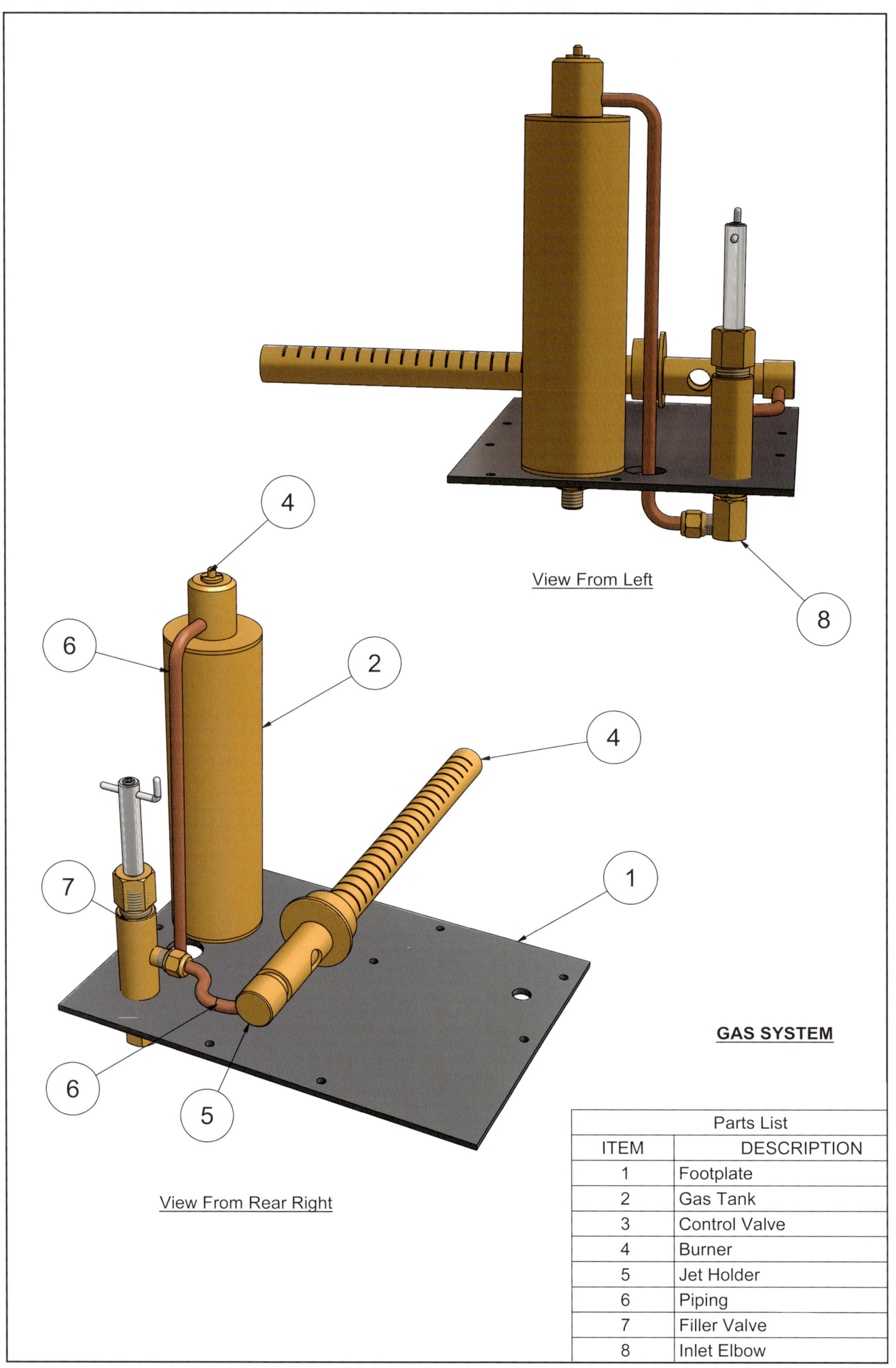

View From Left

View From Rear Right

GAS SYSTEM

Parts List	
ITEM	DESCRIPTION
1	Footplate
2	Gas Tank
3	Control Valve
4	Burner
5	Jet Holder
6	Piping
7	Filler Valve
8	Inlet Elbow

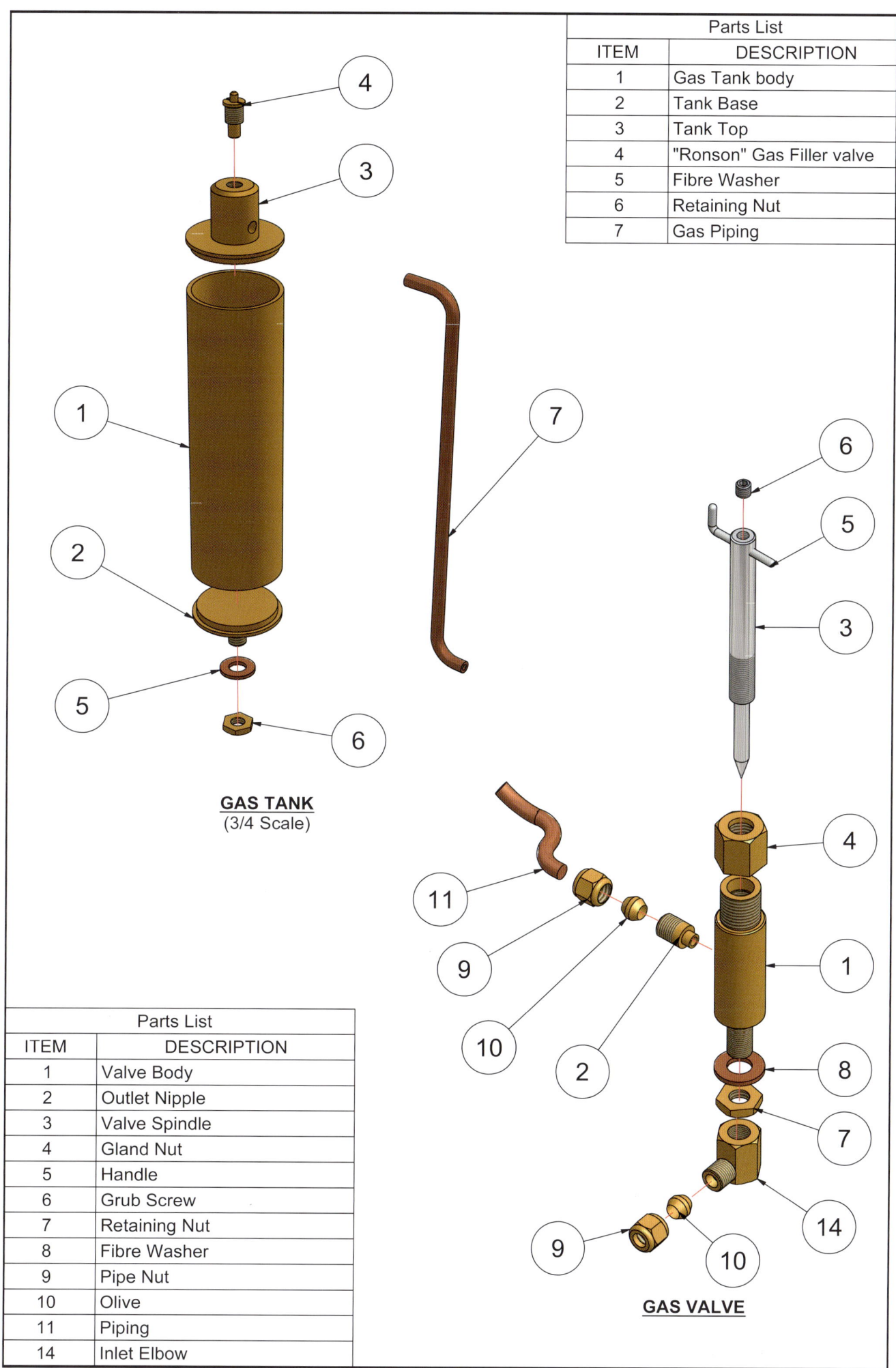

Parts List

ITEM	DESCRIPTION
1	Gas Tank body
2	Tank Base
3	Tank Top
4	"Ronson" Gas Filler valve
5	Fibre Washer
6	Retaining Nut
7	Gas Piping

GAS TANK
(3/4 Scale)

Parts List

ITEM	DESCRIPTION
1	Valve Body
2	Outlet Nipple
3	Valve Spindle
4	Gland Nut
5	Handle
6	Grub Screw
7	Retaining Nut
8	Fibre Washer
9	Pipe Nut
10	Olive
11	Piping
14	Inlet Elbow

GAS VALVE

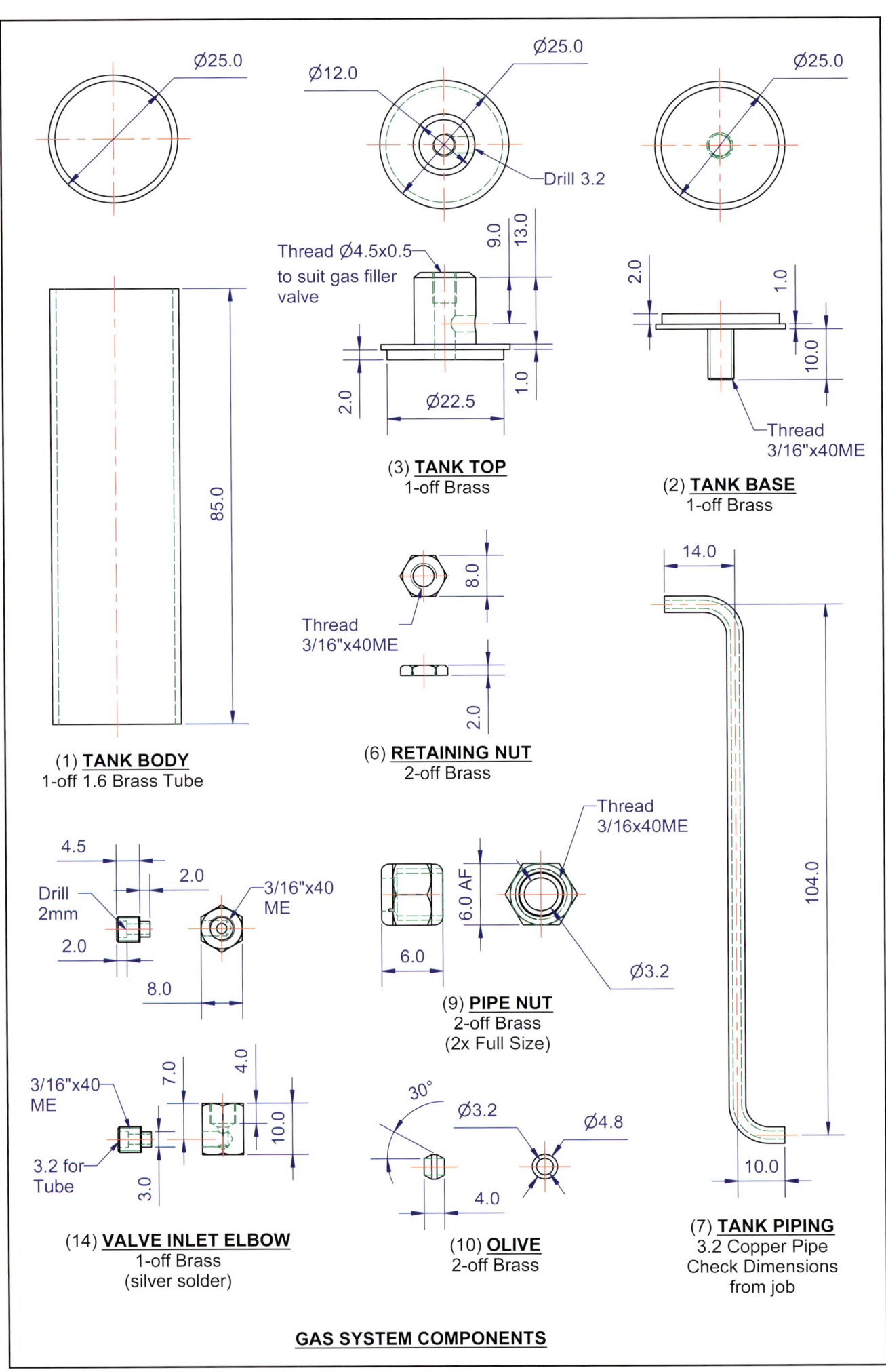

Ø25.0

Ø12.0

Ø25.0

Drill 3.2

Ø25.0

Thread Ø4.5x0.5
to suit gas filler
valve

9.0

13.0

2.0

1.0

10.0

2.0

Ø22.5

1.0

Thread
3/16"x40ME

(3) TANK TOP
1-off Brass

(2) TANK BASE
1-off Brass

85.0

8.0

Thread
3/16"x40ME

2.0

14.0

Thread
3/16x40ME

(1) TANK BODY
1-off 1.6 Brass Tube

(6) RETAINING NUT
2-off Brass

6.0 AF

104.0

4.5

2.0

Drill
2mm

3/16"x40
ME

2.0

6.0

Ø3.2

8.0

(9) PIPE NUT
2-off Brass
(2x Full Size)

3/16"x40
ME

7.0

4.0

10.0

3.2 for
Tube

3.0

30°

Ø3.2

Ø4.8

10.0

4.0

(14) VALVE INLET ELBOW
1-off Brass
(silver solder)

(10) OLIVE
2-off Brass

(7) TANK PIPING
3.2 Copper Pipe
Check Dimensions
from job

GAS SYSTEM COMPONENTS

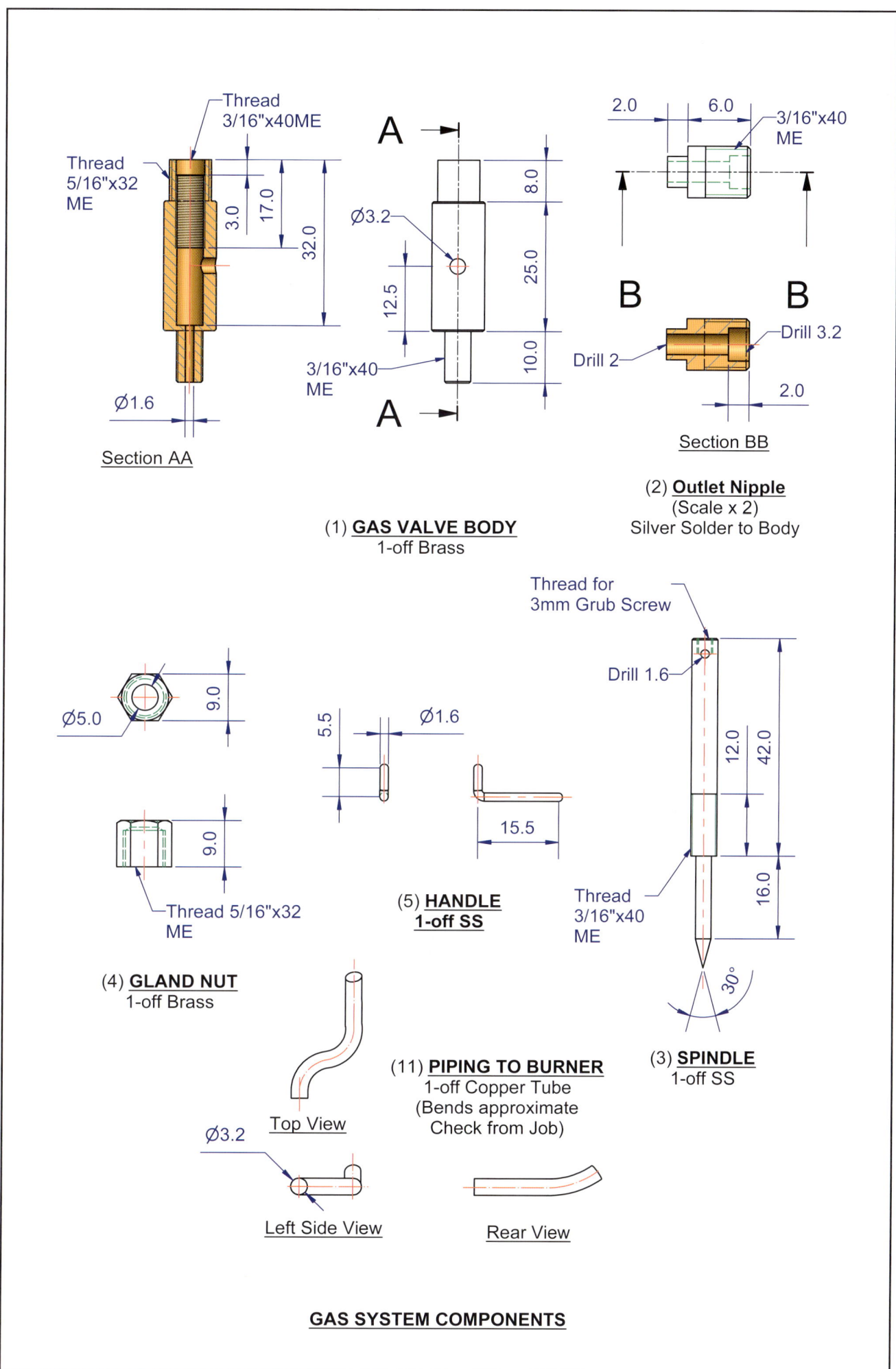

Thread 3/16"x40ME

Thread 5/16"x32 ME

3.0
17.0
32.0

Ø1.6

Section AA

A
A
Ø3.2
8.0
25.0
12.5
10.0
3/16"x40 ME

2.0 6.0 3/16"x40 ME

B   B
Drill 2   Drill 3.2
2.0

Section BB

(2) **Outlet Nipple**
(Scale x 2)
Silver Solder to Body

(1) **GAS VALVE BODY**
1-off Brass

Ø5.0
9.0
9.0
Thread 5/16"x32 ME

(4) **GLAND NUT**
1-off Brass

5.5 Ø1.6
15.5

(5) **HANDLE 1-off SS**

Top View

Ø3.2

Left Side View

(11) **PIPING TO BURNER**
1-off Copper Tube
(Bends approximate
Check from Job)

Rear View

Thread for 3mm Grub Screw
Drill 1.6
12.0 42.0
16.0
Thread 3/16"x40 ME
30°

(3) **SPINDLE**
1-off SS

GAS SYSTEM COMPONENTS

Parts List	
ITEM	DESCRIPTION
1	Burner Tube
2	Collar
3	Jet Holder
4	Jet

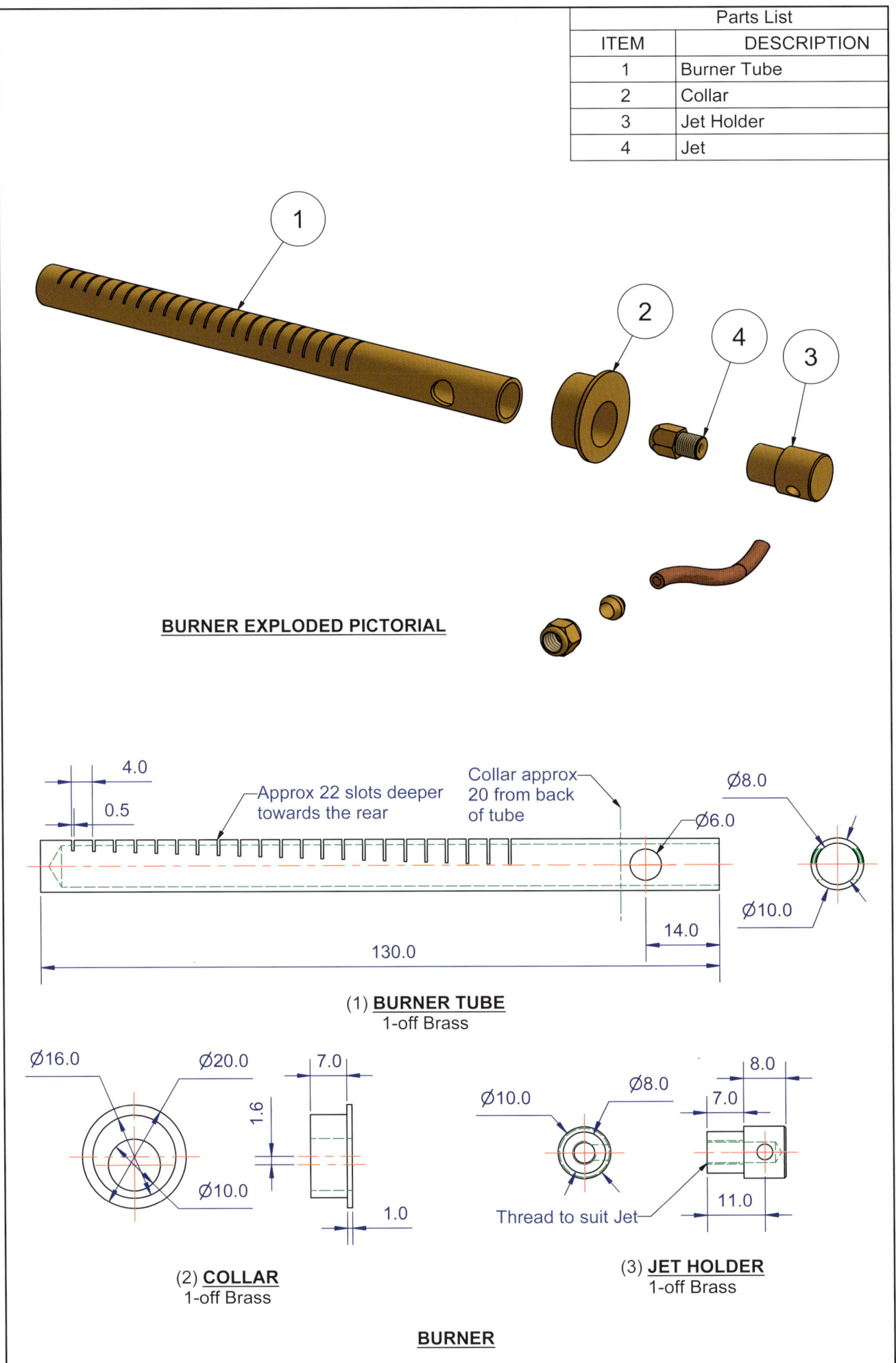

BURNER EXPLODED PICTORIAL

4.0

0.5

Approx 22 slots deeper towards the rear

Collar approx 20 from back of tube

Ø8.0

Ø6.0

Ø10.0

14.0

130.0

(1) **BURNER TUBE**
1-off Brass

Ø16.0

Ø20.0

7.0

1.6

Ø10.0

1.0

(2) **COLLAR**
1-off Brass

Ø10.0

Ø8.0

8.0

7.0

Thread to suit Jet

11.0

(3) **JET HOLDER**
1-off Brass

BURNER

The gas system

The gas system which supplies heat for the boiler consists of a tank, regulating valve and poker style burner. The gas used is butane which is obtainable in convenient sized cans from camping stores and tobacconists. Also available is a mixed gas consisting of 80% butane and 20% propane. It is alright to use this mix, but pure propane should never be used, nor mixes with greater than 20% propane.

The builder must satisfy himself or herself that any regulations which may be in place concerning gas tanks are followed. In the course of construction the integrity of the tank should be proven with a hydrostatic test, or whatever any regulations which are in place demand. In use, the gas systems on locomotives have proven to be safe and reasonably reliable but as we are dealing with flammable gas and heat, care must be exercised to avoid mishaps. (When we consider that we are allowed to carry plastic cigarette lighters filled with butane in our pocket it puts the situation into perspective.)

Tank

The tank body is made from 25mm diameter x 1.6mm brass tube. Cut to length and face both ends. For the top, grip a piece of 25mm diameter brass rod in the chuck and turn to 12mm diameter for 14mm and chamfer the edge. Drill 3.7mm to a depth of 20mm and tap M4.5mm x 0.5. (This is a metric fine thread and is the thread on the gas filler valves. This is not a commonly used size and taps can be difficult to obtain but it is necessary to have one for this thread, and also the gas jet may use the same thread.)

Part off and reverse in the chuck to turn the shoulder which fits into the tank body. Turn the base in the same way, threading the bottom ³⁄₁₆" x 40 ME.

Cut the outlet pipe of ⅛" copper to length, bend to shape and then silver solder the pieces of the tank together. (**Photo 4.4**)

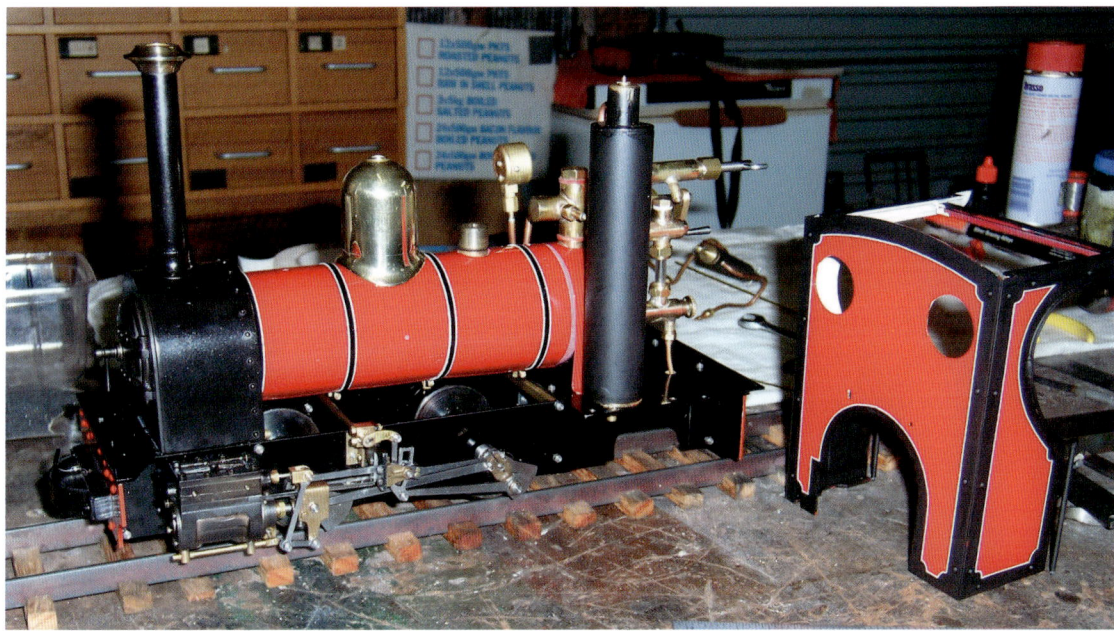

4.4 — Gas tank mounted on the footplate

Gas valve

Sometimes the gas valve is placed at the top of the gas tank with a knurled adjusting nut, which can look a bit out of place, so the valve for "*Eric*" has been placed on the footplate and has an adjusting handle which resembles a hand brake handle. The valve design is similar in many ways to the throttle valve.

Grip a piece of ⅜" brass rod in the chuck, face the end and drill 4.0mm to a depth of 30mm. Drill for a further 15mm with a 1.6mm drill. Form the valve seat with a "D" – bit to a depth of 32mm. and tap ³⁄₁₆" x 40 ME for a depth of 17mm. Relieve the first 3mm of this thread. Turn the outlet nipple and the gland nut from brass and then the spindle, making this in the same way as the throttle valve spindle. Silver solder the outlet nipple onto the body then the valve is mounted through the footplate and held with a nut and fibre washer.

Burner

The burner can either be made from a length of ⅜" diameter brass tubing with a plug silver soldered into the front end or from a piece of ⅜" solid rod drilled ⁵⁄₁₆" (8mm).

If you take the drilled option, you will need to drill very carefully or the drill will wander and finish up off centre, or worse, coming out the side. To help avoid this use a new drill which will have cutting edges of equal length. Also drill slowly and withdraw the chips frequently.

Drill the 6mm air holes in the tube, taking care as the material is quite thin and then cut the slots. These start off shallow and increase to about half depth at the back. A "Junior" hacksaw blade with the set ground off the sides of the teeth will give a slot of about the correct width.

Turn the collar from brass, part off and then drill and preferably ream the hole for the burner tube. The burner tube needs to be a good fit in this hole and the collar needs to be a good fit in the boiler flue tube otherwise the burner will dip down rather than sit in the centre of the flue. The jet holder is turned from brass and is threaded according to the jet that you use. (**Photo 4.5**)

4.5 — Poker burner tube

CHAPTER 5
Assembling, Painting, and Finishing

Assembling

Usually the whole locomotive is assembled, tested and run for a period before dismantling, cleaning up and painting. If you are *very* confident you might paint everything before running it for the first time!

Assuming you are going to have a trial run before painting, we are at the stage where the chassis has been completed and is running on air and all other parts are completed and ready to assemble. This includes lagging and cladding on the boiler and the gauge glass assembly. To assemble the gauge glass, cut off a piece of glass tubing to length. To do this, using the edge of a fine file, carefully file a line or groove around the glass. Holding the tube with your hands protected by some rag, gently snap it. If you have a sharp edge on a grinder stone you can carefully run the glass around on that, but be aware of the dangers. Slide the glass down through the top fitting where it should line up without any forcing whatsoever with the bottom fitting. If it doesn't line up, the fittings can be carefully tweaked so that it does. Insert some twists of thread tape into the gland nuts and screw up hand tight. Other packing which can be used is an "O" – ring or a slice of silicone tubing. Each has its followers.

After fixing the smoke box assembly onto the front plate, mount the boiler by sliding into the smoke box and fixing with the two 8 BA screws through the footplate. Set up the throttle valve into the steam manifold, fix the lubricator through the footplate and run the steam piping. At this stage the union nuts can be tightened with the olives inserted. They need to be done up quite tightly but as was said earlier with the steam unions they can be done up and undone several times and still be steam tight. Fix the gas tank and the gas valve through the footplate, the burner into the boiler flue and connect the gas piping. Mount the pressure gauge and blank off the steam line on the other side of the manifold. (This outlet is for a whistle which we will describe later if you wish to fit one.)

The locomotive is now ready to test under steam, after which when everything is working satisfactorily, we can fit the cab and side tanks. For a first steam test mount the chassis up onto blocks of wood as you did for the air test, after everything is working satisfactorily it can be given a run on the track.

Fill the boiler with distilled water until the level is towards the top of the gauge glass, fill the gas tank with gas and the lubricator with steam oil.

Open the gas valve and you should hear the gas hissing into the flue tube. Put a light to the top of the chimney and the flame should run down into the flue tube with an audible pop. It may be necessary now to turn the flame down a little. If it doesn't want to pop down the chimney, you may have to take the front off the smoke box and light it from there. The flame should be burning in the flue tube with a nice blue crescent shape. (Use a mirror to check through the smoke box.) Also be careful that the flame doesn't burn in the smoke box.

As the water heats and steam pressure starts to build up there will almost certainly be a few leaks from the pipe unions. Tighten these up as necessary. If the gauge glass leaks be very careful when tightening up the nuts. They should never be very tight and it is probably better to shut the flame off and put in some more packing and adjust the nuts after things have cooled down.

Working pressure is 35psi (250 kPa) so slightly above this pressure the safety valve should start to blow off. The safety valve can be initially set with cold water using your boiler test pump, but final adjustment is made under steam pressure.

Now that steam pressure is up, any leaks have been sorted out and the safety valve is operating correctly we can open the throttle slightly and clear condensate from the steam line and cylinders. Because the cylinders are cold, the first lot of steam will condense to water and this will continue until they become hot enough. Full size locomotives and larger models have drain cocks on each end of their cylinders, and although some 16mm models do have working drain cocks they are not really necessary. Turn the wheels gently by hand and condensate will start leaking out. It will spit up the chimney and generally make a mess. It may help to move the reversing lever into reverse and back again, but eventually the condensate will clear and the motion will turn on its own, running for the first time under steam! Close the throttle back to reduce speed and adjust the gas so that the minimum is being used to maintain pressure. Adjust the cylinder and valve glands if necessary until everything settles down. After this, the locomotive can be tested on a track and run around a few times to take away any stiffness and run the motion in. Keep an eye on the water level in the boiler and top up as necessary through the Goodall valve.

This really is a good time to paint the loco rather than be tempted to mount the cab and tanks. If you do mount the body work however, then at least you will be sure that it, and all the pipe work fits properly.

Painting

This is a stage that can make or break a model. Considering the large number of hours that you have spent getting the model to this stage, it seems a shame to spoil everything with a bad paint job. Like most processes if a few simple rules are followed you are almost guaranteed of success.

The following suggestions are not the words of an expert. There are many different approaches to arriving at a good paint finish and many people have their own favourite and highly successful techniques all backed up with sound theory. Maybe the end result has been enhanced with failing eyesight, but the approach outlined here has worked well with a minimum of fuss. However you do it, one of the most important rules is don't rush things. It will take several days or longer, most of it spent waiting for paint to dry. Organize to do some odd jobs around the house, take your wife/husband to the movies, go fishing, do anything, but don't rush each coat. Give plenty of time for drying.

Be aware that paints and solvents have some nasty ingredients, so take care at all times to follow manufacturers' instructions with regard to handling, using and disposing of these materials. These instructions should be considered when carrying out any suggestions which may given here.

We will assume that the chassis has already been painted so we need to do the smoke box assembly and the body. The inside of the cab usually has black up to about half way and cream above this. It also looks better to paint the gas tank and lubricator satin black as it helps to hide them. (**Photo 5.1 & 5.2**)

5.1 & 5.2 — Cab interior showing cream and black painted sections

The different styles for the cab and tanks we will discuss are: (a) single colour; (b) single colour with lining and (c) Two colours separated by lining. All parts will need to be initially primed.

The techniques apply to any small locomotive and the photographs used for illustration are of "Elliot", an 0-4-0 saddle tank locomotive which has as its prototype a small Peckett locomotive now preserved on Victoria's "Puffing Billy" Railway. The paint scheme is two tone green separated by white lining.

If you have never painted a model like this before, then it is suggested that you have a thorough practice session on some trial pieces before tackling the real thing. If you are going to apply lining, then have a good practice of this as well.

If we break the whole process down into its components, we have:

    (1) Preparation of the surfaces to be painted;
    (2) The paint and its application;
    (3) Curing or drying.

(1) Preparation: The surfaces to be painted have to be free of grease, oil and any other dirt or impurities, and they have to be sound and free of any scale or significant scratches. We also have two different materials: brass and mild steel. Generally they each have different requirements.

Set up an area suitable for painting. There must be adequate and appropriate ventilation, and nothing which will be affected by overspray. You have to be able to leave the job for the paint to dry, in some cases for several days. For the first few hours, until the paint is touch dry, there has to be no dust flying around. After this the job needs to be placed where it won't be bumped or otherwise be in the way. This may sound rather obvious, but if we have a workshop where space is a bit tight, it is surprising how quickly a pleasant painting job suddenly turns sour when a beautifully painted item gets knocked to the floor, or rolls over into some metal filings!

Completely disassemble all parts. After testing and running the locomotive, there will be plenty of oil, grease and dirt to be removed. Each part needs to be thoroughly cleaned with degreaser, such as paint thinners. (Do not use detergent.) A way to do this is to place the job in a good sized plastic container and use a combination of pouring, brushing and wiping all surfaces. Use a good quality brush, not one which drops hairs and most importantly don't use rags which shed lint and fluff. It will remain stubbornly on the surface after it is dry. After cleaning, set the pieces aside to dry thoroughly.

Next, the pieces have to be set up or held in a position for painting. This is another seemingly obvious requirement where disaster strikes if we don't adequately prepare!

Some of the considerations here are: Do we have to paint two sides of a piece and if so how will we turn it over? Can we do the lot by hanging or holding the piece up or would it be better to do one side, let it dry then turn it over? What masking, if any, is required? Will another section be affected by overspray? Is the piece so small and light that the jet of paint will blow it away? In other words, the pieces have to be securely held in an appropriate position before the spraying starts. They can be hung by wire, jammed onto a stick, held with blue tack or simply placed in position, as long as they are in the position you want them for spraying and they are secure from falling.

As I don't have a purpose built spray booth, I apply the paint outside and then after it is touch dry take it to a safe spot in the workshop until the paint is fully dry. This raises the next important factor: the weather. Unless you have the luxury of an air conditioned spray booth area, you just cannot paint on bad days. Resist the temptation, don't do it! Bad days are windy days, rainy days, hot days and cold days, which in some parts of the world doesn't leave many painting days. Also don't paint towards evening. There must be sufficient time for the paint to tack before the cold or damp of evening sets in.

So now we have the pieces clean and grease free, set up ready for priming.

(2) Paint and its Application: There are essentially two types of paint which are suitable for our use. The first is the paint usually obtained from hobby shops especially formulated for models. The well known brands are of high quality and are obtainable in a vast range of colours. They have to be applied by air brush, although some colours are available in small spray cans. The second type of paint is that found in hardware or automotive shops in spray cans. Some of these are completely useless. Do not use the cheap and nasty ones as they are just that. The most successful ones seem to be the automotive paints, and again only use well known brands, even though you may cringe at the price. Remember how little the cost is in relation to the overall value of your locomotive!

Within all of these paints there is another division. There are enamel paints and there are acrylic paints. (It will be stated on the can.) You can use both types on the one model, although be aware that enamel can be sprayed over the top of acrylic but *acrylic can not be sprayed over enamel,* as they are not compatible and it would result in watching the whole lot crinkle before your eyes. It is truly an amazing sight.

Air brushing is very popular and has many advantages. Although it is fiddly and requires careful cleaning up, if you are happy using an airbrush then it is probably the best way to apply the paint. It means you can use high quality model paints with their greater range of colours. As not everyone has an air brush and compressor, we will describe using spray cans although most of the processes will be the same.

The first coat will be primer and a badly applied prime coat will ruin the model almost as much as a badly applied top coat. It is essential to use an etch primer on brass and it is also works well on the mild steel smoke box. You may have a favourite brand, but I have had no failures with "PowerPlus" automotive touch-up paint etch primer. (I have no connection with this brand or any others mentioned other than a satisfied customer.)

There are high temperature paints available which would seem to be ideal for the smoke box, but I have found that they don't always work as well as some other paints. VHT brand "Epoxy" paint in satin black has worked very well for the smoke box and although it is supposed to need no primer, the best results have been obtained using the etch primer as well. Therefore set up the smoke box together with the body parts, apply etch primer and allow to dry. When spraying, apply several thin coats rather than one thick one. Allow a few minutes between coats which allows the paint to set a little before the next coat and helps to avoid runs. You don't want too thick a coat of primer, so don't overdo it. It dries quite quickly so you don't have to wait too long before the next coat. Follow manufacturers' instructions and also do a couple of test pieces as you go along. (**Photo 5.3**).

Painting the inside of the cab black on the bottom half and cream on the top half means masking which is a fiddly but necessary process. Buy a good quality, low tack specialist masking tape and paint the inside of the cab before going to the outside.

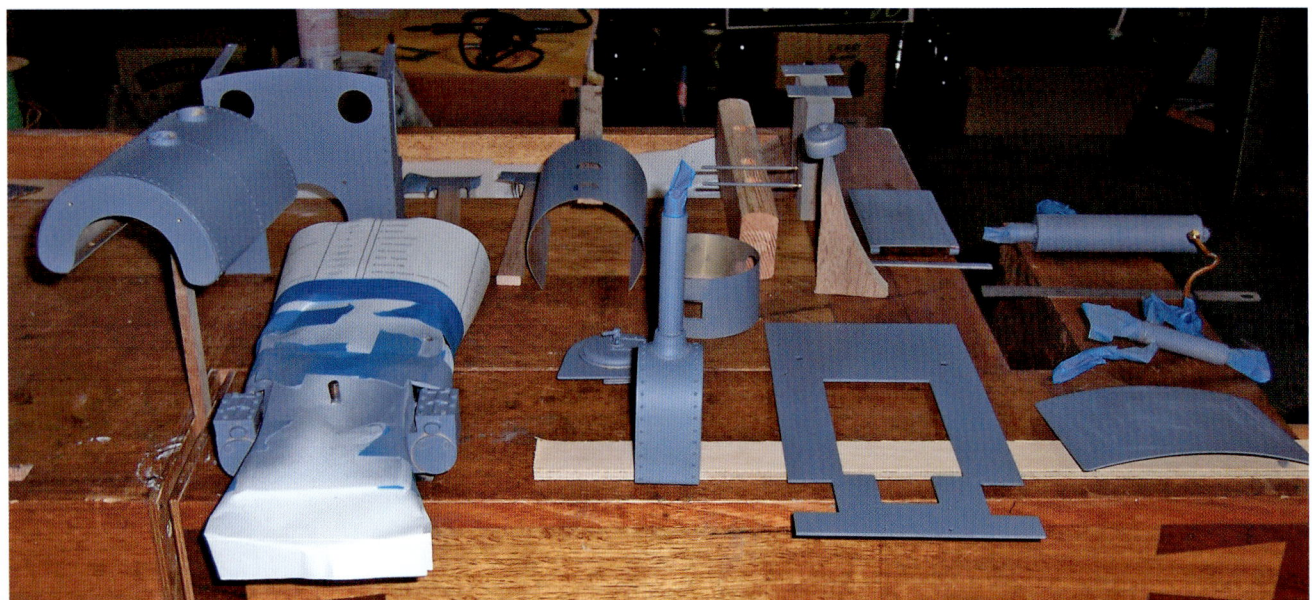

5.3 — *Etch primer applied*

Paint the cream colour first and for this you will need to mask so that paint doesn't reach the outside surface of the cab. Apply masking tape onto the outside faces so that it overlaps the edges a few millimetres and also cover the round windows from the outside. Although not essential, mask the bottom half where the black is to go. Apply a few coats of cream being careful not to get too much build up on its edge where the black is to go. Let the paint tack and then carefully remove all the masking tape and put aside to dry for several days. Always remove masking tape as soon as possible, as it gives a softer edge and also avoids the possibility of the tape pulling chips out of the edge of the paint which can happen if you wait until it has dried hard.

When the cream is thoroughly dry, mask as before, this time placing the tape onto the cream where it is to join with the black. This is why we have to let it dry so completely and why we use a low tack tape, because if the cream isn't dry it will pull off when the tape is removed. The entire cream section has to be masked against overspray, and rather than run strips of tape over the entire surface, fold a piece of paper and tape that into position, taping around its outside. Pay particular attention to masking in the internal corners otherwise black paint will creep down the corner onto the cream.

Spray the cream, allow to tack, remove the masking tape and paper and again allow to dry for several days.

While using the black paint for the inside of the cab, the smoke box, lubricator, gas tank, roof and footplates can be painted. The paint suggested for these parts takes longer to dry than some of the other types and isn't fully hard for a month or so, although it can be used long before this. After this time, though, it has been found to cure to a very hard wearing surface.

Single colour paint scheme

If you are going to have one single colour, with or without lining, the next coat will be the final colour coat. Set the pieces in position again and using either acrylic or enamel in the colour of your choice, spray several coats as before. You will want to build up a final coat which is thicker than the primer, but again, build it up in several thin coats. It is probably better to put a few coats on, let them dry totally and then apply a few more. (Read the recoating times carefully. It is vital to follow them.) Before putting on the second lot of coats, examine for any runs or gaps. If there are gaps, make sure they are covered next time although if there are runs, there isn't much you can do about them. For a bad run in an obvious spot you might be able to lightly rub it with very fine wet and dry after the paint is totally dry and remove the worst of it, but if you apply thin coats with each spray and leave a few minutes between each one you should avoid them in the first place.

If you have made a complete mess with lumps of fluff and runs all over the place there is nothing for it but to remove the lot! This seems unthinkable, but isn't as bad as it seems. (How do I know?) Take the offending part back to the plastic tub and apply plenty of thinners to remove the lot and start all over again, you will be happier in the long run.

When you are happy with each part, allow to tack, remove any masking tape and allow to dry. If you are settling for a single colour you can now assemble the model and you are ready to go. If you want to apply line work over a single colour it can be done now. (The way to do this will be described in the next section.)

Lining out will take quite a bit longer, particularly if using two colours, but it is well worth the extra wait. After all, a week or two longer for a paint job which will last for years shouldn't be too much of a problem.

Two tone paint scheme

When applying a two tone colour scheme with lining, the steps will be to apply:

(1) The inner colour. (Usually a lighter colour);
(2) The outer heavier colour;
(3) Lining;
(4) Tranfers or decals (if applied);
(5) Clear overcoat.

After setting up the pieces securely, spray the lighter colour which is to go on the inner panels. Don't overdo the thickness of this coat, and it doesn't have to completely cover to the edges, as the next colour will do this. Spray just sufficient thickness of paint for a good covering of colour. Put aside and allow to cure, according to the manufacturer's instructions. (**Photo 5.4**) This is one of the times when you should go fishing.

5.4 — The first colour applied

After this coat is fully cured we have to mask the panels and apply the outer darker edgings. A good material to do this is known as "frisk". It comes in sheet form and is a low tack type of contact paper which is used as a masking when artists paint air brush pictures. It is obtainable from artists' suppliers. The shape of the panel is drawn onto the frisk, cut out accurately and placed in position on the job. The best way to draw the shape is with a CAD program on your computer which is then printed directly onto the masking. If CAD isn't available then it can simply be drawn by hand using a fine tipped permanent marker as the frisk has a plastic type of finish. (**Photo 5.5**)

Apply the masking, and make sure that it is pressed down well around the edges so paint can't creep underneath. Spray the second colour on; again don't overdo the number of coats, particularly try not to get a thick build up around the edges of the masking. Remove the masking as soon as the paint has started to tack. Starting to lift the masking is tricky but can be done by taking a pointed cutting knife, sticking it into the mask in from the edge a little and carefully lifting away from the job. Again put the pieces aside and go fishing. (**Photo 5.6**)

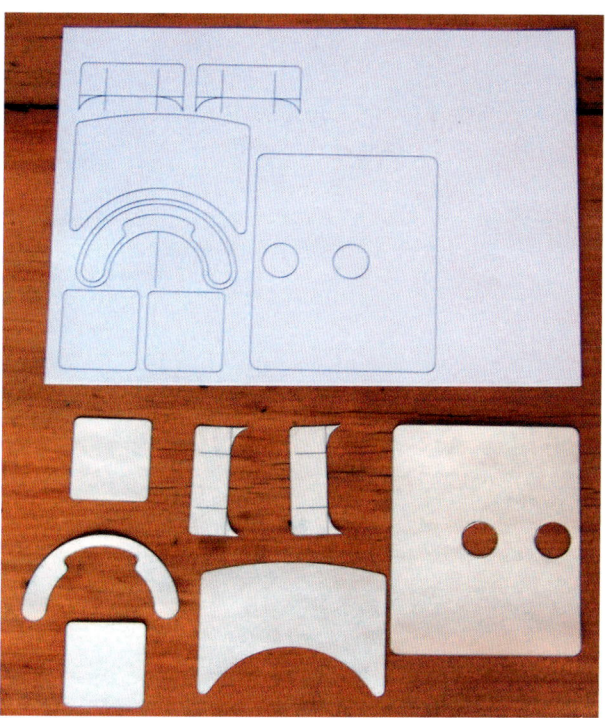

5.5 — The masking panels printed on and cut out of plastic sheets

5.6 — Second colour applied

Lining

As with most things, if we have good tools and equipment and everything properly set up then the lining will work out well and turn a good model into an outstanding one. There are three main requirements for successful lining:

    (1) The pen;
    (2) The ink; and
    (3) A definite path along which to draw the pen.

At the centre of the operation is the pen. Traditionally bow pens as used in draughting offices many years ago were used and with a skilled operator can still do a good job. A pen especially made for lining out models is produced in England called "Bob Moore's Lining Pen" It comes in different sizes to produce different width lines, 0.5mm being the best for our size of model. Another cheaper option is to make your own from a "Rotring" or other draughting pen. This involves attaching the tip (which comes in various sizes) onto a small reservoir which holds the paint and fixing it onto a handle. Yet another pen is available in art shops very cheaply which is similar in principle to Bob Moore's, but the smallest size available is 0.8mm and this generally produces too thick a line.

Whatever pen you choose to use, the requirement is very simply that will produce a nice even line of about 0.5mm width as you draw it along the paint work.

Having acquired a pen that will do the job, the second essential requirement is suitable paint. The lining pen instructions call for enamel paint with a couple of drops of lighter fluid added to help it flow. This of course works after some practice and experimentation. One of the biggest problems when using enamel paint however is that if you are lining onto a job which has been painted with enamel, then you will be lining along the masked edge of the second coat of paint. I have found that this edge takes a long time to dry, even up to a couple of weeks or more, so that as the lining is applied it crinkles if the paint underneath has not fully cured. (This doesn't happen of course if you are just doing a simple line over a single colour.) Also, when using enamel paint, if you make a slip or mistake it can be difficult to wipe off or otherwise correct.

Whilst enamel paint is probably the most durable paint to use for lining, it presents some difficulties, so it is worth looking at alternatives. There are many different types of water based acrylic paints and inks available from art suppliers. Provided they are of good quality and therefore contain plenty of fine pigment, they can be used in our lining pen, thinned down if necessary. The two types I have used are "FW Acrylic Artists Ink" which is purchased in a small bottle and can be used without thinning, and "Jo Sonja's Artists' Colours" which come in a tube, are paste consistency and need thinning with a compatible flow medium. Experiment until you have a fluid which flows easily from the pen but is not so thin that it doesn't contain enough pigment to cover properly. If the paint has difficulty "starting" to flow then wet the end of your finger and gently wipe the tip onto it. This should start the pen flowing. A big advantage of using the water based paint is that if you make a mistake, it can be immediately and easily wiped off with a damp rag. Also the problem of the paint crinkling over the top of the previously applied paint is eliminated. It is of course essential to apply a clear sealing coat over these materials.

Finally, even if the above two items are in order, we can't hope to create a neat line without a definite guide to follow. Free-hand along a hand held ruler or similar just won't work. We have to make a template of the shape we want to draw out of rigid plastic sheet, about 0.010" – 0.015" (0.3 - 0.4mm) thick. If you have already done a CAD drawing of the panels, then this is perfect to reproduce again and print onto the plastic sheet, otherwise draw the same shapes by hand. These are then cut out very carefully, particularly around corners and held in position on the job using blobs of blue tack. This is ideal as it holds the plastic away slightly from the surface. You then have a template around which you can draw the pen. (**Photo 5.7**) Try to complete as much as possible in one smooth action without lifting the pen. Stops will be necessary but a little practice beforehand should help you to do a good job. After completing the lines, carefully remove the plastic sheet and again put aside to dry. The water based paint will be dry very quickly, but if you have used enamel paints they will need several days before the next step. (More fishing or jobs around the house.) (**Photo 5.8**)

5.7 — *Applying the lining*

5.8 — *Lining completed*

Transfers (decals) and finishing

Transfers or decals can now be applied. There are two types: water slide and dry rub. Various crests and numbers are available in both types and they should be applied according to the suppliers instructions, but be particularly careful when applying any finishing varnish. Generally a water based varnish is the safest to use, but follow instructions and practice on a test piece.

The final operation is to apply a coating of clear over the whole painted surface. (Other than the satin black areas.) Depending on which brand of clear used, you can finish with a matt, satin or gloss. I have usually finished with gloss and good results were obtained with Dulux clear enamel. It cannot be overstressed that you should have one of your practice pieces to use as a trial before doing this. Just imagine a beautifully lined and finished paint job doing a massive crinkle up in front of your eyes!

Nameplates

A finishing touch is to apply nameplates. The name of the locomotive, if it is to have one, and the builder's plate on the side of the cab crisply etched in brass sets the model off nicely.

NAMEPLATES (Twice Full Size)

Many articles have been written about etching brass for nameplates, so we will give only a brief description here.

Starting with a cleaned and polished piece of flat brass slightly bigger than required and about 0.6mm thick, the design of letters, numbers and border is put onto the surface in the form of an acid resist. There are two main ways of doing this, both using materials which are obtainable from electronics suppliers and which have been developed for making printed circuit boards. For both systems, the pattern has to first be produced using drawing or lettering software on a computer.

ARTWORK FOR NAMEPLATES

Method 1: This method uses a photosensitive coating, purchased in spray cans. Following the instructions provided with the material, spray onto the brass plate and allow to dry. Having printed the artwork onto clear film, place it over the brass and expose to sunlight or UV light for the specified time. The brass is now placed in a developing solution for a given time when the image will be seen to appear. It is now ready for etching.

Method 2: An iron-on process is used for the second method. Sheets of paper which have been coated with a blue coloured heat sensitive material have the design printed onto them. The design has to be reversed (see examples above) and is printed using a photocopier or laser printer. Again, instructions are provided, but this printing process is critical to the success of the operation. Experimentation with printers will be necessary to find one which produces a print which stands up to the next process of ironing. Place the printed image onto the brass, cover with paper and iron the image onto the brass. Again follow the instructions and be prepared to experiment. After this process is successfully completed, we have the brass ready for etching.

Etching is the same for both methods and involves immersing the brass into a bath of etchant, usually ferric chloride, being sure to follow all safety instructions. The piece needs to be agitated and should be lightly brushed with a paint brush to remove the bubbles which form. Etch as deeply as possible, stopping when the etch is starting to eat under the edges of the letters.

Remove the piece, rinse and dry thoroughly then give a very light coat of etch primer. After this is dry, spray with the background fill colour, usually red, black or green. Let this dry completely then lightly rub the surface face down onto 800 – 1000 grit wet or dry paper which is held face up on a flat surface. The paint should rub off the highlights and leave the fill colour in the recesses. Brush the plaque lightly to clean it and leave to dry again as the edges of the paint will have been disturbed. After a couple of days it can be sprayed with a clear coating.

To mount the plates, make the back surface rough by scratching with the end of a file or similar and also roughen up the area of paint work on the locomotive where the plate is to go. This means scratching right through your beautiful paint job, so make certain it is in the right spot! Apply the plates using 5 minute epoxy very sparingly.

Dummy mounting rivets or screws can be added by drilling and inserting them in the ends of the plate before mounting. They can be glued in with epoxy also. (**Photos 5.9 & 5.10**)

5.9 — Nameplate

5.10 — Works plate

Part 2

OTHER VARIATIONS, DETAILS AND PROTOTYPES

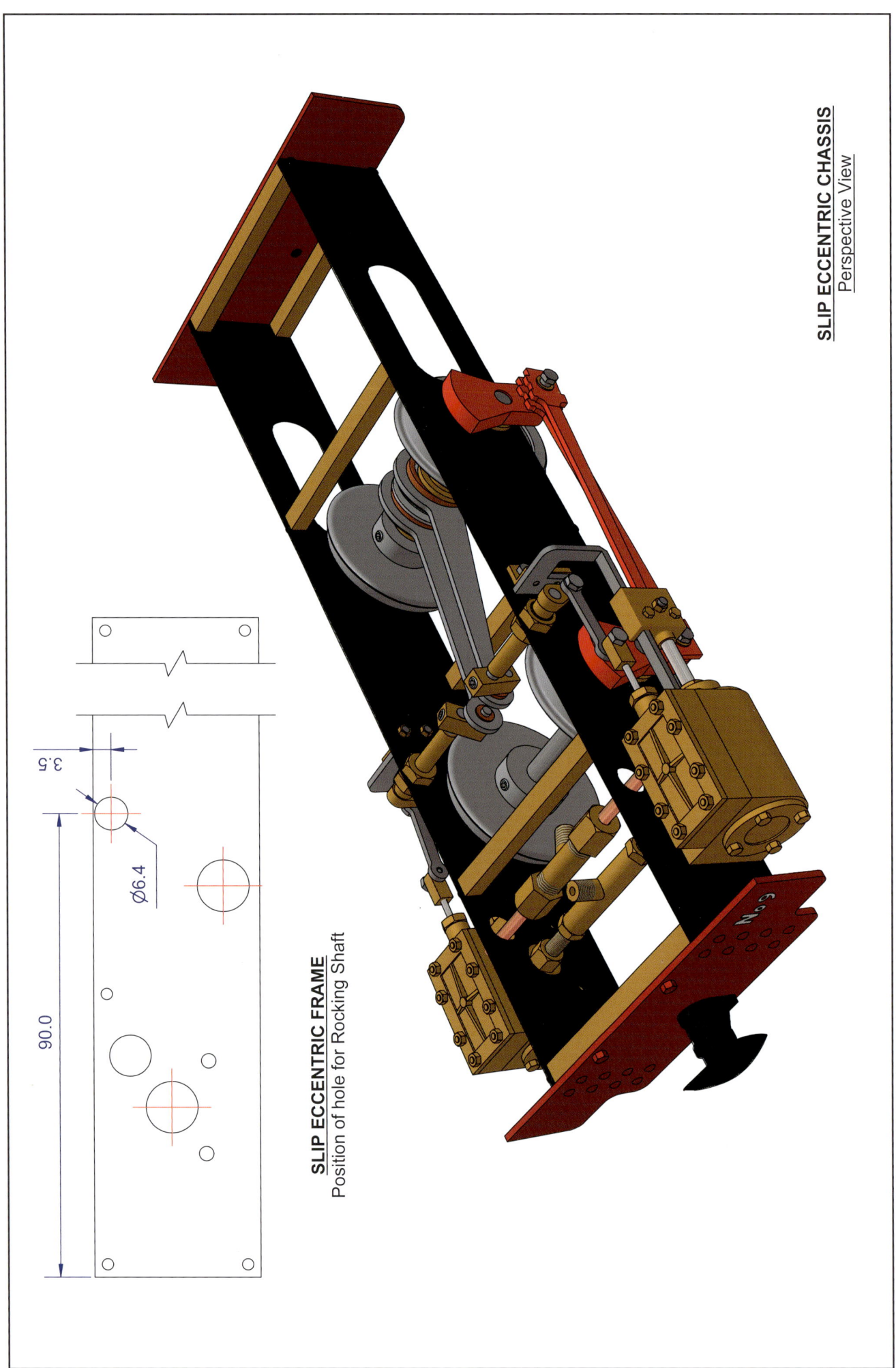

SLIP ECCENTRIC FRAME
Position of hole for Rocking Shaft

Ø6.4

3.5

90.0

SLIP ECCENTRIC CHASSIS
Perspective View

CHAPTER 6 – Slip Eccentric Chassis

Many prototypes had inside valve gear, often Stephenson's, mounted between the frames. The valve chests were either bolted onto the inside of the cylinders with the valves driven directly from the eccentrics, or sometimes they had the valve chests placed on top of the cylinders with the valves driven by rocking arms.

It is outside the scope of this book to describe inside Stephenson's Valve gear, but we will describe a simple slip eccentric valve gear which has the eccentrics between the frames and could be used to model a prototype which originally had an inside valve gear.

Also, some people may not want to tackle the many fiddly components included in Walschaerts valve gear and the slip eccentric offers a less complicated alternative.

Most of the components used in building "*Eric*" can be used, so we will describe the alternative parts and any variations necessary.

The rolling chassis

The rolling chassis is the same, except it is necessary to fit the eccentrics and rods onto the rear axle before fixing the cranks. Also there is a ¼" (6.4mm) hole drilled in the frames for the rocking shaft bearings. You can make all of the components for the chassis, but don't do the final assembly until after the valve gear is made.

Cylinders and valve chests

The cylinders are the same, and the outside shape of the valve chests is the same, but the chests are "turned over" so that the valve centreline is brought closer to the frame. This means that the steam inlet hole is drilled on the side nearest to the valve. The valve crosshead is different and it is necessary to make a pair of valve connecting rods from 1.6mm mild steel.

Motion bracket and crosshead

The motion bracket has a simpler outline and the crosshead is simpler in that it doesn't have the drop arm for the combination lever.

Eccentrics

Grip a piece of mild steel of around 20mm diameter in the 3-jaw chuck and turn to 16mm diameter for 5mm. Part off or hacksaw off, reverse in the chuck and clean up the back, gripping in the three-jaw so that the centre position will be shown. Mark a centreline on each and centre punch 2.0mm from the centre. (This gives a valve movement of 4mm.) You could mark out to slightly more than 2.0mm to allow for fitting losses and future wear. Also centre punch a mark 5mm from the centre opposite the first mark to locate the ³⁄₃₂" hole for the slip pin. Mount the eccentric with back facing out and the shoulder hard on the jaws of the four-jaw chuck and set it up so that the 2.0mm centre punch mark is running true. Drill and ream ¼" to be a sliding fit on the axle. Grip in the machine vice and drill the ³⁄₃₂" hole into which a ³⁄₃₂" pin is fixed with Loctite™.

Eccentric straps

These can be made in various ways, and could be made with split main bearings so that they can be added after the frames are assembled and therefore removed if required, but we will make them simply from flat mild steel with bronze bushes which can be inserted with Loctite. Make them the same way the rods are made in that the holes are made first before shaping the outside. When fastening the large bushes, make sure they are square in the holes and don't forget they must be assembled onto the eccentrics and axles before fixing the frames together.

Slip collars

These can be made from brass or mild steel, but brass would be easier to machine. Turn to the sizes shown and ream ¼". Mark out and remove the cutaway to produce the shoulder as accurately as possible. Either a hacksaw and file may be used, or the collars can be set up in the milling machine. The eccentric is set to an angle of advance of 90 degrees plus the lap, to the main crank pin, and this is how we arrive at the position for the shoulder.

We are at the stage where the frames could be permanently assembled together, but it is probably better to complete all of the parts of the valve gear and have a "dry run" assembly to make sure that everything fits properly. It is not very pleasant tapping pins out and disassembling Loctite joints!

Rocking shaft

This is simply a shaft with an arm at either end which transfers the motion from the eccentric straps to the

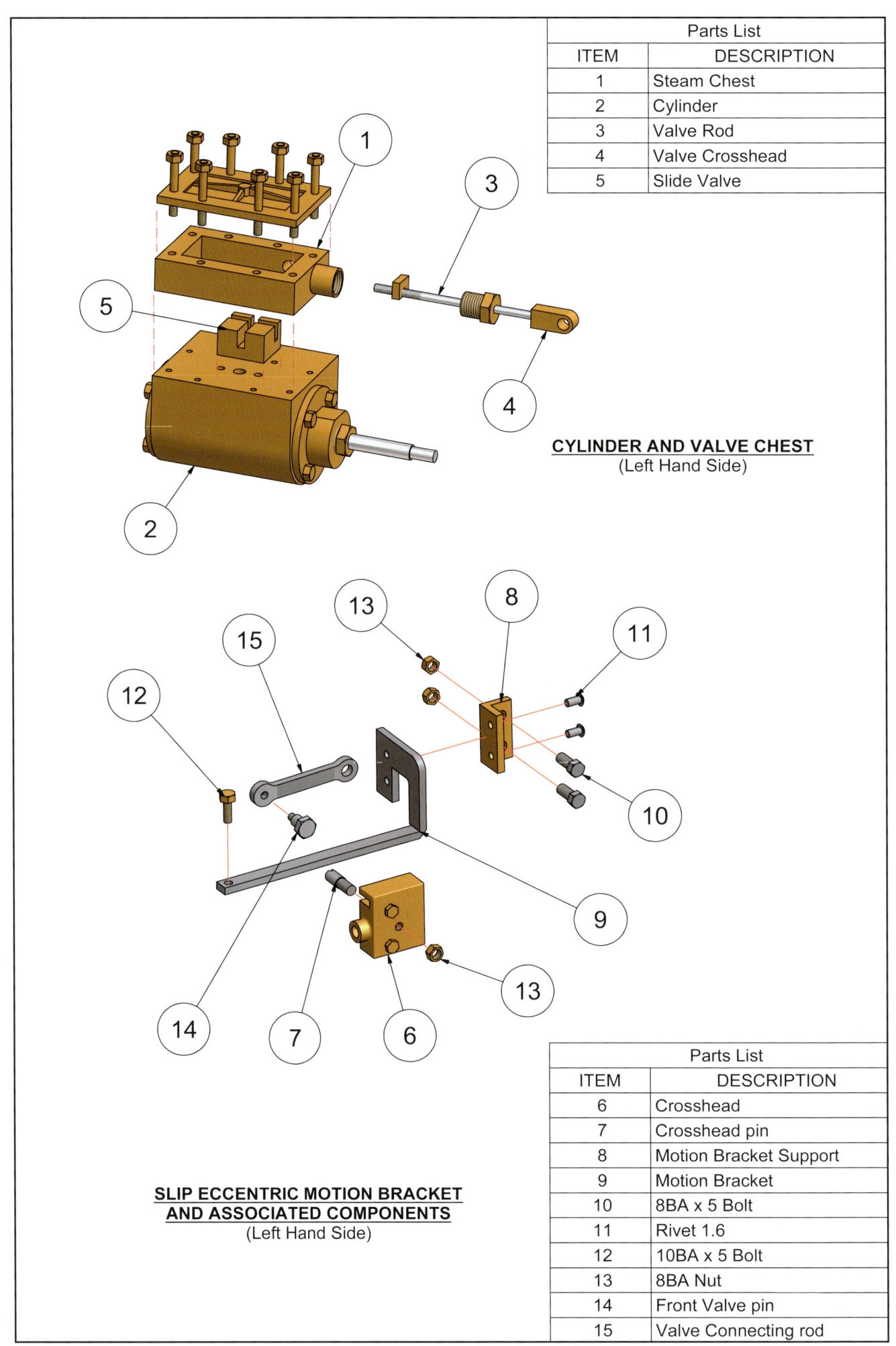

Parts List	
ITEM	DESCRIPTION
1	Steam Chest
2	Cylinder
3	Valve Rod
4	Valve Crosshead
5	Slide Valve

CYLINDER AND VALVE CHEST
(Left Hand Side)

SLIP ECCENTRIC MOTION BRACKET
AND ASSOCIATED COMPONENTS
(Left Hand Side)

Parts List	
ITEM	DESCRIPTION
6	Crosshead
7	Crosshead pin
8	Motion Bracket Support
9	Motion Bracket
10	8BA x 5 Bolt
11	Rivet 1.6
12	10BA x 5 Bolt
13	8BA Nut
14	Front Valve pin
15	Valve Connecting rod

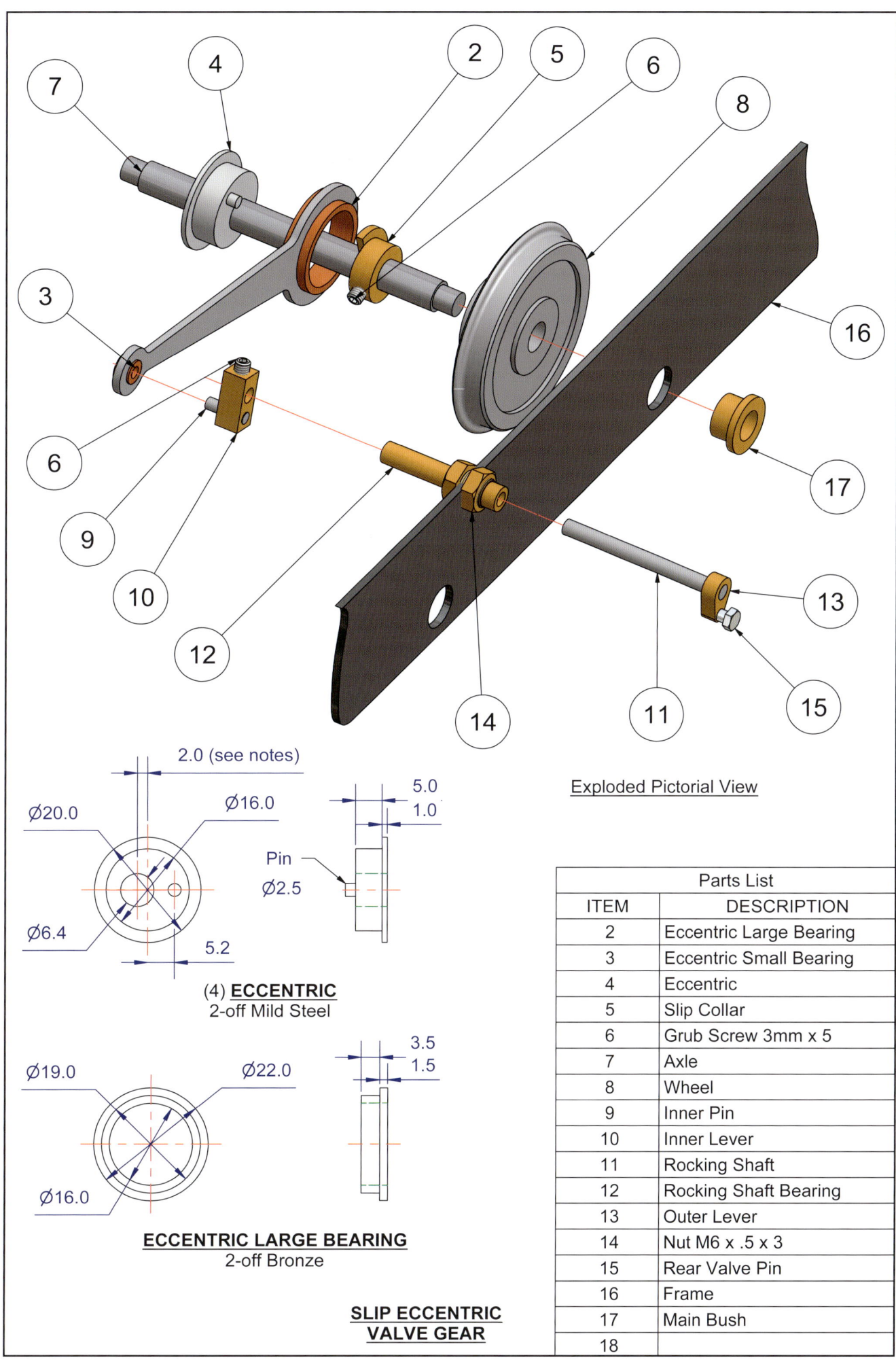

Exploded Pictorial View

(4) ECCENTRIC
2-off Mild Steel

2.0 (see notes)
Ø20.0
Ø16.0
Ø6.4
5.2
5.0
1.0
Pin
Ø2.5

ECCENTRIC LARGE BEARING
2-off Bronze

Ø19.0
Ø22.0
Ø16.0
3.5
1.5

**SLIP ECCENTRIC
VALVE GEAR**

Parts List	
ITEM	DESCRIPTION
2	Eccentric Large Bearing
3	Eccentric Small Bearing
4	Eccentric
5	Slip Collar
6	Grub Screw 3mm x 5
7	Axle
8	Wheel
9	Inner Pin
10	Inner Lever
11	Rocking Shaft
12	Rocking Shaft Bearing
13	Outer Lever
14	Nut M6 x .5 x 3
15	Rear Valve Pin
16	Frame
17	Main Bush
18	

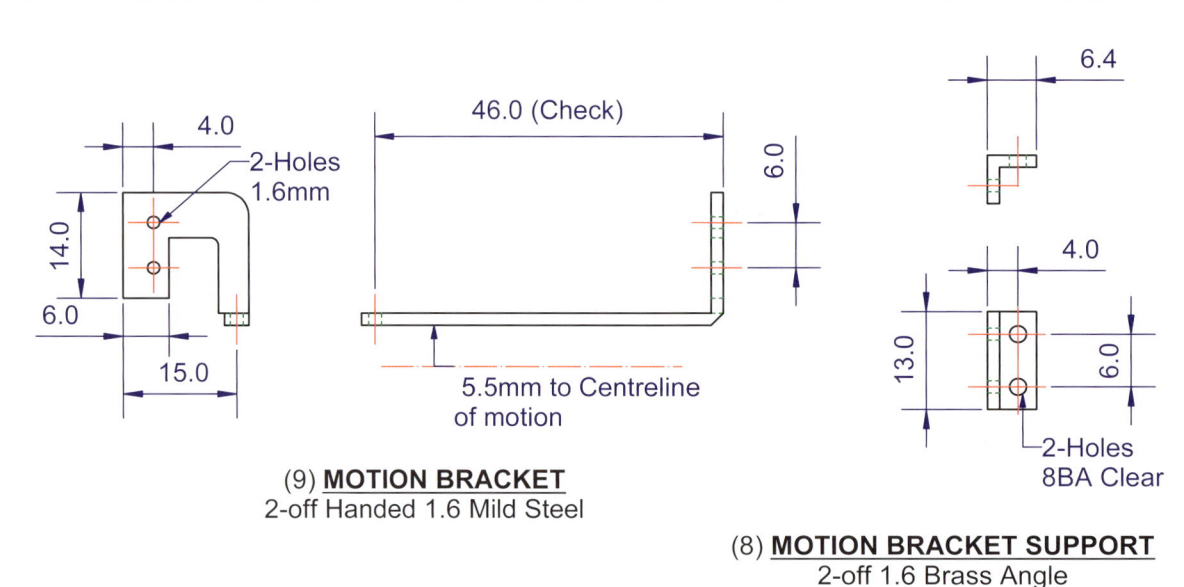

2-Holes 1.6mm

4.0

14.0

6.0

15.0

46.0 (Check)

6.0

5.5mm to Centreline of motion

(9) **MOTION BRACKET**
2-off Handed 1.6 Mild Steel

6.4

4.0

13.0

6.0

2-Holes 8BA Clear

(8) **MOTION BRACKET SUPPORT**
2-off 1.6 Brass Angle

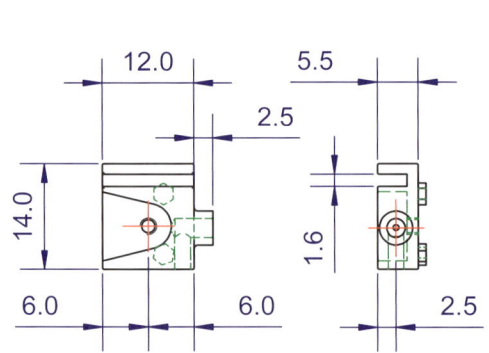

12.0

2.5

14.0

6.0   6.0

5.5

1.6

2.5

Pictorial View

(6) **CROSSHEAD**
2-off Handed Brass

1.0 (Approx)

R2.5

10BA

Ø2.5

R2.5

20.2

(15) **VALVE CONNECTING ROD**
2-off 1.6 Mild Steel

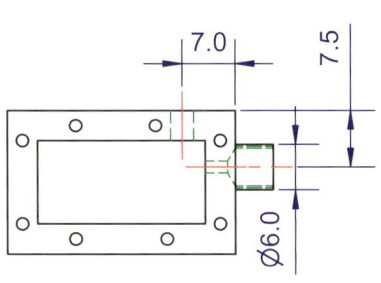

7.0

7.5

Ø6.0

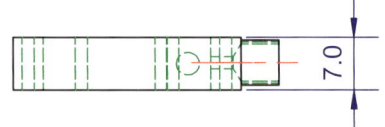

7.0

(1) **STEAM CHEST**
2-off Brass

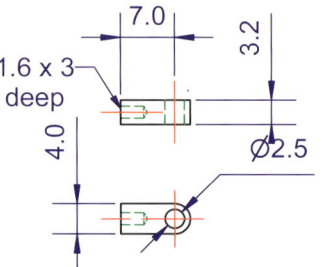

7.0

3.2

1.6 x 3 deep

4.0

Ø2.5

(4) **VALVE CROSSHEAD**
2-off Brass

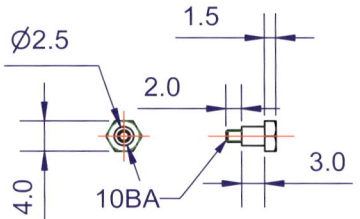

Ø2.5

1.5

2.0

4.0

10BA

3.0

(14) **FRONT VALVE PIN**
2-off Mild Steel

SLIP ECCENTRIC COMPONENTS

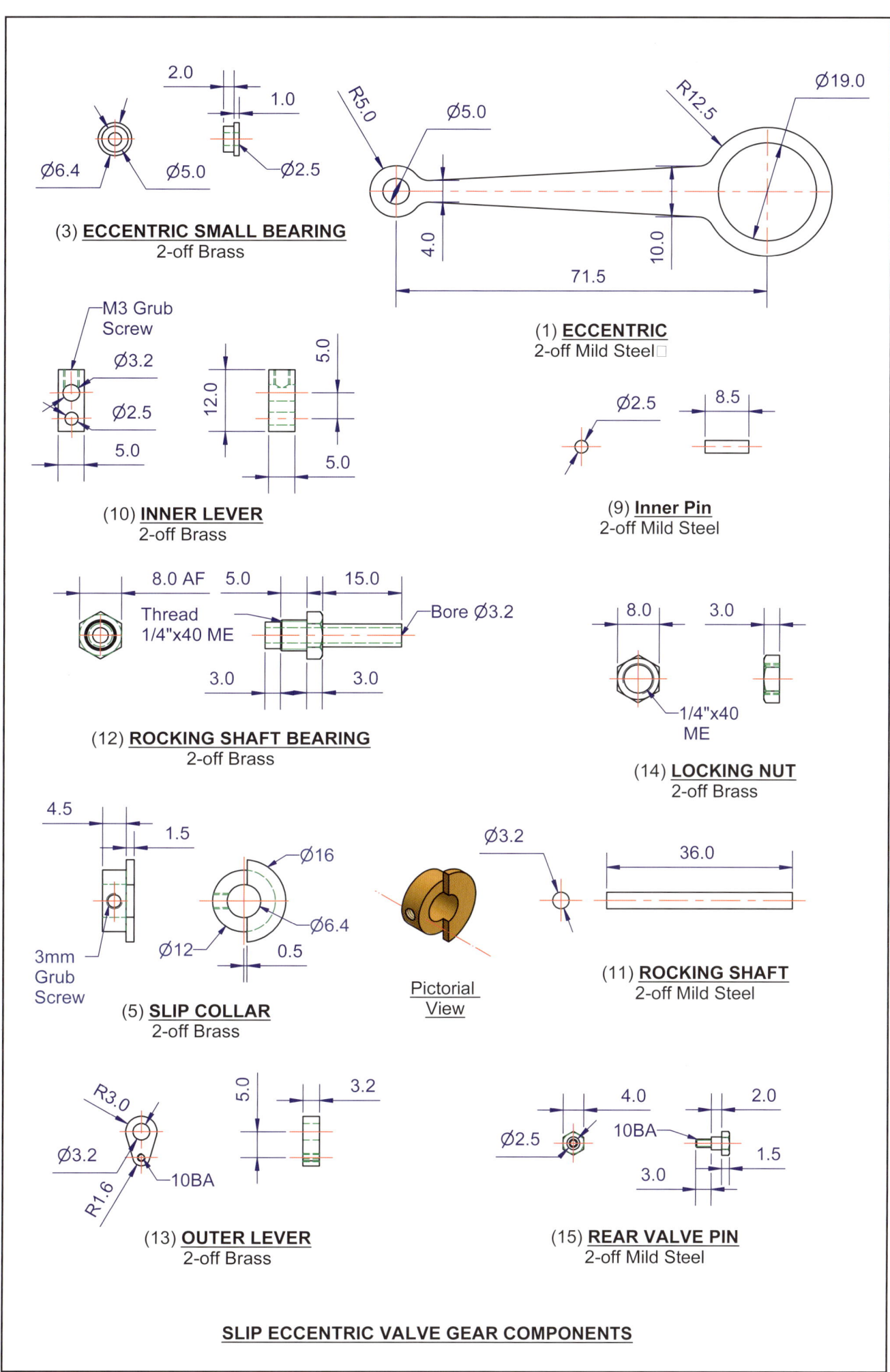

2.0

1.0

Ø6.4   Ø5.0   Ø2.5

(3) ECCENTRIC SMALL BEARING
2-off Brass

R5.0   Ø5.0   R12.5   Ø19.0

4.0   10.0

71.5

(1) ECCENTRIC
2-off Mild Steel

M3 Grub
Screw

Ø3.2
Ø2.5
5.0

5.0
12.0
5.0

(10) INNER LEVER
2-off Brass

Ø2.5   8.5

(9) Inner Pin
2-off Mild Steel

8.0 AF   5.0   15.0

Thread
1/4"x40 ME   Bore Ø3.2

3.0   3.0

(12) ROCKING SHAFT BEARING
2-off Brass

8.0   3.0

1/4"x40
ME

(14) LOCKING NUT
2-off Brass

4.5   1.5   Ø16

12.0   Ø6.4
Ø12   0.5

3mm
Grub
Screw

(5) SLIP COLLAR
2-off Brass

Pictorial
View

Ø3.2

36.0

(11) ROCKING SHAFT
2-off Mild Steel

R3.0
Ø3.2
R1.6   10BA

5.0   3.2

(13) OUTER LEVER
2-off Brass

4.0   2.0

Ø2.5   10BA

1.5

3.0

(15) REAR VALVE PIN
2-off Mild Steel

SLIP ECCENTRIC VALVE GEAR COMPONENTS

valve rods. One of the arms is made adjustable to help with fine tuning the valve setting.

Prepare the shafts by cutting two pieces of 1/8" diameter mild steel to 36mm and facing the ends. The outer levers can be made from brass by marking both out on a piece of ⅛" thick brass. Drill and tap all the holes before cutting out. (**Photo 6.1**). Make the inner levers from ³⁄₁₆" square brass, drilling the two holes in each at the same setting to ensure they are parallel. The ³⁄₃₂" pin can be silver soldered or held in place with Loctite. Drill and tap for the 3mm grub screw in the end.

The shaft is inserted 2mm into the outer lever and silver soldered. This leaves a 1mm recess into which the solder can flow.

Rocking shaft bearings

Mount a piece of 8mm brass hexagon in the 3-jaw chuck and turn to 4.5mm for 17mm. Part off to 28mm, repeat for the other part. Reverse in the chuck and turn ¼" for 8mm. Thread ¼" x 40 ME and relieve the thread from the first 3mm to 4.5mm diameter. Turn a nut 3mm thick from the same material. These fit into the ¼" holes in the frames. (**Photo 6.2**)

6.1 — Tapping outer levers

6.2 — Rocking shaft bearings

The chassis can now be finally assembled before setting the valves and testing on air.

Setting the valve timing

To set the valves, leave the steam chest covers off so that the valve movement can be seen, holding the chests onto the cylinders with a couple of temporary screws. Set one side at a time, and in the forward direction.

There are three places where adjustments need to be made. Firstly where the valve spindle screws into the valve nut; secondly the inner arms of the rocking levers on the shaft, and finally the slip collars on the axles.

Firstly, with the outer lever of the rocking shaft in a vertical position (as close as possible, by eye) adjust the spindle in the valve nut so that the valve is centrally placed over the ports. Next set the inner rocking arm lever perpendicular to the axis line from the rocking lever to the main axle and nip up the grub screw. (Again, do this as close as possible by eye.) Doing the right hand side first, turn the wheels until the piston is at the rear of its stroke, that is with the crank to the rear. When the crank is at this point the aim is to have the pin of the eccentric hard up against the slip collar and the valve just cracking open the rear steam port. Rotate the slip collar until this happens and nip up the grub screw. Now, turning the wheels in the forward direction, the valve movement should be about 4mm and at each end of the piston stroke, the valve should be cracking open the steam port. Repeat for the other side and if all has gone as it should, the valves should operate for either forward or reverse. Make any adjustments as needed.

The steam chest covers can now be fitted and the chassis set up for testing on air.

CHAPTER 7 – Other Details

Prototypes which have inside valve gear were briefly mentioned when discussing slip eccentric valve gear in the previous chapter, and now we will look at some distinctive features and details which other styles of locomotive may have so that with this information and an understanding of the techniques described to build "Eric" in the first part of the book, you should be able to construct a model of almost any type of narrow gauge prototype.

Crosshead and guide bars

The John Fowler locomotives on which *Eric* is based usually had a single guide bar to provide support for the crosshead and this guide bar was fixed from the rear of the cylinder to the motion bracket. Other makes of locomotive, notably Hunslet and Peckett had two guide bars, one above and one below the crosshead. This was the case irrespective of whether the locomotive had inside or outside valve gear.

Shown are two different styles for double guide bars and crosshead, one for use when Walschaerts valve gear is used and one for inside, or in our case slip eccentric valve gear. The guide bars themselves are simply 1.6mm mild steel, 3.2mm wide and are fastened onto the rear cylinder cover with a 10BA bolt in the same way as described for *Eric*. A second flat will have to be machined on the bottom of the cover exactly opposite the top one, again 5.5mm from the centreline.

Because of the small size, it would be very difficult to provide a bolted fastening for the back of the guide bars onto the motion bracket, so because the forces on them are very small on our size of locomotive, the back end can be left to float in the small recess in the guide bar. A dab of epoxy or super glue could be used but it would be unlikely to last.

Different wheel arrangements

Another significant variation with prototypes is the wheel arrangement. Generally a locomotive is either 4-coupled (4 driving wheels) or 6-coupled (6 driving wheels). Additionally it may have a leading or trailing bogie or pony truck. We will describe a 6-coupled chassis and a trailing pony truck.

The trailing pony truck can have either inside bearings or outside bearings and drawings are provided for both styles. The bearing styles varied with different makers and the ones shown here are styled after the trailing pony on a Bundaberg Fowler. (**Photo 7.1**) The bearing is made up from brass and drilled to provide the bearing for the wheel set. The wheel sets can be purchased at a reasonable price or made up to the dimensions shown.

7.1 — Trailing pony with outside bearing

The bogie frame is made from 1.6mm mild steel and in the case of the outside bearing unit, is bolted through onto the bottom of the bearing and for the inside bearing unit the hexagon is silver soldered to the frame. A support post is screwed into the frame and is adjusted so that it just contacts the bottom of the footplate.

For a coal fired boiler (to be discussed later), it is necessary to provide clearance for the ash pan, so an alternative design is given for this.

A suggested design for a 6-coupled engine is given. The essential difference is in the wheel spacing and therefore the rod sizes. The valve gear remains the same except for the eccentric rod.

Saddle tanks

Many narrow gauge locomotives carried their water in saddle tanks and these are not too difficult to build. Ours doesn't have to carry water, so construction is considerably simplified.

Mark out and cut two identical ends from 1.6mm thick brass. Cut two lengths of brass tubing which are silver soldered into position on the outside curves. Cut an extra piece of tubing or solid rod to the same length to support the ends while soldering. (**Photo 7.2**)

7.2 — Framework for saddle tank (the middle tube is a temporary support).

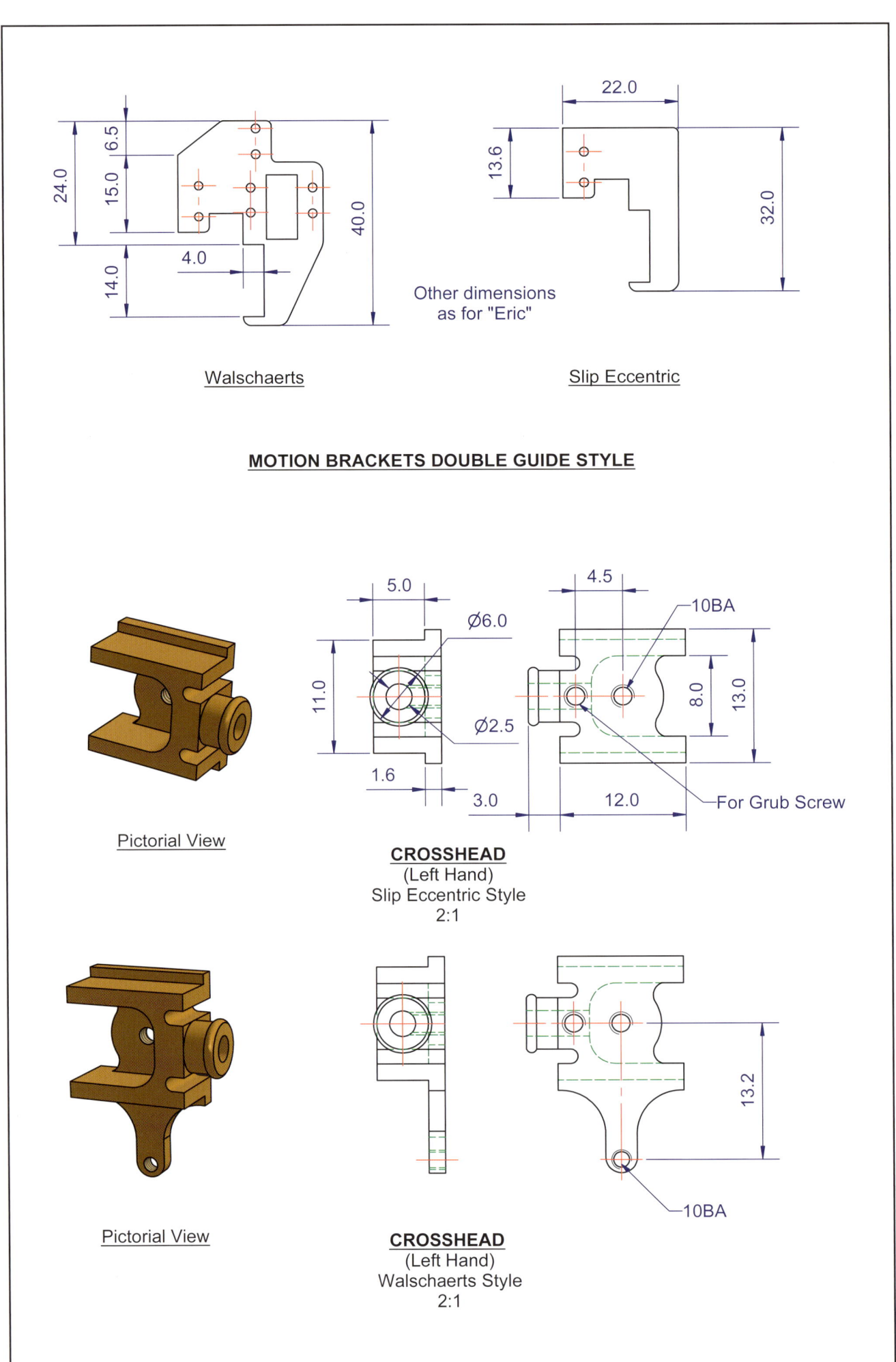

Walschaerts

Slip Eccentric

Other dimensions
as for "Eric"

MOTION BRACKETS DOUBLE GUIDE STYLE

Pictorial View

Ø6.0

Ø2.5

10BA

For Grub Screw

CROSSHEAD
(Left Hand)
Slip Eccentric Style
2:1

Pictorial View

10BA

CROSSHEAD
(Left Hand)
Walschaerts Style
2:1

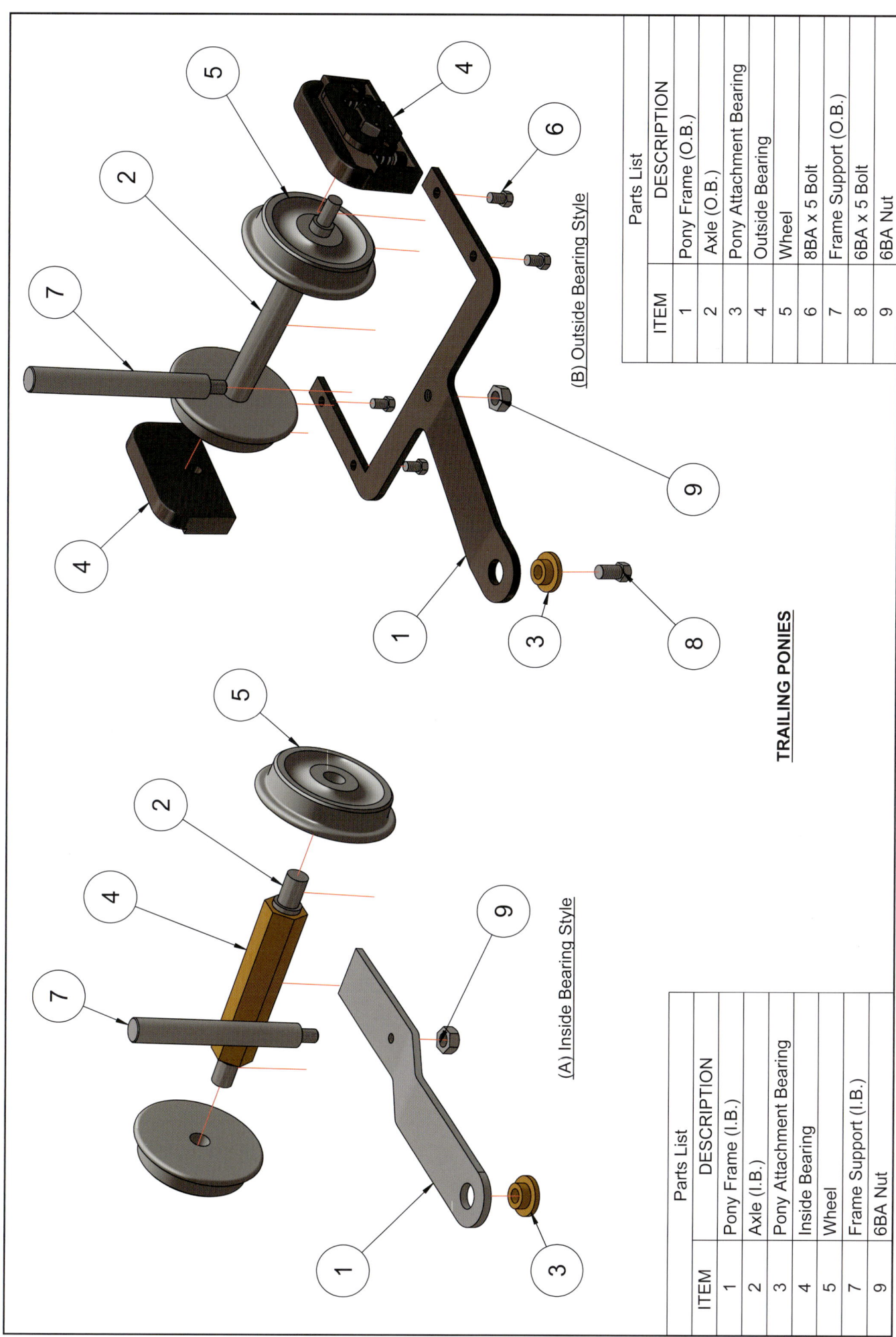

(A) Inside Bearing Style

Parts List

ITEM	DESCRIPTION
1	Pony Frame (I.B.)
2	Axle (I.B.)
3	Pony Attachment Bearing
4	Inside Bearing
5	Wheel
7	Frame Support (I.B.)
9	6BA Nut

(B) Outside Bearing Style

Parts List

ITEM	DESCRIPTION
1	Pony Frame (O.B.)
2	Axle (O.B.)
3	Pony Attachment Bearing
4	Outside Bearing
5	Wheel
6	8BA x 5 Bolt
7	Frame Support (O.B.)
8	6BA x 5 Bolt
9	6BA Nut

TRAILING PONIES

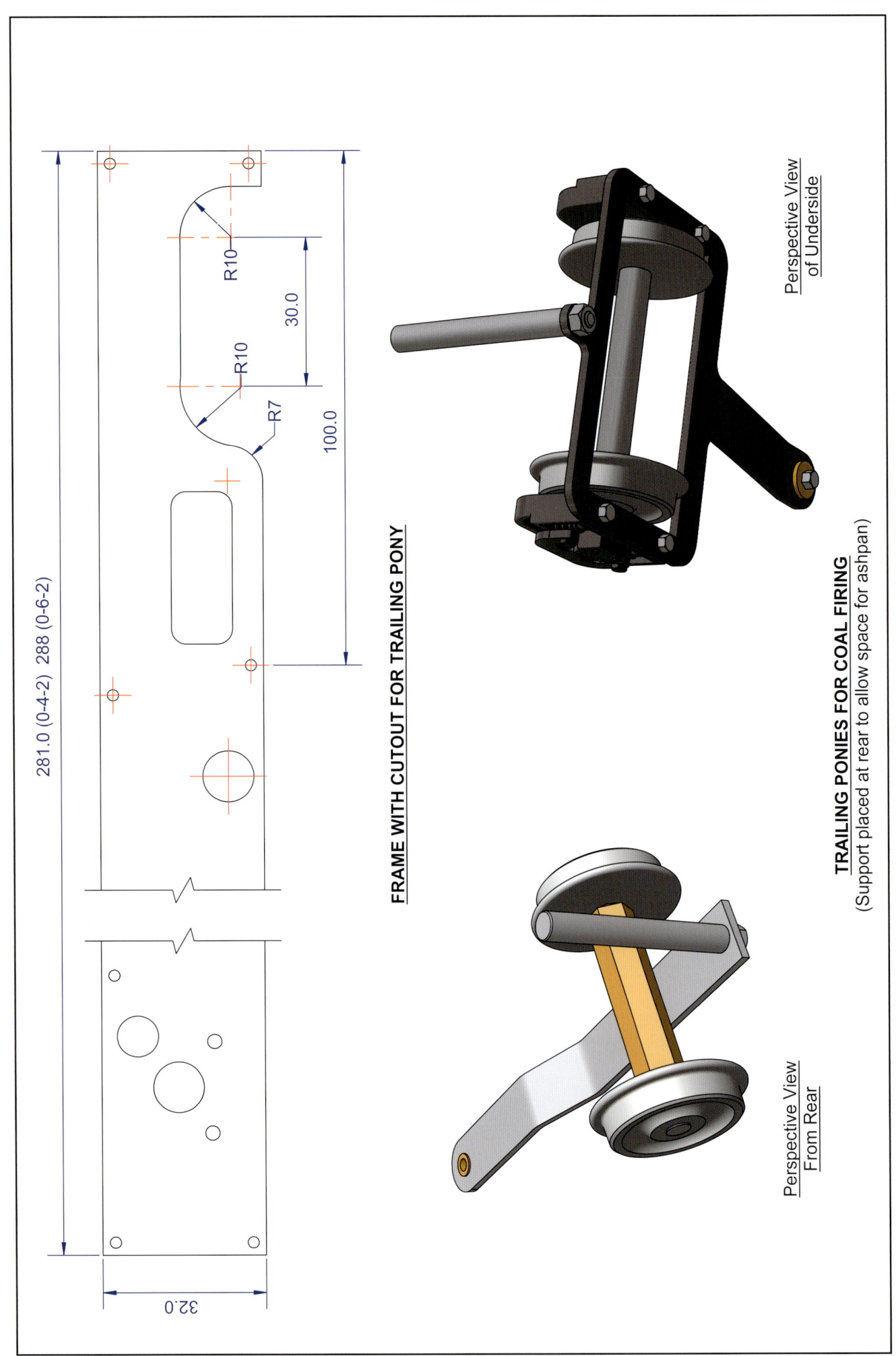

281.0 (0-4-2) 288 (0-6-2)

R10

R10

R7

30.0

100.0

FRAME WITH CUTOUT FOR TRAILING PONY

32.0

Perspective View
of Underside

TRAILING PONIES FOR COAL FIRING
(Support placed at rear to allow space for ashpan)

Perspective View
From Rear

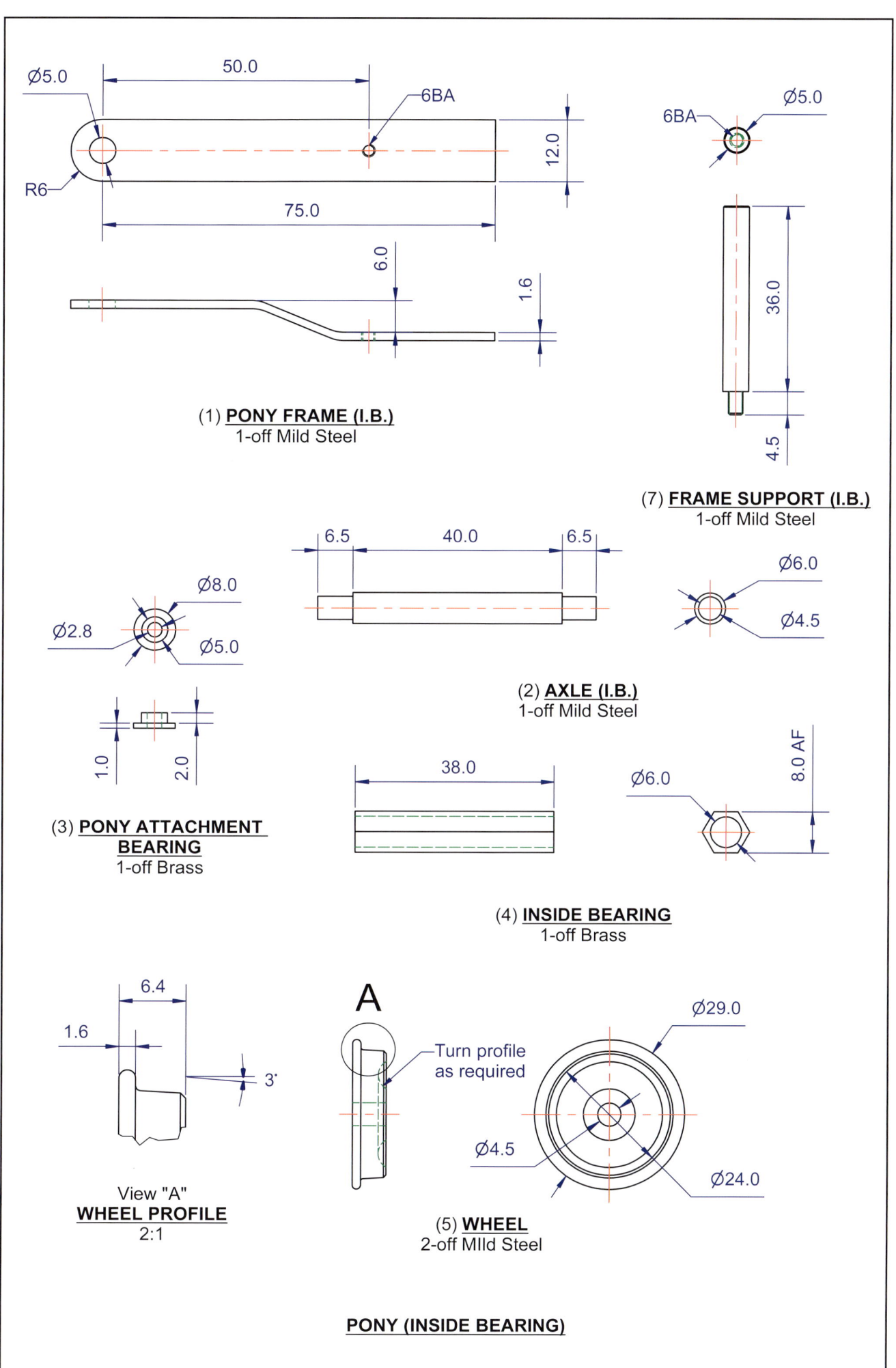

(1) **PONY FRAME (I.B.)**
1-off Mild Steel

(7) **FRAME SUPPORT (I.B.)**
1-off Mild Steel

(3) **PONY ATTACHMENT
BEARING**
1-off Brass

(2) **AXLE (I.B.)**
1-off Mild Steel

(4) **INSIDE BEARING**
1-off Brass

View "A"
WHEEL PROFILE
2:1

(5) **WHEEL**
2-off MIld Steel

PONY (INSIDE BEARING)

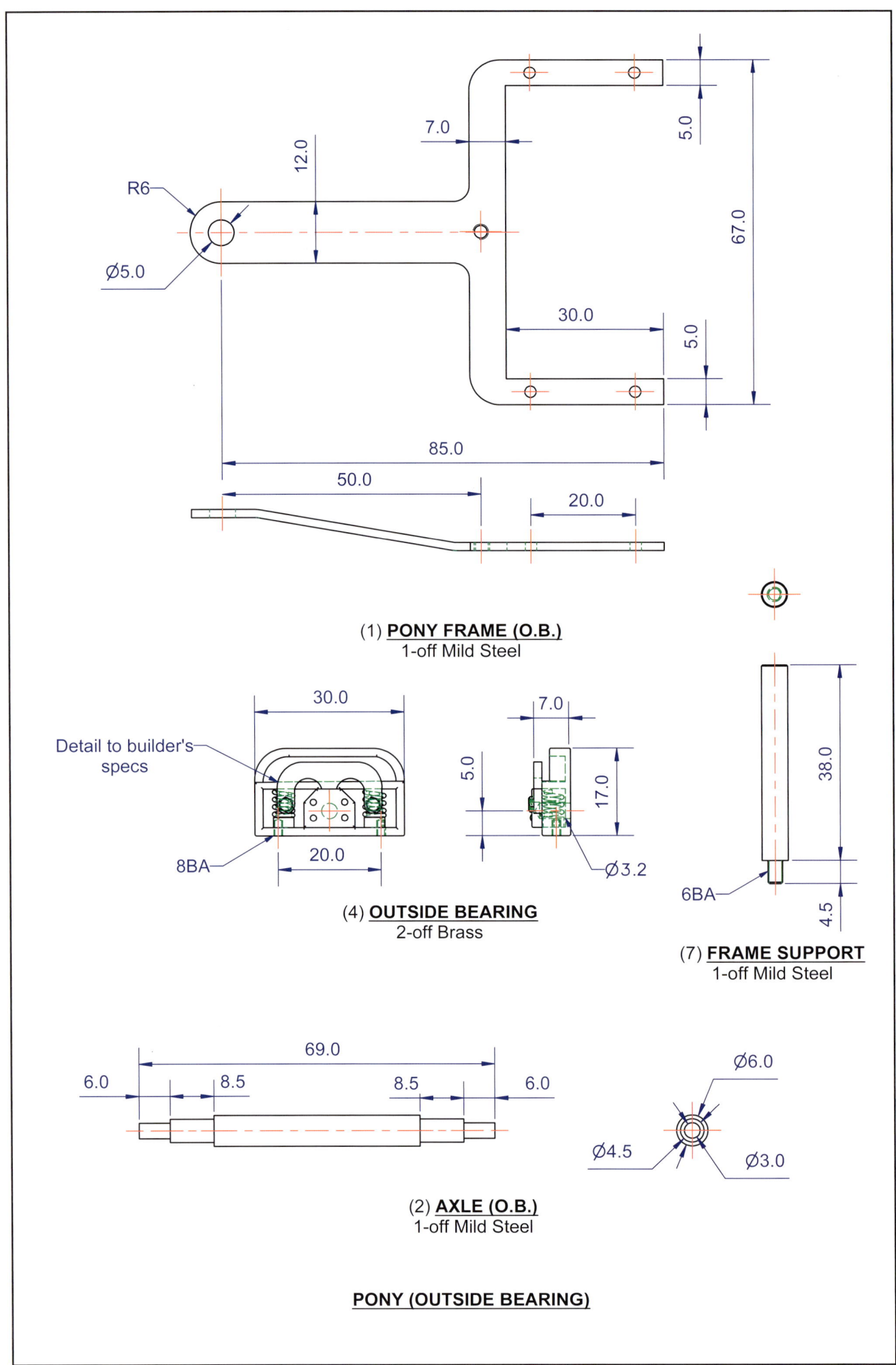

R6

Ø5.0

12.0

7.0

5.0

67.0

30.0

5.0

85.0

50.0

20.0

(1) **PONY FRAME (O.B.)**
1-off Mild Steel

30.0

Detail to builder's specs

7.0

5.0

17.0

8BA

20.0

Ø3.2

(4) **OUTSIDE BEARING**
2-off Brass

38.0

6BA

4.5

(7) **FRAME SUPPORT**
1-off Mild Steel

69.0

6.0

8.5

8.5

6.0

Ø6.0

Ø4.5

Ø3.0

(2) **AXLE (O.B.)**
1-off Mild Steel

PONY (OUTSIDE BEARING)

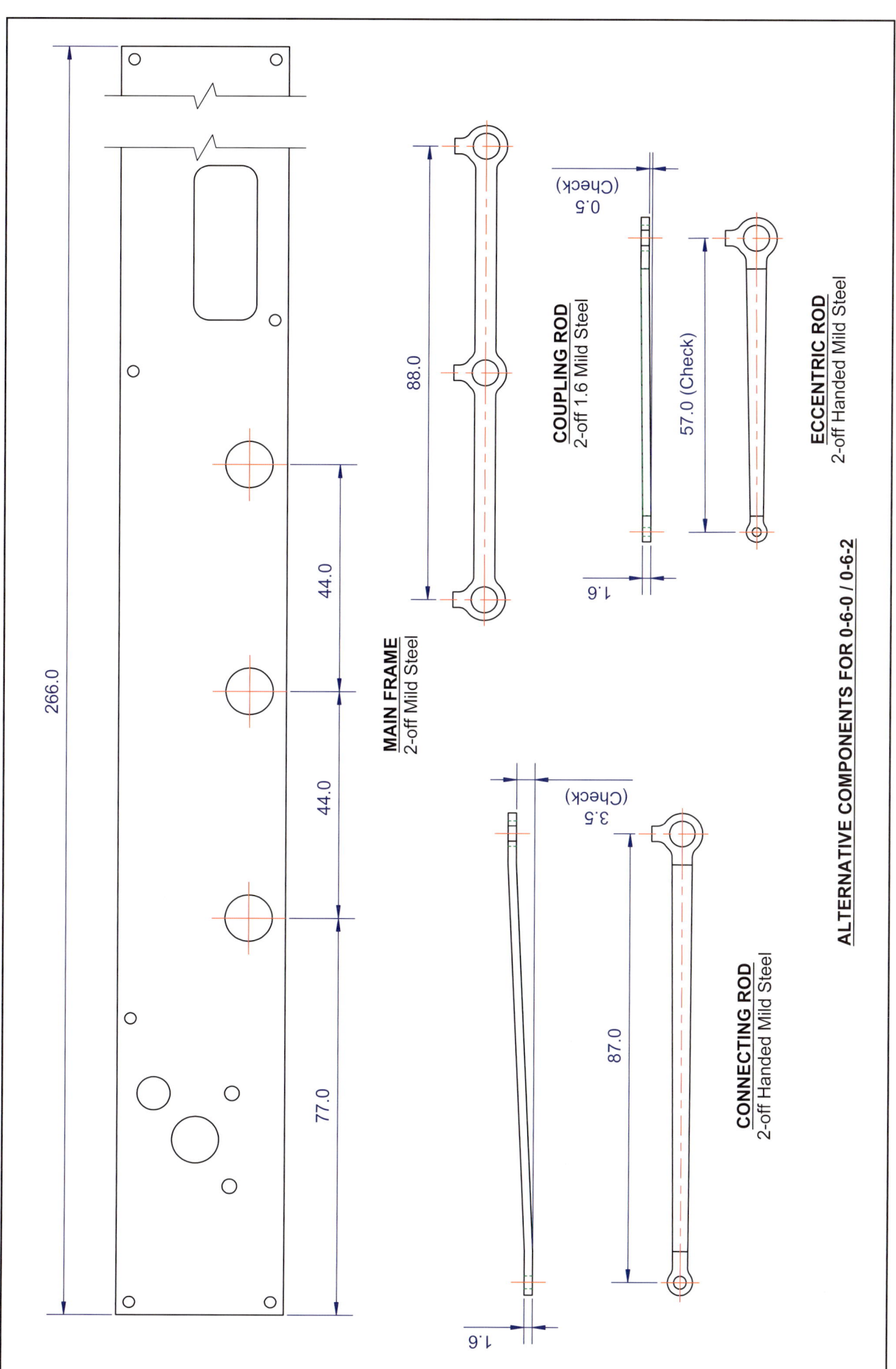

MAIN FRAME
2-off Mild Steel

266.0

44.0

44.0

77.0

88.0

COUPLING ROD
2-off 1.6 Mild Steel

0.5 (Check)

1.6

57.0 (Check)

ECCENTRIC ROD
2-off Handed Mild Steel

3.5 (Check)

87.0

1.6

CONNECTING ROD
2-off Handed Mild Steel

ALTERNATIVE COMPONENTS FOR 0-6-0 / 0-6-2

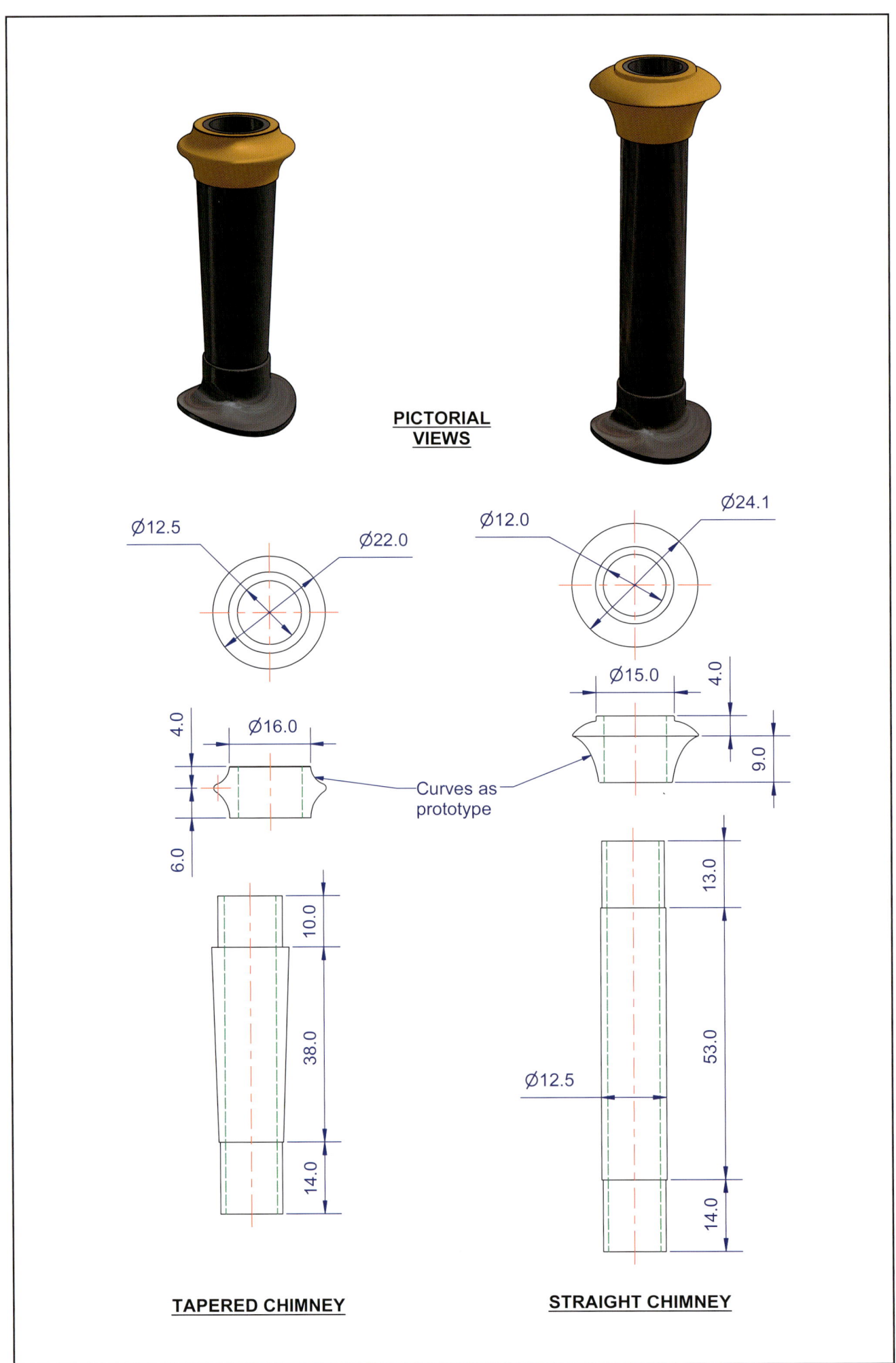

PICTORIAL VIEWS

Ø12.5 Ø22.0

Ø12.0 Ø24.1

4.0
Ø16.0
Curves as prototype

Ø15.0
4.0
9.0

6.0

10.0
13.0

38.0
53.0

Ø12.5

14.0
14.0

TAPERED CHIMNEY

STRAIGHT CHIMNEY

7.3 — Soldering the saddle tank

7.4 — Tubes for safety valve and filler valve viewed from underneath

Measure for the outer sheet, mark out and cut to size, punch for rivets and drill the holes for the safety and filler valves. Bend this around formers until it is a good fit over the tank framework. Using a combination of clamps and/or tape, secure the outer sheet firmly in position and soft solder it to the framework. It will be necessary to do this in stages, moving the clamps and applying new tape as necessary. Generally, tack in various places and then do final runs of solder in short lengths. (**Photos 7.3**)

7.5 — The finished tank in position

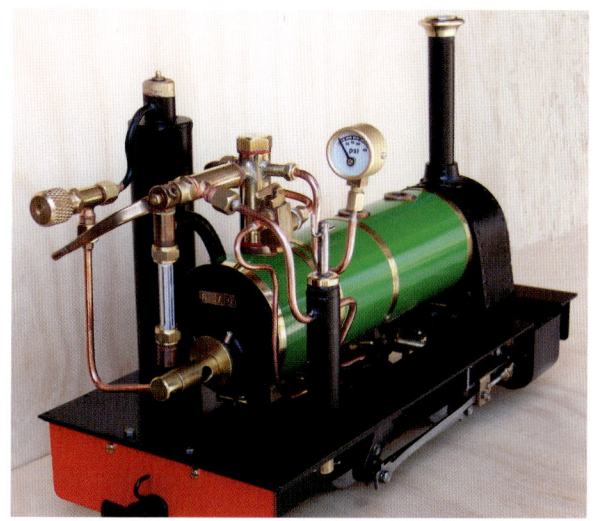

7.6 — The finished locomotive before saddle tank and cab are fitted

7.7 — The completed paint job

Cut two short brass tubes to length which will fit over the safety valve and the filler valve. (**Photo 7.4**) Soft solder these into position.

The tank is fixed into position on the locomotive by a bracket riveted onto the front of the tank and bolts passing through the spectacle plate. (**Photo 7.5**)

Photo 7.6 shows the finished and painted locomotive before fixing the cab and saddle tank and **Photo 7.7** the completed locomotive

Chimney

Chimneys are important to the look of a locomotive. In a full size engine, it is also an important part

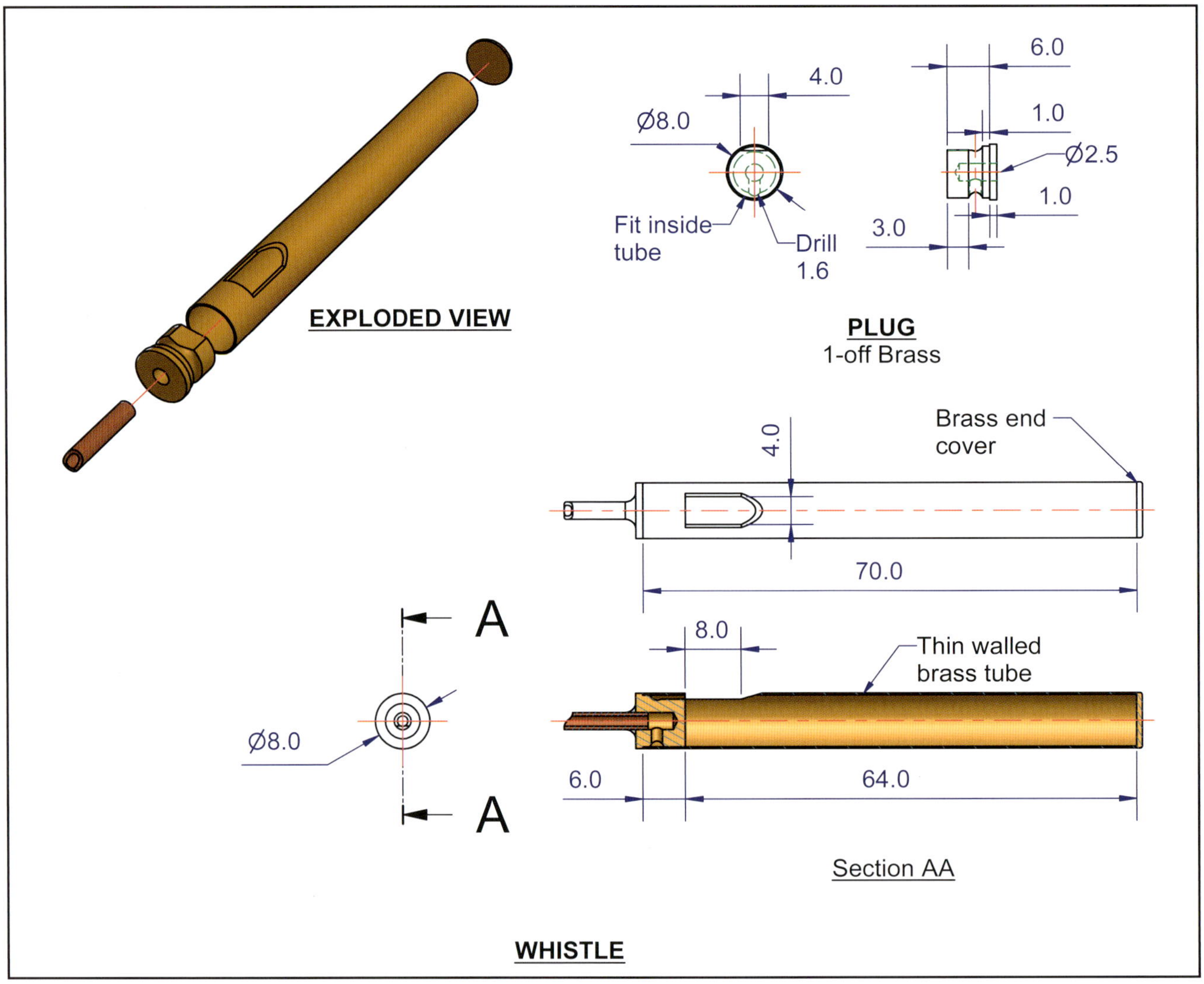

EXPLODED VIEW

PLUG
1-off Brass

Ø8.0

Fit inside tube

Drill 1.6

4.0

6.0

1.0

Ø2.5

1.0

3.0

4.0

Brass end cover

70.0

A

A

Ø8.0

8.0

Thin walled brass tube

6.0

64.0

Section AA

WHISTLE

7.8 — Victoria's "Puffing Billy" NA class locomotive showing the straight chimney with polished cap

of the draughting for the fire. There were many different shapes of chimney and many railway companies had their own distinctive style. If you are building a particular prototype then you will no doubt copy its chimney shape. "Eric" is shown with a spark arrestor type of chimney, so included are drawings of conventional ones suitable for different prototypes. Chimneys are either tapered or straight and the cap shape varies and is sometimes polished brass or copper. (**Photo 7.8**)

Whistle

No locomotive is truly complete without a whistle! For the whistle to be big enough to work, it has to be much bigger than a little scale size whistle sitting on top of the boiler. The whistle shown here should give a nice crisp peep and with an operating valve made from a Schrader tyre valve core you should be able to vary the tone almost like a real one. There is room to fit the whistle either between the frames or to either side as shown in **photos 7.9, 7.10 & 7.11**.

The whistle itself is made from thin walled brass tube. The length of the whistle should be an even multiple of the aperture length; in this case 8 x 8 equals 64mm. The aperture is carefully filed down to be 4mm wide and the outer end is

7.9 — A whistle nestled between the frames under the footplate.

7.10 — The whistle between the frames in front of the cab.

7.11 — The whistle placed under the footplate outside the frames

filed clean and sharp. This is a critical part for the tone and some experimentation may be necessary. A flat is filed onto the plug exactly the same width as the aperture and this must line up when soldering together. As there is not much heat at the whistle, soft solder will be adequate.

There are different ways of making a valve for the whistle and here we have incorporated a complete Schrader tyre valve. These valves come in a short or long form and are very handy as a source of springs and spindles. A conventional valve with a ball and seat could be made using a valve spring, but this design uses the valve complete which is readily purchased from auto parts supply shops.

Making the valve is relatively straightforward except for the thread. If you can obtain a tap (0.209" OD x 36 TPI, UNS) it will be easy, but if not, some compromise will be necessary. An M5 x 0.8 is fairly close, and you will notice that there is only a very short length of thread on the valve, so drill the 15mm long hole with a tapping size drill, tap it M5 x 0.8 and then open out all but the last 5 or 6mm with a 5mm diameter drill. This should enable the Schrader valve to be inserted and screwed in so that the black seal just seats. After this it will be necessary to use a bigger, say 6mm thread when inserting the actuating lever cap.

The valve screws onto the steam nipple coming out of the steam manifold with a thin backing nut to lock and seal.

Cylinder drain cocks

When the steam valve or throttle of a locomotive is first opened and steam travels along the cold steam lines into the still cold cylinders, it condenses into water. This water is incompressible, so if it is not removed not only will the engine not start, but in large cylinders the end covers could possibly be blown off. For this reason, full sized locomotives and large models have cylinder drain cocks which are opened when steam is first admitted to the cylinders and are left open until the engine has warmed up. For small models such as ours, this is not absolutely necessary as we can push the engine along by hand and clear the water through the exhaust. Lots of water will dribble and spit out of the chimney but it will do no more harm than deposit oily water all over the clean paintwork.

Nonetheless, if we can provide cylinder drains then not only do we avoid making a mess of the paintwork, but it is another system used on full size locomotives we can add to our models to improve the realism. On a cold day it is very impressive to have your locomotive chug off with steam blowing from the cylinder drains, just as in full size!

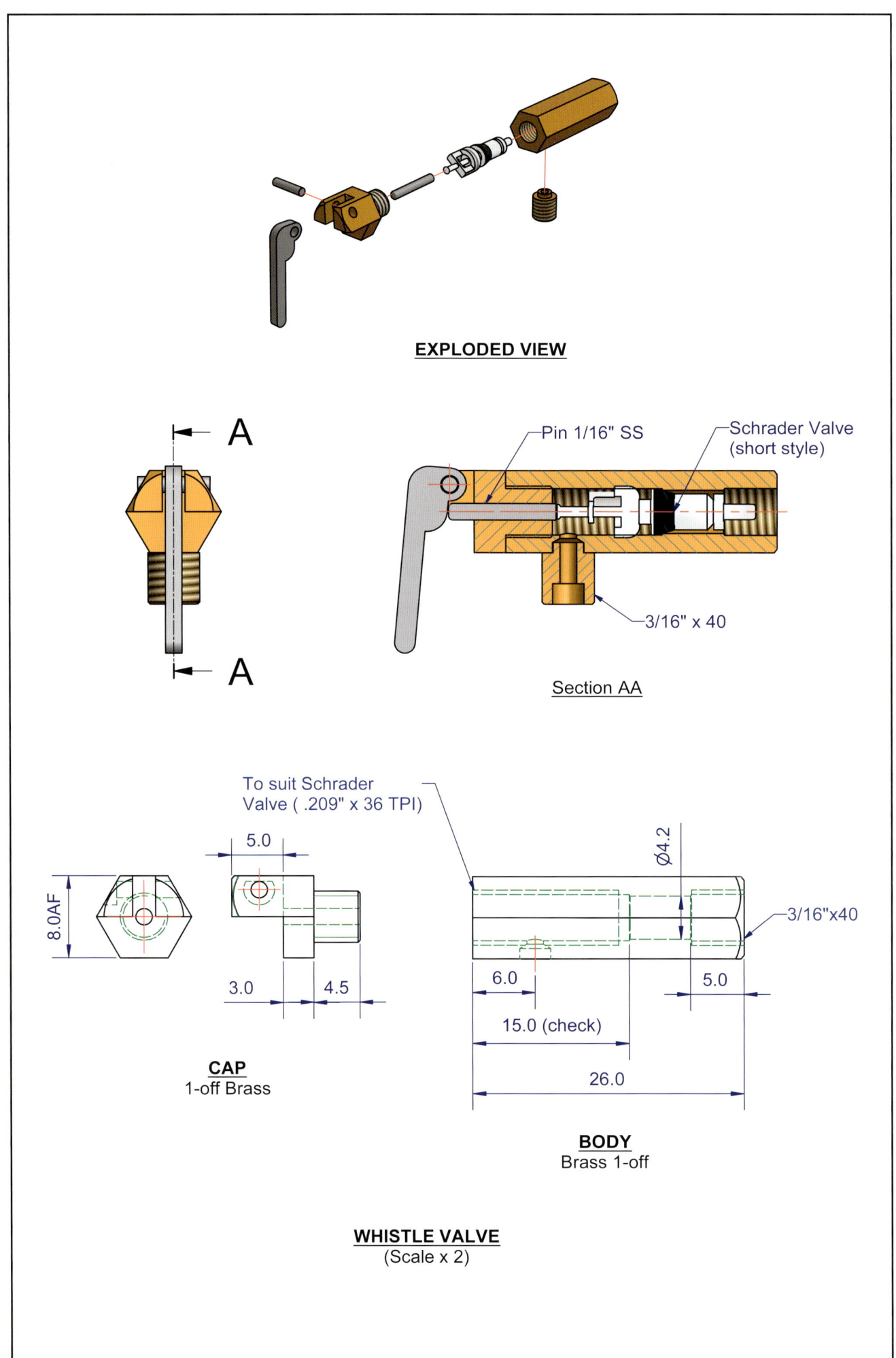

EXPLODED VIEW

A

A

Pin 1/16" SS

Schrader Valve
(short style)

3/16" x 40

Section AA

To suit Schrader
Valve (.209" x 36 TPI)

8.0AF

5.0

Ø4.2

3/16"x40

3.0   4.5

6.0   5.0

15.0 (check)

26.0

CAP
1-off Brass

BODY
Brass 1-off

WHISTLE VALVE
(Scale x 2)

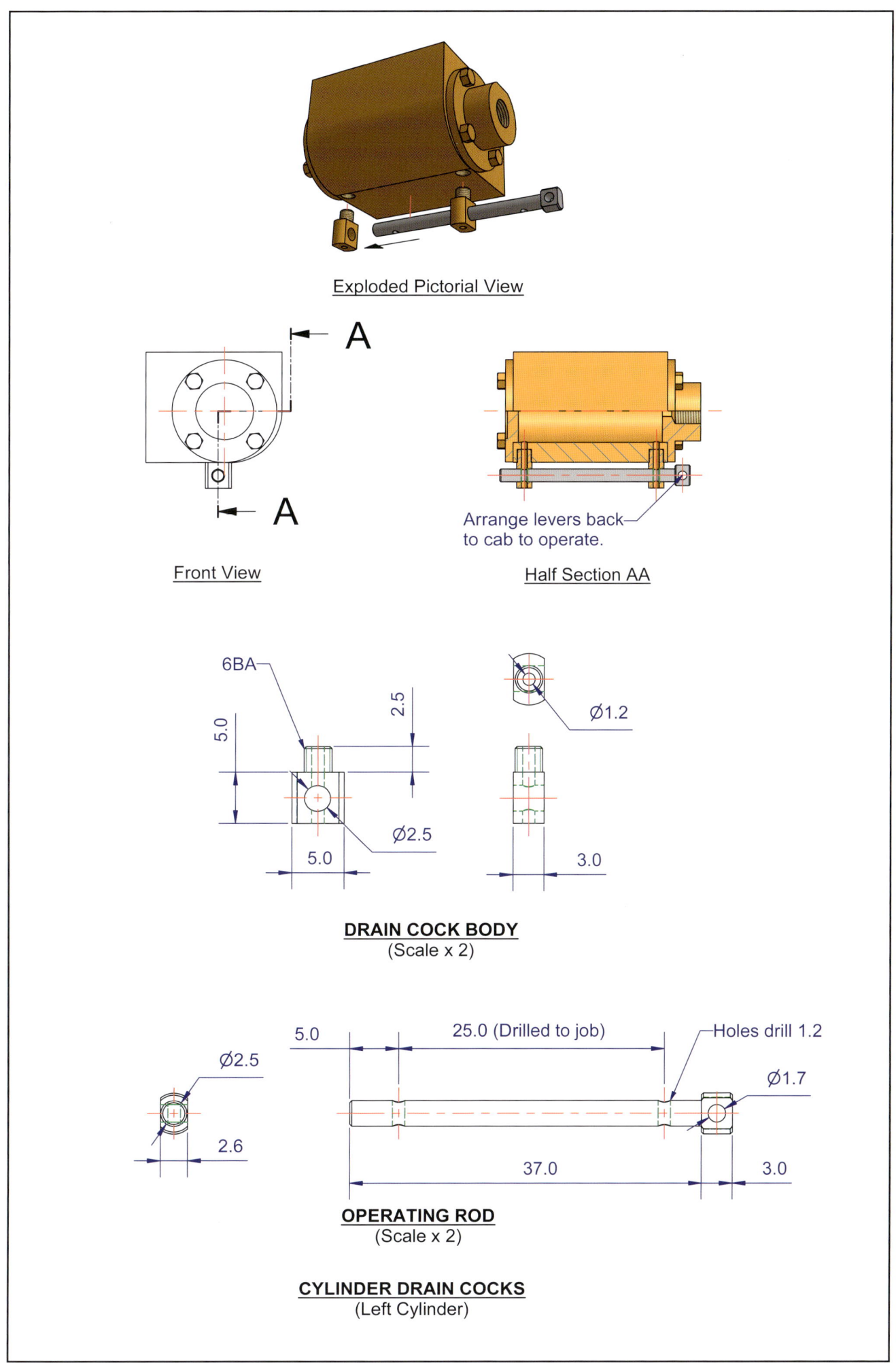

Exploded Pictorial View

A

Front View

Arrange levers back
to cab to operate.

Half Section AA

6BA

5.0

2.5

5.0

Ø2.5

Ø1.2

3.0

DRAIN COCK BODY
(Scale x 2)

Ø2.5

2.6

5.0

25.0 (Drilled to job)

Holes drill 1.2

Ø1.7

37.0

3.0

OPERATING ROD
(Scale x 2)

CYLINDER DRAIN COCKS
(Left Cylinder)

7.12 — The cylinder drain cocks

7.13 — The cylinder drain cocks and operating levers viewed from underneath. They are in the closed position and the holes can be clearly seen

It is a little difficult to fit working drain cocks to such a small cylinder and not look oversize, but this design works well and isn't too much out of scale. They can be made to be operated at the cylinder itself, but it is well worth the extra effort to run levers back to the cab so they can be opened and closed from there.

Mark out the position of the two holes on each cylinder so that the 1.2mm drain hole is as close as possible

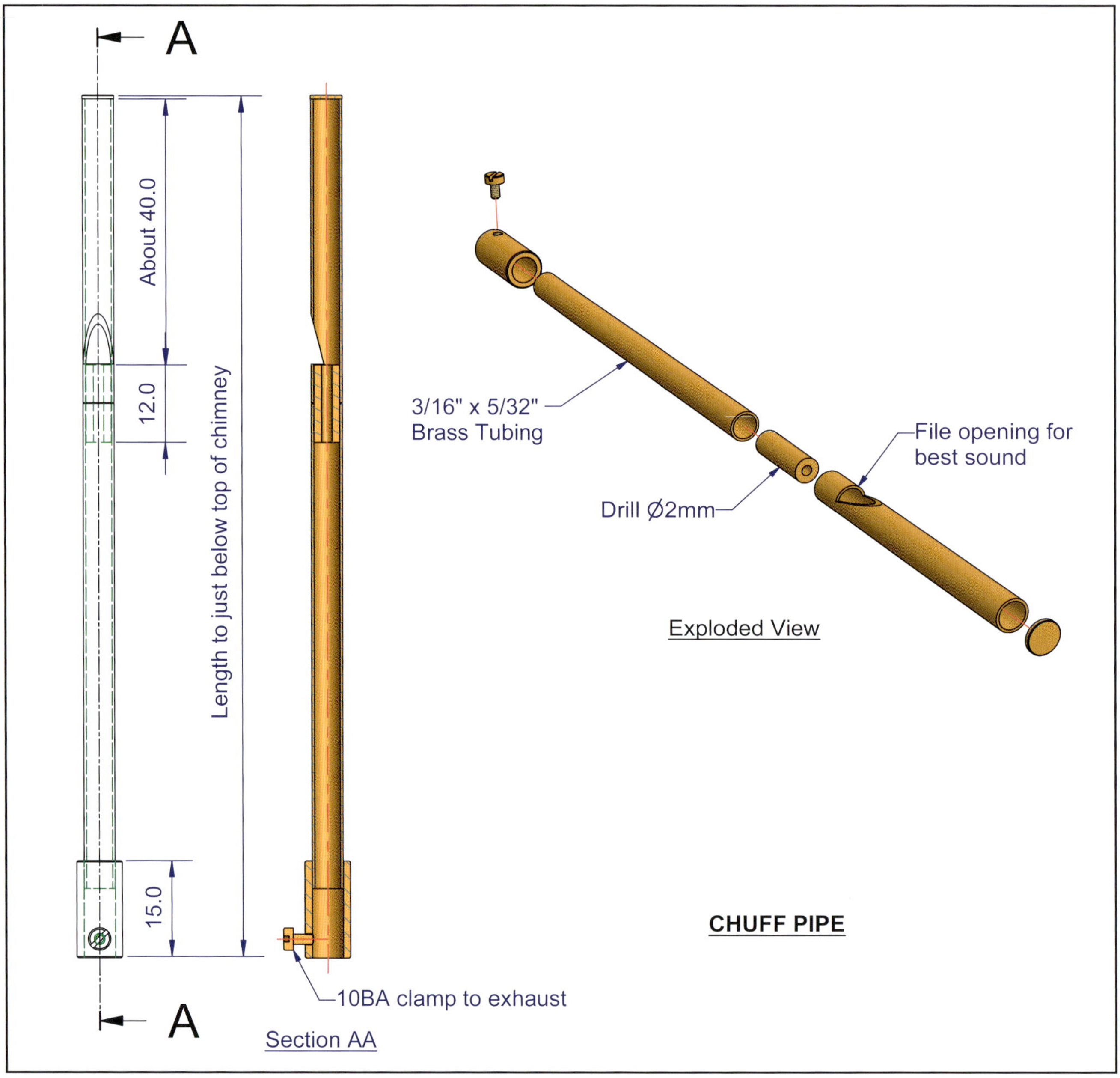

About 40.0

12.0

Length to just below top of chimney

15.0

10BA clamp to exhaust

Section AA

3/16" x 5/32" Brass Tubing

Drill Ø2mm

File opening for best sound

Exploded View

CHUFF PIPE

7.14 — The chuff pipe fixed onto the exhaust stub.

to the end of the bore just inside the spigot of the cover. After drilling these holes open them up with a 6BA tapping size drill to a depth of about 2.5mm and tap 6BA.

Make up the cocks from 5mm brass but leave them round at this stage and do not drill the 1.2mm holes through the centre. Screw them in, securing with high temperature Loctite or even silver solder and file or mill two flats on the cocks bringing them to 3mm thick.

Grip the cylinders vertically in a vice and drill $^3/_{32}$" (2.5mm) down through both cocks in the one setting to form the hole for the operating rod. Make up the operating rods from stainless or possibly bronze rod. It would be better to use $^3/_{32}$" rod and solder the head onto this rather than try to turn a larger rod down.

Mount the cylinders, insert the rods and make up a system of levers back to the cab so that the rods move freely back and forth. Once this is done, move and lock the levers into the open position and carefully drill from the bottom through both the cocks and the operating rod, joining up with the hole into the cylinders. If necessary remove the rods and clean off any burrs. (**Photos 7.12 & 7.13**)

A "Chuff" pipe

When you think of steam trains you remember the wonderful "Puff-Puff-Chuff Chuff" sound. It is definitely an essential part of the atmosphere. On our size of locomotive we can get a reasonably good sound by using a "Chuff" Pipe. As well as enhancing the exhaust sound a chuff pipe helps to keep the spent steam oil from coming out of the chimney all over the paintwork. Sometimes it also seems to condense the steam at the top of the chimney and provide a better steam effect.

There have been many different designs for a chuff pipe and this one was shown to me by Paul Trevaskis of Rishon Locomotives. It is quite simple to make, and fits over the stub of the exhaust pipe where it comes off the exhaust tee. Make sure that all components are silver soldered together as it gets very hot in the smokebox and soft solder would melt. (**Photos 7.14 & 7.15**)

7.15 — A "Chuff" pipe

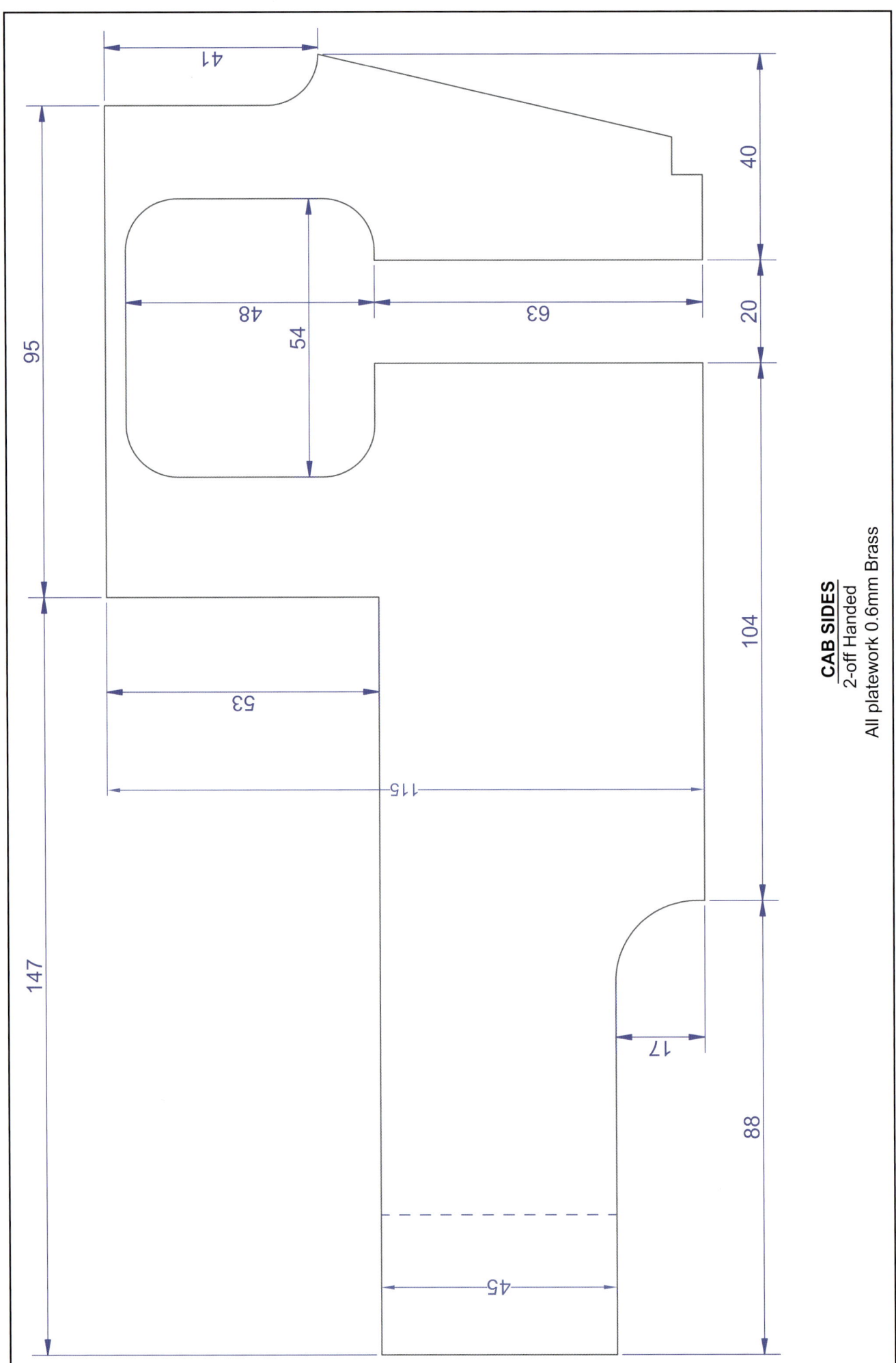

CAB SIDES
2-off Handed
All platework 0.6mm Brass

CHAPTER 8 – Other Prototypes

The Original *"Edwin"*

The original *"Edwin"* (**Photo 8.1**) was a freelance model based on the Bundaberg Fowler. Eight of these fine locomotives were built by the Bundaberg Foundry under license to John Fowler & Co (Leeds) Ltd in England. Their wheel arrangement was 0-6-2 (except for one which was 0-4-2), and they all gave good service in Queensland sugar mills. Most have been preserved and many are running in tourist railways today.

8.1 — "EDWIN" simmering in the siding

"Edwin" was designed as an 0-4-0, although the body closely followed the prototype. Included here are drawings of the cab and tanks for *"Edwin"*.

By building *"Edwin"* as an 0-6-2 and adjusting the tank and cab sizes to suit, a close representation of a Bundaberg Fowler would result.

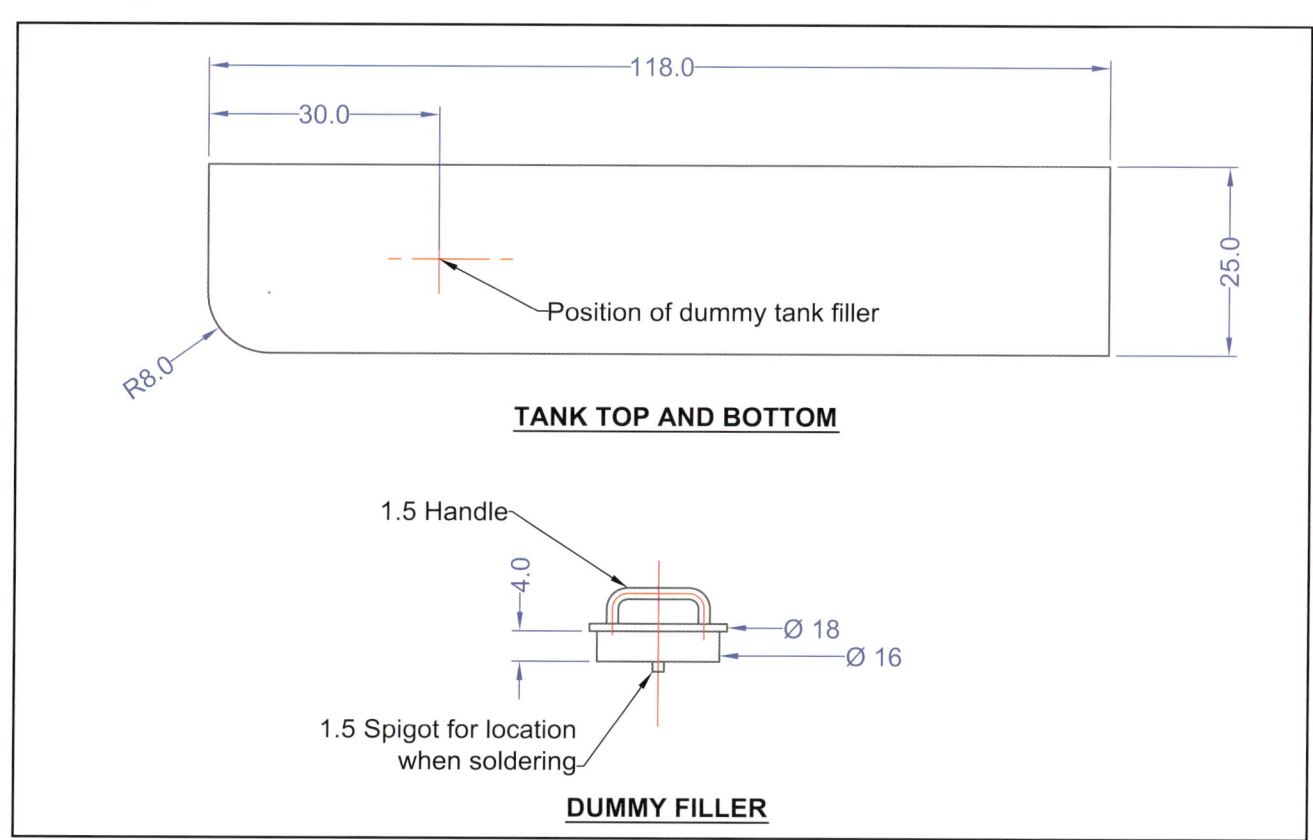

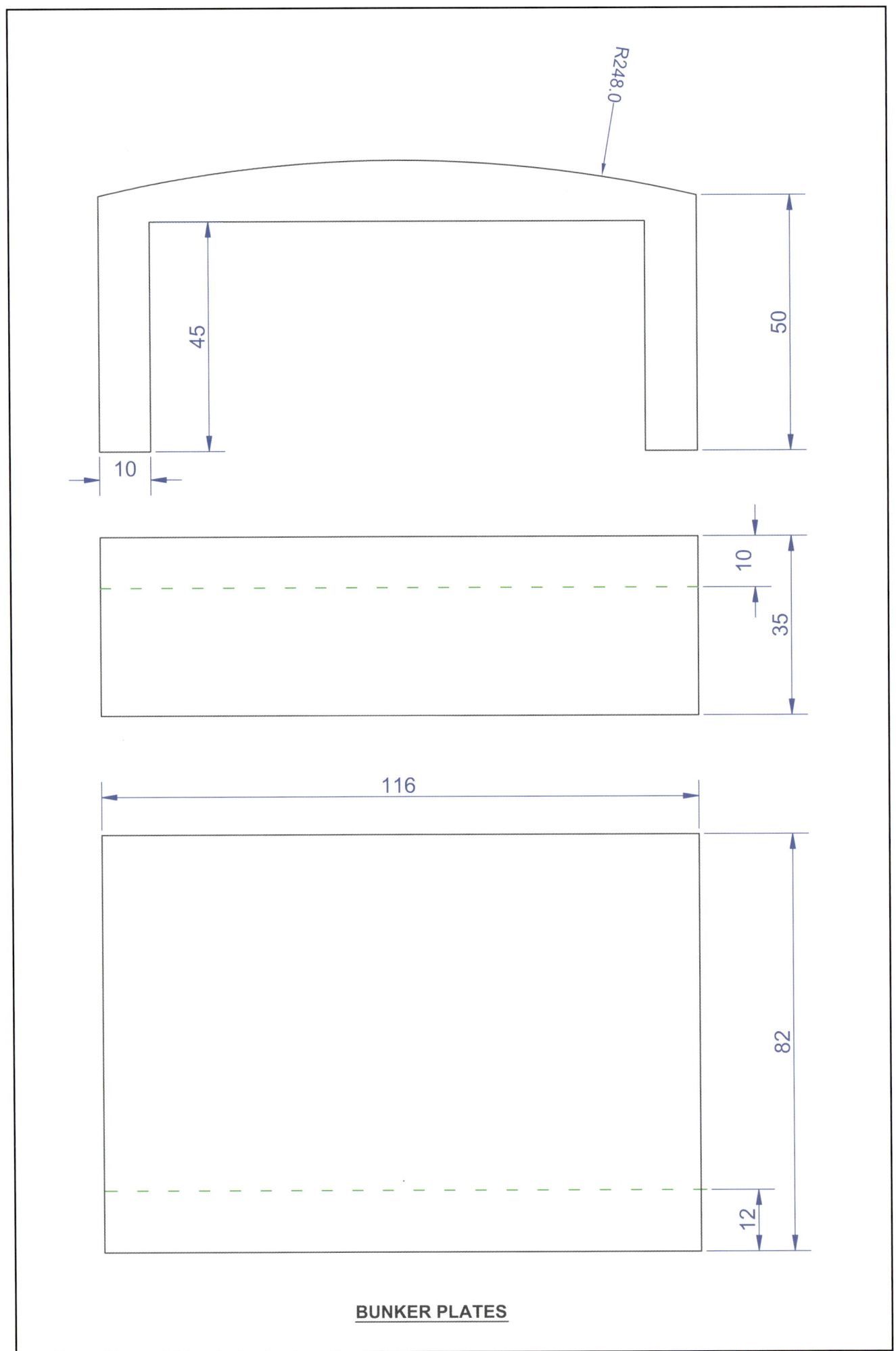

BUNKER PLATES

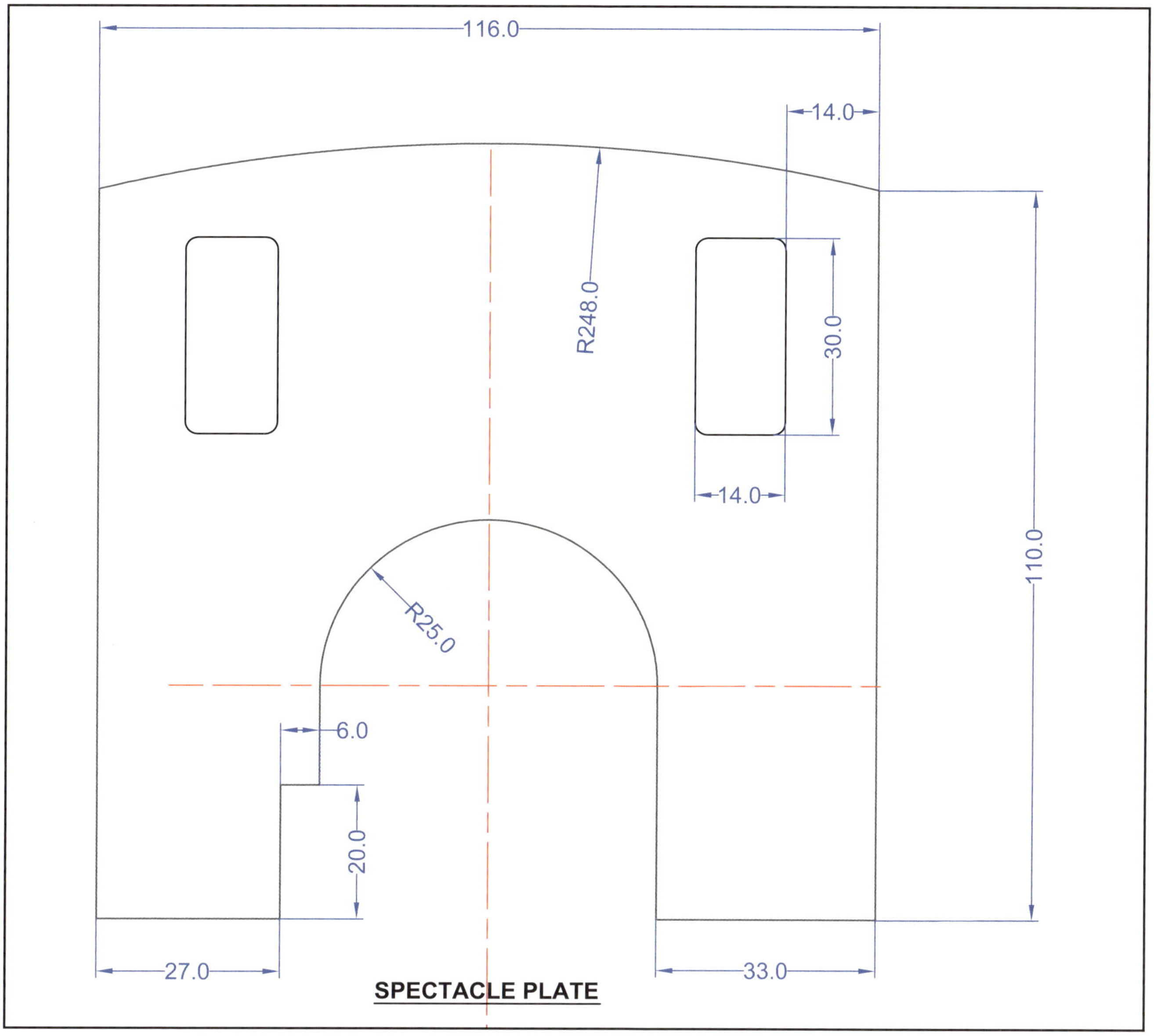

The diagram shows a SPECTACLE PLATE with the following dimensions: 116.0 (overall width), 14.0, R248.0, 30.0, 14.0, 110.0, R25.0, 6.0, 20.0, 27.0, 33.0.

SPECTACLE PLATE

Manufacturers' works drawings and photographs

In order to build a model of another prototype, once you have selected the locomotive that you like, there are various sources where information can be found to enable a fairly close copy of the original. Works drawings are invaluable and copies of these are often reproduced in books. Copies of many John Fowler locomotive works drawings are currently available from the Museum of English Rural Life in Reading, U.K. The General Arrangement drawing shown on the next page is of John Fowler locomotive Works No. 20763 "Airdmillan" which was built for the Kalamia Sugar mill in Ayr, North Queensland. It is very similar in design to the later "Bundaberg Fowlers". This drawing can readily be scaled from the wheel gauge which was 2'-0" in the prototype and is evident in the top view.

Builders used to take a "works photograph" of completed locomotives and many of these are available (**Photo 8.2**). Catalogues of these can be purchased for a selection of Hunslet and Bagnall engines and as these works photographs are usually taken side on, they provide a useful reference. Either the drawings or photographs can be enlarged in a photocopier to the required

THE HUNSLET ENGINE CO. LTD *Engineers* LEEDS ENGLAND

0-4-0 TYPE

OIL BURNING TANK ENGINE

8.2 — Works photograph of a Hunslet "Waril" class 18 inch gauge locomotive

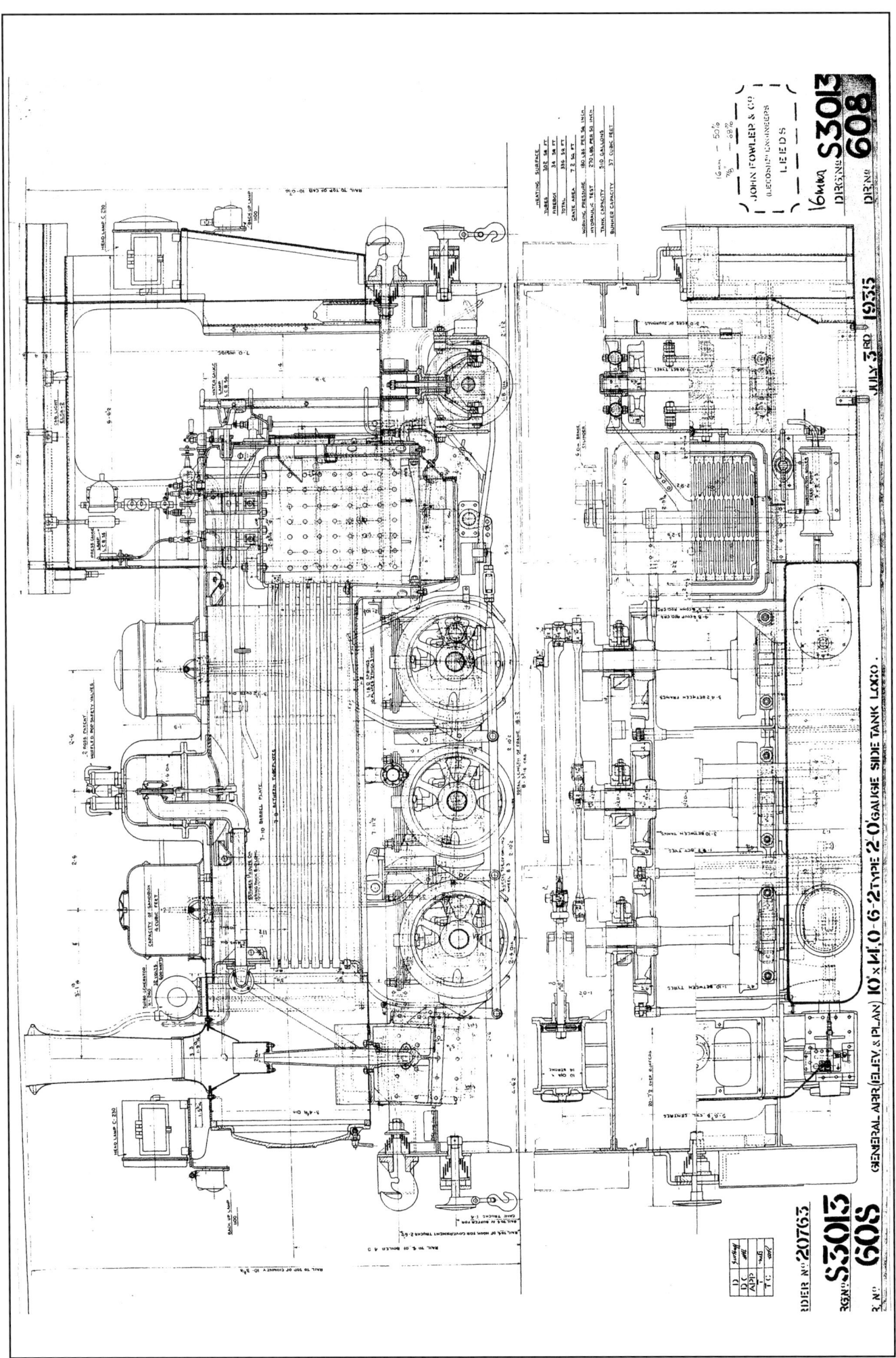

scale after which sizes can be taken from them. With a photograph it will be necessary to have a reference to scale from, for example the full size measurement of the wheelbase may be given. Divide this measurement by 19.06 for 16mm scale or 13.86 for ⅞ scale. Measure the wheelbase on the photograph and divide it into the figure just obtained. This will give the enlargement required in a photocopier to bring the photograph to the size of your model.

This works photograph is of a "Waril" class Hunslet. Two of these charming little locomotives have been preserved and it is a prototype which is frequently modelled. To determine the proportions for a model of this locomotive, it is stated in the catalogue from which this photograph was taken, that the wheelbase is 3'-6" and the height of the chimney top from the rails is 8'-0". From these two measurements, we can readily scale a photocopy to give us a good guide to the size of our model.

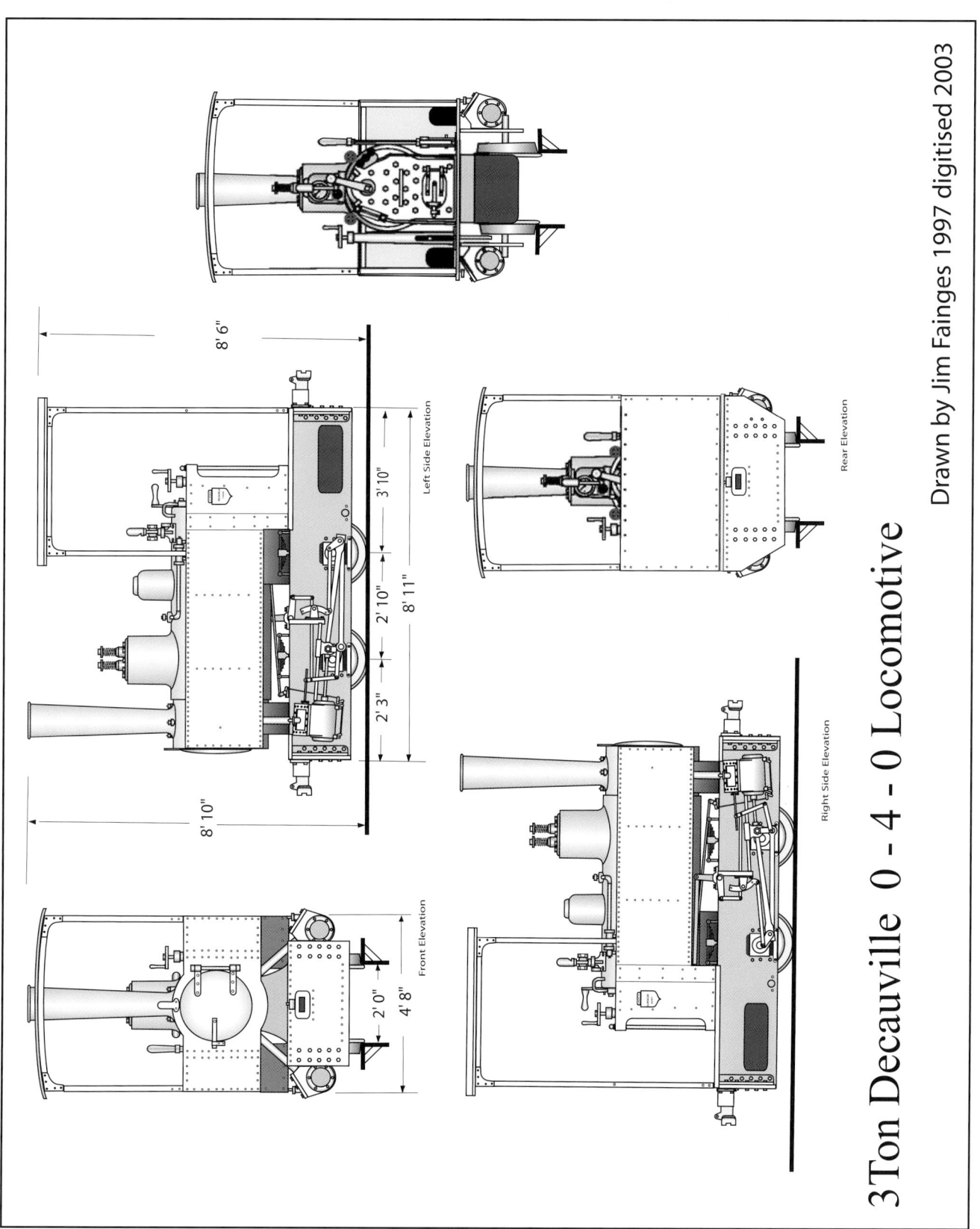

Drawn by Jim Fainges 1997 digitised 2003

3 Ton Decauville 0 - 4 - 0 Locomotive

Jim Fainges of Brisbane has produced a set of drawings of Queensland narrow gauge locomotives and rolling stock and he has generously made this magnificent resource freely available on the Internet at:

http://zelmeroz.com/albumquery/fainges2.htm

Shown on the previous page is an example of one of his drawings, a 3-ton Decauville locomotive.

Provided you are not fanatical about accuracy, the general approach is to build the chassis for the appropriate wheel arrangement and then add the body, making any small adjustment to the scale which is necessary to fit them together. (**Photo 8.3**)

8.3 — No.5, Paul Blake's Innisfail tank engine built with sizes taken from drawings and photographs.

CHAPTER 9 – Laser Cutting and Lost Wax Casting

The construction notes for building *Eric* in Part 1 described the making of parts from solid material. This is perfectly feasible and cheap, but very labour and time intensive.

Lost wax casting

The casting and subsequent machining of suitable components can reduce manufacturing time considerably. The full size engines were built using many castings and larger models invariably use them. These large castings are produced using conventional foundry methods of sand casting which would produce quite a rough finish in the small sizes we require, however, lost wax casting which is a very old process and which is used predominately for producing jewellery is ideal. For our purposes castings can readily be produced in brass or bronze.

Lost wax casting is a process which can be done in the home workshop, but the process can be somewhat involved and suitable equipment is required. It is possible however to make a pattern or master and send it away to a specialist firm for producing the mold and subsequent castings. There is an economy of scale involved, but if you need more than one or two parts the process is worthwhile particularly when the saving in time is taken into account. (**Photo 9.1 & 9.2**)

When making a master pattern it must be borne in mind that there is shrinkage of around 4% during the casting process so the size of the pattern has to allow for this, and because heat is used in the moulding process it is preferable to assemble the master with silver solder. The largest size of object which can be handled is limited, although this varies between manufacturers and also affects the price considerably.

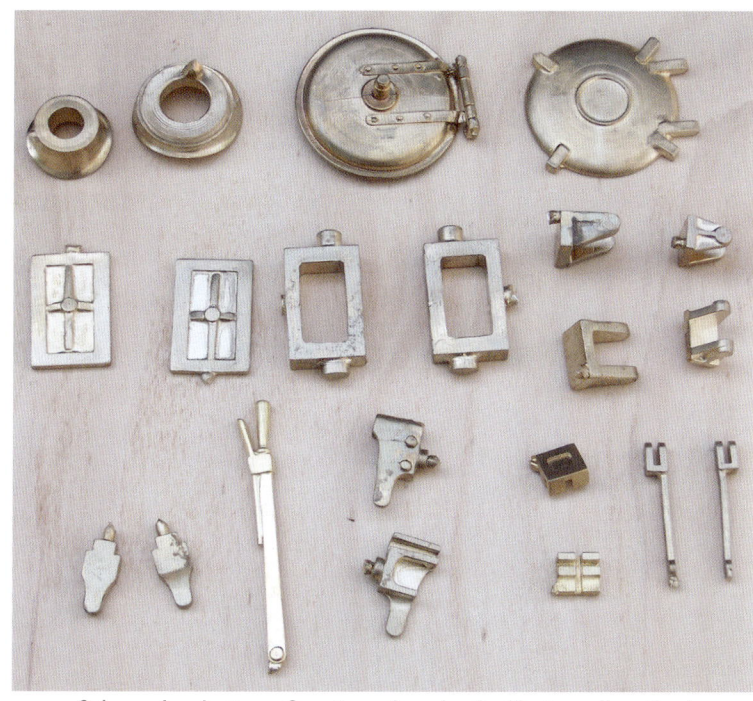

9.1 — A selection of castings done by the "lost wax" method

The general process involves making a rubber mould from your master which is retained by the foundry for your future use. This attracts a one-off moulding fee. From this mould, wax patterns are produced which are then set in a refractory material. The refractory material is fired and the wax burnt out after which the casting is poured. The refractory is then broken away leaving a finely finished casting ready for machining as necessary.

9.2 — A pair of cylinders machined from lost wax castings

Laser profiled components

While casting has been around for a very long time, laser cutting of parts is a relatively new process which can produce components from sheet or flat metals to very fine tolerances and with an excellent finish. (**Photo 9.3**)

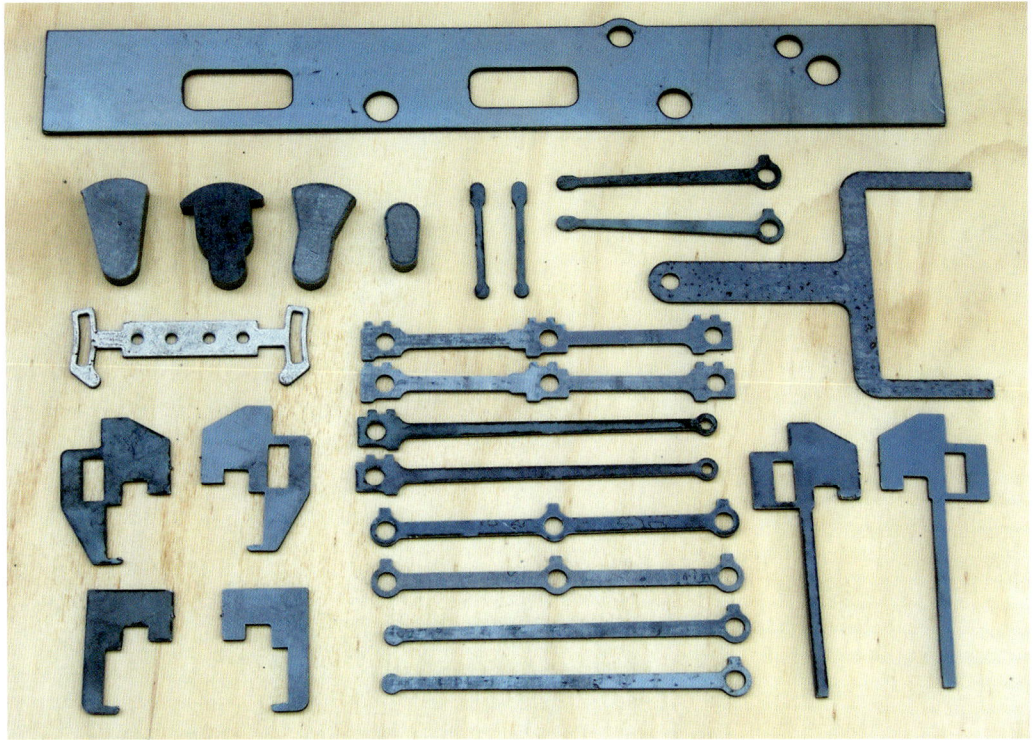

9.3 — An assortment of laser cut components

It is particularly valuable for components in the sizes we are using and vast savings in time can be had. Accuracy is another major benefit. For example the holes for the main bearings can be cut in the main frames and also the bearing holes in the coupling rods can be cut. Because the centre distance for these holes has to be identical, the accuracy of laser cutting guarantees that the hole spacing will be precise which helps greatly with the wheel quartering process.

Anyone with expertise in CAD drawing can have these produced by drawing the outline of the part required, usually as a DXF file and presenting to a laser cutting firm for processing. Again cost is related to the number of components required. One of the biggest problems is that the parts we require are quite fiddly and in relatively thin material and therefore not a very attractive job for many laser cutters who most of the time work in heavier materials with larger components. Never the less, if you can find a willing company it is well worth the expense of having parts cut by this method.

CHAPTER 10 – Coal Firing

Coal firing is said by many people to be the "ultimate garden railway experience". Whilst gas fired boilers provide a quick and clean way to have a steam up, the sights, sounds and smells of running a locomotive on coal are a lot closer to the "real thing". How much better is the pungent smell of burning coal to the smell of butane as it loudly hisses away? What about the enhanced plume of steam and smoke, particularly on a crisp winter's day? (**Photo 10.1 & 10.2**). If you like "fiddling" with your locomotive then you will certainly enjoy coal firing.

10.1 — Raising steam on a crisp winter's morning. As pressure builds the blower is opened and a rich smell of steam and coal smoke issues from the chimney.

10.2 — Not only does it look good ... but what a wonderful smell!

It used to be considered that trains of this size were a bit too small to run effectively on coal and that those that did were being operated by highly skilled almost magic operators. It does take a little more concentration to keep the engine steaming well, and there are a few extra items to add to the locomotive, but it is not all that difficult either to build or to run.

Besides needing a different design of boiler, with coal firing it is best to feed water continuously into the boiler rather than topping up at stops and for this we use an axle pump fitted between the frames. To supply water to the pump the loco must carry water either in its own saddle or side tanks or in a tender, and we also need a bypass valve in the system to control the varying amounts of water required. The only other requirement is to provide a draught up the chimney. This produces a vacuum in the smoke box which in turn draws air through the grate under the fire and provides oxygen for effective combustion of the coal. When the locomotive is moving, this draught is provided by the exhaust and when stationary by a "blower" which is simply a jet of steam directed up the chimney.

Coal–fired boiler

As mentioned previously with the gas-fired boiler, when making a coal-fired boiler it is the responsibility of the builder to determine whether there are any statutory requirements associated with its construction or operation. The sequences and methods of construction given here are offered as a guide only and the builder must make sure that he or she understands the processes involved in its construction and operation and be aware of and adhere to any suppliers or manufacturers' instructions regarding the equipment and materials being used. Again, the AMBSC Code Part 3 — Sub-Miniature Boilers has been used as a guide in the design of this boiler. The equipment and many of the techniques of construction used are also discussed in the section on the gas-fired boiler.

The boiler consists of two separate parts, a main pressure shell and a firebox, the firebox being mechanically fixed onto the pressure shell. Because the firebox doesn't have to hold any pressure and will be mechani-

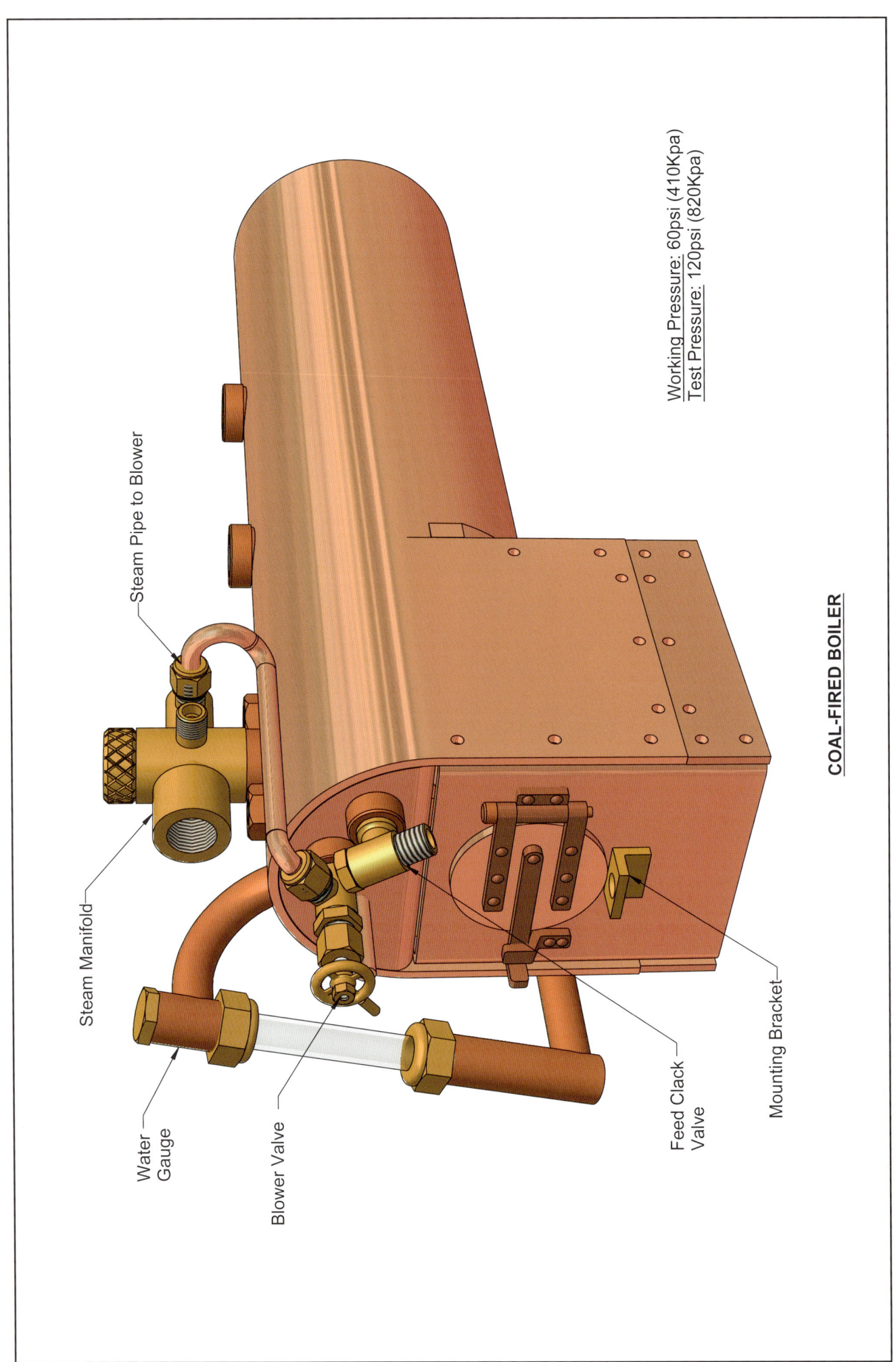

Steam Pipe to Blower

Steam Manifold

Water Gauge

Blower Valve

Feed Clack Valve

Mounting Bracket

Working Pressure: 60psi (410Kpa)
Test Pressure: 120psi (820Kpa)

COAL-FIRED BOILER

cally fixed to the pressure shell rather than soldered, it does not form part of the pressure vessel and so does not have to be tested.

Pressure shell

As boilers become larger and more complex, it is necessary to divide the construction into steps with the components being heated up and silver soldered in several stages. This increases the complexity and to some degree the difficulty of the job, but with this design we are able to assemble all of the components of the pressure shell before any silver soldering is done so the chance of some parts slipping or being soldered out of position is greatly reduced.

10.3 — The firebox fixing bracket can be seen just under the fire door

formity to the Code.

Fixing the boiler to the locomotive is straightforward. The front end slides into the smoke box which allows movement for expansion and the back is fixed to the footplate with a screw through an angle bracket fixed to the back head. (**Photo 10.3**) The footplate is simply a rectangle of 1.6mm thick mild steel screwed into the main frame spacers with a cut out to accommodate the firebox, lagging and cladding. (**Photo 10.4**)

The sizes given in the drawings were determined for a particular locomotive and it will be necessary to check all of these to fit the boiler to your particular job. The shell can be lengthened or shortened to suit, but the diameter should remain at 2" (50.8mm). Also the firebox size can be altered although it and the lagging (which will be discussed later) have to fit between the frames. The spacing of the crown sheet stays is important so if the firebox is lengthened and the crown sheet is consequently made longer the number and position of the stays will need to be checked for con-

10.4 — Footplate showing the cut out for the firebox

Start by making the bushes, stays and nuts. The bushes are made from phosphor bronze and should be made a firm fit in their holes. The stay nuts are from copper or phosphor bronze and do not have to be precise hexagons, they may be simply filed to shape, or at a pinch could even be left square. Make the stays them-

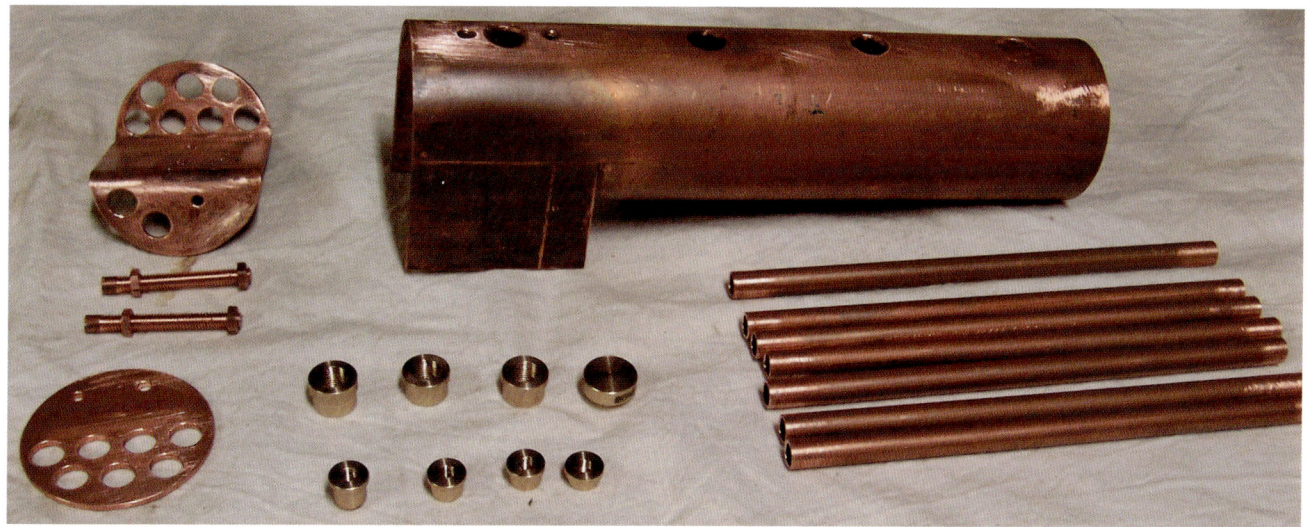

10.5 — Components of the pressure cell ready for assembly

selves by threading some copper rod 2BA, leaving them a bit longer than shown so that a screw driver slot can be cut in the top to enable them to be screwed home.

Mark out and drill the cylindrical shell for the bushes, also drill and tap 2BA for the stays. Mark out, cut and fold out the pieces to form the top of the firebox sides. (**Photo 10.5**)

The front tube plate and the combined back head/crown sheet/rear tube plate are made from 2mm thick copper. In order to drill the front tube plate without any mishaps it is a good idea to drill it while marked out on the sheet and before cutting out so that there is room to securely clamp it onto the drill table. The rear tube plate which is part of the crown sheet and back head can be clamped to a block of wood after bending and safely drilled. (Photo **10.6**)

Once the holes are drilled, the front tube plate can be cut round, making it a firm fit into the front of the boiler tube. This helps to keep things firmly together while soldering. The crown sheet piece can be finally fitted so that it too will be a neat fit.

10.6 — Drilling holes in the rear tubeplate

Note that these plates are set in a millimetre or two from the ends of the main tube which will allow a good fillet of solder to form.

After these are fitted we need to tap the two holes in the crown for the stays, and this is done by holding the crown sheet firmly in its position and drilling and tapping down through the previously tapped holes in the boiler shell. The crown can be held in position by lightly clamping at the back head and wedging a piece of wood down the boiler tube from the front which will hold the crown against the top of the shell.

The whole pressure shell can now be assembled and provided all fits are firm there should be no chance of anything shifting or getting out of place.

Firstly place the crown sheet / back head piece into position and screw in the two stays together with their locknuts. These should be sufficient to hold the crown sheet securely in place. Next silver solder a length of ³⁄₃₂" copper tubing into the blower valve bush, and then insert the bush into the back head along with the feed clack bush. Insert a piece of ⅛" copper tubing for the steam pipe into the hole in the back head. Both of these tubes should be left plenty long enough to go through the front tube plate to be cut to length later.

Next fit the fire tubes and the front tube plate. The tubes will have to be a firm fit otherwise they will fall out just when you don't want them to. Position them so that they protrude from the front tube plate level with the front of the shell. To make fitting easier, the steam and blower tubes can be made a loose fit in their holes when the tube plate is placed in position.

Drive wooden wedge between crown plate and boiler tube.

Tap 2BA right through into crown plate after which stays are screwed in.

TAPPING CROWN SHEET FOR STAY BOLTS

The pressure shell is now ready for soldering. While it would be possible to add the tubes for the gauge glass it would be better to leave them off at this stage and solder them on as a separate item later.

The first application of solder will be to the front tube plate. Apply flux to all joints, holes and bushes over the entire shell. Stand the structure up on the back end, making sure it is secure and not balanced precariously, ready to fall over. Also make sure that the tubes are supported underneath at the back tube plate as well, just in case they want to slide out

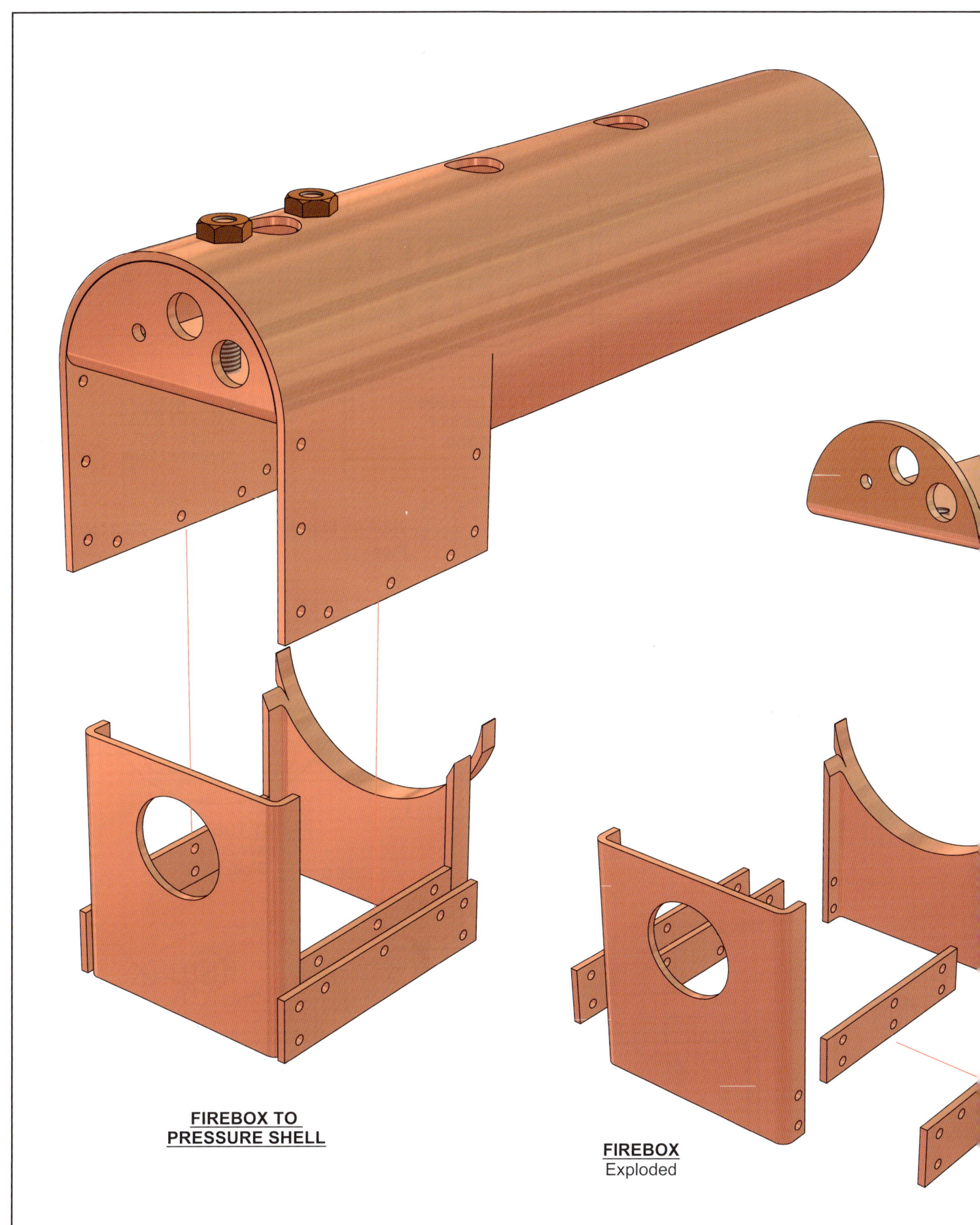

**FIREBOX TO
PRESSURE SHELL**

FIREBOX
Exploded

COAL FIRED
Assem

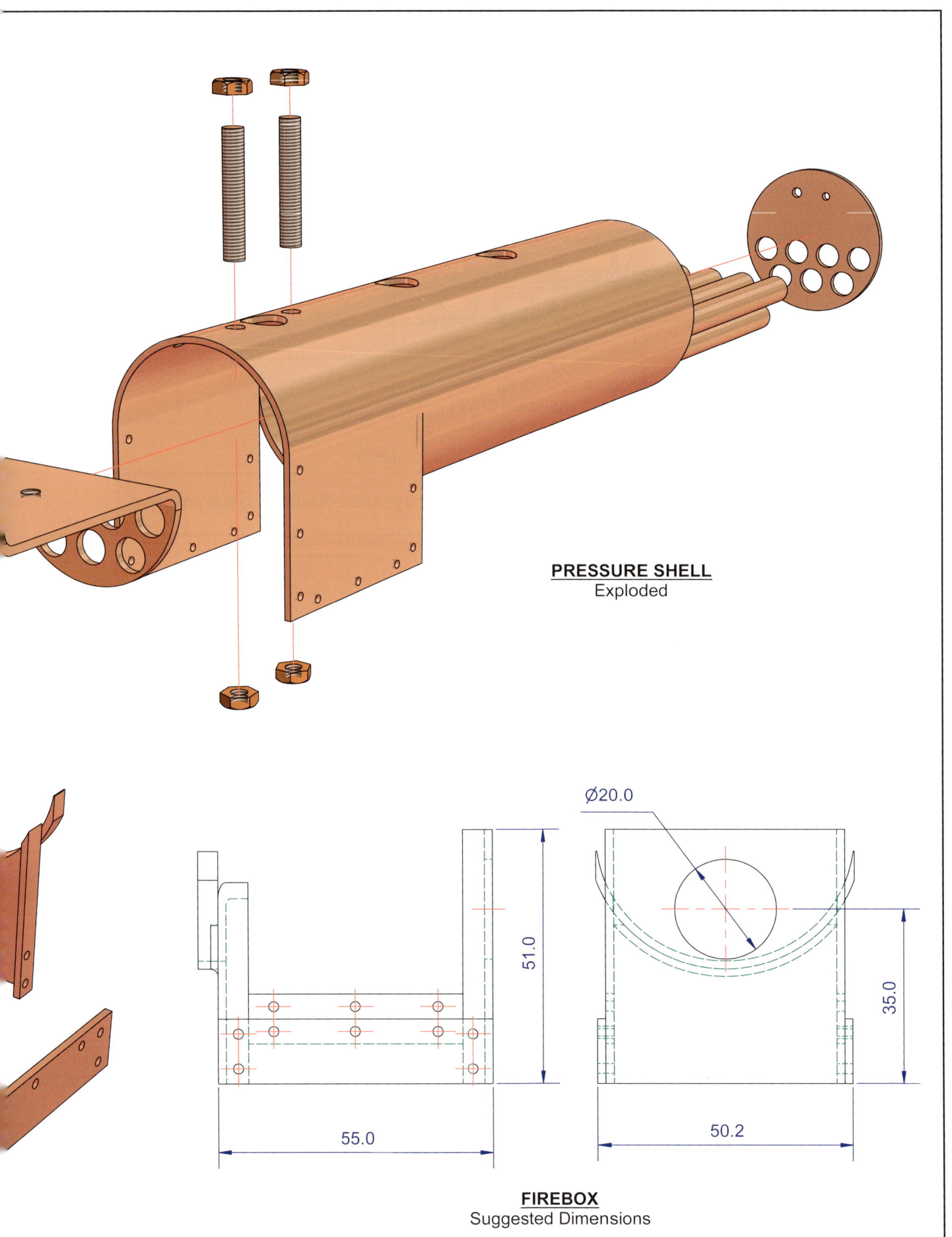

PRESSURE SHELL
Exploded

Ø20.0

51.0

35.0

55.0

50.2

FIREBOX
Suggested Dimensions

BOILER
ly

when heat is applied. Put pieces of solder around the tubes as was described for the gas fired boiler and also have a stick ready to apply more as necessary.

Using a large tip for the gas torch, heat everything up gradually, eventually concentrating the flame to the top of the shell and the tube plate until solder runs thoroughly around the tube plate, the tubes and the piping, adding more solder from the stick as necessary. Remember that this is a very bad time to try and economise on solder!

Let the boiler cool to a safe temperature and then place in the pickle bath. Examine the joints and if all looks well we can move on to the next step.

Again apply flux to all joints including the front tube plate that you have just done. Stand the structure on its front end making sure it is well supported. The joints to be soldered on this heating will be those all around the back tube plate / crown sheet / back head, the back head bushes and the bottom stay nuts, so where possible place pieces of solder where required.

Heat the boiler as before again heating gradually and then concentrating the heat onto the areas to be soldered. The most difficult parts are the two edges of the crown sheet which will be standing vertically. This will cause the molten solder to want to run down and accumulate at the bottom of the joint in the vicinity of the tubes so if you keep feeding solder in it will just run away. To help avoid this happening, the joint between the crown sheet and the top of the firebox sides needs to be a good fit. Also don't overheat the area. As soon as the solder flows properly into the joint move the flame away. Don't forget to solder the steam pipe into the back head as well as the bushes.

After you have finished, let the boiler cool down and place in the pickle bath. After thoroughly washing and cleaning the job examine it and you should be able to see whether the joints are satisfactory. If there is any doubt at all, re-flux everything and heat up again. If there appears to be a problem along those longitudinal joints between the crown sheet and the firebox, it may help to lay the boiler on its top, so that these joints are horizontal, but be careful not to overheat the tube plate and back head or the solder will run out of these joints and cause problems there.

After this area appears satisfactory, the next heating will be done to insert the lower gauge glass pipe. Before soldering this, and the top pipe, solder the two vertical gauge pipes on to their respective tubes and the small optional support bracket onto the lower one.

Apply flux to all joints again and laying the boiler in a suitable horizontal position solder the lower ¼" gauge pipe into its hole. Let the boiler cool and pickle again as before.

Finally heat up and solder the bushes and the stay nuts along the top of the boiler. Let it cool before placing in the pickle bath and then clean up everything by giving a rub over with a scouring pad so that the entire structure is clean and bright and all joints can be seen clearly. Now is the time to give the boiler a hydrostatic test. The "official" test should be done by a club boiler inspector, but you can make up a rig for testing in the workshop by making a small hand pump similar to those used in larger models as hand pumps. One can be made in much the same way as the axle pump but with a handle to operate the ram. A grease gun has even been converted successfully to make a test pump. Make up the necessary fittings to connect the pump and a pressure gauge to the boiler and plugs for the other bushes and openings. The boiler needs to be pumped up with cold water to a pressure twice that of the working pressure which it should hold for a period of 10 minutes, during which time it is inspected for leaks. There should be no leaks or weeps whatsoever, and if there are any then you will need to correct them by emptying the boiler and heating all over again at the offending joint, but let's hope that won't be necessary! (**Photo 10.7**)

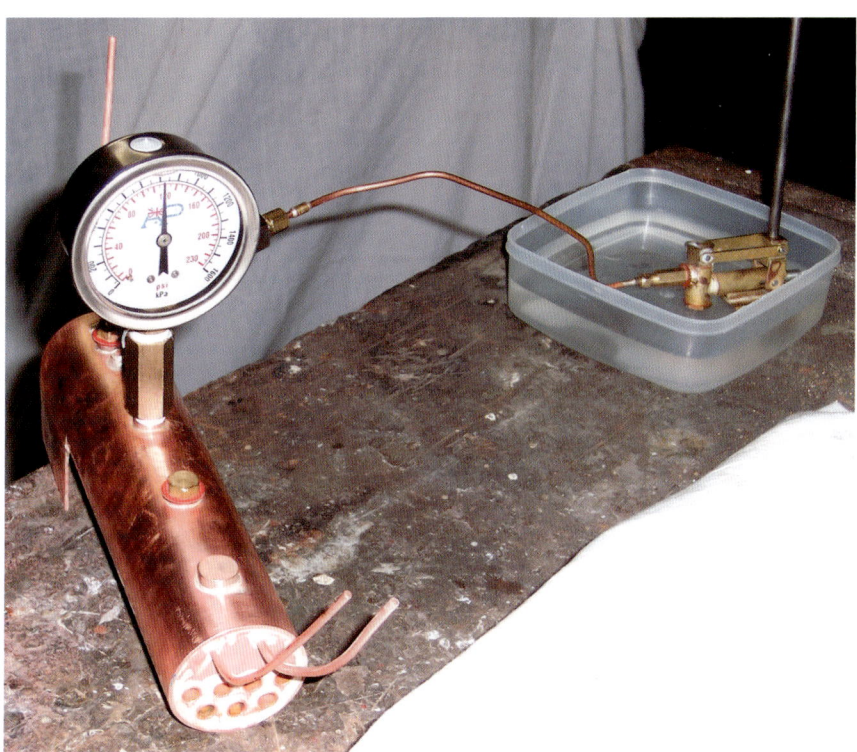

10.7 — A rig for carrying out a hydrostatic test in the workshop. The final test should be performed by a club boiler inspector.

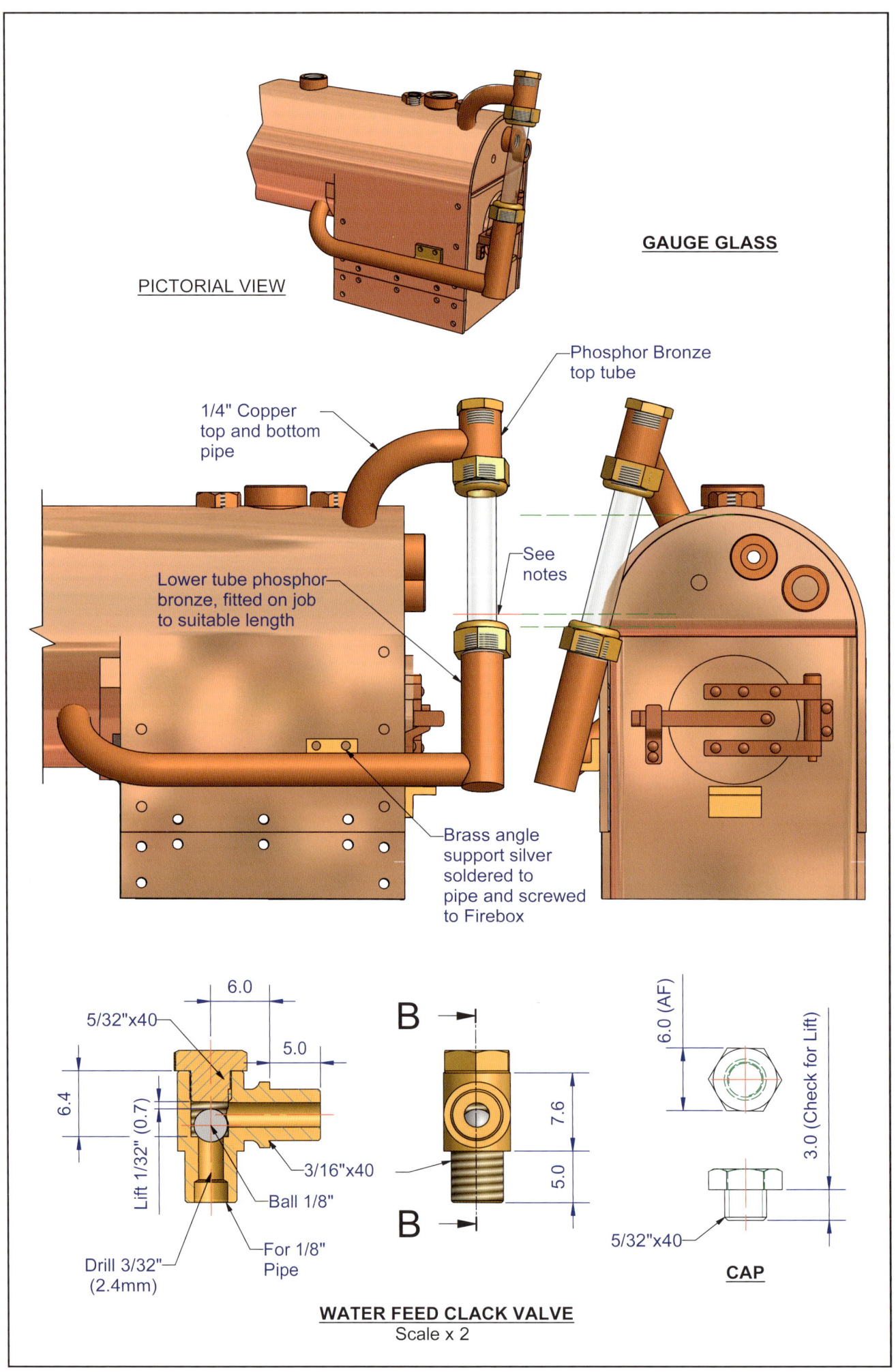

PICTORIAL VIEW

GAUGE GLASS

Phosphor Bronze
top tube

1/4" Copper
top and bottom
pipe

Lower tube phosphor
bronze, fitted on job
to suitable length

See
notes

Brass angle
support silver
soldered to
pipe and screwed
to Firebox

6.0

5.0

5/32"x40

6.4

Lift 1/32" (0.7)

3/16"x40

Ball 1/8"

Drill 3/32"
(2.4mm)

For 1/8"
Pipe

B

7.6

5.0

B

6.0 (AF)

3.0 (Check for Lift)

5/32"x40

CAP

WATER FEED CLACK VALVE
Scale x 2

Firebox

The other main part of the boiler is the firebox. Because this is a dry sided fire box, in use it will become very hot, so if it is simply silver soldered together, it may become hot enough to melt the solder. Therefore it is better to assemble the pieces using rivets, which can simply be short lengths of 3mm diameter copper rod, hammered into countersinks on both ends. This will securely hold everything together and form a perfectly adequate seal along the joints. Having said that, the throat at the top of the front wall of the firebox is silver soldered in position. The purpose of this piece is to help provide a seal where it contacts the boiler shell.

Make up all the components for the firebox including the fire door, which can be made round or rectangular according to taste, as long as it is big enough to take the loaded shovel with reasonable sized pieces of coal. The height of the bottom of the fire door should be just below the level of the bottom of the fire tubes. Assemble it onto the boiler using rivets and where it meets the boiler shell and the back head it can be sealed using fireproof putty such as that sold in fireplace shops for sealing stoves. Drill and tap the mounting holes for the small bracket which supports the bottom gauge glass pipe. This can be fitted now, but it would be easier to fit it after the boiler is lagged.

When fitting the glass for the gauge the top and bottom tubes have to be perfectly lined up otherwise the glass will break. To do this there should be plenty of movement possible by carefully twisting and bending these tubes slightly. When the alignment is correct insert the glass using suitable packing as described for the gas fired boiler.

It is a requirement of the boiler Code that either a mark is made on the glass or that the bottom gauge glass nut is no lower than a level which is 10% of the distance from the top of the crown sheet to the inside of the top of the boiler shell. This is to help in keeping the water level at a safe height above the crown sheet.

Lastly, the boiler assembly has to be lagged and the cladding fitted. It is easier to make the cladding in two sections with the join being around the spectacle plate where it won't be noticed. Also this allows us to use felt lagging for the front shell section and ceramic fibre sheet over the firebox.

There is no need to fix the lagging and cladding over the firebox as it will be held in position once it is inserted into the cut out in the footplate. To make it easier to assemble it is possible to hold it together with a little adhesive such as white wood work glue or even tape which will just burn away after a few steam ups.

Use a few turns of ordinary craft felt for lagging the barrel, cutting out the holes for the bushes as necessary. This also can be temporarily held in position with glue until the cladding is fixed. (**Photo 10.8**)

Grate and ash pan

The grate and ash pan are made as one unit which makes it easier to insert into position. The grate is made to fit loosely into the bottom of the firebox and the whole unit is held in position with a 1/16" stainless pin passing through both of the frames and the tube between the sides of the ash pan.

Barrel Lagged with 2 or 3 layers of felt, covered with brass cladding.

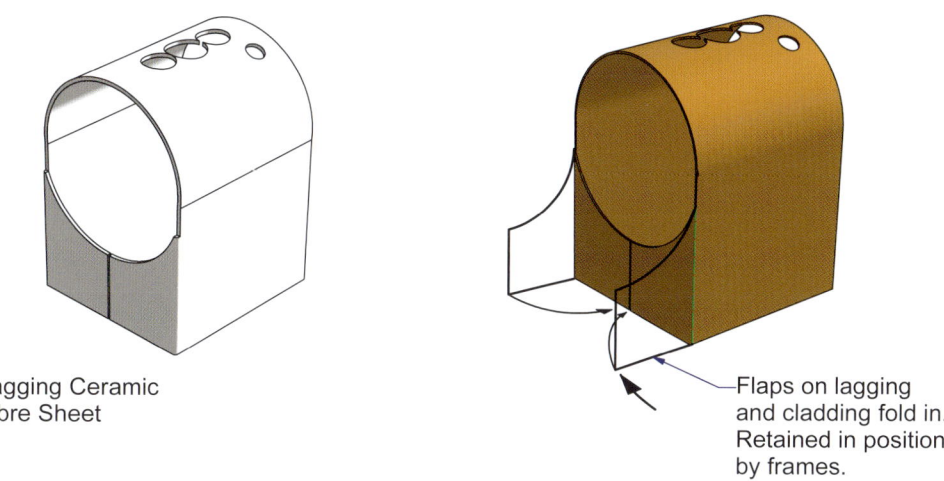

Lagging Ceramic Fibre Sheet

Flaps on lagging and cladding fold in. Retained in position by frames.

BOILER LAGGING AND CLADDING

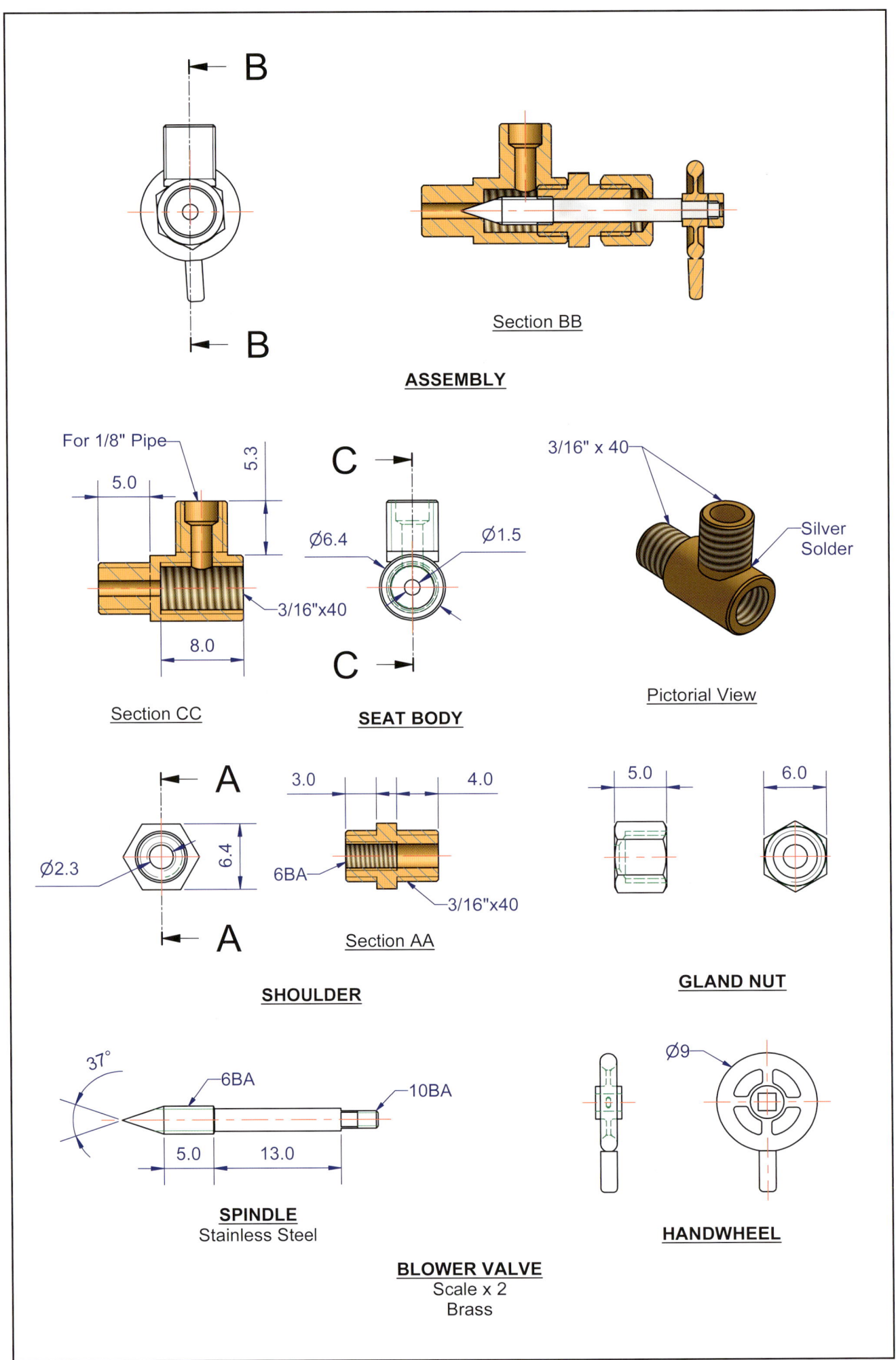

B

B

ASSEMBLY

Section BB

For 1/8" Pipe

5.0

5.3

3/16"x40

8.0

Section CC

C

C

Ø6.4   Ø1.5

SEAT BODY

3/16" x 40

Silver
Solder

Pictorial View

A

A

Ø2.3   6.4

3.0   4.0

6BA

3/16"x40

Section AA

SHOULDER

5.0   6.0

GLAND NUT

37°

6BA   10BA

5.0   13.0

SPINDLE
Stainless Steel

Ø9

HANDWHEEL

BLOWER VALVE
Scale x 2
Brass

10.8 — *This view from underneath shows an axle pump and the suction line from the tank along with the discharge pipe to the bypass valve. Also the ceramic fibre sheet lagging can be seen around the firebox.*

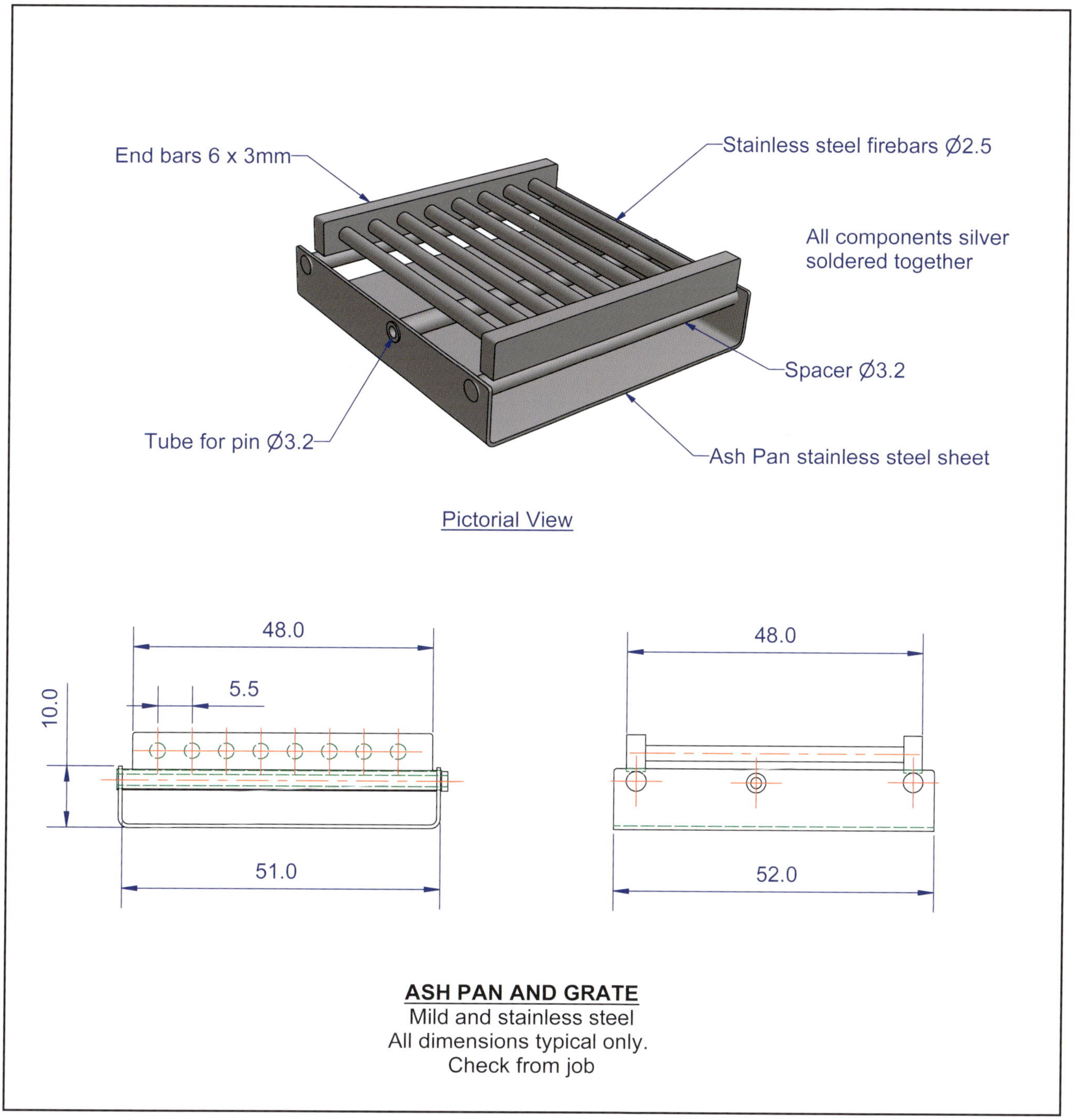

End bars 6 x 3mm

Stainless steel firebars Ø2.5

All components silver
soldered together

Spacer Ø3.2

Tube for pin Ø3.2

Ash Pan stainless steel sheet

Pictorial View

48.0

5.5

10.0

51.0

48.0

52.0

ASH PAN AND GRATE
Mild and stainless steel
All dimensions typical only.
Check from job

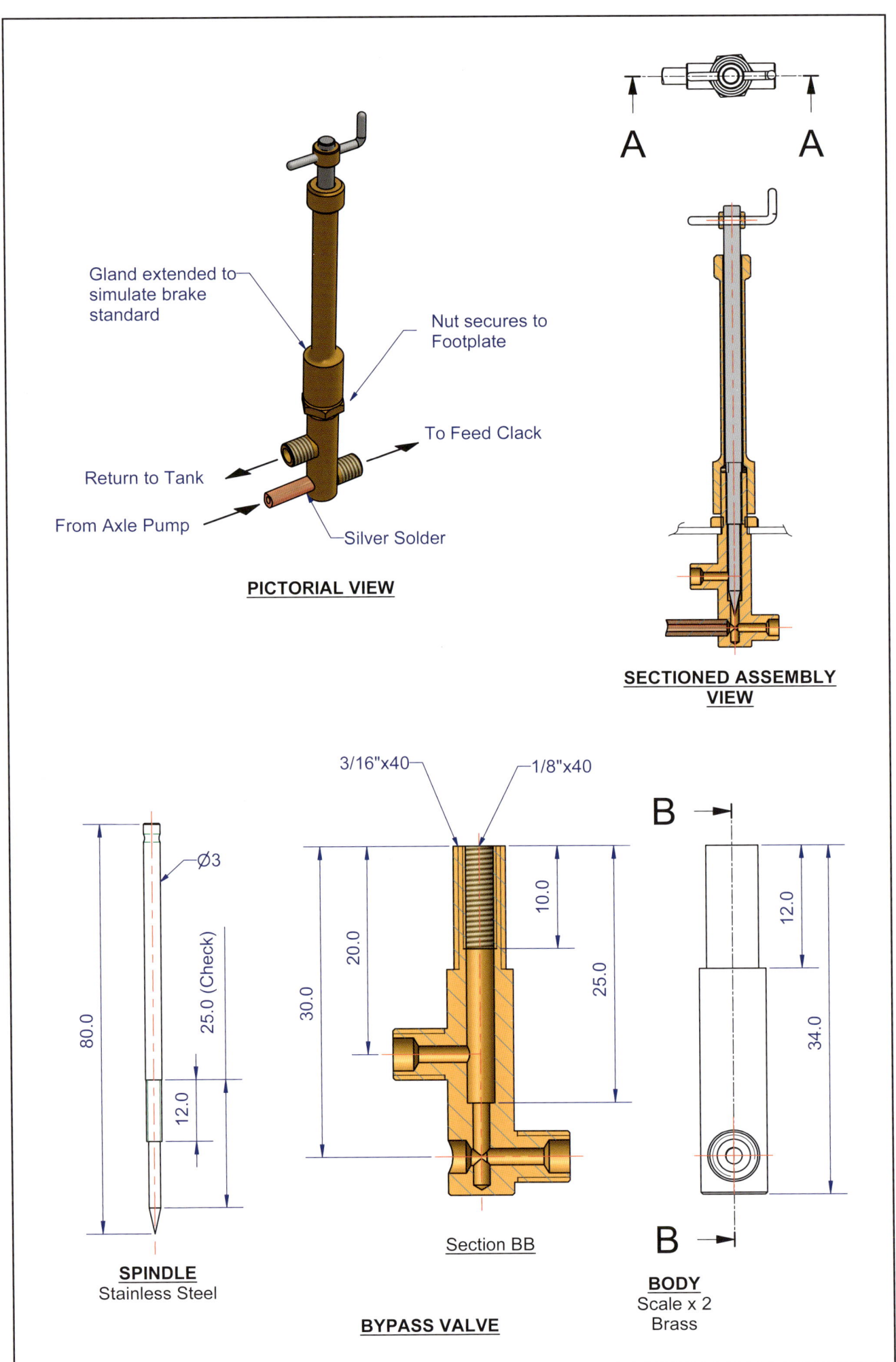

Gland extended to
simulate brake
standard

Nut secures to
Footplate

To Feed Clack

Return to Tank

From Axle Pump

Silver Solder

PICTORIAL VIEW

**SECTIONED ASSEMBLY
VIEW**

Ø3

80.0

25.0 (Check)

12.0

SPINDLE
Stainless Steel

3/16"x40

1/8"x40

10.0

20.0

30.0

25.0

Section BB

B

12.0

34.0

B

BODY
Scale x 2
Brass

BYPASS VALVE

Axle pump

The axle pump is located between the frames and can be positioned anywhere convenient (where it will fit) and driven from any axle .(**Photo 10.9**) The photograph shows a pump for an 0-6-0 engine with the eccentric on the rear axle and the pump stay bolted between the first and second axle. The clack box is just ahead of the front axle. It is convenient to thread the outside of the pump body so that it can be screwed into the stay and held in position with a lock nut. A

10.9 — Axle pump fitted between the frames on an 0-6-0 locomotive.

pump of the size given provides sufficient water so that it just keeps ahead of usage, depending how often the safety blows and how often the blower is used. If the water level starts to fall because a lot of water is being used then the boiler can simply be topped up by hand through the Goodall valve. If the water level rises too much, then the bypass valve can be cracked open and some water is diverted back to the tank.

The pump and clack box are reasonably straight forward to make, but be sure to make the inlet and outlet caps on the clack box the right length to give the correct lift for the balls. When you have turned the valve seats using a "D"-bit, place a ball (preferably not one you will use in the pump) onto the seat, hold a rod onto it and give it a smart tap with a hammer to form the seat. The clack box is attached to the pump by a length of 1/8" copper pipe which provides enough flexibility to be able to locate it where it won't be in the way.

The water inlet and outlet connections to the pump are made with banjos, the lower one feeding from the side tanks or tender. With side tanks, there is a balance pipe across from one tank to the other and the inlet to the pump is taken from this line by means of a tee piece.

The outlet goes from the pump to the bypass valve from which one line goes to the boiler clack valve and the other to one of the side tanks or back to the tender.

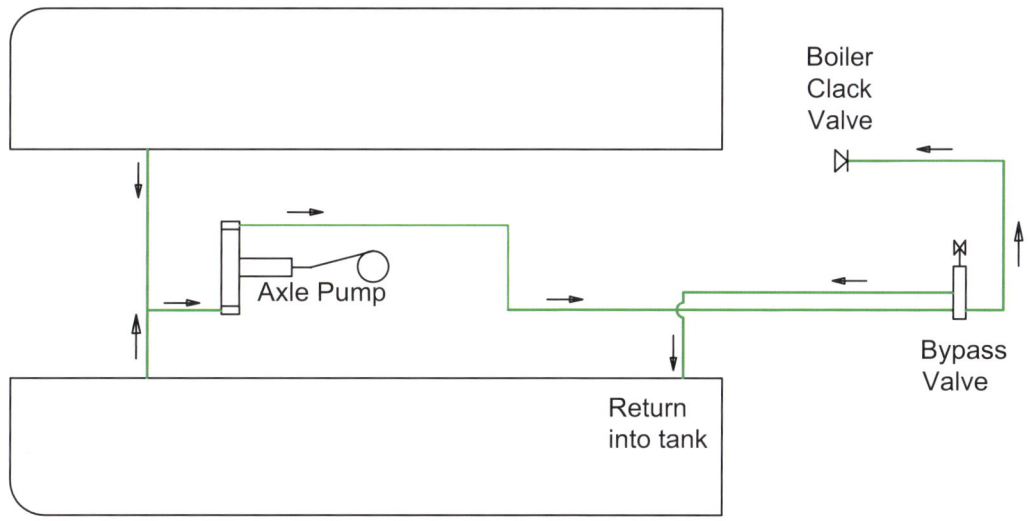

Boiler Clack Valve

Axle Pump

Return into tank

Bypass Valve

PIPING DIAGRAM FOR COAL-FIRED BOILER

Bypass valve and boiler feed clack

When making the bypass valve the main thing to watch is that the length of the valve spindle and its corresponding thread in the body are of the correct length, otherwise it is straightforward as is the boiler feed clack. (**Photo 10.10 and 10.11**)

Smoke box fittings

There are three requirements in the smoke box: a blower pipe, a blast nozzle on the exhaust and a petticoat pipe.

The requirement for the blast nozzle is to have the exhaust discharging straight up the chimney through an opening of about 1mm diameter. If you have a ³⁄₁₆" x 40 thread coming off the exhaust tee as described for "*Eric*" then you can screw a short length of ¼" brass pipe over this with a 1mm hole drilled at the top. The

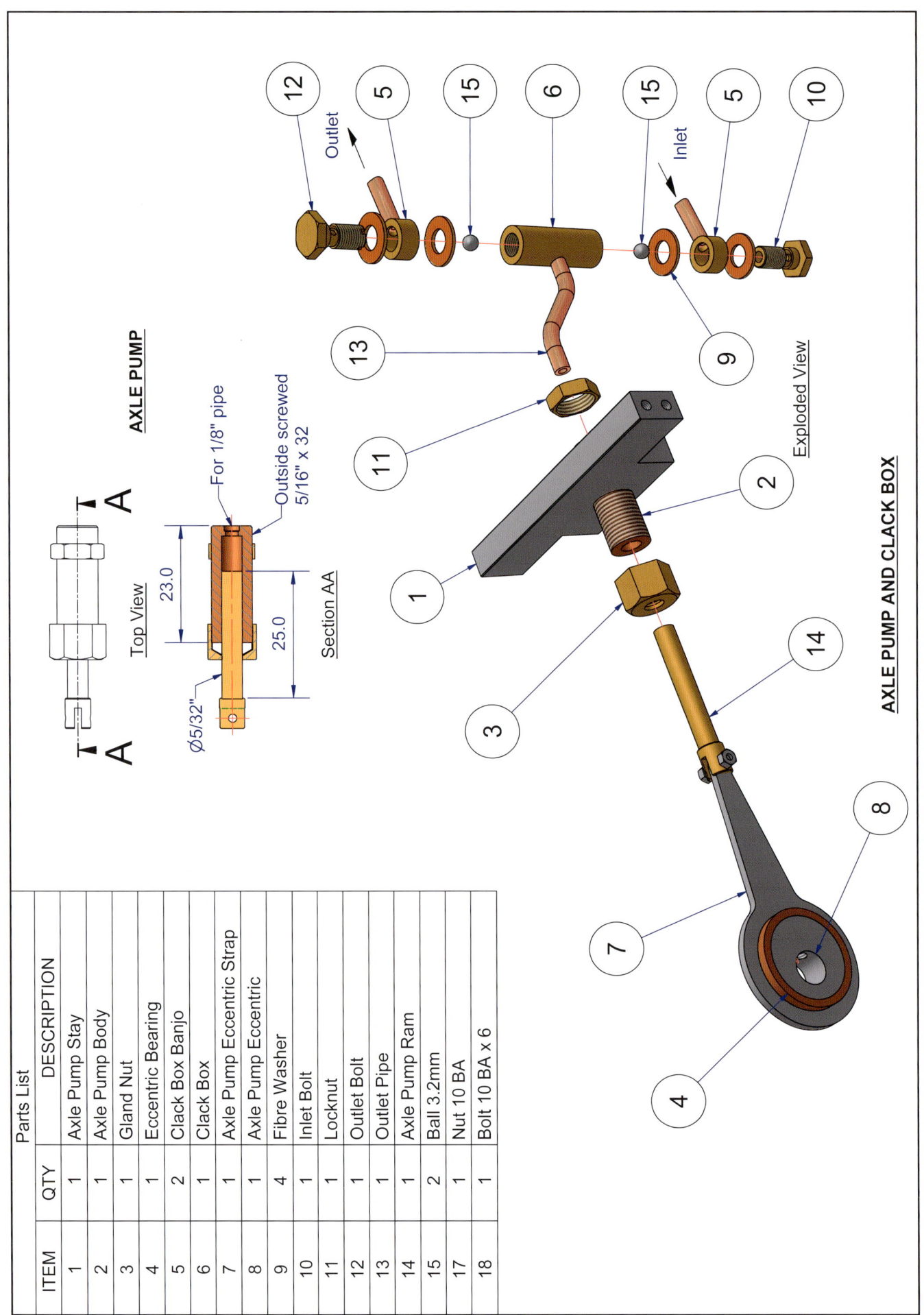

AXLE PUMP

Top View

Section AA

For 1/8" pipe

Outside screwed
5/16" x 32

23.0

25.0

Ø5/32"

Outlet

Inlet

Exploded View

AXLE PUMP AND CLACK BOX

Parts List

ITEM	QTY	DESCRIPTION
1	1	Axle Pump Stay
2	1	Axle Pump Body
3	1	Gland Nut
4	1	Eccentric Bearing
5	2	Clack Box Banjo
6	1	Clack Box
7	1	Axle Pump Eccentric Strap
8	1	Axle Pump Eccentric
9	4	Fibre Washer
10	1	Inlet Bolt
11	1	Locknut
12	1	Outlet Bolt
13	1	Outlet Pipe
14	1	Axle Pump Ram
15	2	Ball 3.2mm
17	1	Nut 10 BA
18	1	Bolt 10 BA x 6

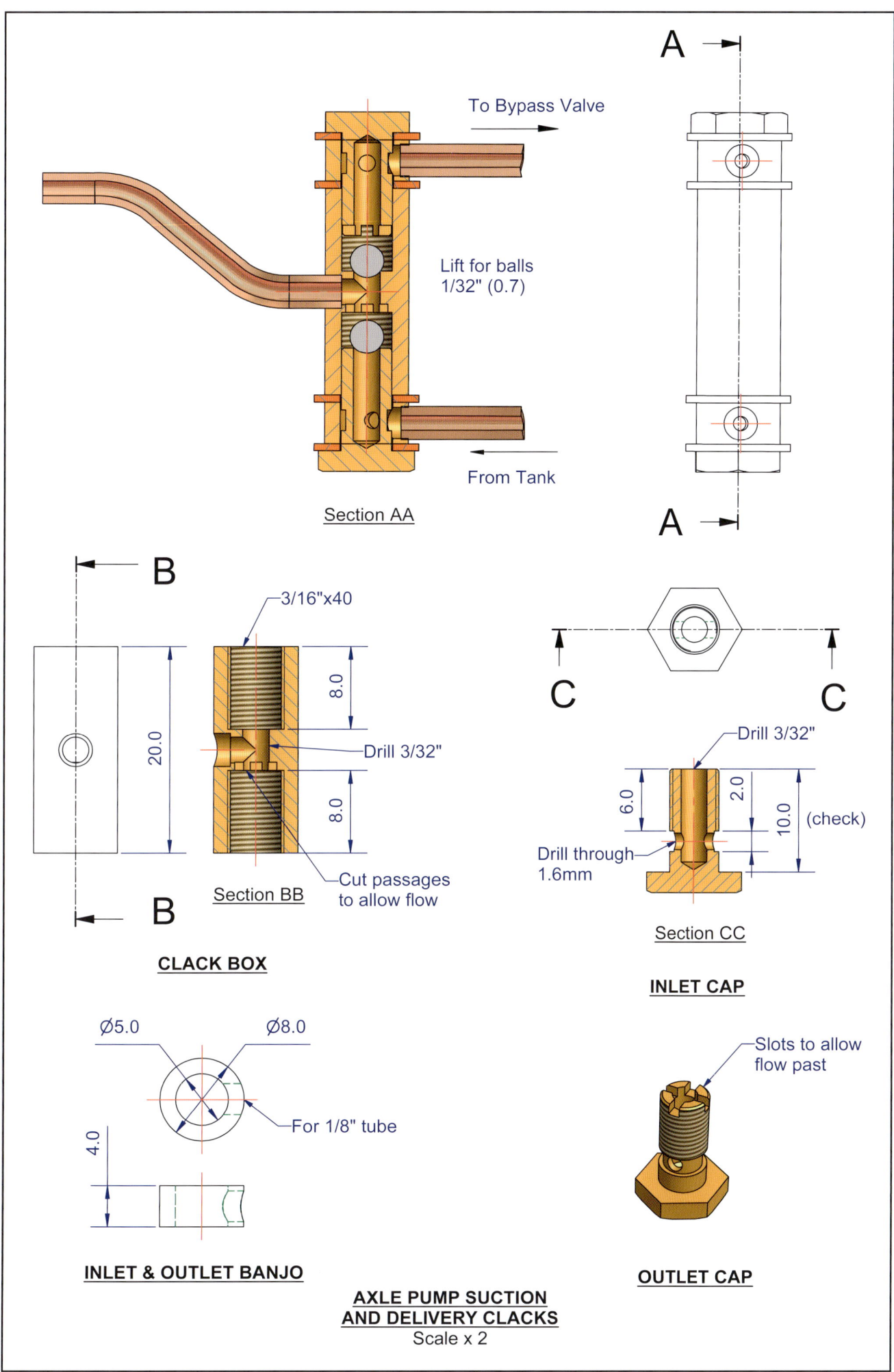

To Bypass Valve

Lift for balls
1/32" (0.7)

From Tank

Section AA

A

A

B

3/16"x40

8.0

20.0

Drill 3/32"

8.0

Cut passages
to allow flow

Section BB

B

CLACK BOX

C

C

Drill 3/32"

6.0

2.0

10.0

(check)

Drill through
1.6mm

Section CC

INLET CAP

Ø5.0

Ø8.0

For 1/8" tube

4.0

INLET & OUTLET BANJO

Slots to allow
flow past

OUTLET CAP

**AXLE PUMP SUCTION
AND DELIVERY CLACKS**
Scale x 2

10.10 — Bypass valve

10.11 — Back head fittings and a nice glow to the fire

exact height of this nozzle may need to be arrived at by trial and error, but should be about one third to a half the smoke box diameter.

The petticoat pipe is the short length of pipe which protrudes down into the smoke box from the bottom of the chimney. Rather than a straight piece of pipe which is adequate for a gas–fired locomotive, we need to form a bell mouth on the end which helps to provide a venturi effect. Use a length of copper pipe for this and form the bell mouth by hammering the end over a cone shape such as a lathe centre. It will need to be annealed a few times as you do this.

10.12 — A view into the smokebox showing fittings

The accompanying photo shows a glimpse of the petticoat pipe at the top with the steam pipe curling down to the cylinders so as to be clear of the exhaust blast. It is difficult to see, but the blower pipe exits close to the left side of the blast nozzle which in this case is a short length of brass drilled in the bottom to fit over the exhaust stub and drilled 1mm at the top. It is clamped in position with a 10BA bolt. The blower itself is simply the end of the $^3/_{32}$" copper tubing positioned so that it points up the chimney. (**Photo 10.12**)

CHAPTER 11 – Running and Maintenance

Equipment

Running a steam locomotive may seem a little daunting at first, but it soon becomes second nature, and with a locomotive of the size we run in the garden, there is very little that can go wrong.

With gas firing, you only need a few minutes to get things ready, so a short run before dinner or when time is tight is easily done.

The items needed are:

- A water filler bottle. This is simply a small plastic sprayer bottle purchased from a hardware store. Remove the spray nozzle and fit a length of plastic tubing ending in a fitting which seals onto the Goodall valve;

- Distilled water or filtered rain water;

- A small oiler for the motion. An ideal item for this is a small syringe purchased from a medical supplies shop. Get one with a large diameter needle; the whole outfit costs only a few dollars. Use ordinary lubricating oil;

- An oil bottle for filling the lubricator with steam oil. This can be a small oil bottle with a spout or again a syringe can be used. Steam oil is much thicker than lubricating oil, so a larger diameter outlet helps it to flow. This oil is to lubricate the pistons in the cylinders so be sure to use proper steam oil as it is formulated to be effective when mixed in with the steam. Ordinary lubricating oil will not do the job;

- A lighter. Any barbecue or stove type of gas lighter will do, but get one which produces a flame, not just a spark.

Gas firing

Place the locomotive onto the track, ahead of your rolling stock and fill the boiler with distilled water to about half way up the gauge glass. The water will expand as it heats up but there will also be losses when warming through and removing condensate, so about half way up the glass is a good point to start.

Drain any water from a previous run out of the bottom of the lubricator and top it up with steam oil. Replace the cap and close the drain.

Fill the gas tank with butane. You may need an adaptor or extension piece to connect the gas bottle to the filler valve, but this is just a length of 3mm brass rod, drilled out slightly to fit onto the filler valve on one end; on to the gas bottle at the other and drilled right through about 1.5mm diameter. The end that fits over the gas bottle outlet can be drilled out to take a small "O" ring inserted to help form a seal.

Open the gas valve a little and light up. Place the lighter over the chimney and the flame should "pop" down into the fire tube and light the burner. You will become familiar with the sound it makes when it lights properly. If the flame doesn't want to pop down into the chimney then you might have to open the smoke box and light from there. If this is the case, as soon as the burner is alight close the door and let the flame settle down. Different locomotives have different characteristics, so you will need to become familiar with the behaviour of each

11.1 — Peter Uscinski's grandson gives the job his utmost attention while oiling Peter's "Edwin" before a run.

one. Be very careful that the flame is alight properly in the fire tube and not in the smoke box. You will need to adjust the gas valve. It can be turned up fairly high while raising steam but after the boiler is up to pressure and the engine is running, it should be turned down as low as possible to conserve gas.

While the boiler is heating, oil around the motion, putting a drop or so of oil onto all the bearings and running gear. (**Photo 11.1**) After about five minutes or so, pressure will start to show on the pressure gauge at which time you can open the throttle slightly and move the loco forwards and backwards by putting into gear and pushing by hand. This should clear condensate from the steam lines and the cylinders.

Check the safety valve operation by continuing to raise steam until it blows and then check the water level, topping up if necessary to a reasonably full glass.

Now your loco is ready to couple up to the rolling stock and go for a run. You can, if you wish, at this point turn the fire off and top up the gas tank which will give an extended run. If you do this then just wait a few moments after re-lighting to let the flame settle down.

From here it is a simple matter of watching the water level and topping up as necessary and keeping the gas pressure as low as possible to maintain pressure. As the locomotive heats up the gas tank also heats up which raises the pressure of the gas slightly so you will need to turn it down a little as the run proceeds.

To shut down before the gas runs out simply close the valve. If the run finishes after the gas runs out you will need to allow the gas tank to cool down before refilling with butane.

Coal firing

Coal firing requires a bit more fiddling and concentration than gas to ensure a smooth run. With gas you can almost "set it and forget it", but if you do this with coal you will probably lose the fire and have an ignominious return to the steaming bay.

In addition to the items listed above for running a gas fired engine, for coal-firing you will need:

- A small battery driven fan to attach to the chimney for starting up;
- A suitable shovel or scoop to add coal to the firebox;
- A rake for the fire which can just be a piece of wire with a small bend in the end;
- Coal and/or char depending on availability of good steaming material. (This will depend on where you live.) Break it up into pieces which easily fit through the firebox door; about ⅜ to ½" should do.
- Charcoal broken up to about the same size. This is soaked in either kerosene or methylated spirits for starting up. Methylated spirits is cleaner than kerosene but you have to be careful not to put the burning shovel back into the container as the fumes are very flammable.
- An optional item is a pair of tight fitting gloves such as riggers gloves to protect your hands from the hot fittings in the cab. (**Photo 11.2**)

Drain and fill the lubricator, fill the side tanks or tender with distilled water and top up

11.2 — water bottle, charcoal and coal, starting up fan, shovel, oiling syringes and lighter

the boiler water to about half a glass. Have your coal or char ready in the tender or wagon. Make sure you have the grate and ash pan in position and fill the firebox to the bottom of the door with pieces of soaked charcoal.

11.3 — The starting up fan sitting on the chimney

Place the fan in the chimney, switch it on and light the charcoal with a lighter through the firebox door. After making sure it is well alight, close the door and oil around the motion. (**Photo 11.3**)

Wait. Wait until the whole firebox is well alight. You will hear it crackling and underneath you should be able to see it glowing through the ash pan. Only then, start adding a few lumps of coal, leaving the door open for as little time as possible. (**Photo 11.4**)

After several minutes the charcoal will have started to burn away and be replaced by coal. The pressure will start to rise on the gauge and when this happens you can remove the fan and open the blower. As the blower uses steam, the water level will need to be watched. In fact you will need to monitor the water level very carefully all the time. It cannot be allowed to fall below the level of the crown sheet either when raising steam or when running.

As the pressure rises the condensate can be cleared by pushing forwards and backwards a few times. Let the safety valve blow to check its operation, add more coal to the fire and generally set the fire up so that you feel you have control. The blower should be cracked on just enough to keep the fire burning well without continually blowing the safety valve and the firebox should be full to just under the door.

11.4 — Shovelling coal into the fire

Couple up your train, check the water level, open up the throttle and move off. When running, the exhaust will provide a draught up the chimney to draw the fire, so you might be able to completely close the blower valve. Try to achieve a balanced situation where the pressure is maintained without blowing off, the water level remains constant and as little blower as possible is used. Add coal regularly, the old saying is "add a little, often." If your engine is a good steamer you will probably find that while running it will maintain pressure without the blower open at all, and you may even find that it produces too much steam in which case you can open the fire door slightly. This draws cool air across the fire and gives you some control.

One of the big variables will be the track you are running on. If it is a simple, level track with gentle curves then it will be much easier to balance the steaming of the engine, but if there are variable gradients and tight curves more attention will be needed. Which of course you will remember is one of the reasons why you were attracted to coal firing in the first place!

After the Run

When the run is finished, let the engine cool down.

If it is gas fired, all that is needed is a gentle wipe down to remove dirt and oil. The boiler water should be completely replaced every so often so that there isn't a build up of solids in the water. This can be done by turning the loco upside down and draining out. You may like to develop a system where you drain and replace the steam oil in the lubricator after the run. This way it is ready for next time.

For a coal fired engine, after it has cooled down and the fire has gone out, remove the ash pan and grate and dump the ash. Be careful as it may still have some burning embers. Open or remove the smoke box door and rake out the ash. There will be quite a build up as the ash is sucked forward with the draught. (**Photo 11.5**) Clean the tubes through with a flue brush. Depending on the size of the flue tubes, many sizes of rifle cleaning brush are available and one of these is ideal, preferably a brass one. While doing these cleaning operations it is a good idea to use a vacuum cleaner rigged up with a small diameter tube in the end of the suction pipe. (That is, it is a good idea if the domestic authorities don't come into conflict.) After cleaning all the cinders and ash away,

11.5 — You can see how ash builds up in the smokebox

wipe the paint work gently to remove oil and dirt. There will be a lot more of this with a coal fired engine. Again drain and refill the lubricator ready for the next run.

Radio control

A detailed description of installing radio control into the locomotive is outside the scope of this book; however we will discuss some of the basic principles which should enable a straightforward installation to be undertaken. (**Photo 11.6**)

Manual control of a locomotive is in some ways a little more like the real thing, particularly when using coal firing, but nonetheless it can be very convenient and much easier to use radio control, particularly when running on a track with variable gradients and curves.

The essential components of a radio control installation are:

- Transmitter;
- Receiver;
- Servos.
- Batteries

The transmitter is held by the operator and has two or more channels, each one of which operates a function on the loco through a servo.

The receiver is located on the train; it has an aerial and receives the signals from the transmitter, sending them to each servo as required.

11.6 — The author's grandson operating the radio control as the train approaches the embankment.

The servos are mounted on the locomotive and each one operates a function such as; throttle, reverse lever, whistle, drain cocks, or whatever is required. They have a tiny motor which drives an arm which is linked to the item being controlled.

There are two sets of batteries required, one set is used in the transmitter and the other on board the train to power the receiver and drive the servos.

Radio gear can be purchased as a set, or the individual components can be bought separately. As space is limited for installation, it is better to use a small receiver and small or mini servos; however, if the gear is bought as a set, it usually comes with a large receiver and servos so the small ones would then have to be bought as an extra.

A basic radio installation will control the throttle and the reverser, so only two servos will be needed. A simple two channel transmitter could be purchased, or if you have an eye on future expansion to other functions it may be more economical to buy one with four or more channels.

The servo can be positioned anywhere where it can be linked up to the item it is to control and where it will be out of the way of other components such as the gas burner. The throttle servo can be mounted under the footplate with the control arm operating through a slot, it can be above the footplate over to one side clear of the burner or it can be mounted up onto the roof frame. A servo operating the reverse gear can be located in the cab or it can be positioned in a side tank, either operating back to the reversing stand or directly connected to the weighshaft with the reversing lever disconnected.

The receiver and batteries can be mounted in either tank or possibly under the roof or footplate. The aerial wire can be wound onto a small rectangle of thin ply and positioned under the roof or in a tank. It is also possible to house the receiver and batteries in a tender or separate wagon. (**Photo 11.7**)

11.7 — Radio receiver and batteries housed in a separate wagon. The aerial is coiled under the false coal load and the control arm for the throttle can just be seen.

To mount the servos, they usually have two holes for mounting screws and these can be screwed directly into the footplate or tank sides, or they can be screwed to brackets which are in turn fixed to the locomotive. Double sided tape or adhesive has been used, but this can be unreliable, particularly where there is heat.

Troubleshooting

Once you are familiar with your locomotive and have run it a few times there is very little to go wrong. Always check that bolts and screws have not come loose, particularly in the motion and that no leaks develop in any of the pipe unions.

With a coal fired engine the pump clack valves and feed water clack valves may leak or stick from time to time, but this often corrects itself. Otherwise they just need taking apart to check.

The burner is about the only item likely to give trouble with a gas fired locomotive and usually it is only a blocked jet. This can be cleared by taking the jet out and blowing back with gas from a can.

When you are making the burner, occasionally you might have difficulty in getting it to light properly and burn smoothly. This can sometimes create difficulties and there can be a bit of mystery surrounding the problem. In response to this issue, Paul Blake wrote an article describing factors which affect satisfactory burner operation and the article is reproduced here.

The Black Art of Butane Burners
by Paul Blake

Any enthusiast who has worked with small scale live steam has probably come across the butane burner. This is a wonderful invention which breathes life into our tiny locos and has many advantages. It is clean, reliable and easily controllable. More importantly the fuel is as cheap as chips down at the local Asian Supermarket.

We see these devices burning beautifully and reliably in commercial locomotives such as the Roundhouse brand and we marvel at the efficiency of them and their simplicity. But those of us who have attempted the building of one often find that they are not as simple as they look and achieving an easy lighting and efficient burner is sometimes frustratingly difficult. Anyone who doubts this to be the case should scan through the pages of magazines about garden railways to see how many times problems with butane burners are mentioned.

Well we have studied them in great detail during our journey building small scale live steam and we have concluded - Butane Burners are indeed a Black Art. But like all Black Arts they do give up their mysterious secrets from time to time and we have decided to write down what we know or have learned.

Our starting point was the Argyle *Philadelphia* design which used ¼" heavy wall tube 55mm long with 16 slots at 3mm centres using 0.010" (0.254mm) saw width (note that this is a very narrow saw width like a razor saw — by comparison a junior hacksaw will cut a slot about 0.7mm and a normal hacksaw about 1mm).

The thick wall tube recommended for that design was found to have an ID of ⅛". We found that in our experience the *Philadelphia* burner as built lit easily and burned well but did not create enough steam for continuous running particularly with a load. This is where the Black Art bit starts as some builders have used this design and had no problems and Gordon Watson of Argyle Locomotive Works built literally hundreds of this model.

Extensive testing and talking suggested that the burner tube was not large enough in diameter resulting in restricted availability of oxygen.

Subsequent experimentation lead to drilling out the ID of the tube to ³⁄₁₆" and opening up the slots with a junior hacksaw blade with the "set" ground off giving a slot width of about 0.6mm. It should be noted that the ³⁄₁₆" ID must be drilled before cutting the slots otherwise you will end up with a tangled mess. Please don't ask how we know this!

This size of burner held steam and was just adequate in a ⅝" flue tube, but for a ¾" flue tube something larger was needed.

In all this experimentation we learned some other basic rules for the Black Art of Butane Burner Design:-

- The gas jet must point directly down the center of the burner tube. To achieve this you need a close fit of the jet holder in the mixing chamber housing.

- Generally the burner slots should taper from just cutting through the burner tube at the front end to approximately half way through the tube diameter at the back. This encourages a more even flame.

- Generally the burner should light easily through the chimney or from the smokebox (i.e. "pop back") with the face of the gas jet positioned about ⅓ʳᵈ into the air breather hole from the rear.

- A larger burner tube ID provides a more efficient burner.

- Termimesh (fine stainless steel mesh) either inserted inside the burner tube or wrapped around the outside can quieten noisy burners (but not always).

- If at first the burner does not light or burn efficiently replace the jet. If this does not work try another jet. In other words have a small supply of jets (they are cheap) and try several before you call your burner a failure. We cannot explain this except by suspecting poor quality control (to be fair it must be hard to achieve such accurate tiny orifices).
- A blocked jet can be cleaned by blowing butane back through it from the face
- We have no idea why this works, but a recalcitrant burner has been coaxed into working by first lighting it out of the boiler.

After building many live steam locos between us and studying burners in several factory locos we have arrived at the following formula:-

- Outside Diameter ⅜" Inside Diameter ¼" (at least)
- Length of burner tube 80mm to 100mm depending on boiler size
- About 24 slots at 4mm centers cut with a junior hacksaw with the set ground off
- Within this burner design we have used the following jets depending on how much heat is needed: G, GN or HM. These jets are readily available in Australia from larger camping stores. They have a M4.5x0.5 thread

This burner design fitted to a number of locos provides more than adequate steam and has to be turned down so far when steam has been raised that it operates very quietly.

The above mentioned jets are part of a range with the following specifications:-

- E   0.10mm x 3.32mj/hr
- FM 0.13mm x 5.28mj/hr
- G   0.15mm x 6.80mj/hr
- GN 0.17mm x 7.72mj/hr
- HM 0.18mm x 9.08mj/hr

The first figure is the diameter of the jet orifice and it is presumed the second figure is the gas usage and potential heat output.

It is noted that the standard Roundhouse jet is 0.20mm (with a 1BA thread), but in practice the HM jet provides a significant amount of heat.

The final critical issue is the temperature of the butane gas. On cold days (which are rare in most parts of Australia) butane gas loses pressure as it gets colder. Occasionally this becomes so severe that the burner will not function properly and like the "watched pot" will not boil.

Several remedies are available the first of which is to use butane with a small amount of propane added (commonly about 20%). This is available in most camping stores. Propane is not as susceptible to the lowering of pressure effect and therefore these mixes perform better. Please note that pure propane or propane in higher percentages **must not be used under any circumstances.**

The second remedy is to ensure that your gas tank is located close to the boiler so that some warmth is transferred into the gas tank as the boiler temperature rises. This of course does not overcome the problem at first light up. Other more radical solutions include locating the tank in a water bath in the tender but we have not found such requirements necessary in our climate.

A quick fix that works is to simply wrap your fingers around the tank for a couple of minutes to transfer some body heat. This is usually effective enough until some heat builds up in the boiler.

If you follow these guidelines in the building of a butane burner and its operation you should find that the black art is mastered and you will have an efficient and reliable firing system for you small scale locomotive.

Part 3

ROLLING STOCK

SIMPLE WAGONS AND CARRIAGES

CHAPTER 12 − Introduction

12.1 — A variety of rolling stock behind the early morning mixed.

Now that you have built a working locomotive, let us complete the picture by making some wagons and carriages to haul.

There is a large range of fine quality rolling stock available "off the shelf" for garden gauges, both in ready to run form and kit form, and many people go for this option if they don't have much time to spare. The problem here is that as your train starts to reach a realistic length, the contents of your wallet starts to drain out proportionally, so your train remains quite short, or you remind yourself that you are a Model Engineer, and it shouldn't be too difficult or time consuming to make some wagons yourself.

As mentioned before, people generally seem to come from one of two directions into Garden Railways. Either they move up from smaller indoor electric gauges, or they are escapees from the outdoor passenger hauling gauges of 5 inch and 7¼ inch. Your approach to carriage making will depend on which of these directions you have come from, so our methods will be something of a compromise between modeling and engineering.

In this section, we will look at how to make a basic chassis, both a 4-wheel and a bogie, and present some ideas showing how to add cosmetic details and build wagons or passenger carriages onto the chassis. It is not intended to present a detailed step-by-step how-to-build description as we did with the locomotive, but rather to provide ideas to set you thinking and creating, to suit your own needs and resources. Any dimensions given will be suggestions only, and you may vary these to suit your circumstances. Remember we are modeling Narrow Gauge prototypes, so we do not work to any "standard" size, the prototypes did not have any particular standard, and neither do we. However, when scaling down 2'-0" gauge using 1:19, remember that the track gauge comes out to 32mm, so you will need to adjust to 45mm if that is your gauge.

Tools and materials

In addition to a metal lathe and basic metal working tools, it is also necessary to use some woodworking tools, and the methods you use will depend on your skills and what you have available. A small band saw or scroll saw would be extremely useful, although handsaws can be used if these are unavailable. To rip lengths of timber to use as small planks, etc, a hand power saw attached to a universal bench such as a Triton® can be used. Working with woodworking tools has its dangers, and all manufacturers' instructions and safety advice should be thoroughly understood and followed. Any jigs or aids which might be set up should be used with extreme care.

Adhesives will be used and good choices are PVA woodworking glue and epoxy; either slow curing or the "five minute" type would be suitable.

Design

Before starting to make anything, we should think about what we are trying to achieve, so it would be helpful to go through a simplified design process. For our rolling stock, we can do this by considering two things:

(1) Function, and
(2) Appearance.

(1) Function refers to the working aspect of the item, and some of the requirements to be considered here are the ability to:

- Run smoothly around the track without jumping off;
- Couple up to the train;
- Withstand derailments and bumps and
- Withstand handling and transport

(2) Appearance refers to the aesthetic side of things, and this will vary greatly depending on your objectives, particularly those relating to how detailed and true to scale you want your wagon to be. Some of the items here are:

- Type of coupling;
- Body panel details such as individual planks or plain sides;
- Metal work, rivet and bolt detail, door handles, ventilators;;
- Wheel springing- dummy or real;
- Glazed or blank windows;
- Paint job and
- Transfers, numbers or letters.

Essentially we are aiming to produce a "working" chassis with only just enough engineering sophistication to allow it to fulfill its function, and then adding on whatever cosmetic bits that suit our fancy. Your objectives, imagination and resources provide the only limits to what you can build.

You can use many resources to decide on how your wagons or carriages should look. Ideas can come from:

- Real life, where you might measure and photograph operating stock;
- Magazine photographs of both real and model railways;
- Other models or
- Plans from magazines or the Internet.

Chapter 13 – Basic 4-Wheel Chassis

Base

The base can be a very simple affair, essentially consisting of a rectangle of 6mm or so plywood with the axle horns or bogies attached, and strips of wood glued to the ends and sides to cover the ply edging. Suggested dimensions for an open wagon or small closed van are shown.

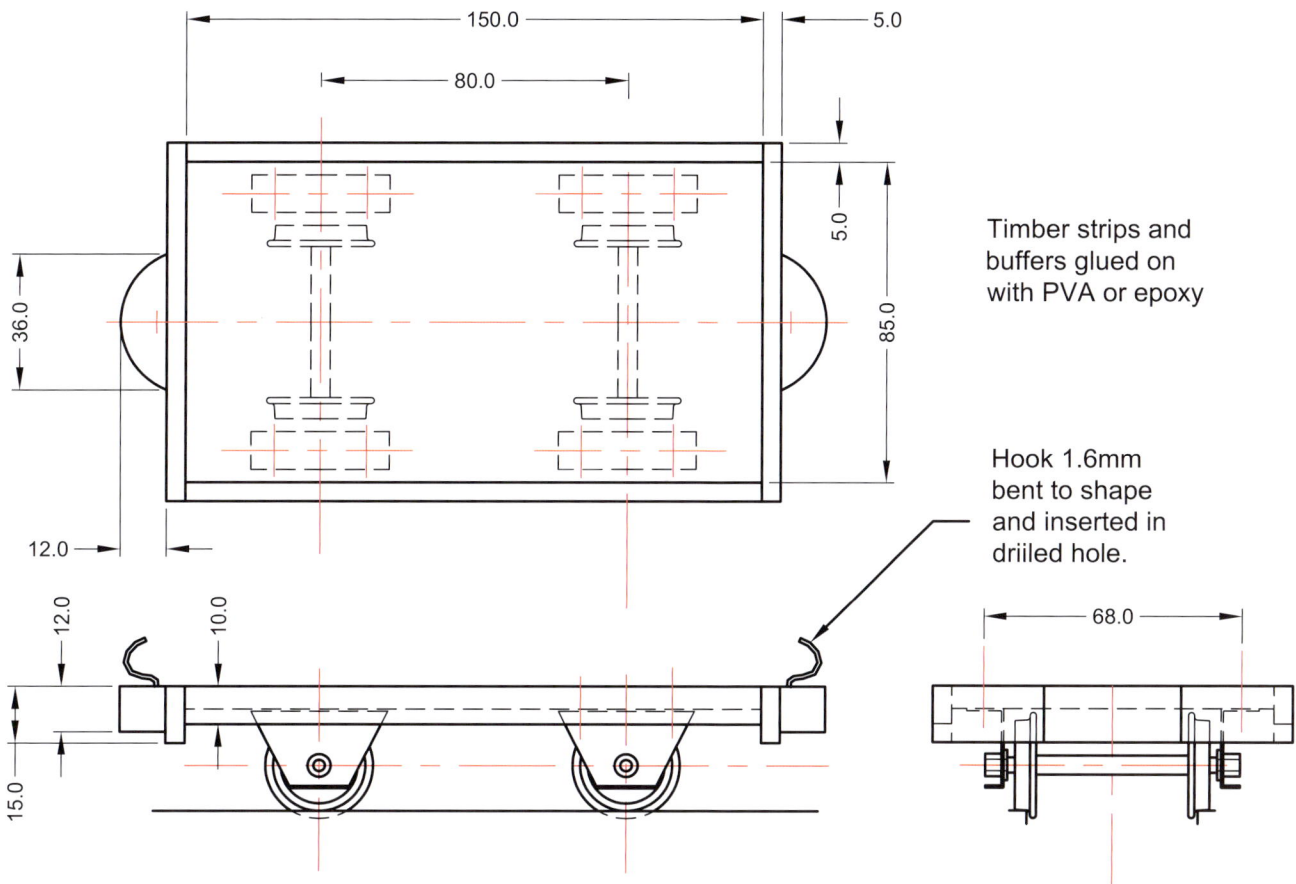

Timber strips and buffers glued on with PVA or epoxy

Hook 1.6mm bent to shape and inserted in driiled hole.

4 WHEEL WAGON CHASSIS

Scale: Half Full Size

You will now need to make a sketch or two showing your coupling height in order to arrive at a suitable wheel diameter and the dimensions for the axle horns. (**See drawing**) We can position the lower edge of the plywood at the coupling height, although there is room for variation here, depending on what type of coupling you are using. A simple and effective coupling system can be a curved pad of timber and a hook, similar to that used on the cane railways.

Axle horns

The function of the axle horns is to retain the bearings, keep the wheel-set in the right place under the carriage, and support the weight of the wagon. We are not carrying passengers or heavy loads, so they only have to be strong enough not to bend, twist or collapse under the weight above them when being used and during handling. You may like to make them from something like 1.6mm thick material here, but in practice steel

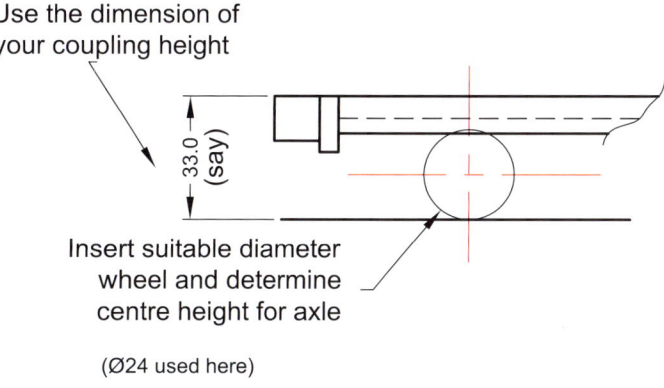

Use the dimension of your coupling height

Insert suitable diameter wheel and determine centre height for axle

(Ø24 used here)

SKETCH TO DETERMINE WHEEL DIAMETER AND AXLE HEIGHT

or brass about 0.6mm thick is perfectly adequate and much easier to cut and bend. In fact we can use tinsnips. If you make cosmetic cut-outs in them, then they probably should be no less than about 1mm thick.

Each horn is a separate piece and is folded where shown and screwed into the plywood using small round head screws or through bolts.

Mark out the pieces on a strip of material, (**see drawing**), drill for the axle bearings and screw holes and then cut out. If you opt for the cut-outs, then these would need to be chain drilled and filed, or you could use a piercing saw.

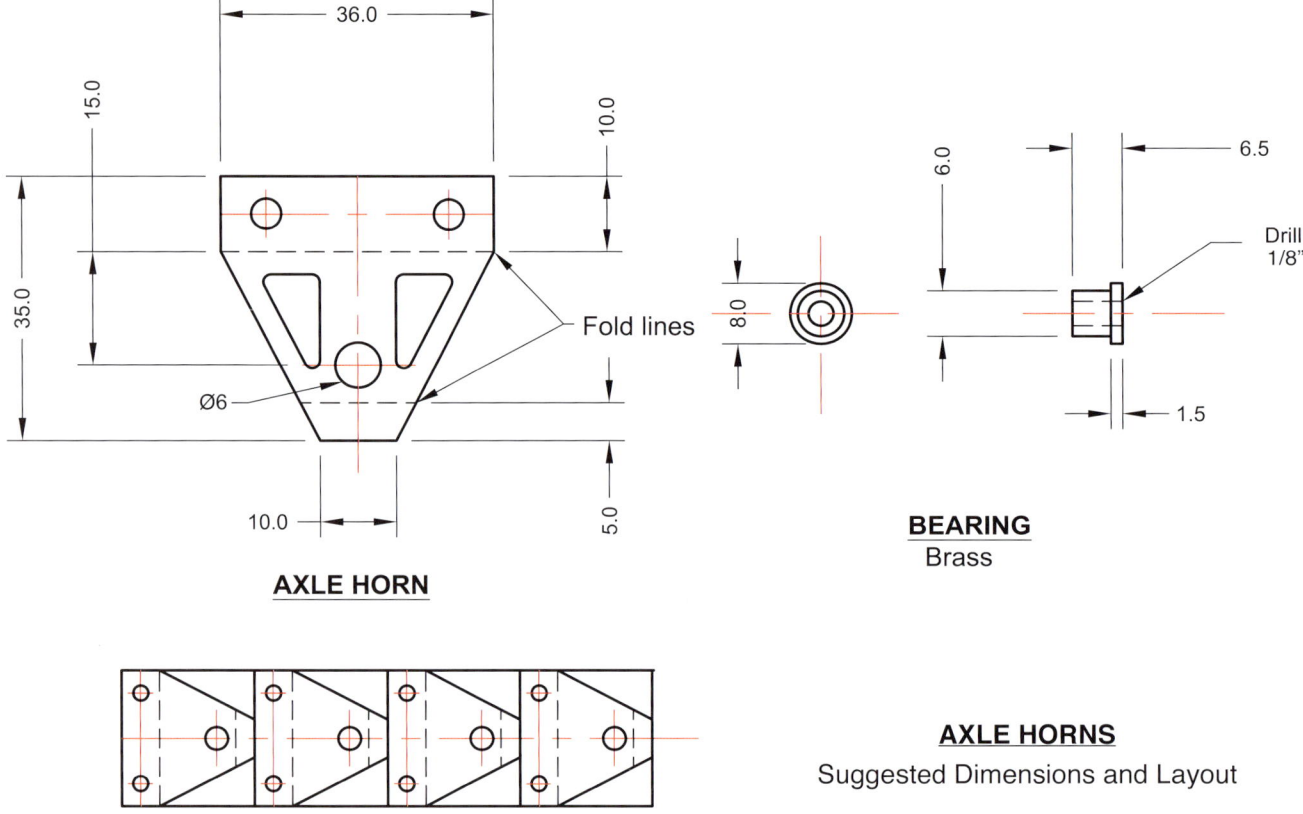

AXLE HORN

BEARING
Brass

AXLE HORNS
Suggested Dimensions and Layout

The bearings are made from brass and are drilled through ⅛ inch to take the axles. We really don't need fine tolerances here, so make sure the axles turn freely in the bearings.

Wheels

You may wish to purchase your wheels, even if you make the rest of the wagon, as they are quite time consuming to make, and are readily available at a reasonable price. They come as pairs of wheels mounted on an axle, the wheels being of various diameters, generally requiring ⅛ inch axle boxes.

If making them, the dimensions given earlier for the trailing pony wheels and axle for the locomotive can be used. You may wish to use other diameters for the wheels, but other dimensions remain the same.

To make a wheel, mount the rod in the 3-jaw chuck, face the end and start the axle hole with a centre drill. Drill ⅛ inch to a sufficient depth. (How many wheels you make in one setting will be determined by how large your lathe is.) Turn the wheel profile and tread. The outside radius of the flange can be filed. Part off if your lathe is sturdy enough, or if not, hacksaw the wheel off. Repeat for as many wheels as you need and then reverse them in the chuck, face the rear surface and file the radius on the flange.

The axles can be gripped in the 3-jaw and the shoulders for the wheels turned to a sliding fit for Loctite, making the back to back distance as accurate as you can, but bearing in mind that to fulfill their function, they don't have to be to the thousandth of an inch!

Assembling the basic chassis

The best time for painting is before things are fully assembled. You might like to paint some items as you go along, but at this stage, we will leave the painting to be discussed later.

The end and side cover strips and the buffer blocks can be glued on, making sure the edges of the ply wood are flat and square.

Place the bearings into the axle horns with Loctite and leave to cure. Mark out with pencil under the plywood where the horns are to go and drill pilot holes for the screws. All that is required here is some accurate marking out from the centre line. Screw in the horns on one side and then insert the wheels and screw the other side on.

You should now have a chassis with free running wheels onto which you can add a wagon or carriage body and any cosmetic details you require. (**Photo 13.1**)

Casting cosmetic springs

Many different styles of axle horns and axle boxes were used on rolling stock, particularly Narrow Gauge. Most, if not all, used some form of springing which helped to keep the wagons from falling off the track.

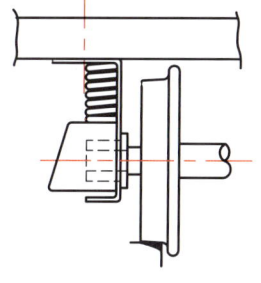

13.1 — Axle horns in position with simple dummy springs

Having described how to make a basic 4-wheel chassis, we will now look at the steps to adding on some simple details such as dummy axle boxes and springs to make the model look a little more realistic. Remember, the style, shape and sizes given are suggestions only, and if used, will produce a model that could be loosely described as "stand-off scale".

The springs and axle box assemblies we are going to describe, become add-on units that are simply glued onto the axle horns using epoxy. I can hear the big gauge model engineers drawing a deep breath and shaking their heads at the thought of it. "Certainly not strong enough for my railway!" The fact is, however, that from a functional point of view it definitely is strong enough, provided there is an adequate gluing surface, because they don't do any work, they just hang there.

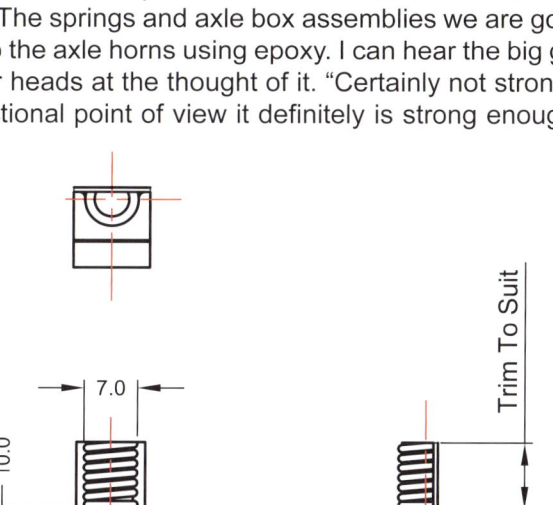

DUMMY SPRING PATTERN

The assemblies could be totally fabricated from brass, steel or aluminium four to a chassis, but that would be a time consuming way to do it, therefore we will describe how to cast them from a master pattern, using a low melting point metal such as white metal, or a jeweller's alloy. The process involves making a solid pattern, making a two part silicone rubber mould from it, and then pouring the molten metal into this.

The pattern

When making patterns for sand casting, the patterns have to be carefully constructed so that they can be removed from the mould without breaking away the sand. However, when using a rubber mould, the mould itself is flexible, and we don't have to be as particular about the pattern shape, although there are still limitations that we need to be aware of. Firstly, although the rubber mould is flexible, you must keep undercuts to a minimum. If the mould has to flex too far, it may break, or you may have difficulty removing the pattern and later the finished job. Secondly, don't use thin sections; otherwise the metal may not flow into them. Complex shapes can be cast, but the simpler they are, the simpler the mould can be, and the less chance there is of a failure. If you are going to cast a large number of pieces or if you want fine detail then it would be better to use a centrifugal casting process which is beyond the scope of this book.

Probably the most straight forward type of pattern to use is one with a flat back, and for both of our examples this is the type we will use.

Straight compression spring

This can be made up from brass and soldered together. Firstly shape the axle box and cut the backing piece from a piece of 0.6mm sheet. The spring can be wound up from a piece of 1.6mm brass, or a bonze welding rod. Wind it around a length of about 3mm diameter rod, and wind sufficient turns to provide a spring long enough for your purposes. Now very carefully file or grind off one side of

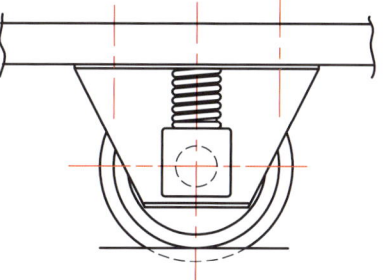

AXLE HORN AND SIMPLE SPRING ASSEMBLY

the spring to form as large a flat as you can without going right through. Cut off a short length of the 3mm rod to fit into the spring and assemble the pieces, laying them back down on a firebrick. Apply soft solder flux and gently heat the parts with an LP torch. Feed in soft solder to hold the parts together and then keep feeding it in to fill up any gaps and form fillets down the side of the spring. Alternatively a bolt of the correct size cut almost in half gives a close representation of a spring.

Leaf spring

This can be fabricated again from brass and when it is loosely assembled, laid down flat onto a firebrick for soldering. Make sure that plenty of soft solder flows between all the parts and fills any gaps. (**Photo 13.2**)

We now have two flat backed patterns around which we will form a two-piece rubber mould.

13.2 — Brass pattern for leaf springs

The mould

The mould is made from a grade of silicone rubber which is able to withstand the temperatures of the molten metal. It is quite readily available from the appropriate hobby and craft suppliers and is a red coloured Dow Corning 3120 RTV Silicone Rubber. Unfortunately this material is not very wallet-friendly, so we have to use it as economically as possible. It comes in a 1lb (453 gm) plastic container with a tube of catalyst which is mixed in at a ratio of 10:1. Unless you have an accurate set of scales, it can be difficult to mix small quantities, so we will describe how to make our two-part mould using half the batch at a time.

Make an open sided box from a piece of sheet material, folding three corners, and holding the fourth together with strong adhesive tape. Brass, tinplate or anything will do. The sizes suggested in the drawing (110

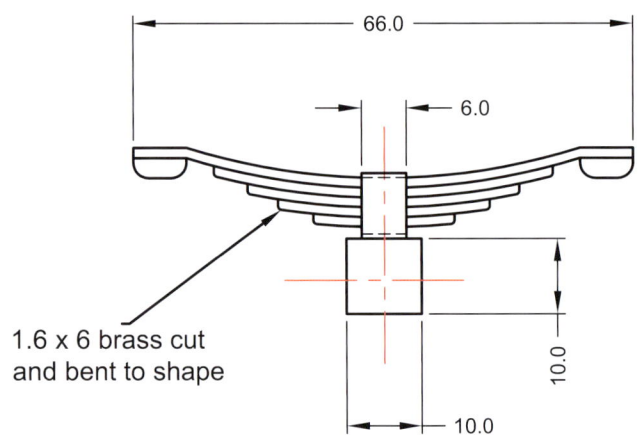

1.6 x 6 brass cut and bent to shape

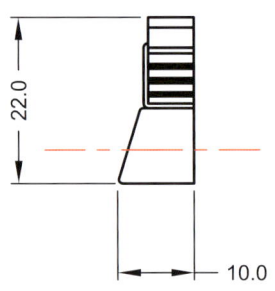

Dummy Spring Pattern
(Dimensions suggested only, can be altered to suit.)

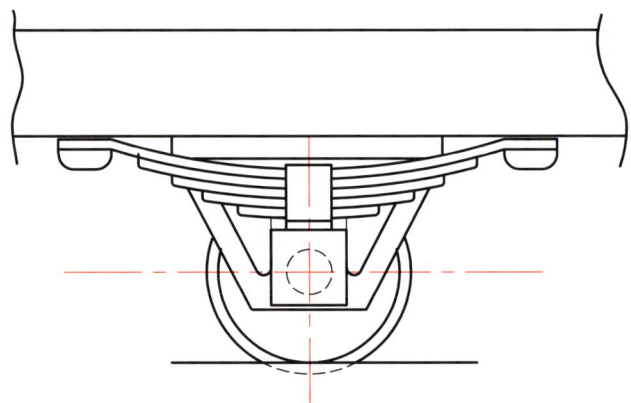

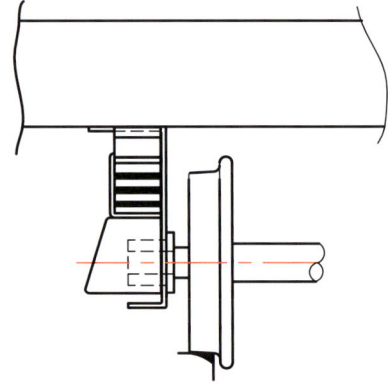

AXLEHORN AND SPRING ASSEMBLY

x 75 x 40) will take approximately the entire batch of silicone, poured in two half pound lots. Place the box down onto a flat surface such as another sheet of tinplate and seal all around the bottom edges with plasticine. Place the two patterns in the bottom of the box with their flat backs downwards and evenly spaced from the sides of the box and each other. Place three or four locating buttons inside the box. They can be turned up from any material in the off cuts bin, and are just truncated cones about 6mm long and diameters of about 8mm and 10mm. They will form tapered holes into which the second half of the mould can locate.

Open the container of silicone and pour out half into a mixing container. Carefully judge and squeeze half of the tube of catalyst in and mix thoroughly, following the instructions given with the material. After mixing, pour it over the patterns and it should half fill the box. Pour slowly and carefully to avoid trapping air bubbles. Poking gently with a piece of wire may help here. After it has cured (as per instructions), free the box from the plasticine and base, take off the tape and free the mould–half. With a little careful flexing, your patterns should come out, leaving a perfect female impression. Now we have to form the other half of the mould, which will contain the sprues and risers, i.e. the channels through which the metal is poured.

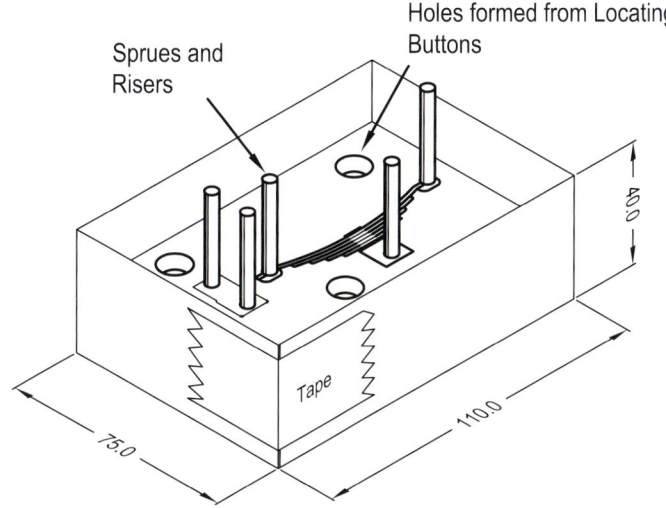

MOULD READY FOR SECOND POUR

Return the patterns into their impressions and place the half-mould down on the bench with the patterns on top. Place the box around it and tape the corner, making sure that it seals around the edges of the rubber. If necessary, plasticine can be used again to ensure a seal. Each pattern needs a sprue to pour the metal in, and a riser to allow the flow through of the molten metal. These can simply be made from a length of 5 or 6mm metal with the end faced off and "super glued" onto each end of the pattern so that the metal will flow through and fill the pattern. Don't be tempted to taper these to make it easier to pour; otherwise you will not be able to get the finished job out of the mould. Make them long enough to stick up above the top of the box. The drawing shows the mould at this stage. When you have these set up, mix the rest of the silicon rubber and pour in to fill the box. Allow to cure, then it can be taken apart and the patterns removed. (**Photo 13.3**)

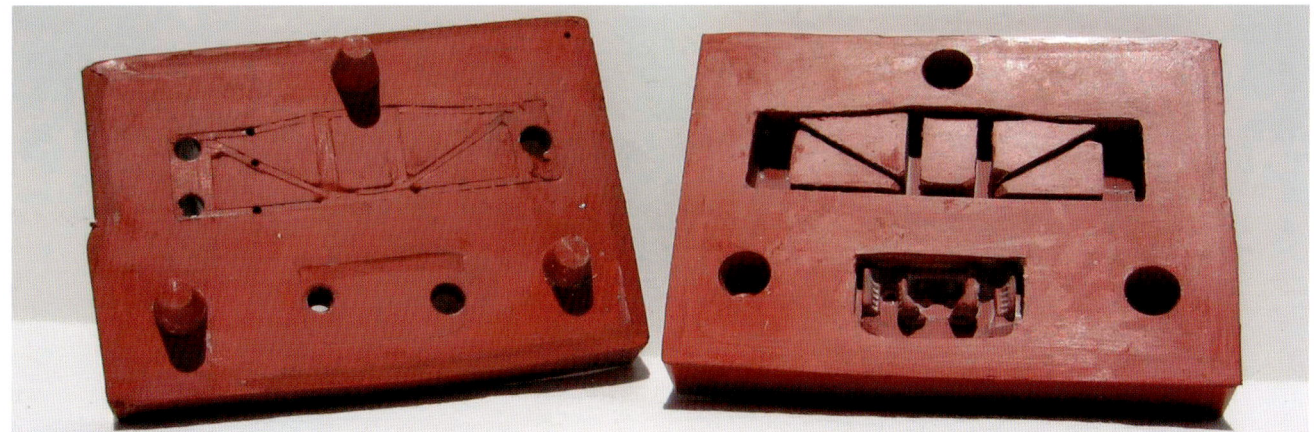

13.3 — Two halves of a mould (in this case for an arch bar bogie and a pony bearing).

Pouring the metal

The metal we use can be obtained from the same craft suppliers as the silicone rubber. Use a metal to suit your purposes, some contain lead which has its dangers, but there are lead-free alloys available. Heating up and pouring molten metal carries obvious dangers if not done properly and carefully. Be absolutely certain that you observe all safety directions given with materials and equipment and that you set up a safe area to heat and pour the metal, which protects against the likelihood of accidental spills. Wear appropriate gloves, eye protection and other clothing to protect you from potential burns. Make sure that you fully understand the processes you are performing and the potential risks involved. The metal we are using liquefies at about 275 deg Centigrade, so if a liquid at this temperature gets away, serious burns could result.

Whilst crucibles to heat and pour the metal can be purchased, you can make one from a suitably sized piece of copper tube onto which is silver soldered a piece of sheet for a base. A handle can be riveted on and the crucible supported in firebricks for heating with an LP gas torch. We will not describe this in detail, and if you do make your own set up, then make sure that it is safe for all stages of the heating and pouring operations.

Assemble the two halves of the mould, giving the pattern cavities and the joining surfaces a dusting of talcum powder, and place in the hearth area for pouring. Only melt as much metal as you need for pouring one of each spring, (this may

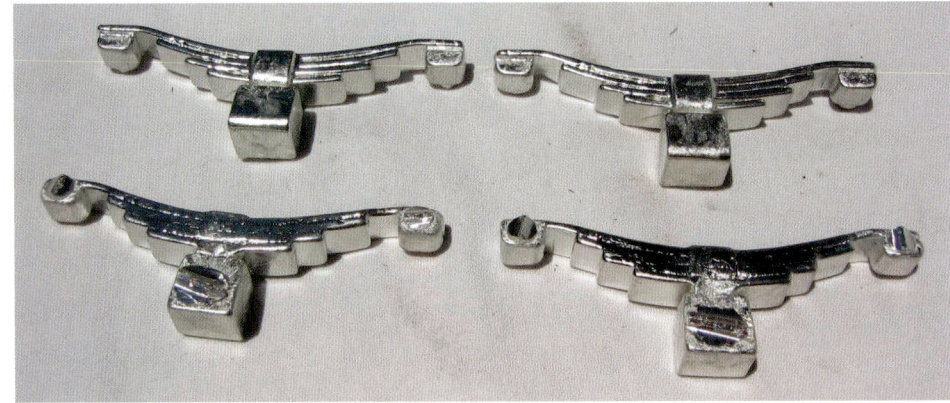

13.4 — Leaf springs fresh from the mould. The bottom pair show the backs.

need to be arrived at by trial and error) then carefully pour it into the sprue until it comes out at the riser. This will happen fairly quickly, and sometimes the castings may not work too well, until the mould has heated up. Don't overheat the metal, turn off the heat as soon as it has melted, otherwise its temperature may rise enough to destroy the mould.

13.5 — Leaf springs glued in position

Allow time to solidify and cool, separate the two halves of the mould and you should be able to pop out two perfect replicas of your patterns. The sprue and riser will be sticking up from the job and these are simply cut off and put back into the crucible for recycling. Repeat for as many springs as you need. (Photo 13.4)

All that needs to be done now is to fit your dummy springs onto the axle horns. To do this, drill a clearance hole for the bearings in the back of the axle box part, (about $\frac{5}{16}$") should do, and epoxy into position before priming and painting flat black. (**Photo 13.5**)

Chapter 14 – Wagon and Carriage Body

It would be surprising to find two people who have exactly the same idea about how a Garden Railway should look. One extreme might be a totally raised track on posts set in the ground with no scenery or line side detail, where running and viewing the train is a priority, and the other extreme might be a track set at ground level, faithfully representing a favourite narrow gauge railway where there are busy scenes at stations, road crossings, tunnels or industrial areas, with scale sized people performing all manner of tasks, (naturally essential to keeping the trains running on time).

The "Brimhillah Railway" is a railway which sits somewhere in the middle of these two extremes, running at ground level through a high rock garden, and then running out onto a raised section for steam raising and setting up. Being situated in a remote area of Queensland where there are cane fields, quarries, timber mills, dairies and some scattered areas of population, very early in its life the directors realised that they would have to provide quite a diverse range of rolling stock to meet all of these needs. The Railway's first engine was an Argyle Philladelphia, a small Baldwin, which was closely followed by two Fowler-style locomotives. With the motive power in order, it was necessary to construct enough rolling stock to meet the demands of a thriving rural area.

In the major population area of the district, a carriage works was established, and we have been describing how they make the basic chassis for their wagons, and now we will look at how the bodies are constructed.

The 4-wheel chassis forms an ideal base for a small narrow gauge wagon or carriage, and we have produced an open wagon for carrying coal, ballast or grain, specialist wagons for sugar cane, enclosed wagons for perishables, mail and a guard and a passenger coach for the school run and general passenger duties. Each one of these requires a different size for the base, but this is just a simple matter of determining what is suitable, again referring to books, magazines, Internet, etc.

An open wagon

There are two main features to the body of an open wagon. The first is the sides (usually timber) and the second is the metalwork which holds the sides together and works any doors or openings with hinges, levers and so on. Here is where you again have to make a decision about how detailed and true to scale you wish to work. At the "Brimhillah Railway" it was decided that economy and speed of manufacture were important considerations, in order that the trains could go into revenue service as early as possible, so a somewhat relaxed attitude to detail was instigated. With this principle decided, work proceeded.

For this, and the other wagons, the sides are constructed from plywood. Around 3 or 4mm thickness is ideal. Run a strip through your saw to the required width to give the height of the wagon and clean up the edges. As wagons were generally made from separate planks held together with metal strapping, we can simulate this planking by inscribing some grooves along the ply. A dull scriber, a blunt nail or some similar tool can be used and is run along a straight edge after first marking out the number of planks required. Measure off the four lengths for the sides and ends and then cut squarely across. Apply glue where the corners will meet and along the bottom edges of the pieces. Place carefully in position and hold in place with masking tape positioned across the corners and also from the sides and ends onto the base. The corners will be reinforced with metal angles, so there should be no need to try and nail or pin them, the glue should prove quite adequate.

After the glue has cured, the ply can be painted and the metalwork applied. This can

14.1 — Wagon with simple detail and plywood sides.

14.2 — Wagon with extra detail and planked sides and floor.

be simple angles and flat straps, or you can apply rivets or nuts, either simulated or real; hinges, pins and whatever takes your fancy. This can be made from around 0.6mm thick brass or steel and is best painted before applying. (**Photo 14.1**)

Of course, there is nothing to stop you building up the wagon from separate pieces of timber as was done in the original, and adding bolt, rivet detail etc. (**Photo 14.2**)

Cane wagons

Many different types of wagon were, and still are used on the cane railways of the world, and some of them make good models when scaled down to 16mm. The older ones were usually made of timber and probably are the best ones to consider for our purposes (**Photo 14.3**). There are some excellent drawings of Queensland cane railway stock available for modellers which have been drawn by Jim Fainges. (Along with his previously mentioned locomotive drawings.) These can be viewed on the Internet at: http://zelmeroz. com/albumquery/fainges2.htm. By following links from the Home Page of these drawings, many other drawings, ideas and information can be found. A copy of an original works-drawing of a Racecourse Mill Cane Truck by Bundaberg Foundry is available at: **http://www.geocities.com/ BourbonStreet/Quarter/2619/cane. gif** These drawings can be scaled to size and then made up to fit onto the basic chassis. It is then an exercise in assembly using small sections of timber and adding metalwork to suit. You

14.3 — Sugar cane wagons

14.4 — Guard's van

will notice different types of axle boxes and again whether you follow these designs closely or not, is up to you.

Covered van or guard's van

No railway which values safety and tradition would be without a guard at the rear of the train, so this wagon will help to ensure your trains run safely. (**Photo 14.4**)

Again we can use 3 or 4mm ply for the sides, but there are separate sections and doors, and strips of wood glued over the planks, simulating the bracing strips which hold the planks together. There is also a partition which divides the guard's compartment from the

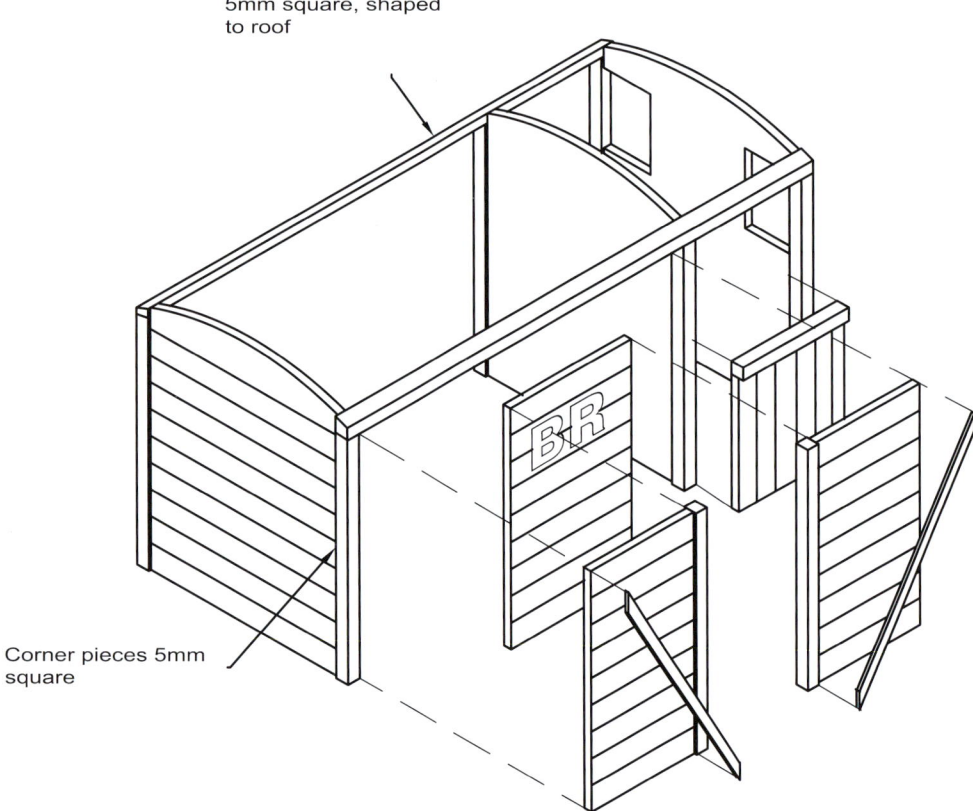

5mm square, shaped to roof

Corner pieces 5mm square

GUARD'S VAN ASSEMBLY

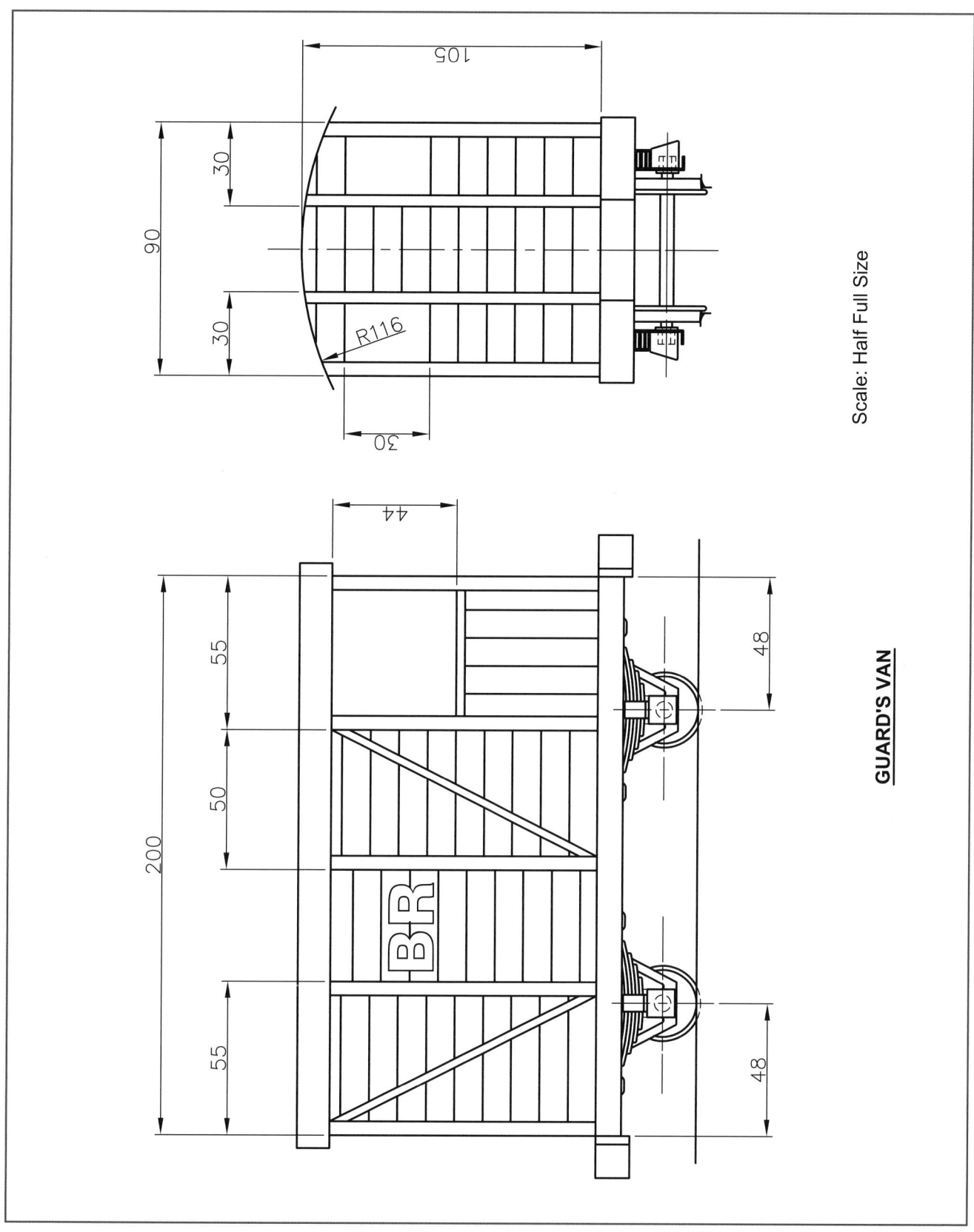

Scale: Half Full Size

GUARD'S VAN

goods section. The drawings show some suggested dimensions and the method of putting the sides together. Again, simulated plank edges are scribed onto the ply. As with the wagon, glue alone should be adequate to hold everything together. The roof can be 0.6mm brass or steel rolled to shape, or thin (1 or 1.6mm) ply with the grain of the outer pieces running lengthwise and held to the curve with masking tape while the glue cures.

Passenger coach

The coach described here (**Photo 14.5**) is modelled after one in use on the Tallyllyn Railway in Wales. Many different ways to model coaches have been devised over the years, and many different materials have been used, from metal to cardboard and everything in between.

A reasonable job can be done in cardboard by printing the sides using a drawing made on the computer and

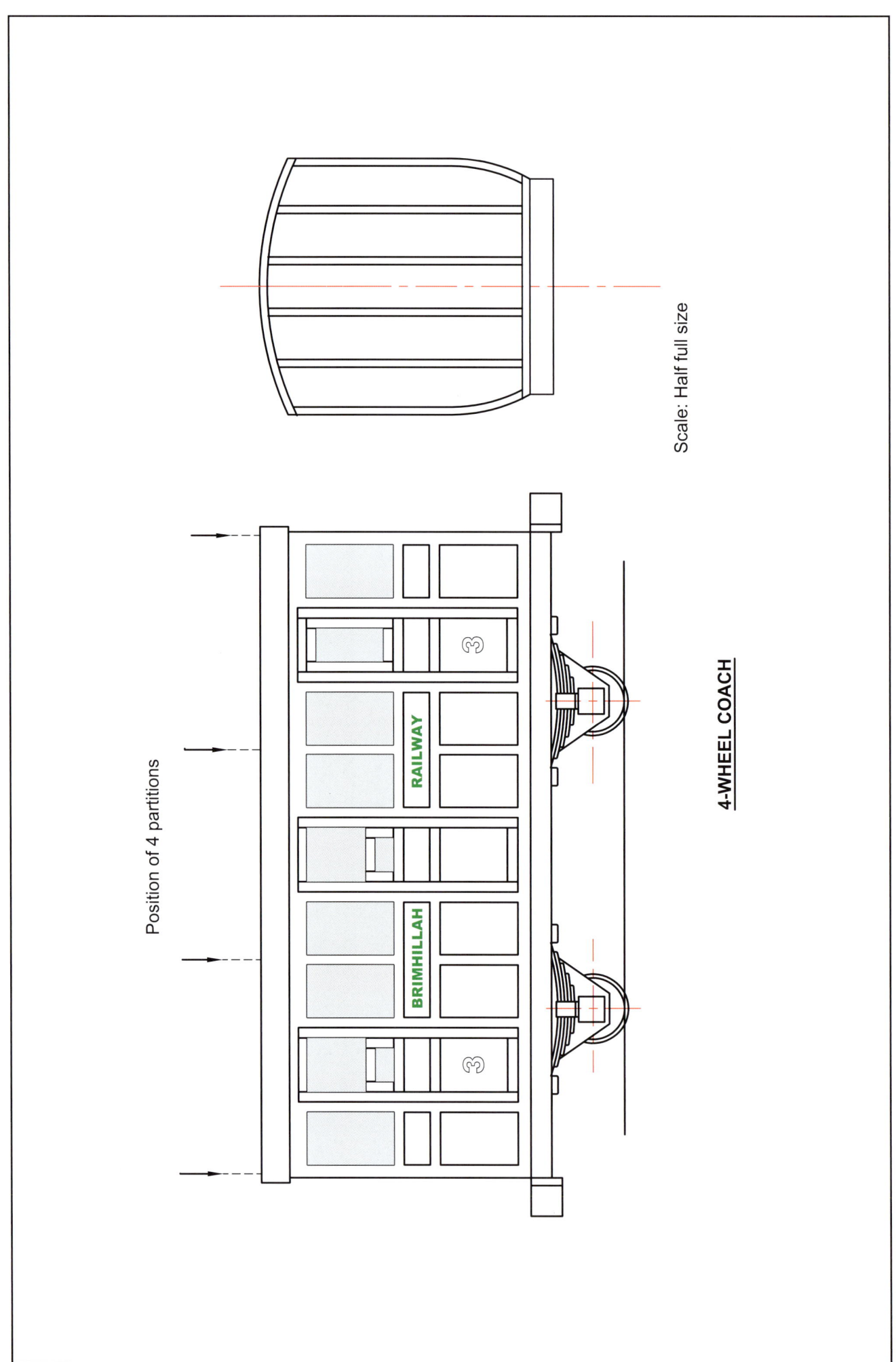

Position of 4 partitions

Scale: Half full size

BRIMHILLAH RAILWAY

3 3

4-WHEEL COACH

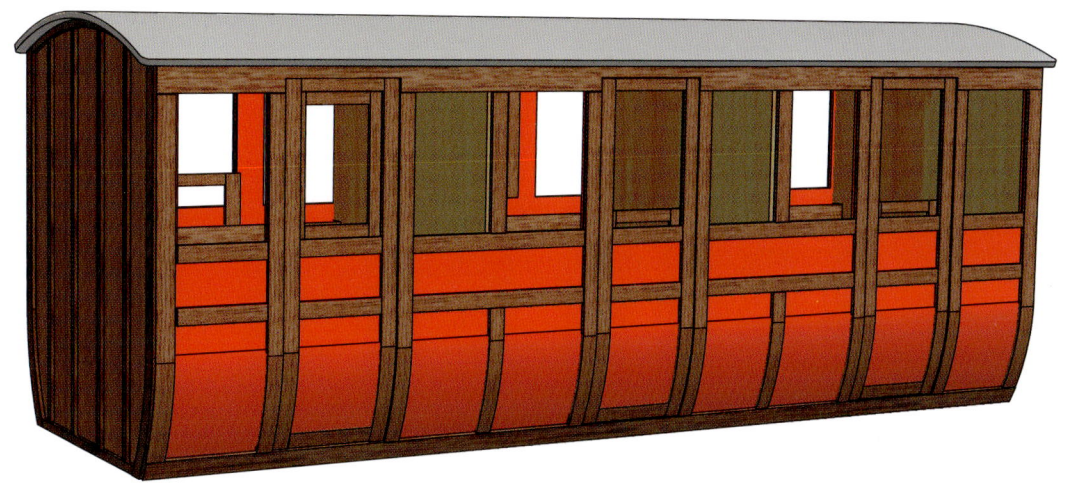

4 - WHEELED COACH BODY

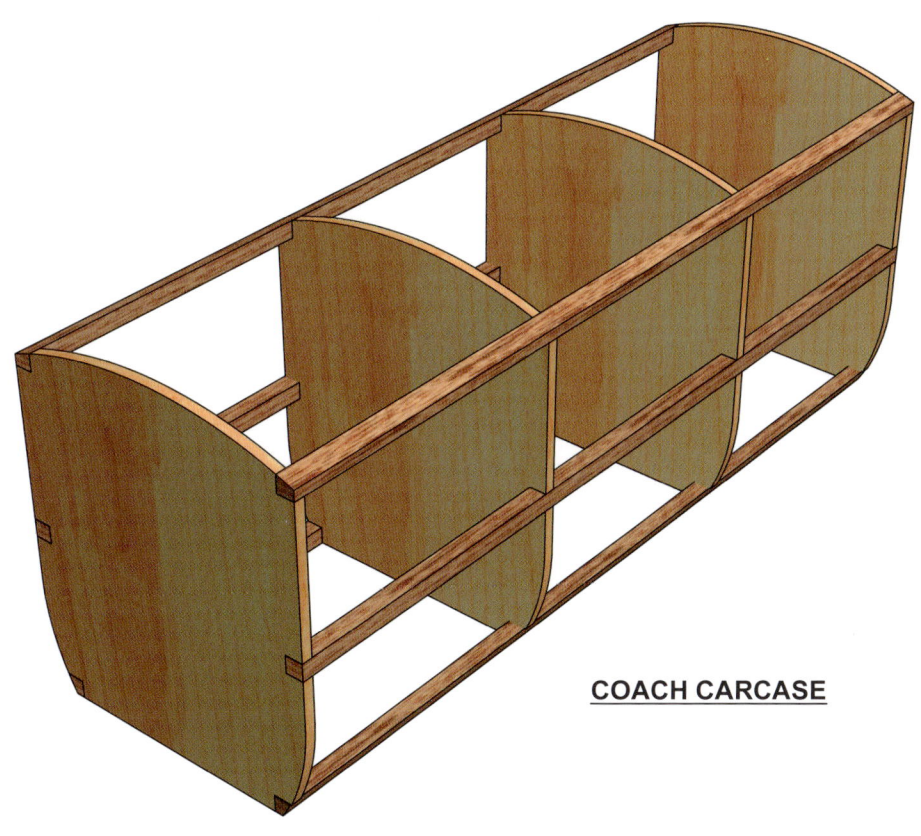

COACH CARCASE

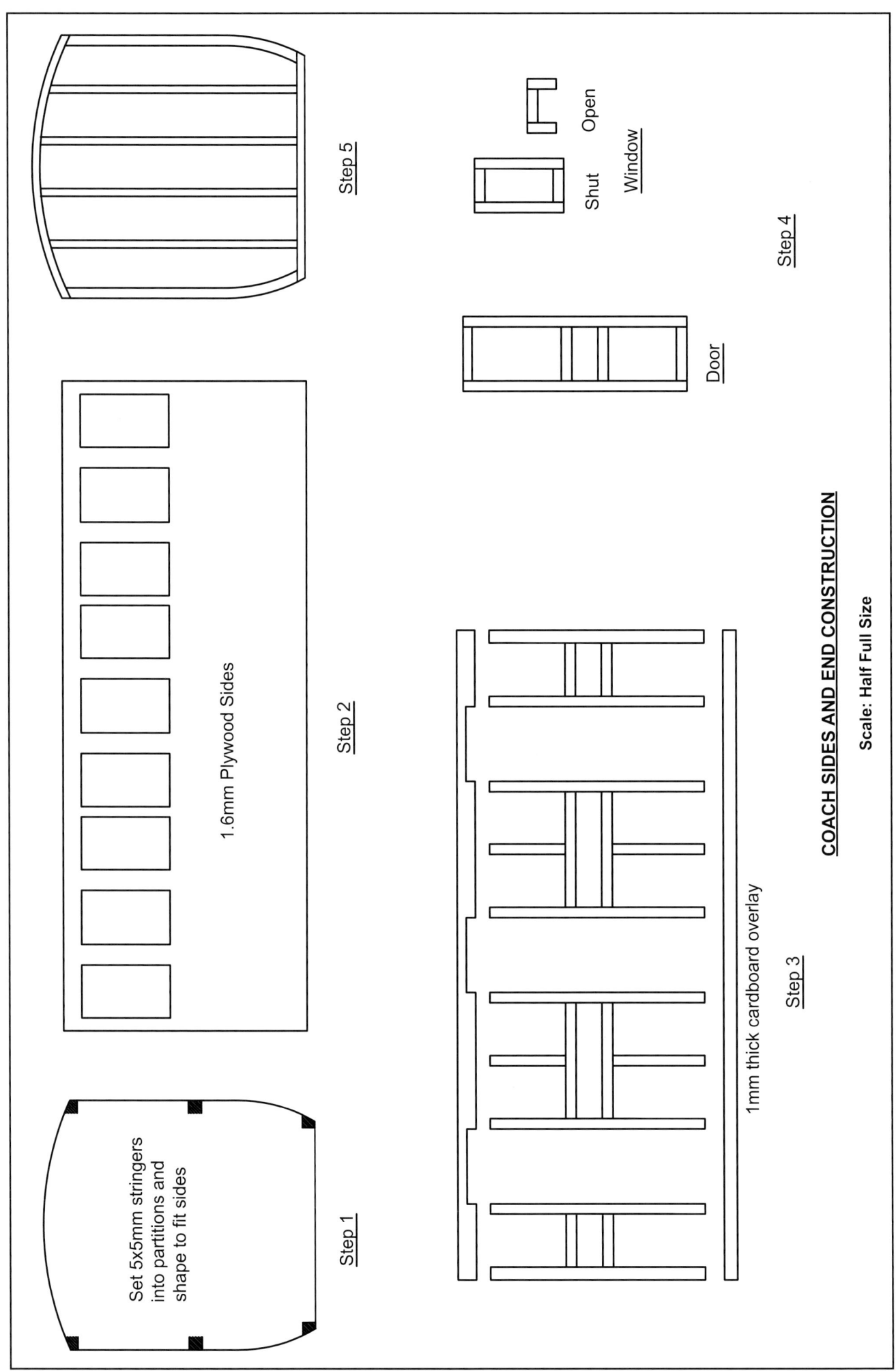

Step 5

Open

Shut

Window

Step 4

Door

Step 2

1.6mm Plywood Sides

1mm thick cardboard overlay

Step 3

Set 5x5mm stringers into partitions and shape to fit sides

Step 1

COACH SIDES AND END CONSTRUCTION

Scale: Half Full Size

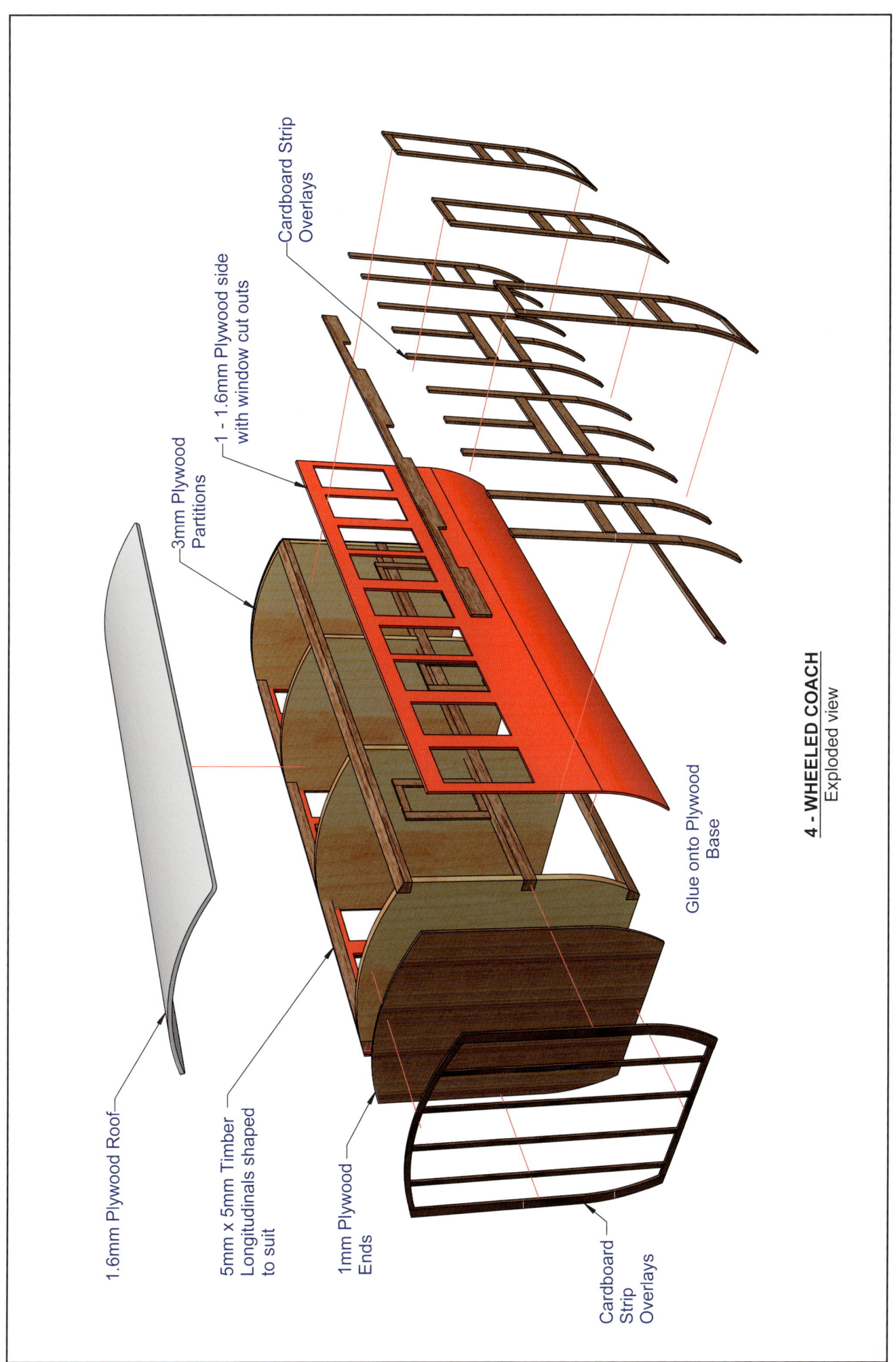

Cardboard Strip Overlays

1 - 1.6mm Plywood side with window cut outs

3mm Plywood Partitions

1.6mm Plywood Roof

5mm x 5mm Timber Longitudinals shaped to suit

1mm Plywood Ends

Cardboard Strip Overlays

Glue onto Plywood Base

4 - WHEELED COACH
Exploded view

an ink jet printer. There are some internet sites which describe in detail how to make cardboard coaches. They are generally a bit flimsy and it is more difficult to attach detail, however, with care, and by painting over with a good coating of clear varnish or lacquer, a reasonable coach can be made. It is also possible to apply a computer printout over plywood for a more rigid job. Photo **14.6** shows a ⅞ scale coach made in this way. An advantage of this method is that crests, text and other detail can be incorporated into the computer drawing.

14.5 — *Passenger coach with plywood sides and cardboard overlays.*

This description will cover making a coach using plywood sides and ends with some details added. A framework of ply and square timber stringers is made, onto which are attached 1.6mm ply sides. Strips of cardboard are glued over this to simulate the timber trim.

Step 1 Make a box frame using 5mm square strips of wood shaped and let into four pieces of ply cut to the shape shown. Two of these will form the ends of the coach, while the other two will be dividers between the compartments.

Step 2 Cut out two pieces of 1.6mm ply taking the dimensions from the frame you have just made, making sure the grain runs long ways. Tape the two pieces together and mark out for the window cut-outs. Apply masking tape to the underside of these pieces where the windows are to be cut out. This will help to avoid the timber

14.6 — *Passenger coach with plywood sides. The colour and graphic detail was printed on photographic paper on the computer and stuck to the ply with double-sided tape. The overlays are cardboard*

breaking away as you cut. An ideal tool for cutting out the windows is a scroll saw, but if you don't have one of these, a coping saw can be used with care. Draw in lightly with a pencil where the coloured panels will be and paint to the colour of your choice. (The prototypes were cherry red). You don't have to be fussy with the edges of these panels because the cover strips will overlap and form clean edges. As we are going to apply a coating of gloss varnish later, matt paint would be the best for this as any transfers you might apply will adhere better.

After the paint has dried the two plywood sides can be glued to the frame. To facilitate gluing the ply to the curve at the bottom firstly put glue only along the bottom stringer and stick the bottom edge of the ply onto this and when it has thoroughly dried the remainder of the side can be glued on, pulling in and holding with strips of masking tape.

Step 3 Timber strips can be used for gluing on the overlays, but it can be difficult to obtain in the sizes we need, and is also difficult to cut neatly. A suitable alternative is good quality cardboard which can be purchased quite cheaply from art shops. Buy a sheet 1mm thick, and using a straight edge and a very sharp craft knife, cut strips to the widths shown for the side strips, and two lengths for the top strips with the cut-outs for the doors. It is convenient to cut these as long strips, cutting them to length as you need them. While they are still in strips, paint them on the faces and sides a mid brown colour. Ordinary acrylic artists paint works well for this. Using PVA adhesive, glue the top and bottom strips on first followed by the full vertical pieces, then the remainder.

Step 4 Using the same material, make the doors, placing on the inside of each one separate pieces for a window, making a couple of them in the open position. Make the side pieces of the windows a bit wider so there will be something to glue them by.

Step 5 Again using cardboard, apply the strips to the ends. The curve for the top, bottom and sides will need to be marked out and carefully cut to shape. The entire end is painted the same mid brown colour as the side strips.

Apply any transfers or lettering you wish and then spray the whole body with several coats of clear varnish. I have had the best results using Dulux Spraypak Clear Gloss. For further detail, you can add door handles and running boards, seats and passengers. The roof can be either metal or ply as for the guard's van, and clear plastic can be used on the inside for window glazing.

A tender

Sometimes narrow gauge engines were initially designed to have their own tender, but most narrow gauge locomotives were self contained, carrying their water in side, saddle or well tanks and their fuel, either coal or wood, in bunkers at the front of the cab. Occasionally small tenders were added to increase the fuel or water carrying capacity and the tender described briefly here is a freelance version of one of these. (**Photo 14.7 & 14.8**)

14.7 — Simple 4-wheeled tender

As the locomotive is coal fired, with its water carried in the side tanks, the tender is used only for coal. It therefore has to be strong enough to take a few knocks and also might have to be able to stand up to some heat, or even hot coals coming aboard. For this reason the tender is made entirely of metal.

The frames and beams are from 1.6mm mild steel held together with square brass spacers in much the same way as the locomotive frame. The wheel sets run in brass bearings which are held in position with Loctite. Onto the outside of these, dummy springs as described for the rolling stock, are fastened with epoxy. (**Photo 14.9**)

The base is another piece of 1.6mm steel fastened through into the spacers with 8BA bolts. The sides can be of brass or steel, although the brass might be easier to work if you

14.8 — Front view of the tender

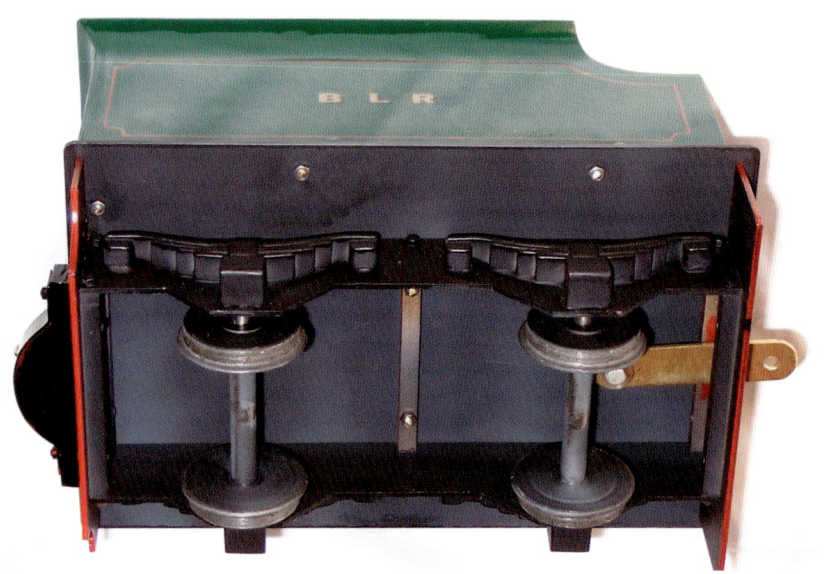

14.9 — Underside view of the tender

include the rolled tops. The corners of the body can be held together with brass angle and this is also used to fasten the sides onto the base. Sizes are not given, as these can easily be decided upon to suit your own purposes.

If required, the tender could be made watertight and divided horizontally so that it could be used to carry water as well as coal.

Chapter 15 – Bogie Wagons

Casting in whitemetal

Whilst there is a little more work involved, it is well worth the effort to make bogie coaches and wagons for your garden railway to add that extra element of realism. If you can't afford the time to make the whole coach, then maybe you could purchase a kit for the body and make the bogies. As mentioned in the introduction, many excellent kits are available and they can certainly speed things up. (**Photo 15.1**)

Many different styles of bogie have been used on both standard and narrow gauge rolling stock, and most of them are suitable for modeling, depending on your requirements. In this article we will describe how to make a simple, freelance arch bar type.

15.1 — Simple bogie cast in metal.

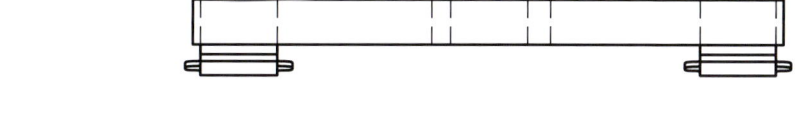

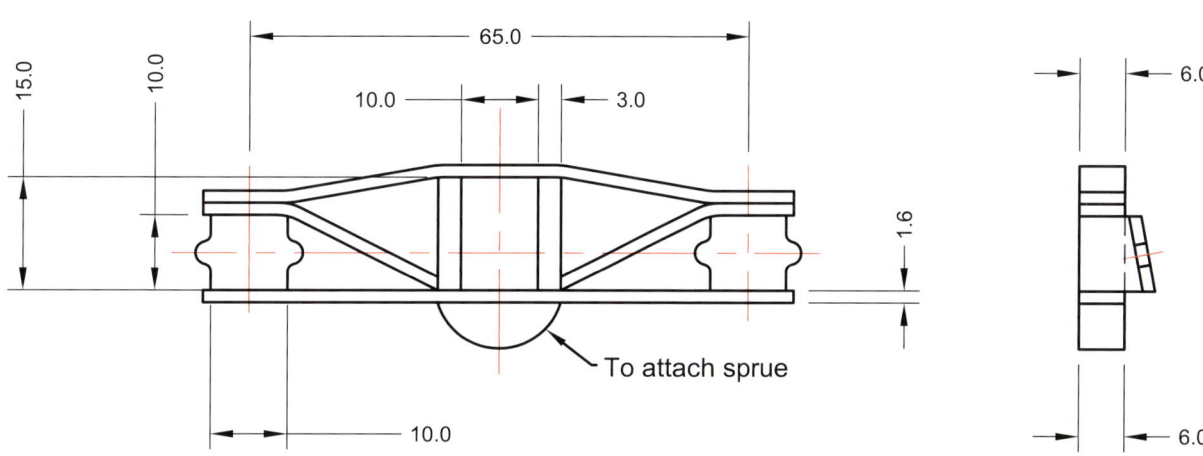

BOGIE PATTERN

(Dimensions suggested only, can be altered to suit.)

The entire unit can be fabricated from flat bar, but as with the spring and axle units we made before, a lot of time can be saved by making a pattern and casting the side frames in whitemetal. The drawing shows the suggested dimensions for a pattern, which can of course be varied to suit. If you decide to fabricate these rather than make castings, then the thickness of the flats could be reduced a little, but for casting it is necessary to provide sufficient thickness to allow the molten metal to flow.

This pattern is flat backed, so the method of making the mould is the same as was described for making dummy springs. However, to assist the metal to flow, as well as making the sections of the pattern a little thicker, the sprue has been placed as an extra piece in the middle of the unit, so the molten metal can flow in both directions from the middle, thus having less distance to travel. This whole sprue piece can then be cut off after

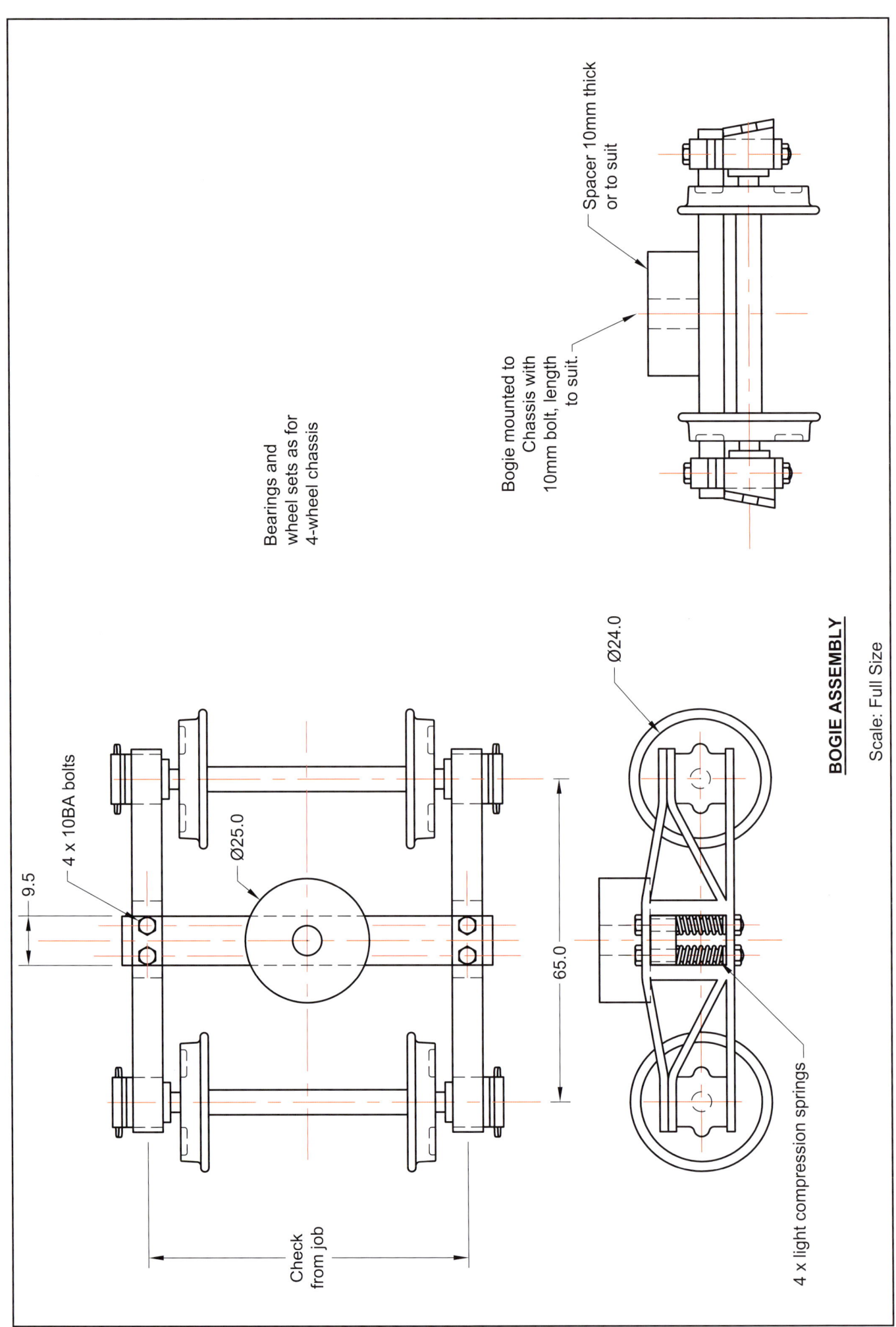

Bearings and
wheel sets as for
4-wheel chassis

Spacer 10mm thick
or to suit

Bogie mounted to
Chassis with
10mm bolt, length
to suit.

4 x 10BA bolts

9.5

Ø25.0

65.0

Check
from job

Ø24.0

4 x light compression springs

BOGIE ASSEMBLY

Scale: Full Size

casting. Place risers at each end of the pattern to ensure the metal flows freely.

After casting the pieces as previously described, cut off the sprues and risers, and generally clean up where necessary. Four will be required for each wagon.

Casting in urethane

An alternative material to whitemetal which can be used successfully in 45mm gauge rolling stock is urethane. This material is a plastic, but is quite tough and perfectly adequate for making components for our size of model, although it might fail if you have a major derailment. It has some advantages in that no heat is involved in the casting process, thereby reducing risk of burns and also a softer grade of mould material can be used which enables us to achieve a greater level of detail as it is possible to have more severe undercuts in the patterns. Furthermore, the urethane flows more readily than molten whitemetal which also enhances the detail. The process of making the pattern and mould is similar; any differences will be outlined in the manufacturer's instructions. The backs of the castings can be drilled in the same way as for whitemetal and a brass bearing can be made a push fit into this hole. (**Photos 15.2 and 15.3**). **Photo 15.4** shows the prototype from which these bogies were designed.

Chassis

A simple rectangle of 6-8mm ply can be used for the chassis. Around 320mm long by about 85mm wide would be suitable, with the centres of the bogies set in 75mm from each end.

Either make or purchase four wheel sets of diameter around 24mm, and make eight brass

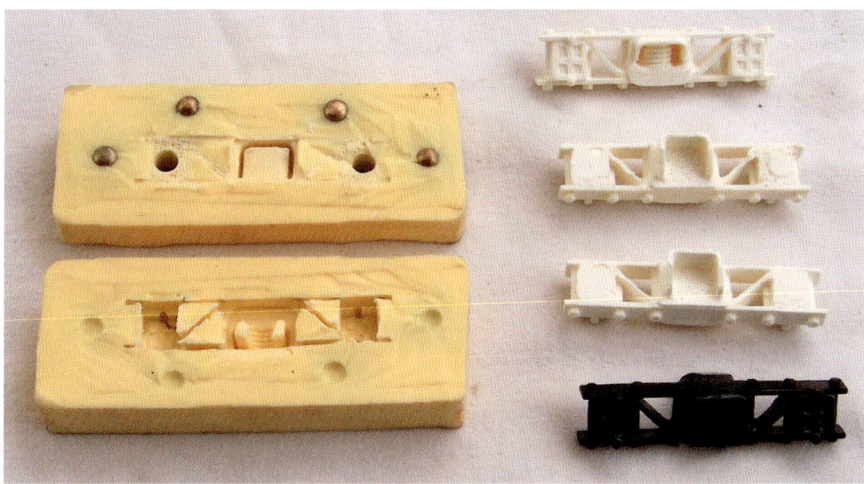

15.2 — Bogie frames cast in urethane together with the mould halves.

15.3 — Pair of bogies cast in urethane.

15.4 — A photograph of the protoype bogie

bearings to suit. Mark out the positions for these on the inside of each bogie frame and drill to a sufficient depth to enable them to be fixed in with Loctite.

For the bolster, use a piece of brass or steel, or even hardwood 9mm x 5mm and cut to 75mm long. For the whitemetal bogies these are assembled as shown in the drawing by fixing with 4 x 10BA bolts and nuts and light compression springs. Check the centre distance for these from your job, but it should be around 70mm. Each bogie assembly can now be attached to the plywood chassis by making a 25mm diameter spacer, placing it above the spacer bar and bolting through. Use washers and either locknuts or Loctite on this central bolt to allow the bogie to swing freely without too much sideways movement. (**Photo 15.5**)

15.5 — Whitemetal bogies bolted to a plywood base.

Coach Body

Onto this basic chassis, you can now build a wagon or passenger carriage, using similar techniques as described for the four wheel wagons and applying as much or as little scale detail as you wish. **Photos 15.6, 15.7, 15.8 & 15.9** show the steps in making an enclosed coach, again based on one from the Tallyllyn Railway. The added trim is cardboard strips cut, painted and glued on as described previously.

Photo 15.10 Shows a bogie wagon built up using strips of timber in much the

15.6 — Bogie coach framework with seats

15.7 — Bogie coach plywood sides

same way as the original would have been made. The bolts added to the metalwork are plastic, and were purchased as a set. Each little bolt is simply glued on with epoxy or super glue before painting over.

The final job with your wagons is painting and they can either be painted smartly in bright clean colours or they can be "weathered" to include dirt, dust, rust, gashes and various other things to show what a hard life they are having.

15.8 — Gluing plywood roof onto coach, the curve being held with tape

15.9 — The completed coach.

15.10 — A bogie wagon with extra detail.

Finally

You now have a locomotive or two and some rolling stock which will give you many hours of enjoyment. You will discover that there are lots of other people with similar interests and you can look forward to many happy meetings at club tracks or in private gardens.

If you haven't already done so, before long you will be casting an eye and a tape measure around your own backyard and looking at the various options for some changes to the garden and a track of your own!

Happy Steaming…….

Appendix

Alternative Boiler Gauge Glass

Some readers may wish to attach a gauge glass onto the boiler using bushes rather than the extended pipes as shown in the main body of the text. Also a blow down valve at the bottom of the gauge can help to clear the glass and give an accurate reading of the water level. In use, however, the gauges as described earlier have functioned well without this, with the movement and jolting of the locomotive as it moves around the track no doubt helping to give an accurate reading.

The designs outlined here provide both attachment by bushes, and a blow down valve at the bottom of the glass.

The gauge glass assembly and fittings as shown are a straight forward exercise to mount on the gas fired boiler, but it is a little more difficult on the coal fired boiler.

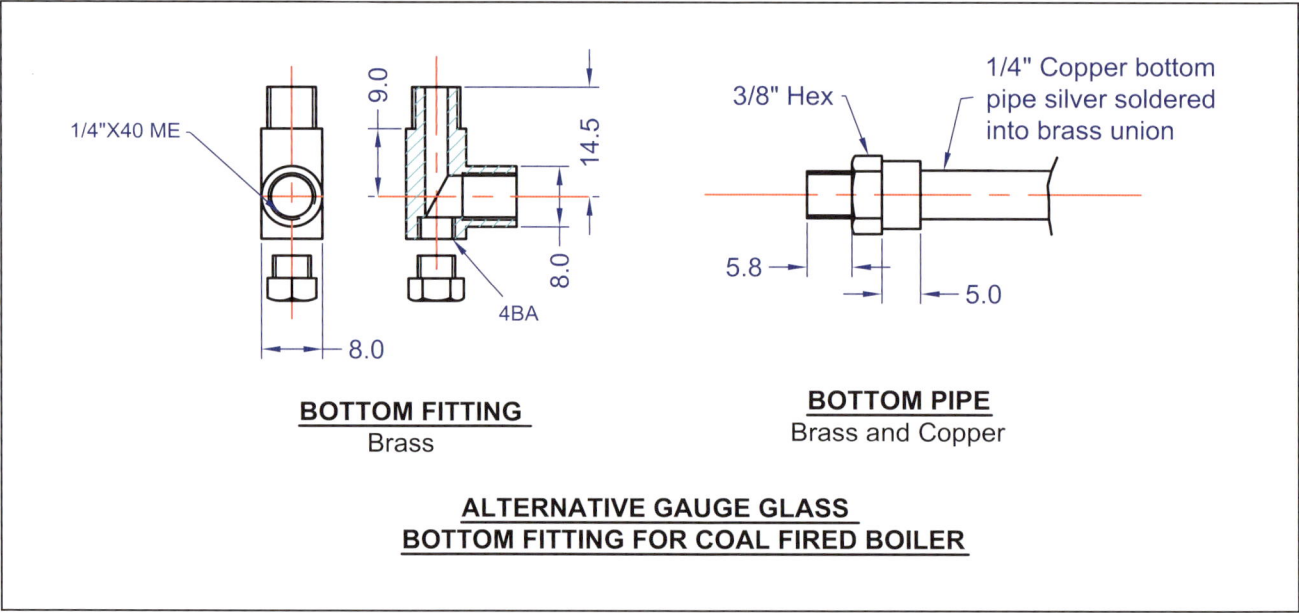

BOTTOM FITTING
Brass

BOTTOM PIPE
Brass and Copper

ALTERNATIVE GAUGE GLASS
BOTTOM FITTING FOR COAL FIRED BOILER

For the coal fired boiler, the drawings show a bottom fitting which screws into the boiler shell for the bottom water end and a brass union which screws into this and into which is silver soldered the bottom copper pipe for the gauge. From here, the pipe can run back and be silver soldered into the lower tube of the gauge as described before without fitting a blow down valve, or if it is wanted to incorporate the blow down valve then a similar union can be silver soldered into the back end of the copper pipe into which the bottom gauge glass unit can be screwed.

The measurements for all of this will have to be taken from the job; you may find that after screwing the copper pipe into the bottom fitting in the shell that it can be bent up a little and hence reduce the length of the bottom tube of the gauge.

Be certain to remember that there must be a clear indication on the glass of the water level at 10% of the distance above the crown sheet.

The photo shows the coal fired boiler after silver soldering with the gauge glass bushes inserted.

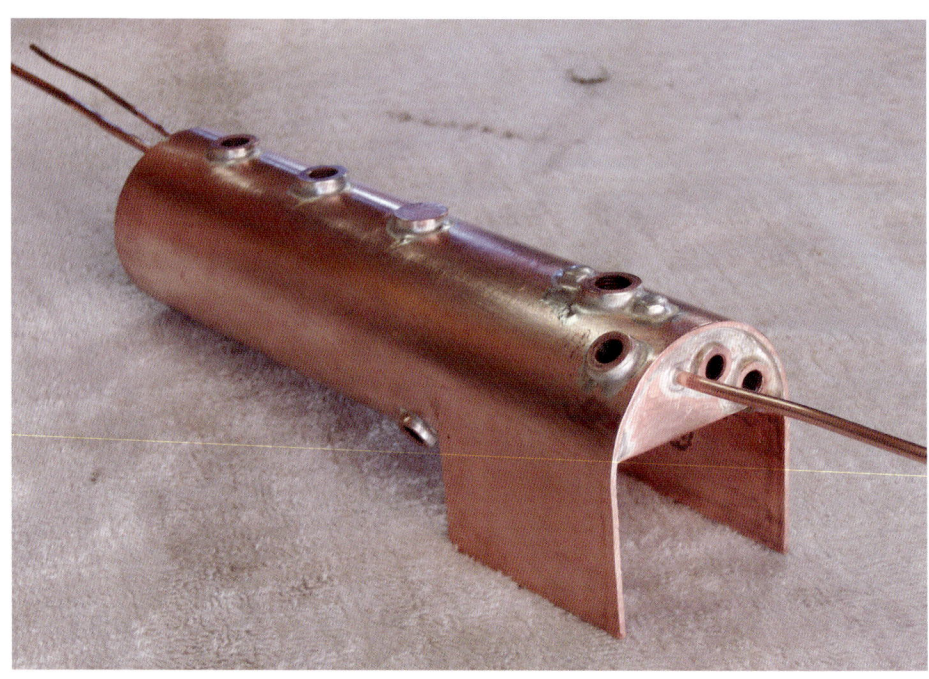

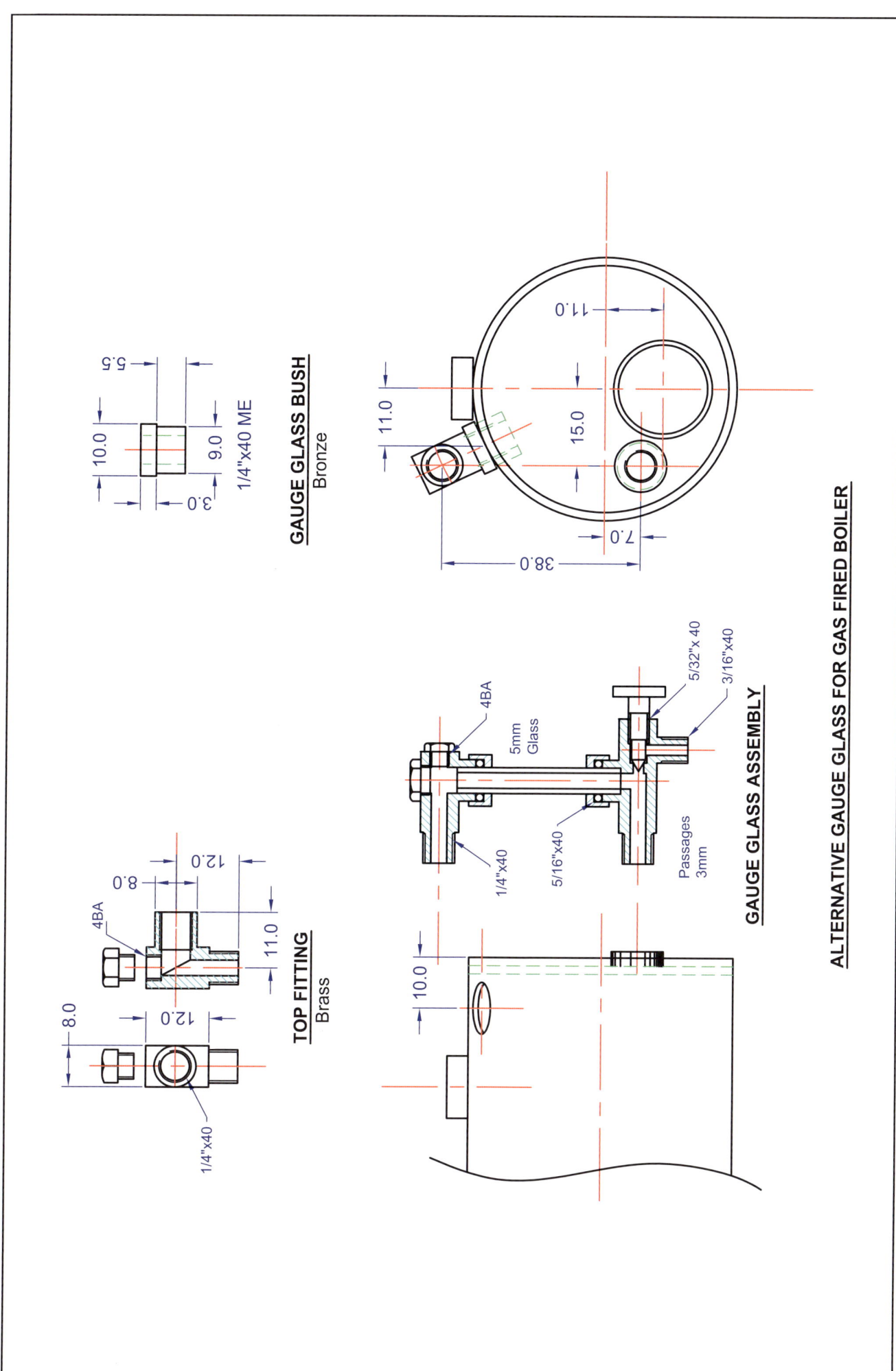

GAUGE GLASS BUSH
Bronze

5.5
10.0
9.0
3.0
1/4"x40 ME

11.0
11.0
15.0
7.0
38.0

TOP FITTING
Brass

4BA
12.0
8.0
11.0
8.0
12.0
1/4"x40

GAUGE GLASS ASSEMBLY

4BA
5mm
Glass
1/4"x40
5/16"x40
5/32"x 40
3/16"x40
Passages
3mm

10.0

ALTERNATIVE GAUGE GLASS FOR GAS FIRED BOILER